CONGRESS
FROM THE INSIDE

Two of SHERROD BROWN'S passions are baseball and politics. He has represented Ohio's 13th Congressional District since 1992, after having served for two decades as a state politician, initially in the Ohio legislature and then as Ohio's Secretary of State. Brown, from Lorain, Ohio, is currently the ranking Democrat on the House Commerce Subcommittee on Health and the Environment. He plays center field and leads off for the Democrats in the annual congressional baseball game.

CONGRESS FROM THE INSIDE

OBSERVATIONS FROM
THE MAJORITY AND
THE MINORITY

Sherrod Brown

The Kent State University Press
KENT, OHIO, AND LONDON

© 1999, 2000, 2004 by The Kent State University Press, Kent, Ohio 44242

Library of Congress Catalog Card Number 2003113910
ISBN 0-87338-792-9
Manufactured in the United States of America

Third edition

07 06 05 04   5 4 3

Political cartoons by Dick Bartlett reprinted with permission.

Library of Congress Cataloging-in-Publication Data

Brown, Sherrod, 1952–
Congress from the inside : observations from the majority and the minority /
by Sherrod Brown.—3rd ed.
p. cm.
Includes index.
ISBN 0-87338-792-9 (pbk. : alk. paper) ∞
1. United States. Congress. 2. Political parties—United States. 3. United States—
Politics and government—1989– I. Title.
2003113910

British Library Cataloging-in-Publication data are available.

To my daughters, Emily and Elizabeth,
who are already pursuing lives of service.
To my mother, Emily Campbell Brown, who helped
to teach them and me about social justice.
And to Connie, who changed my life.

CONTENTS

9

The Mail, the Phones, and Other Things *100*

10

Election 1994 *110*

Part II

11

Intelligence and Surveillance *129*

12

The Coup and the Revolution *133*

13

Storming the Palace: The Government Shutdown *158*

14

The Counteroffensive: M2E2 *177*

15

The Truce *188*

16

The Campaign *199*

17

The 105th Congress *217*

18

Election 1998 and the 106th Congress *225*

Part III

PREFACE

THIS BOOK IS ABOUT POLITICS, elections, governing, and people . . . powerful people. Not a kiss-and-tell, it's an instructive book of what my first terms in Congress were like and what has transpired in the years since.

This story of a newly elected representative navigating his way through Congress begins in hopeful times, when most of us were optimistic that partisan gridlock was over, as a huge, diverse, goal-oriented freshman class was sworn in.

My five completed terms in Congress have provided an interesting perspective in a unique period of congressional history. The 103d Congress in 1993–94, the first time in over a decade when one party controlled the presidency and both houses of Congress, saw a brief period of high public expectation and a longer period of low performance. A decisive portion of the electorate thought that we moved too far too fast, especially on the budget and the crime bill. At the same time, we failed the public by our inability to pass health care reform, in large part because our efforts were characterized as proposing radical reform. And the Democratic president disappointed large numbers of Democrats and enraged Perot voters with his aggressive lobbying for the North American Free Trade Agreement (NAFTA).

My second term saw a group of dispirited Democrats defending our values against a buoyant crowd of Republicans who thought America's political world had changed dramatically, permanently, and irreversibly. Republicans in the House passed, with great ideological fervor, issue after issue. Debate was limited; their certitude and determination were not. They felt certain that they were the vanguard of a movement that would elect a conservative president in 1996 and govern the country with conservative principles well into the next century. Before the government shutdown in late 1995, many Democrats thought they might be right. But by 1996, the Democrats seemed almost ascendant and the Republicans were in disarray. GOP bills died in the Senate or were vetoed by the president. Democrats realized that the public supported them on Medicare, education, and the environment. Republicans who came to Congress in 1994 ended up, to the horror of many of them, passing in 1996 an increase in the minimum wage, strengthening some environmental laws, and appropriating more money for education—not because very many of them wanted to do so, but because they wanted to be reelected.

My third term, when the Republicans held the slimmest majority that either party has held since the early days of the Great Depression, saw a cautious time for an embattled Speaker, a struggle for power among embittered members of the majority leadership, and a Congress that accomplished very little. Congress was to be in session only eighty-nine legislative days in 1997, one of the most abysmal marks in decades. As John Dingell quipped, "Most of those days didn't start until 5:00." And 1998 was even less productive.

Many of the Republican Revolutionaries of the Class of 1994 expressed their unhappiness with GOP leadership and their leadership's unwillingness to pursue the Republican agenda. Lindsey Graham, one of the most outspoken members of that class, muttered, "It's about time to practice one or two things we preach." Ultraconservative Steve Largent, an Oklahoma Republican, after seeing a new round of spending unveiled by fellow GOP Transportation chairman Bud Shuster, proclaimed, "The revolution is over."

In many ways, Congress itself has not recovered from the strategy adopted by Newt Gingrich almost twenty years ago. His years of incessant criticism of Congress enabled Republicans in 1994 to take control of a Congress with which the American public was increasingly angry. Today, and into the foreseeable future, all of us in Congress—Republicans and Democrats alike—must live with the extraordinarily low regard in which the public holds us and the institution to which we belong. And unfortunately, the public is paying the price.

Conflict is inherent to governing, to politics, to policy making. That same conflict, which, productively, can result in legislation and reform, can also incite anger out of legitimate (and illegitimate) differences. Many observers think our zeal and partisanship too childish, that much too often we disingenuously posture for partisan gain. But these displays of passion and anger, and even the barbs, are rhetorical outlets for those same deeply held beliefs. While the words may be vituperative, or even violent and vengeful, they are still only words. On a larger, societal scale this charged rhetoric helps us to avoid a domestic situation such as that in Bosnia or Rwanda, the kind of civil rancor and animosity that can divide and destroy a society.

In the past, underneath the partisan tension there was often a funda-
mental respect and collegiality among members of Congress that crossed
party lines. Unfortunately some of that seems to have vanished. Today we're
less likely to be colleagues _and_ friends. While we may genuinely like one
another, our friendships are usually not deep or long term. One reason for
this shift is explained by my distinguished and thoughtful predecessor, Don
Pease, who told me that members only get to know each other when they
live in Washington and when they travel together. But the daily, fast pace
of modern congressional life and the increasing work load leave little time
for nurturing friendships.

Twenty years ago members and their families typically moved to Washington when they were elected. They socialized on weekends, their spouses
became friends, and their children often went to school together. Also, for
many years, until the early 1990s, members—and often their spouses—
traveled frequently on congressional business (probably too frequently,
especially to places like England, France, and the Caribbean). On those trips
members of Congress had the opportunity to get to know one another
across party lines, off The Hill, on a more personal, intimate basis. Members
travel less frequently today, in large part because of deserved media attacks
on perceived abuses. An unfortunate result of this, however, is that genuine
fact-finding trips important to our national interest have also been sharply
curtailed.

Today, with a society that is more atomized and with members of Congress increasingly isolated from each other, Congress is more partisan, less
civil, less friendly. Unlike in the past, that partisanship is infrequently
buffered or softened by friendship or personal experiences.

And so the inside of Congress revealed itself—its strengths and weaknesses as an institution, its successes and failures, its diversity and its elitism.

Books that influenced what follows range from Richard Fenno's _Home Style,_
which examines the importance of district activities and the image of a candidate at home, to Edward R. Tuft's _Political Control of the Economy,_ which
analyzes the role that national conditions—a seemingly strong economy
with no growth in real income and an unpopular president—played in 1994.
Gary Jacobson's _The Politics of Congressional Elections_ argues the importance
of local factors. Those factors played a significant role even in 1994, especially in the early stages of candidate recruitment and the incumbents' efforts

to keep out good candidates. David Mayhew's *Congress: The Electoral Connection,* which examines the phenomenon that no one felt safe in his or her own district in the 1990s, has also proved influential in the development of *Congress from the Inside.*

When faced with a difficult decision in Congress, I often think back to a beautiful sunny morning in May 1997 when I visited Israel with two friends from Cleveland, Fred Rzepka and Harley Gross. Standing at the shrine at the top of the hill where Jesus delivered the Sermon on the Mount, our Jewish guide handed me a Bible and asked me to read the Beatitudes:

> Blessed are the meek, for they shall inherit the earth.
> Blessed are the merciful, for they shall obtain mercy.
> Blessed are the peacemakers, for they shall be called children of God.

Reflecting on my Judeo-Christian heritage, I thought about a quote from the great Jewish teacher Maimonides:

> Everyone throughout the year must regard himself as if he were half innocent and half guilty. And he should regard the whole of mankind in the same way. If then he commits one more sin, he weighs down the scale of guilt against himself and against the whole world. And he himself causes the destruction of all. But if he fulfills one commandment, he turns the scale of merit in his favor and perhaps he saves the whole world. He by himself has the power to bring salvation and deliverance to all the world.

When faced with a vote in a Congress where class warfare seems to be the order of the day, in a House of Representatives where those with so much already are given even more, in a country where the most privileged are given greater privilege almost every day, the lessons of my faith grow ever more important. And while some use the popular "What Would Jesus Do?" to drive a hard-Right, intolerant agenda, I often wonder what Jesus would really do about the poor, about the meek, about the peacemakers, about those with little.

Through most of my years in Congress, I have been a part of a group called Faith and Politics, a nondenominational prayer and reflection group headed by Reverend Doug Tanner, a Methodist minister. Six or seven of us—Joseph Eldridge, the chaplain at American University; Jack Moline, a rabbi; Representatives Rush Holt and Nancy Pelosi; David Cohen, a human rights activist; and former representative Vic Fazio—meet every Wednesday before breakfast in Representative Pelosi's office for devotions and discussions about our faith, concluding with a prayer. With our all-too-frenetic schedules, it is one of the few times when we have time to reflect, to think deeply, to talk about God, and to examine our values. And twice a year Woody Chamberlain, my pastor from First Lutheran Church in Lorain, comes to my house for devotions. He helps to connect my work to my faith, my hectic life to my spirituality.

Few jobs provide an opportunity for a passion for social justice and spirituality to intersect, and I am blessed to have one of them.

ACKNOWLEDGMENTS

Producing a third edition of *Congress from the Inside* may have been a simpler task than writing the original book, but my appreciation to those who assisted in this effort is just as great.

My special thanks go to all those in Ohio who helped send me to Washington and played a role in my five reelection campaigns. You continue to remind me why we must continue to fight for the principles we value.

My gratitude extends to those in Washington who have mentored me and taught me the ways of Congress. Your guidance has helped keep the message focused and strong. And I thank those around the country who work with me on health care and trade issues. Your commitment to these causes is unparalleled.

Special thanks to Donna Pignatelli, who so adeptly handled what could have been a disaster in redistricting and continues her strong hand at the helm of my office; to Elizabeth Thames, who delivers for so many who have little hope; to Ed Walz, who always has a big idea; to Ellie Dehoney, who knows more about health policy and explains it better than anyone I know; to Tonya Rawe, whose cheerfulness infects everyone; to Diana Milete, whose service has touched so many lives; to Katie Porter, whose compassion for the downtrodden shows every day; to Laura Pechaitis, whose efficiency and steadiness help Ohioans live better; to Pam Walker, whose compassion and kindness shines for all the world to see; to Brett Gibson, who is a fighter for human rights and fair treatment of workers around the world; to Ted Miller, who never misses an opportunity and almost daily creates new ones; to Pat Rogala, whose patience amazes me; to Diana Baron, whose skills remind us always of her value and of her values; and to John Sawyer, who, thankfully, came back; to Rick Diegel, who always fights on; to Vic Stewart, who never gives up. And thanks to Russ Pry and Joe Kanfer for welcoming me to Akron.

I'm grateful to Joanna Hildebrand Craig, whose promotion since the first edition has made her even better, and to Katherine Blauvelt and Jessica McNiece for their insights and suggestions.

I thank John Ryan, whose quest for social justice is unrelenting; Jim Kim, whose skill and compassion as a doctor is exceeded only by his energy and commitment to cure the world; and Joanne Carter, who opened my eyes to the problems of the sick.

Thanks to George Miller, Henry Waxman, and John Lewis, who serve as role models for so many of us, and David Bonior, who taught me how to be a congressman. Many thanks to John Kleshinski, whose steady voice and wise counsel are always just a phone call away.

I thank my wonderful family—my mother, Emily, who never gives up in her battle to improve the world; my brother Charlie, who never lets go; my brother Bob, whose humor and good sense always make things easier; and my daughters, Emily, the union activist, and Elizabeth, whose future is so bright.

My heartfelt thanks go to Connie Schultz, who has taught me so much about writing and even more about so much else.

INTRODUCTION

> There is not a district in this country where many men and
> women would not like to sit where you sit today and would
> run against you any time they thought they could defeat
> you either in the primary or in the general election.
>
> —Speaker Sam Rayburn, opening remarks to
> the House of Representatives, January 1961

> This being the day fixed by the 20th amendment of the
> Constitution for the annual meeting of the Congress of the
> United States, the Members-elect of the 103rd Congress met
> in their Hall, and at 12 noon were called to order by the
> Clerk of the House of Representatives.
>
> —Opening of the *Congressional Record*, January 5, 1993

MY FIRST DAY IN CONGRESS happened to be the most colorful day in
its history. Whites and blacks. Latinos and Asians. Women dressed
in reds and greens. The happy voices of children.

I was one of 110 new members in the Class of 1992. Within four months
three others joined us when two senior Democrats left to join the Clinton
administration and one senior Republican departed to head the Health
Insurance Association of America, which played a big role in defeating the
health care bill. Incoming Democrats—sixty-three of us—were surely the
most representative congressional class America had ever seen and likely
the most diverse group of legislators ever to assemble in a legislative chamber anywhere else in the world: ranging in age from thirty to sixty-six, the
new Democrats were more than one-third women, one-fourth African
American, one-seventh Latino. Incoming Republicans, however, did not
look much different from Congresses of the past: the forty-seven Republicans numbered only three women, two Latinos, and no African Americans.
Of the 110 representatives sworn in on January 5, 1993, nineteen would not
be back to take the oath two years later.

[handwritten marginalia: The battle lines clearly drawn and the results of how many would return was evidence of the conflicted elections]

The camaraderie among members of the House is real. The shallow polit-ical friendliness that the public sees in the parliamentary calisthenics of "my good friend" or "the gentlelady from California" or "my esteemed col-league" reflects the outward courtesy between Members. But genuine affec-tion makes Congress a physical place, where members do slap each other on the back, shake hands frequently, or drape an arm over a colleague's shoul-der. The shared experiences do forge a friendliness that few outside of the institution know or understand. Each member has waged a political war to *terrible* get here, through one election or a dozen. Each knows he or she is fair game for a biting, often unfair editorial. Each knows that spouses and children can be targets of nasty comments in embarrassing situations.

Each also shares membership in a very select organization. Even today, when most of the public has a negative opinion of Congress and low regard for politicians generally, each member knows that many thousands of people in the United States would love the opportunity to serve in the United States Congress, to be numbered among 535 in a nation of 280 million people.

On my first Opening Day, partisanship was subdued. Republicans sat on one side, Democrats on the other. Friendliness between the Members across the aisle was demonstrative, if not typically exuberant. When we were sworn in, everyone stood up together. When the vote for Speaker was made, it was done by a thirty minute roll call, not electronically as is the case for the remainder of the session. That first day in 1993, every Democrat voted for Thomas Foley; every Republican voted for Robert Michel.

The reelected Speaker Foley was sworn in, as is the tradition, by the dean of the House, Jamie Whitten, who was elected to the House of Represen-tatives one month before Pearl Harbor. The Mississippi Democrat, once a staunch segregationist whom the Voting Rights Act turned into a moderate on racial issues, was elected to the House before 83 of us in the freshman class were even born. When asked by another member whether he went back home to Mississippi very often, he answered, "Mississippi? Almost everyone I know in Mississippi has died."

On that day we were sworn in, all of us in the freshman class thought we were part of history. The largest congressional class since 1946, we were elected to change things and to reform the institution.

or so they thought . .

PART I

Energy is the first quality of a statesman.
—Ivan Turgenev, *Fathers and Sons*

1

Election 1992: Getting There

Politics is show business for ugly people.
— Mike Turpin, Oklahoma attorney general

The only cats worth anything are the cats who take chances.
Sometimes I play things I never heard myself.
— Thelonius Monk, jazz pianist

ELECTION NIGHT, as it always is for the winner, was a glorious night. Early in the evening, we knew we had won when the absentee ballots showed us with a substantial lead. Absentee voters, often business travelers and Florida vacationers, are more likely to vote Republican.

Two years earlier, the voters decided they did not want me in office. After eight years as an Ohio legislator and eight years as Ohio's secretary of state, I was defeated in 1990 for a third term as secretary of state. As difficult as election night was in 1990 — as difficult as it was telling my daughters Emily and Elizabeth that we were going to lose, as difficult as it was calling my opponent to congratulate him, and as difficult as it was to stand in front of family, friends, and a thousand Democrats and make a concession speech — nothing hit me as hard as the close of my last day in office. My daughters — Emily was nine, Elizabeth six — were with me as my chief deputy Wayne West and I left the office on that January day. The girls had grown up with me in this office, coming in on Saturdays, attending all kinds of office functions, even playing here in the evening from time to time. Wayne, my daughters, and I walked out of the office at about six o'clock. Wayne and I were talking, and as we approached the elevator, I looked back and didn't see the girls. I walked back down the hall and reentered my office for the last time. Emily and Elizabeth were kissing the furniture good-bye, piece by piece.

Twelve months later, congressional redistricting and the retirement of two veteran northeast Ohio congressmen opened up a new congressional seat. Eight-term congressman Don Pease represented my home county of Richland, where I grew up and which I had represented in the Ohio House of Representatives for four terms, but I had not lived there for nine years because of my service as secretary of state in Columbus. The first redistricting plan kept Ohio's Thirteenth District pretty much intact and included the cities of Lorain, Elyria, Sandusky, North Ridgeville, Brunswick, Ashland, Wadsworth, Avon Lake, Avon, Amherst, Vermilion, Oberlin, and my hometown of Mansfield. When the plan for the new seat seemed headed for approval, I shared with family, friends, and political supporters my intentions to run. I notified the newspapers of the date of my announcement, which would be made at the grade school I attended in Mansfield.

However, a newly revised plan, drawn by the Republicans—apparently with me in mind—took Mansfield out of the district and extended the district almost one hundred miles east, making it probably the most grotesquely gerrymandered district in Ohio. After the first plan had been tentatively approved, one veteran legislator stood up in the Republican caucus in Columbus and thundered, "We spent $4 million to beat that son of a bitch two years ago. Why are we drawing a district for him now?" Lorain County, by far the largest county in the district, was split for the first time in at least one hundred years. The Lorain County Democratic chairman, Victor Stewart, said, "We'll need Houdini to represent the kind of district they came up with here." Others referred to it as the "barbell district," the "turnpike district," and the "roadkill district." One wag wryly commented that the district looked like "something my kid drew with an Etch-a-Sketch."

I had less than a week to decide whether to run in the open seat, which for ten years had included my hometown, or the very Republican Fourth District seat, represented for a decade by Republican Mike Oxley, that now encompassed all of Mansfield. I met with Wayne West, campaign manager Sue Adams, and a couple of friends to discuss how difficult this race would be, based on the Republicans' plan. I decided to run in the open Thirteenth District, knowing I would be called a carpetbagger and an opportunist. (On this I was not disappointed by either the newspapers or other candidates.)

The skills required to run a successful campaign are similar to those necessary for running a business or for being a successful entrepreneur. A candidate needs to raise substantial amounts of capital or campaign money, usually in excess of $500,000. He needs to hire staff and make wise use of volunteers. He must craft a cogent, clear message that is broad enough to appeal to tens of thousands of people. A candidate must budget carefully in order to be able to deliver that message to thousands of voters in a variety of ways—through the mail, on television, on radio, and through printed material distributed by volunteer speakers, canvassers, leafleteers. And he must be able to successfully sell the product—himself—to the public and to the media: one-on-one, at editorial board meetings, through speeches, and in literally hundreds of personal appearances.

Eight Democrats and six Republicans qualified for the Thirteenth Congressional District ballot. A half-dozen more attempted to run but were ruled off the ballot, in most cases for insufficient valid signatures on their petitions. Most of the other Democrats were qualified and articulate but not widely known or able to raise the substantial amount of money necessary for a campaign. My eight years as Ohio secretary of state and my experiences as an officeholder and as both a successful (six times) and unsuccessful candidate (once) helped me substantially. I spent approximately $150,000 and won the primary by almost 25 percent.

As we looked ahead to the general election, my eighty-one-year-old father was not thrilled. He told *Akron Beacon Journal* reporter Regina Brett, "I'm still working for him, that's all I can say. But I'm not glad he's back. I think it's a hell of a way to make a living."

Initially, the most daunting Republican was a very wealthy, former state legislator whose father owned the Cleveland Indians. He, too, moved into the district to run. My daughter Elizabeth worriedly commented on him and his political strength: "You're running against the man who owns the Cleveland Indians. I think all the Cleveland Indians will vote for him." My older daughter, Emily, presciently responded, "That's okay. It's not like there are that many of them." And she was right; he lost the Republican primary to an heiress who had run for Congress and lost three times in a row, spending millions in the process.

Under the direction of my campaign manager and longtime friend, Sue Adams, we organized a 150-mile bicycle trip that took us through dozens of communities in every corner of the district. As Bill Clinton was traveling around and learning about the country by bus, our bicycle trip taught me much about the district and its people. It drew a great deal of media attention and generated an outpouring of grassroots support. Members from a bicycle club joined us in Medina; we played softball with elected officials and community leaders in Garrettsville; in Elyria my daughters did a rap song they had written; we ate breakfast with the county fair board in Lorain County; and we were greeted by a hundred Democrats as we ended our journey in Newton Falls. Almost every stop attracted a great deal of media attention—television at the kick-off at Lakeview Park on Lake Erie in Lorain, radio interviews at several stops, conversations with dailies and weeklies through most of the seven counties. My familiarity with the district from the bicycle trip, from my days as secretary of state, and from our intensive grassroots effort played a significant role in winning the election.

In contrast, my opponent lived in the far-eastern, less populous part of the district and was unfamiliar with most of it. Although she repeatedly labeled me "a carpetbagger, an opportunist, and a professional, career politician," she had not, even by election day, learned much about the district she wanted to represent. At a debate at Oberlin College, the format allowed each candidate to question the other. I asked her to name the high schools in the two largest cities in the district. Her failure even to attempt to answer—or guess—had its effect on the audience.   *intense*

A typical October campaign day started at 4:00 or 4:30 A.M. at the Lorain Ford plant meeting workers. After a couple of hours there, two volunteers and I would go to another plant gate where a later shift started. From there, after a quick breakfast (if we were lucky), I walked through fast-food restaurants going table to table meeting people as they ate. Midmorning usually found us at supermarkets and discount stores, where I stood out front and greeted voters. (More often than not, the manager would throw me out after an hour or so.) Back to restaurants between 11:30 and 1:30. In the afternoon I returned to campaign headquarters to call potential contributors and ask for some last-minute help to buy television time to counter my opponent's ostensibly unlimited bank account. Later in the afternoon I would either go door to door for a few minutes, go back to a supermarket, or return to fast-food restaurants. In the evening, when there were not candidates' nights (which were often attended by more candidates, their families, and their workers than by district voters), I would campaign at bowling alleys. When up to it, I'd stand outside movie theaters when the shows let out or return to headquarters for a late-night campaign meeting.

At one event, a middle-aged woman walked up to me and asked in a friendly voice, "You're Sherrod Brown, aren't you?" I nodded. "You look a lot better on TV than you do in person." Thank you.

During the campaign we unveiled a seventeen-page economic plan and made some very specific first-term promises, promises I knew I could keep: I pledged to pay my own health care until Congress passed universal coverage; to hold regular town meetings and not travel on junkets at taxpayers' expense; to turn back part of my office budget; to turn down any congressional pay raise; to fight for fair trade and an industrial policy; and to end the corporate deductibility for multimillion-dollar salaries. As it turned out, keeping those promises may have been the reason I was reelected two years later.

The North American Free Trade Agreement (NAFTA) was perhaps the central issue of the campaign. Without major side agreements on the environment, worker safety, minimum wage, and guarantees of free elections, I opposed NAFTA. My opponent supported it unequivocally. During my first year in office, NAFTA was to occupy a huge portion of my legislative efforts and ongoing trade interest.

Although being outspent $860,000 to $480,000, we won by 46,000 votes, or 18 percent. And the major issues of health care, congressional reform, and the economy helped Bill Clinton carry the district by five thousand votes, about 2 percent. Interestingly, the Thirteenth District gave Ross Perot his fourth highest vote east of the Mississippi, well over 30 percent in many precincts.

The morning after the election, I was up at 4:00 A.M. at the plant gates thanking voters, many of whom did not know who won because they had gone to bed at nine or ten o'clock. At a morning breakfast, I celebrated with the people I care about the most—my parents, my brothers Bob and Charlie, my daughters, and my niece Tara.

Election day 1992 was over. So now began the next campaign—the campaign for a congressional career. Four major tasks face a newly elected member of Congress: hiring a staff, attending the new-member training seminars, learning about the institution and its players, and campaigning for committee assignments. How the member-elect handles these duties can set the tone not only for the first term but for an entire career.

Soon after the election, newly elected members are handed a 350-page book entitled *Setting Course: A Congressional Management Guide*. In early December, incoming members are first invited to Washington, and then to Harvard, for two weeks of training and issue seminars. Few of us, frankly, knew much about the rules and procedures of the House. Most of us were significantly more conversant with issues, although exposure to some of

America's premier public policy experts showed us how much we still needed to learn. Training—lectures, small seminars, role playing, and hand-outs—helps; but, like most jobs, you don't really learn it until you start doing it.

The new member quickly realizes that he is on his own. One veteran said, "Congress is like 435 separate corporations." From running for political office to running a government office, he is in charge—hiring staffs in Washington and back in the district, budgeting, deciding what issues are important for him and his district. He is running a small business with a $900,000 budget and sixteen or seventeen employees, and his constituents are his customers.

Each week every congressional office receives literally hundreds of letters, dozens of individual problems and complaints, sometimes more than a thousand postcards, petitions with hundreds of signatures, and multitudinous invitations. A member who tries to answer personally all these letters, petitions, and postcards, we were counseled, may be neglecting other legislative business. Conversely, any member, we were told, who does not delegate large amounts of his legislative research or who tries to read every line of every bill—especially outside his committee jurisdiction—cannot do justice to his other work.

Don't overreach on issues, we were told. Dozens of issues are interesting, provocative, important to the district, and challenging. Members who get involved in too many issues are usually effective in none of them. Become conversant on all issues, we were counseled. Be versatile, but pick only two or three to specialize in. As a member gains knowledge and skill about an issue, others will look to him for advice in that area. And, of course, in Congress knowledge is influence.

Much of what we learned centered around the collegiality of the House of Representatives. Get to know people in Congress; think of the membership in terms of spheres. Work with congressmen and congresswomen from your class, from your state, from your region, on your committees, even with those members whose offices are located nearby. Although the seniority system is very much in place, Congress is in many ways a merit system. Lyndon Johnson used to talk about "show-horses and work-horses." Members of Congress, especially those in powerful positions, notice who does the work; who sits through often excruciatingly boring, interminable committee hearings; who is willing to participate day after day in the less-than-glamorous work of the House.

Learn the rules of the House, and learn the reasons for them, we were told. And don't be a perpetual motion machine. As Tip O'Neill said, "The horse that runs fast early fades first." And we were cautioned to move slowly on hiring staff. A full staff is not necessary in the first couple of months because the legislative cycle is not yet in full swing. "Don't hire the mayor's son," we were told repeatedly; that is, do not hire someone that you cannot politically afford to fire.

There are assorted political landmines awaiting new members during the transition period and the first weeks on the job. One is the temptation to talk—and talk and talk—to national media. If the *Los Angeles Times* or *Wall Street Journal* or *Washington Post* writes something complimentary about the new member, the small number of people in the district who read it may applaud. A critical article in a national publication may get wide circulation in the district. Much the same can be said about two newspapers, *Roll Call,* a private, semi-weekly, and *The Hill,* a weekly, which write sometimes substantive, sometimes gossipy stories about members and staff. Congress must be the only workplace in America covered by two full-blown newspapers. All in all, it is much better for members of Congress, especially freshmen, to spend their time with local papers.

A more comical landmine exploded (without serious injury, fortunately) in the face of several incoming members in the early part of the 103d Congress. A reporter from *Spy,* a political humor magazine, for want of a better term, posed as a radio reporter and interviewed a handful of new members of Congress.

Spy: Bill Clinton has proposed lifting the ban on gays in the military. As your state's first openly gay congressman, do you support his position?

A Midwestern Democrat: As my state's first openly gay congressman? Who're you talking about?

Spy: Uh, the story in *USA Today* about—

Democrat: Who is this? This isn't me.

Spy: It's not you?

Democrat: No, no, no.

Spy: Is there another freshman who, uh—

Democrat: If that's true, that's something that's up at the other end of the state.

Spy then asked a series of questions about Fredonia, which, to the consternation of several freshmen, is not a country but in fact a fictional nation created by the Marx Brothers in *Duck Soup.*

> *Spy*: What should we be doing to stop the ethnic cleansing in Fredonia?
>
> A Midwestern Republican: I think anything we can do to use the good offices
>   of the United States government to assist stopping the killing over there
>   we should do.
>
> Another Midwestern Republican: My impression is we've gotta be very care-
>   ful; that effort moving through the United Nations has a great deal of
>   merit right now.
>
> Yet Another Midwestern Republican: Yeah. It's a different situation than in
>   the Middle East.
>
> A Southern Democrat: Yes, and you know, I think all those situations are very,
>   very sad, and I think we just need to take action to assist the people.

And my favorite:

> *Spy*: Are you a dog or a cat person?
>
> A Midwestern Republican: Basically, a dog person. I certainly, though, wouldn't
>   want to offend my constituents who are cat people, and I should say that
>   being, I hope, a sensitive person, that I have nothing against cats, and had
>   cats when I was a boy, and if we didn't have the two dogs, might very well
>   be interested in having a cat now.

And this guy is voting "yes" or "no" on the most important issues facing our
country.

On a more serious note, however, I did learn a telling lesson about Congress and about power. In early December, the representatives-elect spent
several days in Washington. One morning, Cincinnati Democrat David
Mann and I were eating breakfast at a Capitol Hill hotel. Seated at the next
table was former Speaker Jim Wright. No one petitioned him. No one
approached his table. No one was even sitting with him. Three years earlier,
he had been the most influential man in Congress and probably the most
powerful Democrat in America. That December morning Jim Wright sat
alone, largely unnoticed, a grim reminder to a new member of Congress that
fame, attention, and power are fleeting. People's interest in you is directly
related to your position and title; Washington is a tough, unforgiving town.

Government transitions from November to January are almost always more difficult than they appear. In an executive-level office—governor, for example—an entire management team of several hundred administering several thousand employees in several dozen agencies and departments must be hired and trained in a short period of time. Significantly, the hiring takes place without a particularly good understanding of specific job functions. Preparing to take over a congressional office, although of much less magnitude, is not easy. And far too many incoming members impose a deadline on themselves to have an entire staff in place by early January. There is also a great temptation for the new member to bring several people from the campaign to staff the office. Often, the key aide, or the person who will run the office, will be brought from the district; many freshmen bring their campaign manager to Washington with them. More often than not, that is a mistake; most campaign managers, although possessed with considerable political skills, simply do not know Washington and how it works. And if a new member wants to succeed, knowledge of the system is essential.

In the 103d Congress, each member was allocated annually approximately $550,000 for staff salaries for the district and Washington offices, $150,000 additional for postage, and another $172,000 for operation of the office, including computers, district office rental, stationery and office supplies, and travel around the district and between the district and Washington. In 1995 the Republicans changed the process by giving "global" budget to be dealt in any way the members determined. In 2002 the allocation was about $1 million for all office functions—salaries, mail, travel, supplies, rent, etc. Some members are allocated a little more or a little less based on their home district's distance from Washington and rental costs in their districts. Members may hire up to eighteen full-time employees, one employee for every 35,000 people in their districts. During my first term, we spent $265,943 out of $327,450 allotted to us in office expenses; $79,809 out of $304,695 allotted to us in mail allowance; and $1,096,821 out of $1,131,800 allotted to us for clerk-hire. We turned back $321,820, or 18.2 percent of our budget. Many other offices, especially those of new members, turn back some part of their budget.

Seventy Democratic members of Congress were leaving at the end of the year, which meant that a large number of very highly qualified staff people were looking for work. A special room had been set up in the basement of the Rayburn House Office Building with mailboxes and desks for members-elect to process applications and interview potential staff. The mailboxes were stuffed with resumes. I received close to two thousand resumes; most of the new Democratic congresswomen, in this Year of the Woman, as the media termed Election '92, received as many as three thousand job applications. Hundreds of job searchers lined up hoping to meet potential employers, or to simply put their resumes in new members' mailboxes. Most of these jobs paid somewhere between $20,000 and $30,000 a year.

Soon after the November election, when I began interviewing for my chief of staff (most offices refer to the top position as administrative assistant, or AA), I asked three people whom I trusted and who had a good understanding of Washington—my brother Charlie, former attorney general of West Virginia; Steve Elmendorf, soon to be the top aide to Majority Leader Richard Gephardt; and Jackie Gillan, who had worked in Ohio's Washington office—to screen potential applicants. All three looked for potentially good AAs and interviewed those they thought most impressive.

I personally interviewed at least a dozen outstanding candidates for chief of staff and decided on Rhod Shaw, who was highly recommended by Jackie, Steve, and Charlie. Not yet thirty, Rhod had already served as an AA, perhaps the youngest on Capitol Hill, and he was hungry for the challenge of working for a new member, especially one who was going to sit on the Energy and Commerce Committee. He knew how to make things work for people at home—from obtaining a grant for Lorain City Schools to getting the Medina post office upgraded to getting an amendment to a bill in committee to getting quick action from the House Administration Committee for office supplies.

We had several people in place by January; in the district office, we retained three people from Don Pease's staff who did mostly casework, Debra McAfee from Elyria, Diana Milete from Lorain, and Barbara Flowers from Medina. They assisted constituents with social security problems, passports, and other individual matters involving the federal government. We also kept Joyce Edelinsky of Hamden in Geauga County, who had worked for Congressman Dennis Eckart. We brought on board Sam Betounes, a retired autoworker, and Deanna Hill, a math teacher, to run our district office. A few months later, Pat Rogala of North Ridgeville joined us to do casework and scheduling in the district. Ron Orlando, who was key to the Washington transition, had been Congressman Eckart's office manager and now served the same function with us. We also brought two people from the campaign: Margaret Bosela, a campaign volunteer from Lorain County who had recently graduated from Oberlin College, and Tracey Bauer of Elyria, who was a paid campaign worker in the primary and general election. Steve Fought, an old friend from Ohio, put law school on hold and joined us to do press work as well as handle trade and foreign policy issues. Lorain Countian Nancy Ginesta, who worked in Cleveland for our consultant Bill Burges, joined us in Washington. Mary McSorley, the only person in our office with no Ohio connection, came on board to do health care issues, largely because of my assignment on the Health and Environment subcommittee.

For the Washington office, we looked for a blend of issue expertise, knowledge of the district, a sensitivity to people back home, and writing skills combined with a strong work ethic. Thousands of young people from around the country look for opportunities to come to Washington and work on Capitol Hill, and, as in nearly all offices, most Washington staffers are young, single, willing to work long hours, and relatively low paid.

In the end, I suppose smart politicians hire based on their intuition. Apparently, Abraham Lincoln did: President Lincoln was approached by a jobseeker about whom the president's advisers were enthusiastic. After a short interview, Lincoln told his advisers that he was not going to hire him, that he did not like the jobseeker's face. His disappointed advisers were incredulous, telling Lincoln that the man could not help what he looked like. Lincoln replied, "Every man over forty is responsible for his face."

The campaign for committee assignments is the most important task a new member performs between November and January. Every other activity is, in a sense, reversible. An unwise hire can be fixed, often with little damage; an inadequate understanding of House rules and procedures can be compensated for in the first few months of session; understanding of issues can be deepened by reading, studying, and talking with policy experts.

Soon after the November election (or earlier, if their general election races are not difficult), incoming members begin to think about committee assignments. Freshmen are usually appointed to two of the twenty-one full standing committees. During the 103d Congress (1993–94), the House was made up of twenty-three full committees and 118 subcommittees, each with its own jurisdiction and area of expertise. The full committees ranged in size from twelve members on the District of Columbia Committee to sixty-four on Public Works and Transportation. Members from farm states are especially interested in the Agriculture Committee. Westerners think about Interior (renamed Natural Resources and Reserves in 1993) because of federal lands and water issues in their states. Former state legislators who were involved in education issues in their state capital might choose Education and Labor (which Republicans renamed Education and Economic Opportunity in 1995). Members from all parts of the country are interested in Appropriations, Energy and Commerce, Rules, and Ways and Means. These four are generally considered the most prized assignments and consequently generate the most competition for appointment.

Appropriations considers all spending legislation, but it is not quite as desirable an assignment as it once was because government spending is more restrained. It is considered an exclusive committee because none of its members may sit on any other committee.

Energy and Commerce (renamed Commerce Committee in 1995, and then Energy and Commerce in 2001) has "jurisdiction over anything that moves, burns, or is sold," according to the *National Journal.* It is the oldest committee, having been around in one form or another since 1795. It oversees and legislates energy, health care, environment, hazardous materials, recycling, telecommunications, consumer protection, and even toys and defense contracting. One staff person likes to point to a beautiful colored picture of the earth taken from the moon and comment, "That's our jurisdiction." Over 50 percent of all bills in Congress go through this committee, which referees battles among powerful industries, especially in the field of telecommunications. The ten-year fight over deregulation and its impact on AT&T, the Bell companies, newspapers, and cable television prompted Ohio congressman Dennis Eckart to remark that the Commerce Committee too often must choose between "the very rich and the extremely wealthy." The committee's last Democratic chairman, John Dingell of Michigan, is considered one of the most powerful members of the House, and the late Speaker Sam Rayburn was once chairman of this committee. Rayburn and Dingell are primarily credited for having expanded the committee's jurisdiction. In 1995 Commerce became an exclusive committee for newly appointed Democrats, meaning that those members could not sit on Commerce and another committee at the same time.

Rules has few substantive hearings on legislation and is the closest committee to House leadership. It has the power to schedule—or refuse to

schedule—almost all legislation and to formulate the boundaries of debate:
which amendments may be offered, how much debate time each side is
allotted, which motions are allowed. All rules determined by the Rules
Committee must be approved by the full House of Representatives before
the legislation itself is debated. In the past, when controlled by the most conservative members of the House, Rules had stood in the way of the passage
of civil rights and Medicare legislation. Today, in one of the most dramatic
and least-noticed changes in Congress, it generally reflects the will and sentiment of House leadership and the majority caucus. The ratio of majority
to minority members is generally much higher than the whole House to
ensure that leadership can control the flow of legislation. Rules Committee
members sit on no other committees.

Over the years, Ways and Means was considered the most important
committee in the House and its committee room, 1100 Longworth, the
grandest. Its history is certainly the richest. Its roster of chairmen includes
the heavyweights of American government, including future presidents
James Knox Polk, Millard Fillmore, and William McKinley and Chief Justice
Fred Vinson. Its influence, however, is now rivaled by Appropriations and
Commerce. Ways and Means writes all tax laws, which affect everything
from health care to trade to social security. Until two decades ago, Ways and
Means determined all Democratic committee selections. The congressional
reforms of 1973, however, stripped that power from them and created the
Democratic Steering and Policy Committee.

In the 103d, committees were designated "exclusive" (Rules; Appropriations; Ways and Means), "major" (Banking, Finance, and Urban Affairs;
Agriculture; Energy and Commerce; Armed Services; Education and Labor;
Public Works and Transportation), "nonmajor" (Post Office and Civil Service; District of Columbia; Government Operations; House Administration; Merchant Marine and Fisheries; Natural Resources; Science, Space,
and Technology; Small Business; Veterans Affairs), and "major-exempt"
(Foreign Affairs and Judiciary). Once classified as "major," Foreign Affairs
and Judiciary have had difficulty recently in attracting enough members.
Newspapers back home are often critical of a member if his major committee assignment is Foreign Affairs, editorializing about foreign travel and
neglect of the home district. Judiciary has tackled many of the most controversial issues of the day—abortion and gun control—issues many members
would rather avoid.

Budget and Intelligence are special cases. Democratic members may serve only two terms on Budget Committee; they may, however, take a leave of absence from another of their committees and preserve their seniority while serving on Budget. Intelligence is a permanent select committee, of which the Speaker appoints the chairman.

Members typically serve on one major and one or two nonmajor or major-exempt committees. A veteran member assigned to Rules, Ways and Means, or Appropriations must give up all other committee assignments. Each committee in the House is assigned a fixed number of slots or members. Democratic and Republican leadership negotiate committee ratios, how many members of each party will sit on which committees. Through retirements, defeats, or change in committee assignments, all committees in the House—except for Rules—had at least a few openings for the 103d Congress. Energy and Commerce had seven seats to fill.

The Democratic Steering and Policy Committee (the Republicans call theirs the Committee on Committees) is an ad hoc committee that decides which Democrats sit on which committees. In the 103d it was made up of thirty-one members: one elected from each of twelve designated zones or regions of the country; the remaining nineteen were drawn from leadership ranks.

Most members stay on the committees to which they have been assigned in previous sessions, except when they try to move to Appropriations, Rules, Energy and Commerce, or Ways and Means. When a member moves from Armed Services, for example, where he has accrued eight years of seniority, to Appropriations, he starts at the bottom with no Appropriations seniority.

During my fall '92 campaign, I spoke with retiring representative Dennis Eckart about committee assignments. He was the only Ohio Democrat on Energy and Commerce. Don Pease, who represented the old Thirteenth District, was also leaving and was the only Ohio Democrat on Ways and Means. Ohio Democrats Tom Sawyer and Jim Traficant were both interested in Ways and Means, and each had been in Congress for several terms. Ohio already had two seats on Appropriations and surely would not get another. According to Eckart, I had a chance to be appointed to Energy and Commerce.

No incoming Democrat had been appointed to Energy and Commerce in over a decade. Prior to the early 1990s, House leadership did not like to appoint new members to key committees in large part because they were untested under fire. Will the member be able to withstand intense pressure from interest groups? Is he a hard worker? Does he have sufficient party loyalty? What kind of influence will the president have with him? Can he grasp difficult issues? Does he have the political skills to win reelection? Will this committee assignment help him win reelection? Does he have the legislative skills to be an effective member of a difficult committee? A term in Congress before being appointed to one of the key or exclusive committees will usually provide answers to those questions.

2 year period if you're good to go.

But the size and aggressiveness of our class, coupled with the large number of vacancies on the committee, gave me and other new members chances for prime seats. My prospects were considerably heightened by the fact that Ohio, a state with ten Democratic members, had no representation on the Energy and Commerce Committee.

I first had to be "nominated" by the Ohio Democratic delegation. All of Ohio's senior members were satisfied with their committee assignments except Congressmen Traficant and Sawyer. At that point, I did not know the intentions of the other three Ohio freshmen. My first calls were to other Ohio members, all of whom I knew when I was secretary of state. The response was positive. The delegation support was formalized at a meeting in December in the office of Congressman Lou Stokes, the dean of the Ohio delegation, a status granted to him because of his thirteen terms in the House.

Within two days of the election, after making calls to the Ohio delegation, I began the more intensive lobbying of the Steering and Policy Committee members. My first postelection visit to Washington was to see Chairman Dingell. Dingell, a Michigan Democrat who had succeeded his father in Congress in 1955, was seen as tough but fair and as willing to help younger members. His father, he told me, once counseled him to "trust everyone, but cut the cards." He believes, as I do, that one of his major roles in Congress is to help bring industrial America back to a global leadership role, driven in large part by a vibrant auto industry. No one in Congress better understands local politics and the need for all members to tend to their own districts. "Everybody here," he told me months later, "can scratch their fleas the way they want."

Dennis Eckart, a member of Dingell's committee and a close ally, took me in to see the chairman, who was friendly, open, and encouraging. I told him of my interest in serving on his committee and that, "although we might disagree, you will always know where I stand; no surprises." I asked for his support in the Steering and Policy meetings. He was agreeable but noncommittal.

A second key member of Steering and Policy was Vic Fazio, a seven-term Democrat who was chairman of the Democratic Congressional Campaign Committee (DCCC). Of all senior Democrats, with the possible exception of Majority Leader Richard Gephardt, Vic knew the incoming members best: all of us had met him and talked with him; he knew about our campaigns in detail; he watched us under fire. He would be looked to by other Steering and Policy members as the best judge of freshman talent. I had spoken on a couple of occasions to his administrative assistant, Sandi Stuart, who was helpful, encouraging, and decidedly noncommittal.

When I went to Vic's office, I made my best case to be on the committee: Ohio had lost its only slot on Energy and Commerce and, as a large industrial state, was entitled to one. I had the support of the Ohio delegation. My sixteen years' experience in elective office would help me deal with the complex issues on the committee. I had actively supported the Democratic party and its principles all of my adult life. Getting on Energy and Commerce would help me consolidate support in my district, a marginal and tough-to-hold seat. Traditionally, in both parties, leadership was looking for people who respected Congress, not intent on tearing it down. While I ran on a platform of congressional reform, I believed we could accomplish those changes — campaign finance reform, living under the same laws as everyone else, reducing the number of committees and the size of the various staffs — inside the institution.

Probably the most important member of Steering and Policy was Majority Leader Gephardt, who had campaigned for me in my district and who played a major role in putting together the "Speaker's slate," a list of his committee recommendations. Getting on the Speaker's slate does not guarantee an appointment, but, obviously, it helps. When I spoke to the majority leader, he was also encouraging but noncommittal. Gephardt has an extraordinary ability to listen, as good as I have ever seen.

A fourth key member of Steering and Policy was John Murtha, a seven-termer with great political skills. Murtha was dean of the Pennsylvania delegation, which with Ohio made up one of the twelve zones. He is recognized as one of Congress's most effective members, especially in his dealings with colleagues. Once I had won Ohio's support, Murtha stood solidly behind me. He also supported Pennsylvania freshman Marjorie Margolies-Mezvinsky for a seat on Energy and Commerce and made the case that our zone was entitled to two members, as it had been in past years. Murtha was the Speaker's appointee to the Steering and Policy Committee.

I then found out what I could about the other twenty-seven members of Steering and Policy. Ideology was especially important to some members, especially positions on social issues, trade, and the environment. I noticed that one member, Dr. Roy Rowland of Georgia, who was one of only two M.D.s in the House, was born in Wrightsville, Georgia, where my aunt and uncle lived. It turned out, as we spoke on the phone, that he was a cousin of my aunt's husband. The harder I worked, the luckier I got.

I telephoned almost everyone on Steering and Policy, asked for their support, followed up with handwritten notes to each, and then visited almost all of them in their offices during freshman orientation in December. Vic Fazio, I determined, needed special attention. He had grown up in Boston and was an avid Red Sox fan, especially in the 1950s and early 1960s. My brothers and I had packed away, in my parents' attic, several thousand baseball cards from the 1950s and 1960s, and from that trove I located a 1956 Jimmy Piersall card. Piersall, who played center field for the Red Sox and the Cleveland Indians, was known as a zany, sometimes unstable character who played pranks on teammates, his opponents, and even the fans. I sent the card to Fazio with a note: "Dear Vic, Jimmy Piersall said, 'Don't be crazy. Vote for Sherrod Brown for Energy and Commerce.'" (One enterprising reporter, from Lorain's *Morning Journal*, wanted to burn me on an ethics charge; he went to the library to check a baseball card guidebook to see whether the "gift" had exceeded the allowable amount of $250; the Piersall card was valued at seven dollars. Treacherous business, politics.)

The Steering and Policy voting procedure is curious. The election for Ways and Means comes first, then Appropriations, followed by Energy and Commerce. Typically, a candidate for a committee slot is nominated by his zone or regional representative. I was nominated by Pennsylvania's Ron Klink, one of only three freshmen on Steering and Policy. In the first round, with seven vacancies on Energy and Commerce, each Steering and Policy Committee member voted for exactly seven people. Voting for fewer or more candidates disqualifies that ballot. Only the top vote-getter is selected. Freshman Lynn Schenk from California won with twenty-nine votes; I was second with twenty-seven. Each member then cast six votes; I was elected with thirty votes in that round. Three other freshmen—Mike Kreidler from Washington state, Margolies-Mezvinsky, and Blanche Lambert from Arkansas—and third-termers Frank Pallone of New Jersey and Craig Washington from Texas also won places on the committee.

Steering and Policy also makes seniority decisions, which in eight or ten years is important because subcommittee chairs are almost always elected based on seniority. The order of selection in Steering and Policy determines committee rank by class and by election to Congress; that is, among the newcomers, Pallone and Washington ranked first and second because of their congressional seniority, followed by the five freshmen in order of their selection in Steering and Policy: Schenk, me, Kreidler, Margolies-Mezvinsky, Lambert. Of twenty-seven Democrats, I ranked twenty-fourth.

I also got my second committee choice, the Committee on Foreign Affairs. My work in Poland, Russia, and India, coupled with an interest in promoting exports for American business, fit this committee appointment perfectly. There were eighteen vacancies on Foreign Affairs, and only fourteen members requested appointment to the committee. In this case, seniority is determined again by class (freshmen are last); within each class, if there was no contested election for the committee, seniority is drawn by lot. The remaining slots were filled with temporary appointments of four senior members. Of twenty-seven Democrats on Foreign Affairs, I ranked seventeenth.

My third appointment—a temporary one—was to Post Office and Civil Service. That committee interested me because I knew I would likely need to deal with post office problems in Wadsworth, Macedonia, and Middlefield.

My first day on the House floor was thrilling . . . and a little scary. The 258 Democrats gathered in December in the House chamber to listen to and talk with President-elect Clinton. Our seminars were over. Our transition training was complete. Our committee lobbying was done.

Walking around the chamber the first day, I was awed and nervous. Although I had spent two weeks with several dozen freshmen and made friends with many of them, questions gnawed at me when I walked into that august room, when I met several members about whom I had read and whom I had seen on television. And then I thought about the president of the United States coming in to address us—"Do I deserve to be here with all these people? How did I get here? Will I measure up? How was I chosen for this privilege?"

Then I thought about Harry Truman's comments when he went to the Senate, and I laughed to myself . . . and at myself. Truman, on his first day in the Senate in 1935, looked around the chamber and was awestruck. "I can't believe I'm here," he thought to himself. After six months or so serving with his ninety-five colleagues, he walked in one day, looked at the other senators, and thought, "I wonder how they all got here."

2

In the District

In that young and growing Ohio town whose side streets,
even, were paved with concrete, which sat on the edge of a
calm blue lake, which boasted an affinity with Oberlin, the
underground railroad station, just thirteen miles away, this
melting pot on the lip of America facing the cold but receptive Canada—What could go wrong?
   —Toni Morrison, *The Bluest Eye*

The world goes fast, one generation forgets another.
   —Henry James, *The Aspern Papers*

THREE HUNDRED YEARS AGO, King Charles II of England granted to
his colony of Connecticut a huge tract of land in the West. One hundred years later, in 1786, the state of Connecticut, on what was left of this
tract, established the Western Reserve, refusing to cede the land to the federal government and reserving it for its own citizens. In 1792, 500,000 acres
in the Western Reserve, called the Firelands, were given to Connecticut citizens whose property had been destroyed, or burned out, by the British during the Revolutionary War.

In 1800 the entire six thousand square miles of the Western Reserve—
stretching from the Pennsylvania border 120 miles westward, bounded on
the north by Lake Erie and on the south by the forty-first parallel—were
incorporated administratively into the Northwest Territory, three years
before Ohio emerged from it to become the nation's seventeenth state. One
of Ohio's first counties was the Western Reserve's Trumbull County, named
for Connecticut's Jonathan Trumbull, who was the second Speaker of the
House of Representatives (1791–93).

Those New Englanders who settled in northeast Ohio were serious
minded. Ohio would be a land of prosperity only if the settlers made it so.

There was good land, if it was cleared and worked. And these pioneers came to the Western Reserve to settle, to stay. They farmed in Portage and Summit Counties, laid out neat town squares in Medina and Burton, and built whitewashed Greek revival homes in Oberlin and Wadsworth.

All of Ohio's Thirteenth Congressional District is contained within the old Western Reserve. The Reserve's New England heritage can still be seen in the charming communities of Wadsworth, Chardon, Aurora, Medina, and Burton. And eventually to these quaint town squares came an industrial growth fueled by Yankee capitalists and central and southern European immigrant workers.

By the 1930s, the Republican dominance of the Connecticut Yankee had been displaced—compliments of a large dose of class warfare—with an ethnic, class-conscious working class, especially in Lorain County in the west and Trumbull County in the east. A state that produced the Republican nominee for president in 1868, 1872, 1876, 1880, 1888, 1892 (Benjamin Harrison, the nominee in 1888 and 1892, was born in Ohio but lived in Indiana when he was elected), 1896, 1900, 1908, 1912, and 1920 was now voting Democrat more often than not. Northeast Ohio almost invariably produced Democratic margins for presidents and governors.

In 1992, Ohio's Thirteenth District was a little bit of everything: small towns, suburbs, and industrial cities; a huge steel mill in Lorain and small high-tech businesses in Macedonia; auto plants in Avon Lake, Lorain, and Twinsburg and Amish family farmers near Middlefield and Huntsburg; poor communities and the wealthiest county in Ohio (Geauga); direct descendants from the *Mayflower* and recent immigrants from Poland, Hungary, Russia, India, and the Philippines; and just about an even mix of Republicans and Democrats. It is neither Yankee Republican nor ethnic Democratic. Several of the large factories—including George Steinbrenner's American Shipbuilding (Lorain fans of the Cleveland Indians have two reasons to dislike the Yankees' owner)—have closed, but literally dozens of small manufacturing firms have grown up in their place, especially in Medina County. As a result, northeast Ohio has seen a decline in union membership.

The Thirteenth District was home to James Garfield of Hiram, the only member of the House to be sent directly to the White House, and to Toni Morrison of Lorain, winner of the 1994 Nobel Prize for Literature. It is home to several colleges and universities: Oberlin College, the first co-educational college in the world and one that admitted blacks as early as the middle of

the nineteeth century; Hiram College, originally called the Western Reserve
Eclectic Institute, when James Garfield was its president; Lorain County
Community College; and, in Burton and Champion, regional campuses of
Kent State University.

The Thirteenth District boasted Aurora's Sea World and Geauga Lake,
two of the Midwest's premier amusement parks, and the Cuyahoga Valley
National Park, a beautiful federally protected preserve that winds its way
through much of bucolic northeastern Ohio. The largest city in the district,
and my home, is Lorain, which appropriately calls itself "The International
City." On East 28th Street in Lorain sits its history: one of the largest hot-
roll press mills in America. The history of the steel mill is the industrial history of America. Driving three miles along 28th Street, one can only marvel
at its size. Once upon a time, the mill employed twelve thousand people. A
son followed his father into the mill, and his son in turn followed him. That
all ended in 1982.

In 1895, a quiet little fishing and shipping village on the banks of Lake
Erie was about to become a steel town. After being flooded out of the Johns-
town, Pennsylvania, river valley in 1889, steelmaker and streetcar owner Tom
Johnson, who later became one of Cleveland's best mayors, set up a rail mill
in Lorain in order to be close to the Cleveland and northern Ohio market.
Barges carried iron ore from the Iron Range in Minnesota across Lake Supe-
rior down through Lake Huron to Lake Erie and into Lorain to help build
America in wartime and in peacetime. By 1927 the National Tube Company
(Johnson's mill was now owned by U.S. Steel) employed 9,900 Lorainites.

Many of the mill's earliest workers were immigrants, mostly from Italy
and eastern and central Europe. One steelworker told me that when he came
from Greece to this country to work in the mill, he spoke no English. "The
guys next to me in the mill—I think one was a Slovak, and the other was
Polish—we couldn't talk to each other. None of us spoke English. But we
got along and we helped each other." No one then demanded that Congress
make English America's official language. Then, as now, people understood
that learning English was the way to get ahead. In the early days, the sign
outside the employment office was written in six languages: German,
Slovenian, English, Romanian, Hungarian, and Czech. Today, the remnants
of the immigrant waves still sit across 28th Street from the mill. The Slovak
Club, the Czech Grill, the Russo-Slav Club, the Polish Club, the Italian
Club—all of which thrived during the heyday of the mill.

When the mill's workers went off to fight in World War II, wives, mothers, and daughters took their places and helped mobilize America for war. They made bomb casings and pipe for an emergency oil pipeline that was built to move oil from Texas to the East Coast. But when the war ended, the men returned to the mill, displacing those women who wanted to continue working.

In the postwar expansion, U.S. Steel brought hundreds of Puerto Ricans to Lorain. Five hundred came to Lorain in 1947 alone. Today, Lorain boasts the highest per capita Puerto Rican population in the fifty states, prompting Alex Olejko, Lorain's Polish mayor for much of the 1980s and 1990s, to remark frequently, "There are three places to be: Heaven, Puerto Rico, and Lorain, Ohio."

The early 1980s were especially cruel to steelworkers, to Lorain, and to America's industrial workforce. In the first half of 1981, U.S. Steel in Lorain laid off—permanently, as it turned out—almost 10,000 workers, dropping the workforce to 3,500 employees. At about the same time, Steinbrenner's shipyard began to phase out, soon closing and moving to Tampa, killing another 2,000 jobs. Over 10,000 good-paying industrial jobs were eliminated in a city of 80,000 people in a metropolitan area of a quarter-million people. Houses went up for sale, didn't sell, and were foreclosed on. People moved to the Sun Belt, or anywhere else that had more hope than northeast Ohio—which was in those days about anywhere. Many families fell apart when the jobs ended and the money ran out.

But Lorain fought back. Local manufacturing stabilized. Lorain diversified pretty well, promising never to let the catastrophe of the early 1980s happen again. And the steel mill itself is a microcosm of Lorain—hundreds of Puerto Ricans, eastern and southern Europeans, Appalachians, and African Americans, many of whose families migrated from the south.

At the other end of the district—and part of what made Ohio's Thirteenth so interesting to represent for ten years—is part of Ohio's Amish country. The Amish, a largely agricultural people who fled from religious persecution in Switzerland, are known for their thrift, nonviolent philosophy, and self-sustaining communal life-style. Much of their lives center around their religion; their services, conducted in a German dialect, are held in people's homes. They eschew showiness, and the most strict among them reject every luxury. Most do not use electricity and many will not ride in cars (which they call "English taxis"). (The Amish refer to the rest of us as "Yankees" or "the

English"; the rare Amish who abandons the faith and deserts the community is said to have been "yanked over.") In the Yellow Pages for Middlefield, the center of Geauga County's Amish country, a note reads:

> The Amish do not use conveniences such as electricity, telephones or cars because of their religious beliefs. Some businesses in this directory show phone numbers. These are either answering services or phone booths located at the road's edge. If calling, please let the phone ring for a short period of time—the businessman may have to go to the road to answer your call.

In the Cardinal school district in Geauga County, there are about three dozen one-room schoolhouses with thirty to fifty children in each. Many Amish teach their children at home; only a few of the children attend public schools.

Not much interested in politics, the Amish keep to themselves. They sometimes vote on school levies and mental health levies and occasionally express displeasure with an officeholder. When they do vote, they usually do so as a bloc, with direction from Geauga County's thirty-five Amish bishops. Democratic sheriff Red Simmons won election in 1992 partly because of a nearly unanimous vote of the Amish, who resented the Republican sheriff's treatment of them.

The old Thirteenth, referred to by some as the "turnpike district," is long and shaped like a barbell. It surrounds Cleveland's Cuyahoga County, snakes around Akron, and approaches Youngstown, without including any of these cities. A motorist can drive the entire length of the district on the Ohio Turnpike, from Elyria southeast to Newton Falls, leaving the district twice on the way. Its shape is the oddest and most gerrymandered in Ohio. Most importantly, it is far from homogeneous.

Geauga County in the east is generally upscale, white, and conservative. The home of the best maple syrup in America, its farms are tidy, its communities (there are no incorporated cities) quaint and friendly, its suburban homes expansive. Democrats usually have great difficulty here.

Medina County is several counties in one. The city of Medina is the county seat and its second-largest city, Brunswick, the county's largest city and the third-largest in the district, is a bedroom community for several Cleveland auto plants. Many of Wadsworth's citizens work in Akron. Medina County's service clubs, schools, and picturesque town squares hearken back to an America of a half-century ago. Friday night football at any of Medina County's dozen high schools illustrates the region's heightened sense of community. Politically, Medina County leans Republican, although with a very wide streak of independent mindedness. Ross Perot won 30 percent of its vote in 1992, almost beating Bill Clinton.

Only small parts of Portage (pop. 55,000), Summit (pop. 35,000), Trumbull (pop. 30,000), and Cuyahoga (pop. 15,000) Counties are represented in the Thirteenth District. Portage boasts the prosperous, growing community of Aurora; James Garfield's Hiram and Hiram College; and the friendly small towns of Garrettsville, Mantua, Windham, Deerfield, and Randolph. Northern Summit County communities, especially Macedonia and Twinsburg, have attracted dozens of high-tech businesses, and most of these communities, especially the very livable Sagamore Hills and Northfield, look toward Cleveland, not Summit County's own Akron. Trumbull County's Newton Falls, a lovely community twenty-five miles from Youngstown, anchors the eastern end of the district. Cuyahoga County's part of the Thirteenth District splits three cities—North Royalton, Broadview Heights, and Brecksville—and is home to a large veterans' hospital. The Trumbull and Portage parts of the district are, with the exception of Aurora, decisively Democratic; northern Summit County is marginal; and the three Cuyahoga communities are slightly Republican.

Lorain County (pop. 235,000) is the political center of the district. Heavily Democratic, it has been the home of incumbent congressmen, Republicans and Democrats alike, for decades. Its diversity—from the college environment of Oberlin to the bedroom community of Avon Lake; from the rustic tranquillity of Avon to the government center of Elyria; from the lakeside beauty of Sheffield Lake to the fast-growing activity of North Ridgeville; from the industrial and ethnic bustle of Lorain to the quiet distinctiveness of Amherst—brings a richness and a vibrancy that few communities enjoy. It is home to Lorain County Community College, an educational and vocational gold mine for the county, and until recently to five hospitals (which have since merged into three).

Political scientist Richard Fenno, in his trailblazing book *Home Style,* writes that every member of Congress develops his own style at home in his district. Fenno was not concerned with "the world of telephone conversations with the President of the United States nor the world of legislative battle." What intrigued him was "the world of shopping bags" full of campaign material and the local congressional representative's visits to union meetings, farm groups, and Kiwanis Clubs. A member's style—his closest political friends, his support, his central constituency—may tell more about his activities in Washington than anything else.

Although I was not raised in what is now the Thirteenth District and did not live there until I announced my candidacy for Congress, the voters pretty clearly did not perceive me as an outsider: Republicans had drawn my home county, which I represented in the state legislature for eight years, out of the district; I grew up only thirty-five miles from the district; the Thirteenth's second-largest city, Elyria, is similar in many ways to my hometown of Mansfield; I worked on a dairy farm that looked no different from the dairy farms that dot Medina, Geauga, and Portage Counties; and I played high school baseball and basketball (although not particularly memorably) against Elyria High, Lorain High, and Lorain Admiral King. From my years as Ohio secretary of state, a statewide elected office, I knew hundreds of people in Amherst, Brunswick, North Ridgeville, Newton Falls, and all over the Thirteenth District. Nonetheless, it was important that my "home style" reflect what I had in common with the district and its people.

While there is no requirement that a congressman live in his district (he must, though, live in the state), George Mason said at the Constitutional Convention that "representatives should sympathize with their constituents, should think as they think, and . . . should even be residents among them." Surely, the House of Representatives is the people's house. It—not the president, not the bureaucracy, not the Supreme Court, not the federal district courts, not the Senate—is the part of the federal government closest to the people. That means that I *should* come home every weekend, *should* learn the district as intimately as possible, and *should* get to know people from every walk of life.

Over a period of time, sometimes in the span of only a few months, a congressional representative develops a sort of possessive fondness for his district, the same kind of feelings people have for their hometown, with a strong sense of responsibility toward improving it. It means working hard to understand the problems and concerns of people from all walks of life. That is why going home every weekend and living as normal a life as possible are so important.

While shopping with my daughters at my local grocery store in Sheffield Lake one Saturday afternoon, a lady approached me and asked, "You grocery shop?" I wanted to answer, "Who else will? My ten year old doesn't drive yet." A focus group—a more elaborate, more detailed, in-person polling device—conducted by Celinda Lake asked voters in three cities in the United States what it would be like to have dinner at the home of their congressional representative. Almost unanimously, they expected a mansion, servants, and limousine service; they would not know what to call the food that the chef prepared; and after they left the congresswoman would say to her husband, "Boy, am I glad they finally left." Obviously, they have never seen my house, ridden in my car, or eaten the food I cook for my daughters.

Some members, certainly a small minority, I believe, do not look on their districts with the same fondness that I do. One night, riding back from the White House early in 1993, a freshman Republican from a southern state let me in on his stream of consciousness: "Have you found that most of your constituents are ignorant? Don't they grate on your nerves when they don't know anything? They talk for forty-five minutes and have only five minutes' worth to say. How am I going to stand it for two years, let alone ten? Why don't they just leave me alone so I can just do what's right? So I don't have to talk to them." Ten years later, he still represents that district.

In a district like Ohio's Thirteenth, representation means reaching out to everyone. It means town meetings, visits to all its cities and towns, paying attention to those who seem most interested, and searching out those who might be less interested but deserve just as much representation.

It also means seeing what people do for a living. In my first term, my daughters and I watched autoworkers building a Thunderbird on the assembly line in Lorain, with the high-tech paint application and the use of robotics to attach the windshield. I rode the beat with Lorain police officers Steve Curry, Terry Wargo, and Efraim Torres and experienced just a fraction of what police face every day and every night. Hospital administrators in Medina took me into the operating room to watch skillful surgeons insert a prosthetic device in a woman's knee and remove another patient's thyroid gland. And I met and talked with Lorain native Toni Morrison at the Lorain Public Library, where she had worked as a high school student. The opportunity to experience the richness of our society is simply one of the best parts of this job.

Early in my first term, I decided to visit as many companies as possible that had at least fifty employees. Within eighteen months, my district chief of staff, Deanna Hill, and I visited 120 of them and met several thousand people. I learned what they made, what problems the companies and the workers faced, what interaction they had with the federal government. We helped several of them open up markets overseas for exports, others cut red tape, and some expand their businesses. Most of all, I was amazed at the diversity in the manufacturing base in this district.

During my first two years in Congress, I conducted dozens of town meetings, a form of outreach made famous in northeastern Ohio by Congressman Pease. Over the years, hundreds of members of Congress have used them as an excellent way to hear what people are saying, to tell voters what they are doing in Washington, and to defend the controversial votes they cast. That has begun to change, many senior members of Congress will say. Lee Hamilton of Indiana, the top Democrat on the Foreign Affairs Committee during my first terms, told me in early 1994 that he does significantly fewer town meetings because, "in the last six months, people have simply gotten too angry," surely a sign, I realized later, of impending trouble for the incumbent party in the 1994 elections. There is no civility in politics anymore, he says. "There used to be, for example, only four farm groups out there. Now there are dozens, each attempting to justify itself by creating anger at Congress so they can grow, attract membership, and raise money. It's always single issue groups that come to the town meetings, and have no interest in learning anything."

In my first term, most of my town meetings were dominated by pro-lifers or gun enthusiasts. Other people, those less aggressive and outnumbered but interested in discussing health care, welfare, or foreign aid, had sometimes simply gotten up and left in disgust. At one meeting in Medina over a hundred NRA members were present, and the ninety minutes of discussion were all aimed at my vote to ban assault weapons. I closed the rather tempestuous session by joking, "I'm just glad that nobody was armed." Some laughed. Most didn't. At another meeting, in Lodi, a woman named Shawn Vallery set up a VCR in the front of the room and announced that she was going to show a video on abortion. And she did. A year later she filed to run against me. She lost the Republican primary in a fairly close race.

I'm often reminded of a story told by Texas congressman Bill Sarpalius, who, in the heat of a not-very-pleasant town meeting, was interrupted by a minister in the back of the room who thundered, "We didn't send you up there to make intelligent decisions. We sent you up there to represent us."

Some town meetings have been wonderful, though. After two hours at the Greenwood development in Sagamore Hills, I still didn't want to leave. The questions were good; the discussion was provocative; the exchanges were tough, but not angry.

There are certainly other ways to reach out to your constituency. My Washington staff had made a weekly practice of picking out a dozen or so provocative letters from constituents that I would respond to by phone late one evening. And every month or so during my first couple of terms, when everyone else left the office, I opened the mail from the 8:00 P.M. mail drop (mail was delivered to our office four times a day) to get a feel about what people were saying and thinking. Congressman Dan Glickman, a sober-minded and effective member from Kansas and later the secretary of agriculture, recently commented, "I just love opening the mail. I'd come in on the weekend just to open the mail."

And there are other ways, fun ways, to stay in touch with people. I judged a husband-calling contest at the Lorain County Fair, umpired a frog-jumping contest in Valley City, and watched three thousand sets of twins from all over the world in, you guessed it, Twinsburg. And of course there are the parades. On July 4 every year, I walk a parade in Chesterland at 10:00 A.M., hurry sixty miles west to Chippewa Lake to parade there at 1:00 P.M., rush on to Valley City for another later in the afternoon, and then back to Medina for its parade in the early evening. Later in the evening, the community band in Medina traditionally invites the incumbent congressman to direct the band—mercifully for only one song. I have noticed that no one in the band really looks at me while I am "directing." Curious.

But no matter how hard you work, you simply can't please everyone. I received a signed letter from a man in Medina that read:

> The next time you go to a fast food restaurant in Medina, Ohio, make sure you clean up after yourself. My children watched how you left your waste on the table. Remember you're always under the public view of children. My eight-year-old wants to know if you, as a Congressman, get special treatment.
> P.S. If the kids aren't watching you, the Republicans are.

A congressional representative's primary constituency is comprised of his strongest supporters. For me, that means Lorain, with its urban, ethnic, Catholic, minority, working-class dominance; Oberlin, with its liberal, minority, academic makeup; Brunswick, with its base of labor votes; and Elyria, only marginally Democratic but with a solid core of minority and working-class voters. I reach out to these groups through the issues with which I've been involved. Few places beyond the Thirteenth District were hit harder in the last two decades by plant closings, job loss, and economic catastrophe; those in my primary constituency were, in many cases, the victims of those disasters, and they remain among the most vulnerable.

And so they quite rightly want a representative who will fight for jobs. As the 1990 *Almanac of American Politics* outlines, there has been a long history of skepticism toward free trade in the Western Reserve. My predecessor for sixteen years, Don Pease, argued for minimum wage and worker safety standards in our trade policies. In the NAFTA debate during my first term, many of us called for those same conditions—adding environmental safeguards, currency stabilization to guard against peso devaluation, and democratic and labor reforms—to any agreement with Mexico. Those arguments have met with enthusiasm in the Thirteenth District, not just with my reelection constituency but among citizens everywhere, especially in the more conservative areas of Lodi, Spencer, Sharon Center, and Litchfield in Medina County.

A member's personal constituency consists of those people whom he relies on most for political advice and friendship. Many in politics refer to it as a "kitchen cabinet" or "inner circle." These are the people I speak to when facing an intractable problem, looking for an idea, or searching for a creative solution. Although I do not hold regular meetings with my "inner circle," I keep a list in my office and at home of about thirty people I call every few weeks for advice, ideas, and thoughts. When in the district, I have lunch with them, usually individually, and many call me to pass along information they think would be useful to me and the office.

Every weekend, with the exception of one, when my daughters visited Washington, I came home—to listen, to hear people's concerns, to learn the district, and to build those four constituencies: the geographic, reelection, primary, and personal contituencies. A typical weekend looked like this:

Friday:
   Office hours with individual constituents in our Lorain County office.
   Spoke at an assembly at Avon Lake High School on their Government Day;
      then lunch, with students, prepared and served by home economics classes;
      then a meeting with a special class studying the United Nations (who knew
      more about foreign policy, it seemed, than many of us on the Foreign
      Affairs Committee); interestingly, they spoke of the disappearance of the
      Communist Party in the Soviet Union as a simple historical phenomenon,
      not with the emotion that we who grew up with bomb shelters greeted
      its demise.

Did a cable television taping to be broadcast throughout the district.

Attended the Hispanic Festival in Lorain.

Met with Lorain County township trustees in Russia Township near the city of Oberlin.

Had a quick dinner with the Blue Ribbon Committee, a leadership group in Lorain.

Spoke at a literacy award ceremony in Elyria.

Saturday:

Our annual Academy Day, when our office sets up informational seminars for parents and young people who are interested in attending the five service academies: West Point, the Naval Academy, the Merchant Marine at King's Point, the Coast Guard Academy, and the Air Force Academy. We did those in three locations around the district: Oberlin, Medina, and Macedonia.

Did a ceremonial tree planting, in the pouring rain, to commemorate Arbor Day in Parkman.

Eagle Scout presentation in Geauga County.

Spaghetti dinner at a local high school.

Sunday:

Breakfast with the Elyria NAACP.

Attended my own church.

Elyria High School pancake breakfast (which was lunch for me).

CROP walk in Oberlin.

Dinner with a Lorain doctor to discuss Taiwanese-American relations.

Monday:

Presentation at an injured sheetmetal worker's home in the city of Lorain.

Played my guitar and sang Russian folk songs to a third-grade class in Elyria.

Lunch with a Medina doctor about health care issues.

Office appointments in the Medina congressional office.

Speech at Medina hospital to physicians about health care.

Flew to Washington.

When I had free time, I would often hand out issue questionnaires at shopping centers, plant gates, supermarkets, even pancake breakfasts. One man, at a pancake breakfast in Elyria, complained about the cost of printing the questionnaire. (Keep in mind that I was handing them out personally and talking about the issues with people, not dropping 250,000 of them in the mail.) "I'm a retiree, I've worked hard all my life," he growled. "How do you expect me to put a twenty-nine-cent stamp on this? Why isn't there a stamp on it? I could buy a quarter of a gallon of gas for the price of mailing this to you."

While it is true that senior members do not return to their districts as often, and that members who have "safe" seats stay in Washington more, an increasingly larger number of congressmen and congresswomen come home several times each month, especially those whose families stayed in their hometown. In fairness, those members from the far West, whose trips to Washington can take upward of six or seven hours, can hardly afford—in terms of time or in terms of wear and tear on their bodies—to go home every weekend. And more senior members, especially those who are committee chairs or subcommittee chairs, typically have more responsibility in Washington than do more junior members and thus need more time in their Washington offices.

In the end, a congressman hopes for a sense of identification with voters. We try to build some level of trust between ourselves and them. It becomes, we hope, almost personal. We want to hear voters' comments, to hear "Even though I don't always agree with you, I know I can count on you to tell me the truth and to stand up and fight for what you think is right." To my delight, many of my constituents, even ones I've never met, call me by my first name. People want good government, surely, but they also want the personal attention of a sort that only hard work and diligence on our part can give them.

3

In Committee

There are all sorts of ways to get things done in Congress.
The best way is to live long enough to get to be a committee
chairman.

—Congressman Clem Miller (D-Calif., 1959–62)

Eighty percent of success is showing up.

—Woody Allen

POWER AND INFLUENCE RESIDE IN COMMITTEES—where the work is done, reputations are built, and legislative decisions are made. Former Speaker Sam Rayburn said, "A man makes a record in the House the way he does in business or the law or anywhere else. It's hard work that makes the difference." Other members "spot the men who attend a committee session where there isn't any publicity, who attend during the long grind of hearing witnesses. . . . There are only a few men who sit there and watch every sentence that goes into the bill and know why it went in."

In an increasingly complex society and "atomized" Congress where authority is decentralized, specialization and division of labor make the committee system work and allow Congress to function better. In many ways, committee assignments define members in terms of their expertise, interests, influence, and reputations. Most members concentrate on a small number of issues, usually unique to their committee, and come to learn those areas thoroughly. Few other members of Congress will reach their depth of understanding of those issues. If they try to do more, their efforts and expertise are too diluted; ultimately, if Congress were comprised of a bunch of generalists who knew only a little about a lot of things, influence and power and decision making would shift to the president's cabinet, to lobbyists, or to staff.

In ordinary times—the most obvious exception is when the majority changes hands and the new majority forces a reduction in the outgoing majority's slots—members do not usually change committees after their third or fourth terms. Seniority is never transferred from one committee to another, so when a member changes committee, she starts at the bottom of the ladder. Once established, members typically stay on the same two or three committees, gaining insight and developing expertise on issues unique to those committees.

In January 1993, after swearing-in festivities, the first order of business was to organize committees and subcommittees. Majority Democrats met in the room assigned to each committee. After approving the committee rules, and introducing new members of the committee, we chose our subcommittees in order of seniority. A big board was placed in front of us with, in the case of Energy and Commerce, the names of the following subcommittees arranged across the top: Commerce, Consumer Protection, and Competitiveness; Energy and Power; Health and the Environment; Oversight and Investigations; Telecommunications and Finance; Transportation and Hazardous Materials. There were then several slots underneath each subcommittee, ranging from fifteen for Health to seven each for Oversight and Commerce.

After the first six senior members—Dingell, Henry Waxman (Calif.), Phil Sharp (Ind.), Ed Markey (Mass.), Al Swift (Wash.), and Cardiss Collins (Ill.)—chose their subcommittee chairs, each member made his first choice in order of seniority. Once a subcommittee's slots are filled, it is "closed out"; no one else can choose it. Health was the most popular subcommittee because of the attention paid to health care reform by the president, the First Lady, and the media; many of us had campaigned on the issue also. I chose Health and the Environment when my turn came, the next-to-last slot.

During the second round, subcommittee chairs usually pass, opting not to choose a second subcommittee so that junior members can get good assignments. By the time the second round came to me, no one had chosen Oversight and Investigations other than Chairman Dingell, who was its chair. When I chose it, it put me in the position to be the vice chair of the subcommittee.

The process on Foreign Affairs was similar. On that first day, California Democrat Howard Berman, the incoming chairman of the Subcommittee on International Operations, said to me, "You'll love this committee. Foreign Affairs is like graduate school—except there are no tests and no papers." In fact, Foreign Affairs, while without the jurisdiction of the Senate Foreign Relations Committee, proved to be an important and fascinating assignment. From meetings with Indian prime minister Rao to conversations with

King Hussein and Queen Noor of Jordan to discussions with Shimon Peres and Rupert Murdoch, service on the committee gave each of us an excellent understanding of world affairs. Murdoch, with whom three of us, at the invitation of Asia subcommittee chairman Gary Ackerman, had breakfast, showed us his plan to electronically rule Asia, replete with maps, demographic data, and anecdotes—a sort of high-tech version of a strategy meeting with Alexander the Great.

I also had the good fortune to have lunch with Mikhail and Raisa Gorbachev. I spoke with Raisa in my very rusty Russian (I had majored in Russian and East European Studies in college), and she wrote a sweet note in Russian to my daughters. Every Tuesday morning, Foreign Affairs chairman Lee Hamilton held a classified briefing from the Central Intelligence Agency about "hot spots" around the world, where American interests were affected most directly. Equally important, my position on Foreign Affairs gave me the opportunity to assist several businesses in the Thirteenth District in exporting their products around the world, which, in turn, helped create jobs in northeast Ohio. Even on the Foreign Affairs Committee, politics can be local.

Foreign policy has been in large part the domain of the executive branch. The tension between the president and Congress is always just below the surface, usually with some partisan overtones. Chairman Hamilton and ranking Republican Benjamin Gilman in the 103d Congress, however, were two of the least partisan members of Congress, and each has the reputation of being very fair-minded. Gilman said, "Foreign affairs and foreign policy is a matter of consensus. You know the old quotation, 'Partisanship stops at the water's edge.' There has to be a truly bipartisan foreign policy if it's going to work, and that's where compromise comes in, a give-and-take process of evolving consensus."

Complaints from Congress about the State Department and the president's handling of foreign policy are as old as the Republic. Congress is often accused, rightly in many cases, of micromanaging foreign policy, and often the State Department seems slow in moving on anything. Franklin D. Roosevelt complained, "Decisionmaking at the State Department is like watching an elephant get pregnant: everything takes place at a very high level, there's a great commotion, and then nothing happens for twenty-two months."

There were seven subcommittees available on Foreign Affairs—Africa; Asia and the Pacific; Economic Policy, Trade, and Environment; Europe and the Middle East; International Operations; International Security, International Organizations, and Human Rights; Western Hemisphere Affairs. I selected two of them: Europe and the Middle East, and Asia and the Pacific.

Committee hearings usually start with the chair and ranking minority member (usually the member of the minority party who has served on the committee the longest) making a four- or five-minute opening statement about the bill, the issue involved, or even the witnesses. Each member is given the opportunity to make a three-minute opening statement. Opening statements, especially when the committee or subcommittee is hearing a controversial issue and the media are present, can take up as much as an hour—a colossal waste of time for all of us. Too often I have seen witnesses—whose time is as important to them as ours is to us—sit for over an hour waiting for opening statements to conclude before they can deliver their testimony. Witnesses are then given five minutes (although cabinet officials and prominent experts are sometimes allotted more) to present their statements. Often, a witness or a panel of witnesses will submit a much longer written testimony to be inserted in the committee record. At the conclusion of the testimony, each member, either by seniority or in order of arrival at the hearing, is given five minutes to question the witness or the panel of witnesses.

Occasionally two members will engage in a scripted colloquy, a conversation to bring out a point or clarify an issue that the two members want in the public record to illuminate legislative intent, to explain legal intricacies in case of a court challenge, or for newspaper consumption back home. Sometimes, for purposes of inserting remarks in the public record, committee hearings are more scripted than the public knows. Opening statements are often written ahead of time by staff and then read verbatim by the member. Questions are frequently written prior to the hearing, and questions and expected answers are regularly scripted at oversight hearings, especially with friendly witnesses. Reid Stuntz and the staff of the Oversight and Investigations subcommittee of Energy and Commerce were particularly skilled at using friendly witnesses to build a base of information from which to expose a legal, ethical, or political lapse of a hostile witness.

Oversight and Investigations, of which I was vice chair in 1993–94, was chaired by full committee chairman John Dingell. (Until a rules change in 1995, chairs of full committees usually chaired one of its subcommittees.) No one in Congress is as good as Dingell in the oversight role, with his strong trial-lawyer skills and cross-examination techniques. While he and his Oversight subcommittee have been feared for many years, I have seen him—with the right mixture of charm and gentlemanly toughness—excoriate a witness for all to see, though the witness seems not to notice.

My other Energy and Commerce subcommittee, Health and the Environment, is, unlike Oversight and Investigations, a legislative subcommittee; we hold hearings on a piece of legislation and usually bring it to a vote. Chaired by California Democrat Henry Waxman, Health and Environment was one of the two major subcommittees that held hearings on the Clinton health plan; the other was Ways and Means' subcommittee on Health.

Elected to Congress in 1974 and chair of the subcommittee from 1979 until 1994, Waxman has for years been considered one of the most adept legislators in Congress. His efforts have led to mammograms for poor women, significant increases in AIDS research, greater availability of less expensive generic drugs, and a wide array of accomplishments on environmental issues. He is responsible, probably more than anyone else in government, for providing government health insurance for millions of poor children.

Early in the tenure of the 103d Congress, our Health Subcommittee scheduled hearings on the health hazards of exposure to radon gas. Witnesses, including physicians, cancer victims, scientists, government officials, came before the subcommittee to warn us of the harmful effects of long-term exposure to undetected radon, as the public and realtors typically know little about radon risk in their communities and in their neighborhoods. After the testimony, subcommittee staff wrote H.R. 2448, the Radon Awareness and Disclosure Act of 1993, which Chairman Waxman introduced. The bill was intended to provide homebuyers with information about the potential hazards of radon and to improve building codes to ensure that newly constructed homes provide radon abatement in areas of high risk. The bill, upon its introduction and prior to its mark-up in subcommittee—the committee session where amendments are offered and voted on and the bill passes or is defeated—had no Republican support because of active opposition to it from realtors, homebuilders, and some bankers. They contended that provisions in the bill would delay residential real estate transactions for ten days after the initial closing was scheduled because of radon testing requirements in the bill, even in areas where there appeared to be little radon risk. There was also some question that the bill would require multiple radon tests of the same home, all paid for by the seller.

Recognizing the health problems of long-term exposure to radon, Kansas Democrat Jim Slattery and I knew there would be no bill unless we could broker some kind of compromise among environmental groups, physicians, realtors, Chairman Waxman, the Republicans and conservative Democrats, and homebuilders. Our goal was to bring the disparate groups together to help deal with the health hazards of radon gas. The bill we worked out did not please very many. Legislation like this usually doesn't. But Slattery and I believed that the bill we worked out addressed the problem.

During the committee mark-up, we were able to get our agreement approved. The language provided for the distribution of a radon hazard pamphlet to prospective buyers that outlines regions of high risk and methods to remove radon from a home. It also clarifies that the buyer and seller can include radon testing as part of any agreed-to contract. The legislation, as voted out of subcommittee, was passed by the House and Senate and signed by the president.

In mark-ups, members are especially appreciative when others speak out in support of their amendments. It helps to build special, long-term camaraderie among members who will likely serve together on the committee for years.

Full committees, which meet less often than subcommittees, usually do not meet for public hearings. Expert witnesses, concerned citizens, and knowledgeable observers will usually testify in subcommittee, where most of the intricacies and complexities of legislation are explored and examined and where the legislation is rewritten. The bill is usually marked-up or amended in subcommittee and then again in full committee.

While the function of full committee is to markup legislation, occasionally it serves as a backdrop for television and to graphically illustrate a point. Senator Tom Harkin of Iowa, a supporter of corn-based ethanol, once drank a glass of pure ethanol at a committee hearing to underscore its safety and its environmental advantages. Congressman Don Young of Alaska, after enduring testimony from Cleveland Amory about the "cruelty of the steel jaw trap," stuck his hand in one and left it there for several minutes as he continued and completed his testimony. Only later did he admit that it "hurt like hell." And at one Foreign Affairs hearing on exports of pesticides, ultraconservative Republican Dana Rohrbacher of California was defending the use of DDT and expressing concern about the public's and government's "overreaction" in regulating pesticides: "I remember when I was a kid, running behind the DDT truck . . . ." Cynthia McKinney, a liberal Democrat from Georgia, interrupted, "Well, that explains it."

Committee hearings often run interminably long. Sitting there for three or four uninterrupted hours, listening to witnesses explain the intricacies of Medicaid financing is not, to be charitable, the most exciting part of being a congressman. During a lengthy and particularly dry hearing, I turned around to talk for a few moments to my health aide, Mary McSorley, who was seated behind me on the committee rostrum. (Okay, I admit, we weren't talking about health care; we were discussing Mary's upcoming wedding.) Four days later, I received a letter from a couple in Medina. "Dear Mr. Brown," the letter began, "We were in Washington watching your committee hearing. You looked like you were having too much fun. We don't like that."

As well as the committee system works much of the time, it falls short on occasion. The same expertise that brings credibility to the process makes other members all too often fail to question committee decisions when a bill reaches the floor. For example, when a military authorization bill comes to the floor, and some members offer amendments to cut weapons programs, the "experts"—those Armed Services Committee members most familiar with the arcane minutiae of military armaments—almost always defeat the amendments. Armed with Pentagon studies and defense industry statistics, the committee members convince less informed members who are not on the Armed Services Committee that defense cuts are bad public policy. "The experts," a California congressman wrote in the early 1960s, "used everything—insults, superciliousness, patronization, sarcasm. The Defense Department was quoted and re-quoted backward and forward heralding a disaster." Nothing has changed much in the three decades since. In addition, the Armed Services Committee, by its very makeup, is predisposed to higher military expenditures. Those members who choose Armed Services are frequently conservative southerners who often have military installations in their districts. Northern, more liberal members rarely choose Armed Services.

One very obvious exception to that was California Democrat Ron Dellums. A former marine, he came to Congress in 1970 from Berkeley—radically antiwar, militant, outspoken, tall, wearing a dashiki and a huge Afro. (He told me that when he sees a picture of himself then, it makes him laugh. "And all those cats now shave their heads.") He was put on Foreign Affairs in 1971 and spent most of his term conducting hearings on racism in the military, generally angering almost all the military top brass. After his reelection in 1972, he wanted to make a move. The African American chair of

Education and Labor, Los Angeles's Gus Hawkins, didn't want him, Dellums told me, because he was too young, too new, too militant, perhaps too much of a threat. Besides, Dellums did not want to be just another liberal vote on Education and Labor, probably the most liberal committee in the House. So, because of the hearings he had about racism in the military, he picked Armed Services. He told the Black Caucus of his interest, and their membership promised their support. He notified Speaker Carl Albert, who did not say much of anything. Phil Burton, a very liberal white Democrat from California, nominated him for the committee. The nomination went nowhere.

So Dellums went to see Burton to devise a strategy. Burton told him that leadership might, under pressure, finally agree that there should be a black on Armed Services—but surely they would opt for someone else. So whom might they choose? Barbara Jordan, a freshman from Houston, was the likely choice. When Dellums called her, she said she would rather be on Judiciary. Within a year, she achieved fame because of her Judiciary Committee performance during the Watergate hearings, which led to her addressing the Democratic Convention as the keynote speaker in 1976.

Two congressional Black Caucus members, Bill Clay from Missouri and Louis Stokes from Ohio, went with Dellums to see Speaker Albert, Majority Leader Tip O'Neill, and ultraconservative Armed Services Committee chair F. Edward Hebert from Louisiana. Stokes was the nice guy. He solemnly told the leadership that there had never been a black member of the committee; that the military had a large number of black men and women; and that the Black Caucus now numbered about fifteen members, an important part of the Democratic caucus. When Albert and Hebert hemmed and hawed, Clay angrily pointed out that the institution was bigoted, that he was going to the press and call congressional leaders racists. Finally, Dellums was put on the committee, alongside all those southern, pro-military conservatives.

But when he arrived in the committee room the first day, there was no chair. In fact, he and Pat Schroeder, who was right behind him in seniority (she was elected in 1972), had to share a seat—literally. "My right cheek was on one side of the chair and her left cheek on the other," he recalled in an amused tone. In 1993 Ron Dellums became committee chair, with Pat Schroeder next in line.

Amazingly, until Louisiana's Bill Jefferson and Georgia's Cynthia McKinney joined the committee in the mid-1990s (when the Republicans changed its name to National Security), Dellums was the only black Democrat to serve on Armed Services, not because Democratic leadership had denied them, but because none had asked to be assigned to Armed Services in two decades. African Americans have had little interest in it; black members, Dellums told me, want to address issues that are of more obvious and direct interest to their constituents—"jobs, education, health care, fighting drugs. They always wanted to get on those committees, not Armed Services." It takes so much effort to explain why the Armed Services Committee matters to them, he said. "I had to spend a lot of time educating my people about why I was on Armed Services, and why it was important to them."

Seniority, of course, is still very important throughout the institution, especially in the committee process, where rank is determined almost always by seniority. Office selection in Rayburn, Longworth, and Cannon is also determined solely by seniority. Conferees on House-Senate conference committees are determined, for the most part, by seniority. Seats on the Steering and Policy Committee, which makes committee appointments, are more often than not given to members who have served the longest in a state's delegation. Deans of state delegations are accorded deference and powers. Seniority implies an expertise and knowledge that are useful to the institution.

However, committee chairs in some cases have been too old, tired, or lethargic to be effective. Those members who become chairs usually have safe districts, were elected to Congress at a young age, and are bestowed with good health and longevity. During Democratic control of Congress in the 1930s, 1940s, 1950s, and 1960s, they were mostly southerners. When Lyndon Johnson came to Congress as a young staff person in 1931, four committee chairmen were Texans, as was the Speaker of the House, John Nance Garner.

But things have changed. In the 103d Congress, the seniority system was challenged three times—twice successfully, once not. The first was the replacement of Jamie Whitten, longtime chairman of Appropriations who suffered a stroke, by Kentucky Democrat Bill Natcher. Whitten, who served with eleven presidents from Franklin Roosevelt to Clinton, did not contest his removal or Natcher's ascension. Elected to Congress in 1953, Natcher had cast more than eighteen thousand votes in a row, the longest string of consecutive votes in congressional history. He once told Congressman Jack Brooks that "having a perfect record was probably the worst mistake he ever made." A few years ago, Natcher hurried back to Washington after his wife's funeral to cast his vote in the House. Natcher, who wrote a letter at the end of every week to his grandchildren telling about his activities and describing the events of the week, was from a different era: he had no press secretary and sent out no news releases; he never owned a fax machine or ever spent his entire office budget; he regularly raised less than five thousand dollars to get elected, and never filmed a political commercial; and he prided himself on never having missed a day of work. During my first visit to the White House for a meeting with President Clinton and Vice President Gore, Natcher exhorted us freshman members to "do what's right, then go home and explain to your people why you did it. . . . Some votes will take the skin off your back. If you explain, your people back home will put it back on."

The second challenge to the seniority system was attempted by Lane Evans, a Vietnam vet who ran against Veterans Affairs Committee chair Sonny Montgomery. Lane claimed that Sonny's attention was focused on World War II–era and Korean veterans at the expense of Vietnam veterans. His challenge fell a handful of votes short, in large part because Montgomery, who was almost a legend among the older veterans all over the country, had campaigned for members in their districts and helped a number of them with veterans groups.

The third challenge came when Chairman Natcher died in 1994 at the age of eighty-four. Not wanting his consecutive voting streak to end, he was, a few days before he died, wheeled into the chamber, accompanied by two doctors and a nurse, to cast his vote. One particularly insensitive reporter inquired of him as he was lying on a gurney, "Mr. Natcher, is it worth it?" After Natcher's death, David Obey, a fifty-five-year-old Wisconsin Democrat, challenged Neal Smith, a seventy-four-year-old Democrat from Iowa who was first elected in 1958 and who was next in line in seniority, for the Appropriations chair. Obey, who most Democrats thought would be more aggressive, better on television, and more sensitive to other members' concerns and requests, was elected handily.

Minority members and, at least on the Democratic side, moderate and conservative southerners are the strongest supporters of the seniority system in the House. Both groups see seniority as their protector. While the Democrats were in the majority, southern conservative and moderate Democrats feared that more liberal members would take away or refuse to give them chairmanships because the southerners often vote against the majority of Democrats. African American members are only now beginning to reap the benefits of seniority, after wandering in the political and electoral wilderness for decades. Minority members, usually in safe districts, are in a position to be the most senior Democrats on several full committees and scores of subcommittees in the next twenty years.

Interestingly, no other national legislative body in the Western world, or any of the fifty state legislatures, for that matter, uses seniority as the dominant factor in determining committee appointments and chairs. So although there have been some cases where a less senior member has been selected over a more senior member for a chairmanship, the seniority system seems locked in place in the Congress. Too many members of Congress have waited patiently for too long.

4

In the Chamber

Don't forget. This is work.

—Baseball commissioner Bart Giamatti, to his assistant
at a ball game on a beautiful sunny day

Least of all do I admire the puerile, paltry shysters who
constitute the majority of Congress. But I confess frankly
that these shysters, whatever their defects, are at least
appreciably superior to the mob.

—H. L. Mencken

When you first enter the House, your first impression
is of noise like that of sharp waves in a Highland loch,
fretting under a squall against a rocky shore.

—Lord James Bryce

A NEW MEMBER OF CONGRESS, not unlike a visitor in the gallery, is first
struck by the apparent chaos in the House chamber. Perhaps forty or
fifty members will be on the floor, one speaking in the well or at the committee table, a few listening, and several more conversing with each other.
Others can be found in the cloakroom, maybe eating a sandwich, watching
a couple of televisions mounted in the corners usually tuned into floor proceedings, or frequently the news (and occasionally a ball game). Most members are either in committee or in their offices.

The chamber of the House of Representatives is large, about half the size
of a football field. Almost everyone who enters it for the first time, however,
comments that it is not as grand nor as august as it looks on television during the president's State of the Union address. On the wood paneling in
front of the Speaker's rostrum are carved the words: *Union, Justice, Tolerance,
Peace, Liberty.*

While there are no assigned seats on the House floor, Democrats sit to the Speaker's right and Republicans to the Speaker's left. (The political, ideological descriptive terms "right" and "left" come from the French Legislative Assembly, where the radical commoners sat on the left of the hall and the more conservative clergy and nobility sat on the right.) Also, there are various groupings of representatives on the House floor. On the Democratic side, for example, for as long as anyone can remember, southern conservatives and moderates tend to sit in the back in the middle, while the Pennsylvania Democratic delegation almost always can be found in the far back corner.

Above the Speaker's chair can be found the only quote from a former member to be included in the decoration of the chamber, that of Daniel Webster, who served as a Federalist congressman from New Hampshire and later as a Whig from Massachusetts: "Let us develop the resources of our land, call forth its great powers, build up its institutions, promote all of its great interests, and see whether we also, in our time and generation, may not perform something worthy to be remembered."

Only two portraits adorn the walls of the House: one of George Washington and the other of Marquis de Lafayette. Both portraits were hung in the Old House Chamber, now Statuary Hall, where Lafayette addressed the Congress in 1824, the first foreigner to do so. Interestingly, the next foreign dignitary to address a joint session of Congress was Winston Churchill 117 years later, in 1941. The British prime minister surveyed his audience and pronounced, "If my father had been American and my mother British, instead of the other way round, I might have got here on my own."

In recent years, it has become much more commonplace for heads of state to address the House and Senate in the chamber. During my first term, Indian prime minister Rao and South African president Nelson Mandela spoke, and, in a historical first, Israeli prime minister Yitzhak Rabin and King Hussein of Jordan addressed us in the same session. The traditional State of the Union address, delivered to a joint session of Congress every year, is a relatively recent phenomenon. Although Washington and Adams addressed Congress, it was Jefferson who began a tradition of sending a written message to the Congress. In 1913 Woodrow Wilson began the new tradition of delivering a State of the Union address to the Congress. Wilson was also the first sitting president to travel abroad.

The House of Representatives convened for the first time in its present home in December 1857. In those days, members worked at desks in the chamber, which were removed in 1909 when representatives were provided personal offices in the House Office Building, now called the Cannon House Office Building. Other than the Washington and Lafayette portraits, the only objects that were moved from the Old House Chamber to the new chamber in 1857 were the ornate inkwell on the Speaker's desk and the mace, originally a medieval weapon but now the symbol of authority for the House of Representatives. When the House is convened each day, the sergeant at arms places the mace — crafted in 1841 — on a pedestal to the right of the Speaker's chair. When the House resolves itself into the Committee of the Whole House on the State of the Union, the mace is moved to a lower pedestal. Members of the House thus know, upon entering the chamber, whether we are in session or in the Committee of the Whole by simply glancing at the mace's position.

On the ceiling all the way around the hall are state seals in order of admission to the Union. The seals of Puerto Rico and the Virgin Islands are positioned alongside them. Hung in a corner of the Democratic cloakroom is a 1951 diagram of the seals with the order of admission of the states and the predicted order of admission for the territories. Whoever was in charge of putting up the seals four decades ago expected Puerto Rico to be the forty-ninth state, followed by Alaska, Hawaii, and then the Virgin Islands.

The huge glass ceiling in the hall, which for over a century allowed the House to be bathed in natural light, was covered in the 1940s, apparently for security reasons. Around the eagle depicted on the ceiling were forty-eight stars representing the states at that time. In 1962, without changing the design, and two years after Alaska's and Hawaii's admissions to the Union, the stars representing these new states were crowded into the constellation.

Ringing the upper walls of the hall are marble bas-relief portraits of twenty-three of history's greatest lawmakers: from Hammurabi to Jefferson, Solon to Napoleon, Pope Innocent III to Suleiman. Sculpted in the late 1940s from white Vermont marble, they were placed in the House in 1950 during the major renovation of the chamber. The relief portrait of Moses, the "ultimate lawmaker," is located directly opposite the Speaker's rostrum and is the only one not depicted in profile.

On the south wall of the chamber, above the press gallery, is an electronic scoreboard that appears when the House is voting. During a recorded vote, members' names are listed alphabetically; as they cast their votes, a green (yes), red (no), or yellow (present) light goes on next to their name. Electronic votes in the House of Representatives were a long time coming.

It was on June 1, 1869, that a young inventor named Thomas Alva Edison, born twelve miles from my House district in Ohio, got his first patent—for an electrical vote recorder. Edison, who had observed the thirty-minute, cumbersome voting process in the United States House of Representatives, believed his invention could save Congress valuable time. After an unsuccessful approach to the Massachusetts legislature, he came to Washington, where he presented his invention to a House committee. The earnest twenty-two-year-old inventor showed the committee how his machine worked and told them that it would save time for them and their colleagues. The committee chairman responded: "Young man, that is just what we do not want. Your invention would destroy the only hope that the minority would have of influencing legislation. . . . And as the ruling majority knows that at some day they may become a minority, they will be as much averse to change as their opponents." A dejected Edison promised himself that he would never again invent something that had no commercial value.

And so the House continued its cumbersome voting methods. When the House was in the Committee of the Whole, most votes were taken by voice vote: the chairman simply listened to the *ayes* and *nays* and pronounced whether the motion had passed. Unlike today, the ruling of the chair was usually not appealed. When there was a counted vote in the Committee of the Whole, it was done by "teller vote": one Republican and one Democrat stood in the center of the House chamber; those members voting *aye* lined up and walked by as the tellers tapped each of them on the shoulder and counted "one, two, three . . ."; then the *nays* lined up, walked by the teller, and were counted. There were no recorded votes in the Committee of the Whole; the public had no way of knowing how their congressmen voted in the Committee of the Whole unless a local reporter actually sat in the press gallery, watched how a particular member voted, and reported it. According to Indiana Democrat Lee Hamilton, who was first elected to the House in 1964, lobbyists sat in the gallery during teller votes and took notes and kept tallies, reporting back to their associates and membership about how a congressman voted. Congress was thus more accountable to organized interest groups than to the public at large. Hamilton said, by way of example, that there were no recorded votes taken on the Vietnam War for several years. Legislative leadership in both parties made sure of that.

Most of the time voice votes were taken in the full House. Appeals of the

Speaker's rulings, although not frequent, and votes on final passage were taken by recorded vote. A clerk called the 435-member roll alphabetically. When a member did not answer, the member's name was again called at the end of the roll call. The whole process typically took about forty-five minutes. The lengthy and cumbersome voting procedure was adeptly used by civil rights opponents in the 1950s and 1960s. Repeated quorum calls, each lasting about forty-five minutes, slowed House business to a crawl, prompting one southerner to say, "That was our way of filibustering."

In the late 1960s, Congressman Andy Jacobs, a Democrat from Indiana, introduced a bill to install an electronic voting system. Thirty-six state legislatures were already using electronic voting, four of them (Iowa, Louisiana, Texas, Wisconsin) since 1922. After repeated attempts, the bill finally passed. So, 104 years after Edison's invention and attempted sale (the Republic had more than doubled in age!) the House of Representatives installed an electronic voting system. And on January 23, 1973, under the direction of Case Western Reserve University math professor (and former Cleveland Browns quarterback) Frank Ryan, the first electronic vote was cast in the United States House of Representatives.

Congressman Jacobs had been defeated in 1972, so, ironically, when the system was installed he was not there to use it. Two years later, however, Jacobs, whose sardonic wit is almost legendary in the House, was elected again and then reelected every two years until he declined to run in 1996.

Closed-circuit televising of the House began in 1977. Cameras are placed in several locations around the House chamber so that members speaking from the well or from the majority or minority committee tables are facing a camera. Over five hundred small electronic speakers are placed underneath the chairs on the floor of the chamber and in the gallery.

Occasional verbal outbursts or protests come from the gallery, and the Speaker and Capitol police quickly restore order. But a much more serious eruption took place in 1954. Four terrorists, their guns concealed in camera cases, entered the southwest corner of the gallery and opened fire. No one was killed, but five members of Congress were wounded. Since then, security has tightened, cameras are not allowed in the gallery, and a lead shield has been inserted inside each of the seatbacks on the floor. One bullet hole is still visible in a committee table from which Republicans speak.

Off the House floor, the steps connecting the first and second floors on the northeast side of the Capitol tell an interesting story. Over a century ago, Kentucky congressman William Taulbee, a physically imposing man, had been the target of *Louisville Times* reporter Charles Kincaid's unfriendly pen one too many times. Spotting the rather scrawny reporter in the hallway, Taulbee menacingly told Kincaid he had better be prepared to defend himself when he saw him again. The next day, as Taulbee was walking down the stairs after leaving the House floor, Kincaid came around the corner and fired a six-shooter at the congressman. Shot just below the eye, Taulbee died eleven days later, on March 11, 1890, in a Washington hospital. Somehow Kincaid was acquitted by the jury. Sixty years later Taulbee's son John said, "That trial was a farce. [The jurors] were bought off. . . . They were a bunch of 'court hangers.'" As for the congressman, some of his bloodstains could not be washed out of the porous marble steps. They can still be seen on northeast steps nos. 5, 6, 7, and 8 between the first and second floors in the House side of the Capitol. Taulbee's son commented, "It's almost impossible to remove bloodstains when they are left by a person who has been murdered."

The "cloakrooms" off the House floor are each L-shaped (the larger leg is about the size of a small railroad car) with banks of telephones along both sides of one leg, a small lunch counter anchoring the middle, and comfortable sofas and chairs lining the walls of the larger leg. In reality, they are not cloakrooms at all. One for the Republicans, one for the Democrats, there are no places for coats or hats or umbrellas or boots.

In the winter months and in rainy weather, members move from their offices across the street to the House floor in tunnels that connect much of Capitol Hill. The tunnel between Longworth/Cannon and the Capitol is lined with paintings from high school students who have entered them in congressional district competitions. A subway train connects Rayburn and the House floor.

To the consternation of some House members, the United States Senate is called the "upper body." This appellation derives from the body's first quarters: when the First Congress met in New York in 1789, the Senate convened on the second floor of Federal Hall while the House met on the first floor. Many older members of the House have a particularly strong disdain—or perhaps even contempt—for the Senate. Many would concur with the words of Henry Adams in his famous autobiography: "No man, however strong, can serve ten years as schoolmaster, priest, or Senator, and remain fit for anything else." The Senate, veteran House members will say, is viewed by its members as a stopping-off place before going to 1600 Pennsylvania Avenue. Nineteenth-century Speaker Thomas Reed, who referred to the Senate as a "communion of old grannies and tabby cats," wrote a futuristic account of a presidential election conducted by secret ballot in the Senate. Nobody won. Every senator received exactly one vote.

Often, the Senate seems to delay by filibuster or kill legislation that the House has passed with strong majorities. House members know that we, with two-year terms, are closer to the people and typically more responsive to the public will. House members are often more knowledgeable about complex issues, which is usually evident in conference committees between the two houses. But George Washington envisioned the Senate as the "saucer" that cooled the hot tea brewed in the House. The upper body would slow down and dilute public passions passed on by the House. The Senate was to be more manageable, more genteel, more sedate. The House, according to Missouri Democrat Richard Bolling, "is more unruly, more gamey, more susceptible to vagrant gusts of opinion." We would see the Senate play the role of the cooling saucer repeatedly in the 103d Congress, in the 104th Congress, and in the impeachment vote in the 106th Congress in 1999.

In the first four decades of the nineteenth century, as the House grew in size, it became increasingly unwieldy; a boisterous minority could stop floor action, either through a filibuster, by making long speeches, or by offering amendment after amendment. In 1841 the House outlawed the filibuster, a method that gave great power to the minority to block legislation. It also instituted a one-hour limit on speeches, and the Rules Committee was formed to govern the rules of debate. The Rules Committee establishes the floor calendar for the day: what bills will be in front of the House; which bills will be brought up under suspension rules (which requires a two-thirds majority of those present); how much time is allotted to each side for debate; whether there will be a closed rule with no amendments allowed or an open rule with an unlimited number of amendments or a modified open rule with predetermined amendments.

The majority party usually schedules "closed rules," while the minority almost always argues for "open rules," which allow for all sides to be heard on all issues. However, open rules clog the House for weeks at a time on issues that may not be important. A body with 435 members—each free to offer as many amendments as desired, each member free to speak on any amendment—would certainly result in an especially inefficient operation of Congress. Obviously, the majority party must allow for open debate but must also manage Congress so as to accomplish the majority's ultimate goals and the public's desires. When a bill is brought to the floor, the rule that the Rules Committee has attached to the bill is voted on first. If it fails, which is unusual, the bill goes back to the committee for a new rule.

Much of the activity in the House chamber is conducted in the Committee of the Whole House of the State of the Union. Generally referred to as the Committee of the Whole, it was created in the early days of the Congress to work more informally with fewer parliamentary restraints. Today, it is regularly used to allow for freer debate among members. Depending on the rules adopted by the Rules Committee, debate in the Committee of the Whole is often conducted under the Five-Minute Rule. When an amendment is offered, anyone who wants to speak for or against it is allowed up to five minutes to address the committee. If a member wishes to speak for more than five minutes, she may "ask for unanimous consent" for an extra minute or two. If a member wants to speak for a second or third time, she may ask another member to yield part of his five minutes, or she may ask for unanimous consent for more time. At other times, the Rules Committee may write the rules so that each side—supporters and opponents—is allowed one hour. The supporting and opposing floor managers "control" the time. Usually the floor manager in support of the legislation will begin by saying, when recognized by the chair, "I yield myself as much time as I may consume." At the end of her remarks, she will say, "I reserve the balance of my time." The opposition leader will then "yield himself as much time" as he needs. After he concludes his remarks, the floor manager in support of the bill will yield time to others who support the bill. Each side alternates until the time is used up.

By the time most legislation reaches the House floor, it is almost assured of passage, usually in a form very similar to its committee version. There is a deference to the committee structure and to committee expertise that typically makes difficult successful amending of legislation on the floor. Over 95 percent of bills pass on the floor; committees kill, usually by inaction, well over 90 percent of bills introduced, so those bills that do reach the floor are usually in a form that a majority of members can support. Only 4 percent of all bills introduced in Congress pass every hurdle—committee in each house, floor action in the House and Senate, and a presidential signature or override of a presidential veto—and become law.

Throughout the day, members are called to the House for votes. Depending on the importance of the bill, members of the majority and minority whip's operation, or members who are actively supporting or opposing the bill or amendment, will often be stationed by the three or four major entrances to the House chamber. They will be campaigning for votes, sometimes handing out flyers, other times simply informing party members and ideological allies of the issue and suggesting a position. Upon arrival on the floor, members usually know how they are going to vote because the legislative calendar for the day is distributed ahead of time.

Early in the day, I meet with my staff to discuss the day's legislative business—what amendments will be on the floor, how legislation will affect my district, what specific amendments mean to Ohio and the nation. Each of my staffers is assigned a series of issues in which he has gained expertise and can therefore advise me. I also look to other members who have specific knowledge on certain issues and listen to the advice and direction of the committee of jurisdiction. My staff will also collect "Dear Colleague" letters, which are letters from other members advocating a position in support of or in opposition to an amendment or bill.

Arriving in the chamber, members use a plastic card, which resembles a credit card with the member's photograph, to cast their votes. The card is inserted in one of the forty-five little black boxes located throughout the chamber, and the congressman pushes *yes, no,* or *present*. This vote, which can be changed during the fifteen- or five-minute vote, is recorded on a large scoreboard on the south wall of the chamber. Illuminated panels on the east and west walls, located above the floor and directly below the gallery, keep a running tally and note the time remaining to cast votes. Members who have forgotten or misplaced their cards may vote in the well of the House at a table in front of the Speaker's rostrum.

Members usually have fifteen minutes to vote after the initial bell rings. (Most members carry pagers so they can be summoned to the floor for votes.) Once in the chamber, a great deal of legislative business can be conducted. Members will circulate "Dear Colleague" letters or letters to the president for one another to sign. Discussions about cosponsorship of bills take place. The chamber is an ideal place to lobby other members about all kinds of legislative issues; it is the one place where members can almost always locate one another.

At first glance, the influence of the seniority system on the House floor *seems* to be as important as it is in committee. Managers of floor debate— those supporting the legislation and those opposed—are usually committee

chairs, subcommittee chairs, or senior members of the committee of jurisdiction from which the bill emerged. Those most closely listened to in debate are often senior members because of the expertise they have developed.

Nonetheless, Congress has become more and more of a merit system
where hard work is rewarded, where knowledge and expertise usually carry
the day, and where members must bargain with one another to reach agreement on complex issues. Amendments are regularly offered by junior members who have impressive knowledge and expertise about the issues. New
members are not at all bashful about challenging more senior members on
substantive issues, and legislative leaders are listening to younger members
more than in the past, especially because both parties have had large freshman classes in the past decades.

Of course, this "merit system" operates in the framework of political parties. Merit, expertise, and hard work often made little difference in the big
issues in the increasingly partisan environment of the 103d, 104th, and 105th
Congresses, but on less partisan or controversial issues, those attributes can
matter. One of the most interesting legislative skirmishes (notice how so
many legislative and election terms also describe military actions: campaign,
conflict, attack, fight) of the 103d Congress was the battle over the superconducting supercollider (SSC). First submitted to Congress in 1987 at a
cost of $5.32 billion, the world's largest, most advanced particle accelerator
was lauded as the key to a high-tech future. Begun in 1989 in Waxahachie,
Texas, it was the world's grandest engineering project. Congressman Joe
Barton, a conservative Republican who represents Waxahachie, could not
find enough superlatives when he talked about America's future with the
supercollider: "It is the only project in the world with the capacity to unlock
the basic secrets of nature and determine the most basic elements of matter."
And with the supercollider, he vowed, "we will save America's future." The
circular collider, which was to be completed in 1999, would be the greatest
physics project in history: fifty-four miles of fourteen-foot-wide tunnels
under 16,700 acres. The collider was projected to use, upon its completion,
4.2 million gallons of water each day.

The project ran behind schedule and over budget from nearly the beginning. The private contractor hired by the government had charged for
dozens of questionable expenses. The inspector general concluded that $216
million of the $508 million in government reimbursements were excessive
or inappropriate, including $35,000 for a Dallas holiday party and $56,000

for potted tropical plants. By 1993, the cost for completion was estimated to be as high as $12–$13 billion. Opponents—including the National Taxpayers Union, Environmental Action, the Seniors Coalition, Friends of the Earth, and Concord Coalition—joined with many scientists in arguing that the supercollider sucked up too much of America's research dollars, especially at a time when government research dollars were already in short supply.

In the 102d (1991–92) Congress, the House had defeated the project 232 to 181, but Texas senator Lloyd Bentsen had resurrected it in the Senate. Supercollider supporters saved the project in large part by promising that there would be significant foreign investment—approximately $1.7 billion—to help pay the ever-increasing costs; proponents promised that foreign governments, especially Japan and Germany, would become major partners in the Texas project. But by 1993, when Congress was again considering renewal of SSC funding, only India, the poorest of the potential investors, had come forward. More promises by supporters that costs would be reined in and that foreign nations would invest rang hollow to House members, especially the 114 freshmen (four additional new members had been elected to Congress in special elections). SSC was in serious trouble, and by this time Lloyd Bentsen was no longer in the Senate.

Freshman Democrat Mike Kreidler of Washington state, Republican Chris Shays of Connecticut, and I joined with longtime supercollider opponents Democrat Jim Slattery of Kansas and Republican Sherwood Boehlert of New York to lead the opposition to SSC funding. Meeting around a table in Slattery's office in early June 1993, we went over the names of every House member, discussing where they stood, how they had voted on the supercollider the previous year, what approach to take with them, and who should talk to which member. For the next few days, each of us worked our list. We sent out a bipartisan "Dear Colleague" letter—signed by a dozen freshmen—to all new members of the House, asking for their votes: "[The] federal government's cost has increased more than 250% since the project was introduced. . . . The SSC [is] 51% over budget on conventional construction. . . . Please join us in voting for the Slattery-Boehlert amendment to cancel the Super Collider and save taxpayers $8.7 billion."

As the vote neared, we were certain that we had more than enough to win, but we also knew that the larger our victory, the better our chances in a not-particularly-sympathetic Senate. And if we did fail in the Senate, which was likely, an impressively lopsided House vote would give our side more strength to keep SSC funding out of the final bill in conference committee.

In the days leading up to the vote, SSC supporters stepped up their lobbying efforts. Some Congress watchers observed that more lobbyists were hired on this project than on any other single appropriation in recent memory. While we called the huge supercollider "Jurassic Pork," proponents dismissed our contention by claiming that the SSC was not just for Texas; almost every state in the country would benefit. SSC lobbyists brought me a printout of SSC contracts in Ohio's Thirteenth District; twelve contracts—including one to a printer for $47.50—added up to $86,122.77.

The *Waxahachie Daily Light* asserted that the supercollider was not wasteful. Its headline blared, "If SSC's a 'Pork Barrel' . . . 48 States Share in It," which simply confirmed our point that it was indeed pork. The B-1 bomber was once called the perfect weapons system because parts of it, it was said, were made in all 435 congressional districts in the country. The supercollider was almost as good.

Our confidence was buoyed by our whip count: 179 confirmed opponents to funding; 65 leaning against; only 94 certain proponents; and 16 leaning in support of the SSC. Even if we lost all of the 80 or so undecided, which was unlikely, we would still kill the supercollider in the House. So when the vote was taken, even we were surprised by the size of our margin: 280 to 150. We had gone from a fifty-vote margin in the previous Congress to a 130-vote margin. The victory was total: two-thirds of House Democrats voted with us; over half of House Republicans voted to kill the SSC; eighty-two of 114 freshmen voted to eliminate supercollider funding.

Two ancillary factors may have contributed to the one-sided vote: Texas politics and the space station. Kay Bailey Hutchinson, the Republican candidate for the U.S. Senate, was running in a special election to fill the term of President Clinton's new secretary of the treasury, Lloyd Bentsen. Her entire campaign repeated the theme of "Cut Spending! Cut Spending First! Cut Spending Now!" She was elected overwhelmingly, crediting her victory to her and the Texas electorate's fervor to eliminate pork, cut spending, and "get government off our backs." Interestingly, in the tradition of Texas Republicanism, the new budget-cutting senator—on her swearing-in day—was on the House floor lobbying for money for the supercollider.

As many of us considered the funding of this Texas-sized, Texas-pork project, we could only say, "Let the cuts begin." To many members of Congress, these conservative politicians had been given enough. Their antigovernment rhetoric, anger at the federal government, and brazen feeding at the federal trough seemed a bit hypocritical.

Two months after the House overwhelmingly defeated the supercollider, the Senate approved funding, 57 to 42. On October 14, the House-Senate conference committee—mostly supercollider supporters who were appointed by the House and Senate leadership—chose the Senate version and restored funding, causing the usually cheerful, even-tempered New York Republican Sherry Boehlert to snap, "What they did insults the intelligence and integrity of this institution."

When a bill comes out of conference committee, it faces an up-or-down, yes-or-no vote in each house. We needed to reassert House authority to knock out funding, and the only way to do that was to defeat the entire Energy and Water Appropriations bill, of which the supercollider was only a relatively small part. While that was an unusual tactic, it was our only option.

We appealed to House pride, or at least to members' resentment of the Senate ("Don't let the Senate do this to us, and to taxpayers, again!") to enlist support of the 280 colleagues who voted with us in June. When the appropriations bill came in front of us in October, we defeated it again, 282 to 143, an even larger margin. The conference committee would now have no real choice but to delete the funds for the SSC. The superconducting supercollider was indeed dead . . . finally.

At about the same time all this was going on, legislation to fund another expensive high-tech project, the space station, had passed Congress by one vote. Also seen, at least in part, as a Texas project, the passage of the space station helped seal the defeat of SSC: too many new members had campaigned as budget cutters to support two behemoth engineering projects. Ironically, defenders of both the space station and the supercollider tended to be, for the most part, conservatives. Rhetoric aside, most conservatives can be found on the side of the big spenders on defense and big-science pork projects like these.

Earlier in 1993, a more partisan and equally controversial bill came to the House floor. The Motor Voter bill liberalized voter registration by extending registration services at motor vehicle outlets and other places. Democrat Al Swift of Washington state asked me to help him manage the floor debate. As Ohio secretary of state, I had worked with Swift's office on this bill in the 1980s, when President Bush vetoed it. Each side—the Democrats and the Republicans—was given two hours to make its best case. Congressman Swift, chairman of the House Subcommittee on Elections, introduced the bill. After his presentation and Louisiana Republican Bob Livingston's counterarguments, Swift yielded time to other supporters of the bill, usually in increments of one, two, or three minutes. Democratic arguments centered around the seemingly inexorable decline in voter turnout for the last thirty years and how the great majority of people will vote if they are in fact registered. Republicans countered with arguments about potential voter fraud and federal intrusion in state election activities. When Swift had to leave the floor for some pressing business, I was given the opportunity to manage the bill. Although I had spoken on the floor several times, I was nervous and anxious about my lack of knowledge of parliamentary procedures. Fortunately, Swift had a good staff there to help. Passing the House by a healthy margin, the bill also passed the Senate, making it one of the first major bills signed by President Clinton.

I went to the White House bill-signing ceremony—my first. I sat next to Georgia Democrat John Lewis, who, I like to say, is the only person now serving in Congress who was a great man before he got here. At the beginning of the ceremony, an audio recording of President Lyndon Johnson speaking at the signing of the Civil Rights Act was played. I could only imagine what John Lewis—who had been beaten up by white supremacists and county deputy sheriffs perhaps more than anyone else in the civil rights movement—was thinking as his journey to secure the vote for all Americans had reached its final stage.

Floor sessions consume an enormous amount of time. When we are in our offices or in committee and are summoned to the floor, a vote will usually take fifteen or twenty minutes. Committee hearings generally take two or three hours; mark-up can take much longer. During floor sessions or committee hearings, we try to shoehorn meetings with constituents outside the chamber in the Rayburn Room, conversations with other congressmen and congresswomen in the cloakroom, briefings with staff in the office, and discussions with other officials in the anteroom off the Commerce Committee hearing room. Unfortunately, as members rush back and forth from committee to the floor, from meeting to meeting, and from Washington to their districts, there is little time for reflection. Congress and its members are almost always reactive, rarely reflective. Sober, thoughtful analysis of public policy is too often the loser.

During my first year in office, I would often return to the House chamber after dinner to do a "Special Order" with Majority Whip David Bonior or with Ohio representative Marcy Kaptur or freshman colleague Bart Stupak about the North American Free Trade Agreement. Special Orders allow members up to an hour to address the House on a particular issue after the close of legislative business and are done by one person or by a group of members, often in the form of an almost informal discussion, for a longer period. Their purpose is to educate, explain a point of view, and advocate a position to the public via television. Broadcast on C-SPAN, Special Orders are viewed by hundreds of thousands of people.

In the 103d Congress, every incoming Democrat (the majority party always presides over the House and the Committee of the Whole) was expected to preside over Special Orders, which often go late into the night. One evening, in the summer of 1993, it was my turn to preside. Several members spoke for five minutes, a few for fifteen minutes, and a couple more for an hour. Finally, Congressman Bob Dornan, a right-wing, pro-military California Republican (who, during the 1992 presidential race, Bill Clinton suggested looked "like he needs a rabies shot," and who was defeated in 1996 by Loretta Sanchez) rose as the last speaker on the calendar. Dornan took to the floor for an hour to talk alternatively about our role in Somalia peacekeeping, Bill Clinton's draft status, and his own trip to Mogadishu, Somalia's capital. As the presiding officer during Special Orders, the acting Speaker must sit patiently, usually only half-listening (sometimes reading a book, other times signing letters). The camera is always trained on the member addressing the House, or on the empty House chamber. So, as he spoke, Dornan whipped out several pictures he had—of himself in fatigues and of others from Mogadishu—showing them to the camera. Thankfully, and mercifully, his one hour expired soon after. At almost midnight, I adjourned the House for the day.

A "One Minute" is another attempt to reach the public prior to the opening of legislative business. Members are given one minute—alternating between Democrats and Republicans—to speak, usually in the morning. Some of the most partisan speeches in the House are delivered during One Minutes and Special Orders. Through much of the 103d Congress, Democrats used Special Orders and One Minutes to promote Democratic initiatives and the president's program or to criticize and build a case against NAFTA. Republicans, however, used One Minutes and Special Orders to criticize Clinton and the Democratic House: Whitewater, "oppressive majority rule," gun control, health care and "loss of physician choice," "the biggest tax increase in American history," and on and on. Minority Whip Newt Gingrich said during one Special Order that the Clinton health plan "means, if you are over 55 and you need kidney dialysis, you die." Republican One Minutes were structured, well organized, and always "on theme." The Republican Conference, the caucus for Republican members, chose a theme the day before, faxed the message to House Republicans, and often prepared the actual One Minutes for its members. They were almost always negative, virtually always partisan, and nearly always anti-Clinton. One especially vitriolic Special Order prompted Ohio Democrat Ted Strickland, a psychologist, to remark, "Some of the meanest people I have ever met are in the United States Congress, and I worked in a maximum security prison."

The regular, almost daily pounding that President Clinton and majority Democrats took was part of the public discrediting of Democrats that led to the debacle on Election Day 1994.

5

The Budget

It is not whether we add more to the abundance of those who have much; it is whether we provide enough for those who have too little.

—Franklin D. Roosevelt

The flaw in the pluralist heaven is that the chorus sings with a strong upper-class accent.

— E. E. Schattschneider

IN AUGUST 1993, several Democratic members of Congress knew that the vote they were about to cast could hasten the demise of their political careers. Republicans and right-wing talk radio hosts were billing the Clinton budget vote as "the largest tax increase in American history." All of us knew that we would see television ads in the 1994 election trumpeting our votes for "the largest tax increase ever." Nonetheless, 218 Democrats, many of us in vulnerable districts, voted for it because it began to deal with the budget deficit in a decisive way. Moreover, the budget's income tax increase actually affected less than 2 percent of all Americans.

Historically, the president sends a budget—the blueprint of how the government will allocate its resources—to Congress. Although Congress, through the Congressional Budget Office and Appropriations Committee staff, is better equipped than ever to write a budget, the president draws upon his agencies' and departments' resources to tell him their needs and to draft department budgets accordingly. Congress is then charged with writing the budget.

The appropriations process on the House floor involves three actions. First, the Budget Committee passes a budget resolution that serves as a blueprint for all appropriations. A total spending amount is set, and ceilings are imposed on each Appropriations subcommittee in its areas of jurisdiction.

Second, the nonappropriations, authorizing committees of jurisdiction—for example, Armed Services authorizes dollar figures for the defense department—passes legislation that, as President Franklin Roosevelt once said, is in the form of a New Year's resolution: it may or may not be carried out. Third, the Appropriations Committee sends to the floor the actual appropriations bill. When a line item or particular appropriation is increased, a corresponding decrease is necessary to offset that increase in some other area in the subcommittee's jurisdiction. Only when an appropriations bill passes and is signed into law can the government actually spend the money.

When President Clinton and the Democratic leaders in Congress wrote the $500 billion deficit-reduction package, we all knew that it would be a difficult vote. But the problems in the economy were real. In his first State of the Union address in February 1993, President Clinton told Congress and the nation:

> Unless we have the courage to start building our future and stop borrowing from it, we are condemning ourselves to years of stagnation, interrupted only by recession, to slow growth in jobs, no growth in incomes, and more debt and disappointment. . . .
>
> If we don't act now, you and I might not even recognize this government ten years from now. If we just stay with the same trends of the last four years, by the end of the decade the deficit will be $635 billion a year, almost 80 percent of our gross national product, and paying interest on that debt will be the costliest government program of all. We'll still be the world's largest debtor, and when members of Congress come here they'll be devoting twenty cents on the dollar to interest payments, more than half of the budget to health care and to other entitlements, and you'll come here and argue over six or seven cents on the dollar, no matter what America's problems are.

The president was going to make deficit reduction the hallmark of his budget plan and the theme of his first two years in office.

The national debt (the amount of money the federal government owes its creditors) had grown from $1 trillion ($1,000 billion) in 1980 to over $4 trillion when Bill Clinton took office. The debt had increased, on average, roughly $800 million every day for more than a decade. The deficit (the annual shortfall in the federal government's revenues and expenditures) stood at almost $300 billion at the beginning of Clinton's first term. Interest payments alone consumed about thirteen cents of every federal dollar, military spending made up another seventeen cents, and discretionary non-

defense spending took another seventeen cents. All other spending—
Medicare, Social Security, Medicaid, farm subsidies, food stamps—is considered entitlements, which simply means that anyone who qualifies for
these programs is entitled to receive the support from the government, thus
making entitlements the most difficult expenditures to contain.

At the same time, wages in America were experiencing a long-term
decline. In the 1980s, worker productivity increased 12 percent while real
wages increased only one-sixth as much. Income for the wealthiest 10 percent of Americans had risen in the 1980s, while income for the majority of
the rest of the citizenry had declined; the wealthiest 10 percent saw their tax
bills decline in that decade, and the rest of us saw our taxes rise. According
to William Greider in *Who Will Tell the People: The Betrayal of American
Democracy*, "In 1960 the average pay for chief executives at the largest American corporations, after taxes, was twelve times greater than the average wage
for workers. By 1990, it was seventy times!"

President Clinton's budget bill included roughly $250 billion in cuts and
$250 billion in new taxes over a five-year period, a significant tax increase,
certainly, but not the largest in American history (the Reagan tax increase
was larger in real dollars). The bill made major cuts in Medicare reimbursement for doctors and hospitals, reduced cost-of-living increases owed federal employees, and eliminated several dozen federal programs. The bill
increased taxes in three ways: the income tax was increased only for those
whose adjusted income, for a single filer, exceeded $125,000, and for joint
filers, $140,000; Social Security recipients, whose income exceeded $25,000
(single filer) or $32,000 (joint), saw their taxes increase slightly; and the
gasoline tax was raised 4.3 cents per gallon. In the first House-passed version, the bill included a BTU tax—a tax on the energy content of all fuels
measured in British thermal units—instead of a gasoline tax. It was dropped
in the Senate.

Republicans argued that the Clinton budget would destroy any chances
of recovery because tax increases would stop investment and lead to job loss.
They contended that taxing the rich—even as they argued that this was actually a tax on the middle class because it would all be passed on to them—was
penalizing success. They accused Democrats of class warfare by taxing the
rich, again while arguing that the income tax was also being levied on the
middle class. And most vigorously, they argued that the economy would
slow because tax increases take money out of the economy and rob the private sector of investment capital.

Ohio Republican John Kasich compared the budget bill to a "snake bite. The venom is going to be injected into the body of this economy, and it's going to spread throughout the body and it's going to begin to kill the jobs that Americans now have." California Republican Chris Cox called it "the Dr. Kevorkian plan for our economy." Not to be outdone, future Speaker Newt Gingrich predicted that the sky would fall: "This will lead to a recession next year. This is the Democrat machine's recession, and each one of them will be held personally accountable."

Republicans also claimed that the spending cuts were actually reductions in the increase that various federal programs had been promised. In some cases, they were right, although the increases were committed and promised and would have taken effect if Congress had not acted. Although there were several programs that the president proposed to eliminate, some of us freshman wanted to see *more* programs "zeroed out": superconducting supercollider, space station, helium reserve, mohair subsidies, C-17 transport plane, sugar subsidies, tobacco subsidies, and several dozen others.

Clinton's budget bill passed the House in May with $250 billion in cuts, with the majority of the $250 billion in tax increases paid by people earning more than $250,000 per year. (When I went home to Lorain the weekend after the vote, my daughters and I checked out a couple of books at the library, where the librarian told me, "We won't charge you a BTU tax on that.")

Soon after the House vote, the Senate went to work. The BTU tax was stricken, even though most economists thought it fairer, and replaced with a seven-cent gas tax, which would have produced the same amount of money that the BTU tax would have generated. Western senators of both parties balked, as they had balked at Clinton's attempts to force a full market–value assessment on western timber, grazing, and mining interests. The president was forced to back down on both, and the gas tax was set at 4.3 cents per gallon.

By the time the bill passed the Senate and the conference committee had hammered out an agreement, the opposition, led by Republicans and talk radio personalities, was fully engaged. No Republican had voted for the budget in either house. The president knew he had to corral all his votes from Democrats. As the August vote approached, the calls and letters were angry. Talk radio, the *Wall Street Journal,* Republican speeches, and conservative columnists and editorial writers had convinced millions of people that this was the biggest tax increase in American history, that there were no real spending cuts in the bill, and that the middle class was going to be hit especially hard.

The facts decidedly said otherwise. As political analyst Kevin Phillips wrote, "The ultimate fiscal truth of the early 1990s was that for America's two or three hundred thousand somewhat rich or genuinely rich families, combined taxes as a share of income were probably at their lowest point in more than sixty years, whereas for middle-class families, combined federal, state, and local taxes took a higher portion of income than ever before." Only the wealthiest 3 percent of taxpayers would see their income taxes go up, and 12 percent of Social Security recipients would be subjected to a tax increase. The average motorist would pay about three dollars a month in additional gasoline taxes. In my district, the most affluent in Ohio, only 2,400 taxpayers would have to absorb a personal income tax increase. More than 17,000 families would benefit from the Earned Income Tax Credit (EITC), averaging a tax cut or refund of about $1,000 per family.

But people simply did not believe it. In the week before the vote, the Senate switchboard was deluged with over three million calls. Our office received hundreds, most of them opposed, and most of them middle-class taxpayers who were led to believe that their income taxes were going to be dramatically increased. Staff person Larry Callahan had just returned to my office from Ohio by car and had listened to Rush Limbaugh that afternoon. He took forty calls, he told me, where people used almost the identical—and inaccurate—words about the budget bill that Limbaugh had sputtered on the air.

On the night before the vote, one man from Medina who told me he earned $50,000 a year angrily called me a liar when I informed him that he would pay no more income tax. I even promised him that I would pay any increase in his income tax if he had to pay more on the same income. He still did not believe me—but I didn't hear from him the following April. Another man called me a liar because, he said, "You aren't really Sherrod Brown. Those lazy bastards would never take any phone calls from regular people like me. You were just told by him to say that you were him."

Many Democrats in Congress were unhappy with the president's failure to sell the budget plan to the public. He had said that those people making less than $30,000 would get a tax break in his budget plan (the EITC), while only the rich would pay more taxes. His comments were not especially forceful and were easily distorted by his opponents. At a White House reception in the early summer, I spoke privately with the president for a few minutes and told him that people at town meetings were saying things like "Congratulate me. The president says I'm rich. I make $30,000 a year." Clinton bristled, "I never said that." But he still did not make the distinction loudly or clearly enough to break through the din of talk radio distortion and the partisan ravings of the editorial pages of the *Wall Street Journal*. Some Democrats believed that most of the nation's newspapers, with their predominantly conservative, Republican-leaning editorial writers, and the highly paid pundits in Washington might have had a bit of trouble with objectivity in discussing the tax, since most of them, unlike reporters of twenty or thirty years ago, were in an income tax bracket subject to the higher tax.

Those of us who voted for the bill and the tax on upper-income taxpayers simply did not believe that an increase from 35 percent to 38 percent in the top tax bracket would have a significant negative effect on the economy and on job growth. As recently as sixty years ago, the top tax bracket in the United States had been 90 percent; and the upper bracket during America's best economic years, the post–WWII years through the 1960s, ranged from 50 percent to 70 percent. The steepness of the progressive income tax did not seem in those days to hurt the productivity of the wealthiest, most dynamic, most competitive economy on earth. I have never met anyone in the top income bracket who has said, "I don't think I'll work today because I don't want to go into a higher tax bracket." Or, "I think I'll stay home this month because I don't get to keep enough of my money."

The president simply could not get the message out that the income tax part of his budget bill was aimed at only a few. Even many partisan Democratic activists around the country were convinced that their taxes were going to go up. At a Democratic picnic a few days before the vote, I was sitting with a local judge, an autoworker, an attorney, and a county employee— all informed voters. Every one of them thought that their income taxes were going to go up; none, however, was in a high enough tax bracket for that to happen.

The week before the vote, when I told twelve-year-old Emily that I was going to vote for the budget and that this action would hurt me in the next election and possibly cause me to lose, she protested and suggested I vote against it. When I said that it was the right thing, she asked, "Can't you just vote, then, and not tell anyone?"

The pressure leading up to the vote was intense. President Clinton and his cabinet were working the phones calling undecided House Democrats. Hundreds of phone calls each day came into the offices of those who were undecided. Talk radio broadcast the names of the undecided members, putting additional pressure on them. Members lobbied one another. My closest friend in the House, Ohio Democrat Ted Strickland, who came from a slightly Republican district, sent me a "Dear Colleague" letter along with a book written by his wife about children, with the inscription: "We must do what is best for our children and America's future generations. That's why I'm voting for the President's deficit reduction plan." Congressional staff in many cases urged their members to vote against the plan, understanding that a vote in support could send a congressman into political oblivion. Surely the vote was going to be close. Even as the debate was in progress, the angry phone calls continued. Democrat José Serrano, a native Puerto Rican who represents a New York City district, presided over the Committee of the Whole during the budget debate. Both his office and the Speaker's office got several calls from people protesting against a Puerto Rican in the chair. "How can you not have a real American presiding over the very important budget debate?" callers asked. Serrano responded by sending them his Vietnam War service record.

The vote was indeed close: 218 in favor, 216 opposed. All of the 218 were Democrats, many of whom would not return to Congress, probably in large part because of that vote.

When we returned to our districts on the weekend after the vote, most of us had never seen such anger. Freshman Democrat Karen Shephard of Utah, who knew her vote could very well mean she would be a one-termer, had to be escorted to town meetings with armed guards. She was defeated in 1994. Marjorie Margolies-Mezvinsky, from Philadelphia, who cast the 218th vote in the House, had to listen to Republicans in the chamber wave and sing "Bye-Bye, Marjorie" over and over. Her treatment at home was just as hostile, and people's comments were just as vitriolic. In November 1994, Margolies-Mezvinsky lost her seat by a slim margin.

At the Medina County Fair two days after the vote, I was besieged by dozens of voters who simply did not believe me when I explained the spending cuts, the EITC, and the taxes. One man was particularly angry, especially about programs for the poor, and even a bit racist in his tone. After I found out that he was a minister at a very conservative church, I went over to his booth and asked him, "Did you know that there is a New Testament or do you just read Isaiah and Job?" He testily answered me—and I am *not* making this up: "Don't you think that Jesus believed in owning weapons?" And the next weekend, as I was walking in a parade, a dog barked at me along the parade route; its owner smiled (sort of) and remarked, "That's my killer cocker spaniel. He knows about your tax vote."

Usually, people at least understood my vote and acknowledged that I truly believed it was best for the district and for the country, and more often than not they respected me for the decision, even if they did not agree with it. Those members who were more tentative and unsure when they were home suffered politically for their uncertainty at election time. Prior to the vote, I had gone home and argued the case for the Clinton budget in town meetings, at grocery stores, on the phone, at Kiwanis and Rotary Clubs. And right after the vote, at 10:00 P.M., I was on the phone talking to print reporters explaining my vote and arguing that the budget was a significant step toward serious deficit reduction and that it would be the best thing, in the long term, for our economy. The next morning, I was in my office at 6:30 A.M. calling Cleveland, Akron, and Elyria radio stations and explaining my vote on tape for morning drive-time.

By acting boldly and doing what he thought was right, Clinton knowingly courted political disaster. Few politicians understood that better than former Ohio governor James Rhodes. Rhodes, a borrow-and-spend chief executive if there ever was one, was talking to George Bush in 1980 as Bush was trying to generate support for the Republican nomination for president. Bush was elaborately listing his accomplishments and qualifications: Yale graduate, war hero, chairman of the Republican National Committee, successful oilman, ambassador to China, director of the Central Intelligence Agency, member of Congress, and on and on and on. Rhodes, Ohio's governor at the time, reached in his back pocket, pulled out his wallet, and slapped it on the table in front of Bush. "None of that matters. If you put something in here, people will vote for you. If you take money out of this, people will vote for the other guy." The earthy Rhodes, who didn't like Bush's preppy mannerisms, said to reporters after that meeting, "George Bush is the only guy I know who gets out of the shower to take a piss."

President Clinton knew he was taking a gamble by advocating and pushing through Congress a budget with a tax increase and spending cuts when the economy was sluggish. Many economists, he told reporter Haynes Johnson, said to go easy on taxes and set in motion more government spending to restart the economy. By August recess Clinton had passed a budget for the first time since the initial Reagan budget of a decade earlier and had gotten 85 percent of what he had wanted in the bill, even more than Reagan's 60 percent. "This," said Johnson, "is the great gamble Bill Clinton is taking with history."

The Democrats' gamble seemed to pay off in a better economy. Seven times as many people received tax cuts as paid more income taxes; gas prices were actually lower than when the gas tax went into effect; more than 15,000 people in my district refinanced their homes as a result of interest rate reductions brought on, according to most economists, by a falling budget deficit. Government employment actually shrank by almost 100,000 employees over the next year; the budget deficit dropped from $300 billion to $180 billion and was on course to decline three years in a row for the first time since Harry Truman's presidency. And the employment picture dramatically brightened: six million new private-sector jobs were created in the first eighteen months of the Clinton presidency.

Ironically, however, the electoral news was not so good for Democrats. Some members endured negative radio ads in their districts immediately before and after their votes, usually paid for by the Republican National Committee. Fourteen months later, those of us who voted for the bill were pounded with television ads proclaiming that we voted "for the biggest tax increase in American history." Our votes for the Clinton budget became, for the most part, the centerpiece of our opponents' campaigns. Legislators who had wavered or implied that they were going to oppose the bill were, not surprisingly, hit the hardest. One midwestern congressman lost his reelection in large part because of an ad showing him on television—he had made the mistake early in his term of allowing a national television reporter to follow him during his deliberations on the budget—stating his intention to vote against one version of the budget bill and then ultimately voting for the budget on that fateful August day.

The budget vote imprinted on the Democratic majority, however unfairly, an image that President Clinton and congressional Democrats wanted to avoid: that we were old-fashioned tax-and-spend Democrats. As a result, a number of Congress's most courageous members lost bids for reelection: Margolies-Mezvinsky, Shepherd, Strickland, Tom Barlow, and a dozen others. And although clearly the country was significantly better off in the ensuing years because of the Democratic budget, the Democrats paid a price.

6

The North American Free Trade Agreement

The *Times,* the *Post,* the *Wall Street Journal*
Always know what's best for you.
Editorials, op-ed pieces,
If they don't write it, it ain't true!

Free trade's just a dandy concept
Advertisers tell us so.
Don't you question, don't you doubt it.
You're so stupid. You don't know.
　　　—My 1993 song about NAFTA

We pretend to have an agreement.
Japan pretends to abide by it.
　　　— Mickey Kantor, U.S. trade representative

RICHARD NIXON, GERALD FORD, Jimmy Carter, Ronald Reagan, George Bush, Bill Clinton, all of America's major newspapers, almost all of America's largest corporations, the Speaker of the House, the minority leaders of the House and Senate, the Senate majority leader—it seemed as if everyone was for it.

Yet, it was almost defeated. Almost.

In 1991 Congress granted President George Bush "Fast Track" authority to negotiate the North American Free Trade Agreement with Canada and Mexico. It gave the president and U.S. trade representative Carla Hills greater authority in the negotiations. More importantly, it meant that Congress could not amend the NAFTA agreement; we would be faced with one up-or-down vote. The negotiations were completed and the agreement finalized and signed by President Bush in late 1992—in time, it turned out, to be considered by a new Congress and to be managed by a new president.

No trade agreement in recent memory has so captured the American people's attention. During the 1992 presidential election, George Bush actively campaigned for the agreement that his administration had negotiated. Attempting to box in his Democratic opponent, Bush raised the visibility of this complex agreement. If Candidate Clinton supported NAFTA, Bush campaign strategists reasoned, he would alienate his labor base; if he opposed it, he could be characterized as an old-style, protectionist, not-ready-for-prime-time Democrat.

Clinton sidestepped the trap when, in a speech in North Carolina, he announced he could support NAFTA only if it had labor and environment side agreements; that is, labor standards for Mexican workers and environmental safeguards built into Mexican law. Organized labor, strongly opposed to NAFTA, was cautious but not alienated. Clinton business supporters were generally satisfied, and neutral commentators pronounced Clinton even-handed and sober-minded.

The visibility of NAFTA was sharpened even further when independent candidate Ross Perot, a Texas billionaire, made opposition to NAFTA one of the major planks of his campaign platform. Perot argued that the agreement would send hundreds of thousands of good-paying jobs to Mexico. Canada was rarely mentioned.

Although NAFTA ultimately was not a deciding issue in the presidential election, the strategies of Bush, Clinton, and Perot placed the issue prominently on the national agenda for the 103d Congress and the new president. Public interest in NAFTA was further heightened by organized labor. Throughout the debate on "Fast Track" in 1991, the NAFTA negotiations in 1992, and the debate in Congress in 1993, the American labor movement made the defeat of NAFTA its top legislative priority. The United Auto Workers (UAW) and the American Federation of Labor and Congress of Industrial Organizations (AFL-CIO) sent newsletter after newsletter to its membership; sponsored seminars for its shop stewards, business agents, and other union activists; and held rallies and demonstrations at union halls and in front of shut-down industrial plants.

Many of us in Congress—especially Majority Whip David Bonior, Toledo Democrat Marcy Kaptur, and San Diego Republican Duncan Hunter—were also stoking the opposition. We held news conferences, buttonholed other members, made speeches on the floor, and helped organize environmental and citizens' groups against the agreement. On Wednesday nights from late spring through the vote in November, we were often joined on the floor by Ron Klink of Pennsylvania and Bart Stupak from Michigan, two articulate first-year Democrats.

Union involvement, Perot's statements, and others campaigning against NAFTA touched a nerve in a public that for a decade had lived with plant shutdowns, job loss, and a decline in wages. The massive loss of industrial jobs and newspaper stories about relocation of major industrial plants to Mexico turned an anxious blue-collar workforce—union and nonunion alike—into angry opponents of NAFTA. Frustration turned to bitterness as more and more American workers seemed to be forgotten by their government as jobs went overseas, by corporations as their plants closed, and by society as their wages declined.

In July 1993 President Clinton's negotiators, under the tutelage of U.S. trade representative Mickey Kantor, announced that they had arrived at an agreement on labor and the environment. Most observers thought these side agreements were not particularly substantive. Most NAFTA supporters found them not especially bothersome; most of its opponents found them meaningless.

Supporters of NAFTA argued that the long-term economic benefits would outweigh the short-term costs of job loss, although many NAFTA proponents would not even acknowledge short-term job loss. In the end, they asserted, hundreds of thousands of jobs would be created: by eliminating tariffs—a border tax, in effect—on products coming to and from Canada, Mexico, and the United States, more goods and services would flow among the three countries, creating jobs and more prosperity in all three nations. Before NAFTA, the average tariff on Mexican goods sold into the United States was 4 percent, while tariffs on American goods sold in Mexico averaged 10 percent. Eliminating all tariffs would thereby be advantageous—and create more jobs—for the people of the United States.

More prosperity in Mexico, NAFTA supporters contended, would mean higher wages, a stronger Mexican middle class with greater buying power, and a cleaner environment that only a wealthier Mexico would be able to afford. The trade surplus of $2 billion that America enjoyed with Mexico would only grow and mean more benefits for the United States as the Mexican middle class expanded, NAFTA optimists argued. USA NAFTA, a group made up of America's largest corporations, called NAFTA "the best international trade agreement" the United States had ever signed.

Furthermore, with 90 million people just south of our border, Mexico was moving toward democracy. Its president, Harvard-educated Carlos Salinas de Gortari, had a very solid reputation among the American business and diplomatic elite. His dress and his English were impeccable, and his advisers and assistants were Mexico's "best and brightest." U.S. Secretary of the Treasury Lloyd Bentsen frequently said that there was one overriding and compelling reason to support NAFTA, and it was spelled S-A-L-I-N-A-S. The White House told us that under Salinas's rule Mexican productivity had jumped, the economy was being privatized with the selling off of public assets, and democracy was on an inexorable march.

Opponents of NAFTA saw a different Salinas. Despite his urbane image and perfect English, he led a political party—the People's Revolutionary party (PRI)—that had been in continuous power since 1927, longer than any political party in the world now that the Communists had fallen in the former Soviet Union. *The Economist* wrote about claims that 164 members of the opposition party had been killed in the preceding five years. Salinas and the PRI had kept wages low to attract foreign investment and to keep high-value foreign luxury goods as inexpensive as possible for Mexico's elite. But even we, as NAFTA opponents and Salinas detractors, were shocked when Salinas, after his term expired, fled into self-imposed exile.

In spite of sharp Mexican productivity gains, wages declined for the great majority of Mexicans. As Mexican business became more profitable and the country exported more of its products, Mexican workers saw their wages decline by one-third. We knew that unless there were solid side agreements on minimum wage, worker safety, democratic reforms, and the environment, there would never be a middle class in Mexico. NAFTA would simply lock in an exploitive political and economic system.

One of the most troubling results of NAFTA, we predicted, was that Asian firms would use Mexico as an export platform. Before NAFTA, Asian—or European or African—firms could sell into the United States and pay a duty to the U.S. government. Or those firms could build a plant in the United States, hire American workers, and sell their products in our country without paying a tariff. The passage of NAFTA, however, would provide a third, highly profitable alternative to foreign investors. A Japanese firm could build a plant in Mexico, hire workers for one dollar an hour, begin production with few environmental and worker safety restrictions, and sell their industrial products in the United States tariff-free.

NAFTA also meant high-paying American jobs moving south to low-wage Mexico. So with its very weak environment and labor side agreements, NAFTA would help the people of neither country. "It was negotiated," Michigan Democrat David Bonior said on the House floor, "purely in the interest of multimillionaire investors and multinational corporations, at the expense of working people and their families on both sides of the border."

Those investors, multinational corporations, and the Mexican elite were certainly not shy about preparing to take advantage of such an agreement. The Mexican state of Yucatan ran full-page advertisements in American trade magazines beckoning U.S. businesses to journey south: "'You can't cut labor costs 300% [*sic*] in 90 minutes . . .' Yes you can in Yucatan. . . . And you can save over $15,000 a year, per worker." And another ad, showing a concerned Anglo businessman scratching his head, read: "'I can't find good, loyal workers for a dollar an hour within a thousand miles of here.' Yes you can in Yucatan. . . . And you could save over $15,000 a year, per worker."

One other issue troubled many of us who opposed NAFTA. Small Business Committee chairman John LaFalce, a Democrat from Buffalo, held hearings on the potential problems of the weak Mexican peso and on what might happen if the peso were devalued. Economist Jeff Faux presciently wrote in *Dissent* magazine:

> There is the risk of integrating Mexican financial institutions, regulated by a corrupt one-party regime, with an already fragile U.S. financial system. NAFTA makes it much easier for U.S. banks, security firms, and so on, to buy into Mexican industry. This creates the possibility that when the next debt crisis hits, the U.S. government will have to rescue the Mexican economy in order to protect major American banks.

In July I made a speech to the Cleveland City Club calling for a side agreement on currency stabilization. But it wasn't taken seriously, either by a dismissive press or the single-minded Clinton administration. The media were too busy writing and talking about Ross Perot's belief that there would be a "giant sucking sound of jobs going to Mexico" to bother with the more complex issues of potential peso devaluation and the development of export platforms.

Perhaps our greatest difficulty was convincing the nation's media that there were serious, intellectually credible reasons to oppose NAFTA. Nearly all of America's major newspapers editorialized for NAFTA. Ohio's *Toledo Blade,* not among the nation's fifty biggest dailies, was the largest-circulation newspaper in America to oppose the agreement. The media were amazingly cynical about the motives of those of us who opposed the agreement: we were reactionary politicians; we were Luddites standing in the way of progress;

we were anti-intellectuals; we were old-time protectionists; we were stooges
of organized labor. One event especially stood out. Common Cause president Fred Wertheimer—the only man in Washington to have kept his job
for fifteen years without accomplishing the one task for which he was hired,
campaign finance reform—let his elitism show when he unveiled a Common
Cause study detailing the contributions from organized labor that anti-
NAFTA members of Congress had received. Released a few days before the
November 17 vote, Wertheimer and Common Cause forgot to say anything
about corporate contributions to pro-NAFTA members. As a former member of Common Cause, I would hope that he was not thinking of his own
organization's contributors and their interests.

One prominent radio producer asked me, "In your heart of hearts, what
do you really think of NAFTA? You don't really believe those things you say,
do you? You're against it just because you've got labor in your district,
right?" Another reporter from a major national newspaper, who covered my
campaign statements against the free trade agreement, called my office in
February 1993 and asked if I had switched over yet, figuring that a couple
of months in Washington among the free traders in government and the
media would surely help me see the error of my ways. The media attributed
public and congressional opposition to NAFTA to ignorance, jingoism, and
mindless protectionism. Anthony Lewis, one of the *New York Times*' and the
nation's best columnists, said that NAFTA opposition was grounded in "fear
of change and fear of foreigners."

Usually, public discourse on major issues requires that those who advocate change state a compelling case for this change; the burden of proof generally falls squarely on those who want to change the status quo. NAFTA
was different. The media decided that it was up to NAFTA opponents to
prove the negative case. Yet the press gave us little opportunity to make our
case.

Lectures from editorial writers about the desirability of free and open
markets were frequent. Less apparent was their willingness to provide space
for a free and open debate about NAFTA. *Washington Post* editorials and
op-ed pieces favored NAFTA by an almost six-to-one ratio, according to
North Dakota senator Byron Dorgan. FAIR (Fair and Impartial Reporting),
a media-watch group, found that the *New York Times* quoted three NAFTA
supporters for every one opponent in its news coverage. Regional papers
were not much different. When Congressman David Bonior wrote a piece
about NAFTA, the *Washington Post* refused to run the part of it that was crit-

ical of their coverage of the issue. The so-called "liberal media" again took the pro–big business conservative line.

Interestingly, according to political analyst Kevin Phillips, President Clinton enjoyed only one month during his first two years of more positive stories than negative stories on the national news; that was the thirty days before the NAFTA vote, when the president was lobbying Congress daily, calling us one at a time, making deals with individuals or groups of House members, and exhorting the American people to support the agreement.

In spite of all that, as the NAFTA vote approached, both sides believed the opponents were ahead. Clinton and pro-NAFTA members of Congress had claimed during the summer that business was lethargic, that they had not been engaged enough in support of NAFTA. According to the *National Journal,* Jim Kolbe (R-Ariz.), one of NAFTA's most visible supporters in Congress, complained that "they have not been outspoken in supporting NAFTA," and, as a Democratic House member concurred, "the business community has taken a duck. They are not working this issue like labor is. At the early stage, there was a vacuum." NAFTA supporters were dealing with the free-rider problem with corporate America; let the other companies do it while we take care of our unique, more pressing problems, many companies thought.

Our grassroots efforts, however, continued and accelerated. "NAFTA opponents," Georgia Democrat John Lewis asserted, "are passionate about our opposition." Jobs were at stake, world environmental concerns were at stake, issues of human and economic justice were at stake. The other side, mostly investors and corporate executives whose companies would likely benefit financially from the agreement, felt little passion about their support of it. During the August recess, labor activists, Perot's organizers, environmental groups, and Ralph Nader's organization were all involved. At one rally dozens of signs announced that NAFTA meant "No American Firms Taking Applications." At another event steelworkers Larry Ientille, Dominick Cataldo, and Bruce Bostick presented me with a t-shirt that read "Not Another F—— Trade Agreement."

We knew our grassroots efforts were paying off. After the August recess, our anti-NAFTA meetings in Majority Whip Bonior's office were more spirited, more optimistic. *NAFTA NOtes,* a daily newsletter written by Steve Fought of my staff and distributed to anti-NAFTA congressmen and congresswomen, reported positive signs of effective grassroots activity all over the country. One undecided member, returning to Washington, saw a

thousand yard signs on his way from his district home to the airport. Minority Whip Newt Gingrich, a Georgia Republican and NAFTA supporter, said
that there were no more than twenty pro-NAFTA districts out of 435 in the
country. One pro-NAFTA legislative leader said, "I hate weekends. These
guys all come back here and are more anti-NAFTA than they were when
they left D.C."

But after Labor Day, the pro-NAFTA people really went to work. Corporate lobbyists were everywhere. They came in from all over the country
(usually in their corporate, tax-deductible jets) to lobby members in their
offices. They invited us to tour their plants in our districts and told us that
"NAFTA meant jobs" at home. They encouraged and persuaded their
employees to write letters about the benefits of NAFTA to our congressional districts. One day, before visiting a very pro-NAFTA company in my
district, an anonymous employee of that firm called our office and whispered, "We were told by management that we are not to talk to the congressman unless we are pro-NAFTA. The meaning was clear that our jobs
might be in jeopardy otherwise."

Another member received a call on a Friday from the wife of an official
at a Fortune 500 company. She said that in spite of the call that the congressman would receive from her husband on Monday, there were two anti-
NAFTA voters in her house. Indeed, on Monday the company official called
and said that he was pro-NAFTA, as his boss sat there listening.

The grocery manufacturers sent us and presumably every other member
of Congress the biggest food basket I've ever seen. Attached was a note: "All
of this was Made in America. Vote for NAFTA so we can export more of
this to Mexico." We sent it to a homeless shelter, as did every other anti-
NAFTA activist in the House. We also sent out a news release that a Mexican maquiladora worker (in the area where most American companies were
located in Mexico) would have to work two or three weeks to be able to
afford to buy the basket's contents.

Nestle, Inc., one of the big gainers from NAFTA, sent us a large basket
of their products: Quaker Oats, Nestle's Crunch ("It's CRUNCH Time for
NAFTA"), and Capitan Crunch (notice the Spanish spelling, letting us know
that Nestle could sell a lot of cereal in Mexico). That, too, went to a homeless shelter. Not to be outdone, the opposition Coalition for Justice sent a
package of beans and flour wrapped in a newspaper, which represented a
typical meal for the millions of Mexicans living in poverty.

The Mexican government spent $25 *million* to lobby our government. They hired many of Washington's most powerful lobbyists, Democrats and Republicans alike, and paid them generously. One of the reasons that America's trade balance went from a surplus to the largest trade deficit in world history in less than fifteen years is that so many of Washington's highest-paid lobbyists work for foreign governments, foreign-owned businesses, and foreign investors; from 1979 to 1994, registered foreign agents—American citizens representing foreign concerns and lobbying the U.S. Congress or executive branch—increased eightfold!

President Clinton hosted events extolling the virtues of NAFTA together with Nobel Prize economists, with former presidents, and with former secretaries of state. Henry Kissinger, still afflicted with terminal self-importance, solemnly announced, "About once in a generation, this country has an opportunity in foreign policy to do something defining, something that establishes the structure for decades to come." NAFTA opponents hoped and believed that these ceremonies only served to underscore that NAFTA was an agreement of the elite, by the elite, and for the elite.

During the two weeks leading up to the NAFTA vote, the president and corporate America pulled out all stops. Elizabeth Drew wrote in her book *On the Edge* that during the NAFTA fight, "Clinton threw himself into the fight—meeting members of Congress in one-on-one sessions, making many phone calls to them, giving speeches, meeting with opinion leaders, meeting with individual members. Shortly before the vote, there were White House dinners for undecideds." An airport official told the anti-NAFTA forces that there were more corporate jets at National Airport than they had ever seen. Democratic leadership aide Steve Elmendorf told me that he had never seen a bill that the elite of this country wanted so badly. Full-page newspaper advertisements paid for by Merrill Lynch and other financial services companies appeared in *Roll Call,* the privately owned congressional newspaper, extolling the economic growth benefits of NAFTA.

Some NAFTA business supporters even threatened punishment when necessary. Ohio Republican David Hobson held a fundraising breakfast with a dozen or so corporate lobbyists and talked about NAFTA and me. "We can get Brown because of his NAFTA vote. . . . I know you don't want to give to Brown's opponent directly, but we can find a way for you to help." From the look of my 1994 opponent's campaign finance report, many did help directly.

Other meetings were taking place all over Washington. Five undecided Democrats were hosted at the vice president's residence by Pamela Harriman, treasury secretary Bentsen, energy secretary Hazel O'Leary, trade representative Mickey Kantor, and transportation secretary Federico Peña. The CIA conducted a briefing—I'm not making this up—in a dimly lit room in the Capitol with six men in dark suits telling us that defeat of "The NAHF-ta" (in their affected, preppy, establishment manner of speech) had national security ramifications. They seemed unable, however, to answer any questions or offer any information about the dozens of unsolved murders of leading Mexican labor activists, journalists, or political figures. But they did know a great deal about Haiti's Aristide. Many of us walked away, more certain than ever, about the corruption in the highest levels of the Mexican government.

And then there was the grassroots support for NAFTA aimed against those of us who very visibly and loudly opposed the agreement. One unsigned letter to Lorain's *Morning Journal* said, "How dare Congressman Brown criticize three former presidents and imply he is more representative of the working man when he has been attached to the public nipple for longer than I can remember. What a phony." Another, signed and sent directly to me, stated:

> I am writing as a business owner and a Wellesley College graduate majoring in Economics to implore you to reconsider your NAFTA vote. . . . As a graduate of Yale, surely you must be aware of the drastic consequences of Smoot-Hawley tariff act. . . . Your constituency, the working man, may not relate to the textbook reasons for a pro-NAFTA vote, but surely he will reap the benefits of free trade in time to thank you at the next election.

Eight days before the NAFTA vote, on November 9, Vice President Gore debated NAFTA opponent Ross Perot on national television. Undoubtedly, we were ahead; why else would the vice president of the United States debate? Perot was mediocre; Gore was at his best. The vote the following week was going to be very close.

Two days before the vote, President Clinton got on the phone to cajole, make deals, twist some arms. He was still a dozen votes short. In the previous weeks, according to Associated Press, his cabinet made more than a thousand phone calls to House members. And the president also made deals. The Institute for Policy Studies claimed that members got for their districts construction of two C-17 cargo planes; a $10 million trade center in Texas;

air routes to Europe for their district airports; protection for peanut butter, flat glass, durum wheat, sugar, and on and on. Most noteworthy was the president's deal with Florida Republicans to protect—in the name of free trade!—winter vegetables and citrus.

Doonesbury even got into the act:

Clinton: And let's see . . . You would be Rep. Charles Ribbler, am I right?

Ribbler: Yes sir. Freshman from the proud Nutmeg State. You promised me a pair of Presidential cufflinks in exchange for my NAFTA vote.

Clinton: So I did, Chuck! And here you go!

Ribbler: Wow . . . These are GREAT, Sir! Actually, I would've voted for it, anyway, but everyone was getting such cool stuff. . . .

Clinton: I understand.

On November 17, the presidents, banks, newspapers, large corporations, secretaries of state proved to be too much for us. We stationed NAFTA opponents at every entrance to the House floor, trying one last time to convince our colleagues to oppose the agreement. But by then we knew we'd lost. The final vote was 234 to 200. Republicans supported NAFTA better than three-to-one; Democrats opposed the agreement by a three-to-two margin. First-year Democrats voted more than two-to-one against NAFTA, while first-year Republicans supported it two-to-one. In the end, by Election Day 1994, NAFTA did not seem to matter much, at least to candidates for Congress. Few incumbents bragged about their NAFTA vote, and few challengers criticized them for it.

NAFTA did, however, contribute to an anger and a cynicism among labor union members and 1992 Perot voters. Clinton's NAFTA position especially angered a large number of Perot voters. They felt more and more betrayed by their government. Mostly white males, they saw their wages stagnate and their communities' factories close and their president send their jobs to Mexico. They were upset at Clinton because he did not seem to do enough to close the budget deficit (although he did more than twelve years of Republican presidents) or to reduce the trade deficit. An overwhelming number of white, male, Perot voters took out their frustration and anger—about job loss, wage stagnation, the trade deficit, and the budget deficit—on Democratic candidates for Congress.

At the same time, NAFTA dampened any enthusiasm that rank-and-file labor may have felt toward Democrats. Warren Davis, a top UAW official, told me at a summer picnic in Geauga County in 1994, "We wanted three things from the Democrats: health care, striker replacement, and the defeat of NAFTA. We lost all three." And even though most Democrats wanted health care reform, opposed NAFTA, and voted for the bill to ban the replacement of striking workers, we had failed. Health care never got off the ground, NAFTA was pushed through by a Democratic president, and the striker bill that passed the House was filibustered by Republican senators.

Consequently, union members had little enthusiasm for the 1994 elections. Gun owners were angry. Pro-lifers were alienated. Democrats simply had not done enough to generate any real excitement among the rank and file, or even much among union activists. While most still voted for Democrats on November 8, too many did not vote at all.

NAFTA hurt voter turnout among Democratic friends and allies and fueled voter turnout among those who wanted to punish a president they did not like—a deadly combination for the Democratic majority. But it was only three years later, in the first week of November 1997, when 160 House Democrats joined some eighty Republicans in denying the president Fast Track negotiating authority—an extension of NAFTA to other Latin American countries. NAFTA had failed.

7

The Great Health Care Debate

I'm against the Clinton plan. We don't need socialized medicine
in this country. It didn't work in Russia. I'm satisfied with my
health care. I've been on Medicare for 14 years.
> —letter from a Chardon woman

I have to wait two years for Medicare. I don't know what
I'm going to do. But I'm against Clinton's plan; I don't
want the government doing it.
> —telephone call from a Wadsworth man

FOR DECADES, party discipline has been a problem for Democrats. The
party of Henry Wallace and Strom Thurmond in the 1940s and the party
of George McGovern and George Wallace in the 1970s could never have the
discipline that the Republicans held and exercised. Democrats in Congress
were diverse; almost all congressional Republicans were white men. House
Democrats were urban, suburban, and rural; Republican members were
almost all suburban and rural.

Franklin D. Roosevelt could not hold most southerners in his coalition.
Neither could John F. Kennedy. Nor could Lyndon Johnson or Jimmy
Carter, southerners themselves. And neither could Bill Clinton and the
Democratic leadership in Congress. And this split was its most divisive
during the health care debate in the 103d Congress, when Energy and
Commerce chairman John Dingell simply could not assemble enough
Democratic votes to craft a bill that he could accept. The frustration felt by
Democratic leadership was articulated by House Speaker Tom Foley:
"Everybody's exercising sufficient leadership—It's the followership we're
having trouble with."

Comprehensive health care reform was a central part of the 1992 campaigns
of Bill Clinton and the overwhelming majority of House and Senate
Democrats. A year earlier, health care reform as a political issue had captured

the attention of the nation when Senator Harris Wofford, a Pennsylvania Democrat, won a stunning victory over Pennsylvania's former Republican governor. Wofford's line—"If criminals have the right to a lawyer, I think working Americans should have the right to a doctor"—and his support for universal health care coverage were the catalysts that vaulted him to victory. Washington's political pundits realized after Wofford's win that George Bush might indeed be vulnerable in his reelection bid.

Almost every Democratic challenger in 1992 had followed the lead of Bill Clinton and argued for comprehensive universal health care reform. Most of us addressed universal coverage in our campaign speeches, many repeating Senator Wofford's crowd-pleasing line. Although specifics were not often offered (for, as Mario Cuomo said, "you campaign in poetry and govern in prose"), we believed that a mandate for health care reform had been achieved.

By January 1993, as a new administration and a huge new class took office, most of us had health care reform at the top of our legislative agenda, and supporters of health care reform had no difficulty in explaining the problem: 37 million Americans had no coverage; 80 million had preexisting conditions; 72 million Americans had no coverage for increasingly expensive prescription drugs; tens of millions were underinsured; millions more were a catastrophic illness and a pink slip away from financial ruin.

Moreover, health care costs were out of control, putting coverage out of reach for many and crippling expansion plans of small business. Health care cost the American people $900 billion annually; costs were increasing at twice the rate of inflation; state Medicaid and federal Medicare costs were sapping budgets and pushing up the national debt; and the costs to businesses hurt our global competitiveness. Health care costs in 1970 accounted for about 7 percent of the nation's Gross Domestic Product; two decades later they consumed over 12 percent. Perhaps even more troubling, in 1965 federal spending on health care made up only about 4 percent of the federal budget; that number, by 1993, had jumped to 20 percent.

Soon after his inauguration, President Clinton named First Lady Hillary Rodham Clinton to head the newly created President's Task Force on National Health Care Reform. The president pledged that the task force would report its preliminary findings and legislative recommendations to the nation on May 1. By appointing the First Lady to head the effort on health care reform, the president raised significantly the stakes and visibility of the undertaking. Mrs. Clinton and her task force were charged with three goals: universal coverage, controlling costs, and maintaining quality of service. Public opinion polls showed that overwhelming majorities of Americans supported all three goals. The hard part, obviously, was going to be filling in the details.

As the group began its deliberations, it became clear that it would not meet its May deadline. Worse, from a public relations standpoint, the group consisted mostly of academics and government officials. The names of its participants, and even the times and places of the meetings, were also kept secret. Although the drafting of legislation by the president and the executive branch is almost always done by a few people quietly behind closed doors, the scope and secrecy of the First Lady's undertaking almost immediately drew heavy criticism. Its secrecy and its inability to meet its self-imposed deadline gave opponents of health care—and there were many—an easy target.

The secrecy and the delay hurt the president's efforts in other ways, too. Leaks about costs, although often exorbitantly and extravagantly inaccurate, contributed to a fear among the public, a fear stoked by talk radio personalities and other opponents of major change. Other leaks suggested cuts in quality and service and limits on doctor choice. And as month after month passed—May, June, July, August—expectations built and opponents organized.

Before the introduction of the president's legislation, there were two other major comprehensive health care bills under consideration in Congress. One, the single-payer bill, sponsored by Democrat James McDermott, a psychiatrist from Washington state, would have replaced insurance companies with government as the insurer, or payer, and health care would be funded with a payroll tax. McDermott and ninety-one cosponsors argued that the single-payer system would displace the bureaucratic waste of 1,500 private insurers with, in a sense, one government insurance company. Canada, which has single-payer and where survey after survey (in spite of opponents' horror stories) shows great satisfaction with its health care system, has administrative costs less than one-half of this country's. *Consumer Reports,* after studying each health care bill in Congress and endorsing single-payer, also pointed out that Medicare, a type of government single-payer, has only 2 percent administrative expenses. Four years earlier, Chrysler chairman Lee Iacocca had written an article in support of single-payer, arguing that it is good for business and for America's global competitiveness position because health care costs are not so directly attributable to each company and instead spread through the population. The McDermott legislation, which I supported, never came to a vote; even many of its supporters, recognizing the lack of broad-based support for single-payer, were waiting for Clinton's plan to emerge.

Another bill, introduced by Tennessee Democrat Jim Cooper, a member of the Energy and Commerce Committee, provided for managed competition, attempting to impose personal purchasing responsibilities on the health care consumer. Termed by some as "Clinton Lite," it established large health insurance purchasing cooperatives that would act as the large purchaser of health care. Consumers would be provided information on the quality and price of the plans and would choose among them. Although Cooper's plan had support from insurance companies and some southern Democrats, it was never very seriously considered, in large part because it fell short of achieving universal coverage.

By late summer, enough of the president's plan, while not complete, had leaked out that the nation had some idea what was in it. The major thrust and most controversial aspect of the Clinton plan was the establishment of mandatory health alliances in each state to guarantee universal coverage. Large firms that self-insure would be exempt from joining the alliances but would be assessed a 1 percent premium to help pay alliance costs. Everyone else would be required to join an alliance, and businesses and individuals would pay insurance premiums to fund the alliances. Businesses that provided relatively generous health care benefits would save money under the Clinton plan. Businesses that provided no coverage would be subject to an "employer mandate" and would pay for coverage, and their employees would also pay. The Clinton plan dealt decisively with "freeloaders"—businesses that provided no health insurance for its employees and enjoyed a cost advantage over its competition that did; and individuals who had no health insurance and who were taken care of in hospital emergency rooms and paid little or nothing. H.R. 3600 attempted to distribute costs more evenly and equitably throughout society.

In September, the president made an impassioned and—judging by the public and congressional reaction—very effective speech to both a joint session of Congress and the nation calling for comprehensive health care reform. He reiterated the three tenets of his not-yet-released proposal: universal coverage, cost containment, maintenance of high-quality care. The speech was so well received that several leading Republicans began to resume talk about the health care "crisis" and again lent their support to legislation that guaranteed universal coverage.

Finally, in October, the Health Security Act of 1993 was released to the public and introduced in Congress. The work of the task force had been exhaustive; its five hundred members had eleven hundred meetings with every conceivable public and private group affected. H.R. 3600 was 1,342 pages of extraordinarily complex material. Upon the bill's introduction, the First Lady testified in front of several House and Senate committees, including the Energy and Commerce Committee. By any measure, she was terrific! Her testimony, her grasp of details, her memory, her style were lauded by Republicans and Democrats, the media, and everyone else in official Washington. The next hearings, though, with the secretary of Health and Human Services and other administration officials and supporters of the bill, were more telling, for there were no budget figures available to the committee, even after the months of delay. Waiting for the health care bill was like telling a joke; the longer the joke is, the funnier it has to be. People's expectations had been raised (and lowered and raised again) for so long, that everyone seemed disappointed. And by then the opposition had organized, rumors had become fact, inaccuracies had calcified, and fear of radical change had taken hold among large segments of the public.

The health insurance industry, probably the most visible opponent, had been gearing up all year. The Health Insurance Association of America was especially effective with its Harry and Louise campaign, a series of television ads costing tens of millions of dollars and featuring a very earnest, slightly yuppie couple who expressed their fears of big government, loss of physician choice, and diminished quality of care.

Opposition from other organized groups was equally intense, and at least as effective. Almost everyone who opposed the bill and who visited me about health care—from the Washington lobbyist representing a Thirteenth District insurance or health care concern to the constituent from North Ridgeville or Chardon with a packet of special interest information in tow—prefaced their comments with, "I support health care reform, but this bill goes too far." One woman from a Geauga County insurance agency came to my office to talk about health care and made a convincing and passionate plea to "get government off our backs, let us run our business, government should get out of our lives." Before she left, she told me she had one other issue to discuss. "The banks," she said, "are trying to get into the insurance business. We need government to stop them. Can you help?" Now let me make sure I understand this. You want government out of your life and out of your business, except . . . .

Perhaps the most effective grassroots opponent to health care reform was the National Federation of Independent Businesses (NFIB), which spent, according to the Center for Public Integrity, two-thirds of its annual budget, about $40 million, to kill the employer mandate part of the bill. One of their lobbyists commented, "This Congress proved that grassroots lobbying is the only way to be successful on broad policy issues. You have to let the people who are directly affected speak for themselves." Overall, over the first eighteen months of the 103d Congress, special interest opponents to health care reform spent over $100 million to defeat the legislation, retaining more than ninety-seven firms and hiring at least eighty former congressional and executive branch officials. And health care interests contributed more than $25 million to the reelection campaigns of members of Congress.

The sophistication of big-money lobbying reached a new high—or perhaps a new low—in the early 1990s. Several companies were formed, the first one in 1990, to literally stand in line for the rich, the powerful, and the very busy.

During important committee hearings, there is usually a shortage of seats in committee rooms. And, of course, the crowds are almost always the largest when big money rides on the outcome—tax bills, health care legislation, telecommunication issues. Dozens of people line up in front of locked committee doors for hours before a major committee mark-up takes place. Some are tourists, others are students, but most of them have something at stake in what the committee decides.

Before major hearings on the health care bill, observers would notice as many as a few dozen young men and women in these lines. Most were students dressed in blue jeans and sweatshirts, reading, writing, studying for exams. They were paid about ten dollars an hour. On the really big issues, when seating was especially limited, these students would pull all-nighters, waiting outside locked government office buildings, awaiting the buildings' 7:00 A.M. opening. If the nights were cold, they often were paid a little bit extra. They were employed by companies whose sole business was to provide warm bodies to stand in line. These companies were paid twenty-five or thirty dollars an hour by lobbying firms whose principals earned two hundred dollars an hour and up. So it makes sense for everyone who participates: the students who could make a hundred dollars a night, the new congressional stand-in-line company that provides service, and the lobbying firm that can attend the hearing without its highly paid principals and associates spending their valuable time waiting. By the late 1990s, these firms had replaced the students with unemployed, often homeless, Washingtonians.

The opposition to major health care reform was not unlike the opposition to Medicare in the mid-1960s, the last major health care fight in Congress. The guns in the opponents' arsenal in this Congress, however, were bigger and seemed to have better aim. The same arguments used against Medicare in 1965—intrusive government, socialized medicine, fear of government control of doctors, loss of physician choice—were resurrected, dressed up in a more sophisticated suit, and used to hammer the Health Security Act of 1993. In 1993 and 1994, interest groups, with their grassroots component, were able to focus public anger on government and stoke the fears of the public toward Big Brother while deflecting anger and resentment away from insurance providers, drug companies, and the medical community. A pretty impressive feat, considering the public image of insurance companies, pharmaceutical firms, and tobacco conglomerates.

To make matters worse for the president, and to make passage of health care reform even more difficult, his health care plan tagged Clinton with the label of a tax-and-spend Democrat, a big spender, and a Great Society liberal. Interestingly, though, most liberals were not thrilled with his plan and overwhelmingly supported the single-payer bill.

Close to one hundred House Democrats, mostly NAFTA opponents, wrote a letter to President Clinton asking him to take up health care before the NAFTA vote. Others asked that he put his efforts into welfare reform before health care. Most of us understood that the president could ask the Congress only once or twice for a vote "to save the presidency." He had done that with the budget and succeeded with no votes to spare. He would have to do the same, we reasoned, with NAFTA. Health care—the legislation that many thought would define his presidency—would be left, in a sense, to fend for itself. Congress would not likely respond again to a personal presidential plea.

The coverage of the health care debate by the press was another obstacle that Clinton was unable to overcome. The media focus, not unlike coverage of political campaigns, was on the personalities much more than on the issues. Reporters wrote and talked much about legislative maneuverings, less often of the complexities of health care. Little attention was paid to foreign health systems, the examination of which would have been very helpful to the American public. While journalists appropriately wrote stories about political contributions from health care companies to members of Congress, some reporters, such as Cokie Roberts, received huge speaking fees from health care concerns while still covering the health care debate. Moreover, the coverage often gave the most attention to conflict, not dispassionate analysis. The *Washington Monthly,* in an article critical of press coverage of health care, wrote, "Because reporters are attracted by conflict, the people who want to sink major reform—those with stakes in the status quo—have a ready-made ally in any reporter. Consider these *New York Times* headlines, INFLUENTIAL GROUP SAYS HEALTH PLAN SLIGHTS THE AGED; BUSINESS GROUP ASSAILS THE SCOPE AND COST OF THE CLINTON PLAN; LOCAL GOVERNMENTS MAY PAY MORE IN HEALTH PLAN; HEADS OF HMOS HAVE CONCERNS ON HEALTH PLAN; CLINTON HEALTH CARE PLAN MAY CUT BENEFITS TO CHILDREN." And this was the generally subdued *New York Times*. (One newspaper observer said, "The people who read the *New York Times* run the country. The people who read the *Washington Post* think they run the country. The people who read the *Wall Street Journal* think they should run the country. The people who read *USA Today* don't give a damn who runs the country.")

With no Republican votes, and with opposition from four southern Democrats on his Energy and Commerce Committee, Chairman John Dingell simply could not persuade, in the face of intense business and insurance company lobbying, all of the four or five undecided Democrats on the committee. The president had backed off his support of an increase in the minimum wage to woo business in support of his plan, yet to no avail. Dingell scaled down the employer mandate provisions, but also to no avail. Although most were willing to support a bill with employer mandates, the diversity and range of the Democratic philosophy spelled defeat for the president's plan. It was never brought to a vote. The northern and southern wings of the party had again failed to come together.

In the end, the American people were neither convinced nor particularly well educated in the debate. The public desire to keep government out of their lives, at least in a theoretical way, carried the day. Senator Bob Kerry, a Nebraska Democrat recognized as one of the Senate's experts on health care, said after the debate, "I could have scored points in my re-election campaign by running a 30-second television commercial promising to keep the federal government out of Medicare."

Many people believed that the creation of Medicare in the 1960s and Social Security in the 1930s could never have happened if they had been faced with the obstacles that the Health Security Act faced—groups like the NFIB, the tens of millions of dollars spent by interest groups, unrelenting talk radio, and the Harry and Louise ads. Small business groups convinced Congress, and many of their employees, that employer mandates would cost jobs.

While eating a sandwich in a restaurant in Lodi in southwestern Medina County, I heard a story from a young waitress, who by all logic should have supported the bill. As she brought dessert, she told me that although neither she nor her husband (who also worked full-time) had health insurance, "Clinton's bill sucks. If it passes, this restaurant will close, so will the other one in Lodi, and we'll all lose our jobs." Her young son had just been in the emergency room with a broken arm; she was paying twenty dollars a month "until we pay it off." That summer night I realized comprehensive health care reform was probably dead. If we couldn't convince her and millions like her around the country—the people who needed health care the most—that universal coverage through employer mandate made sense, we had failed.

The death of health care reform was greeted with an almost audible sigh by millions of Americans. To many, the Democrats' health care plan was too costly, too intrusive, too Washington. Ironically, Democrats lost the health care debate in two ways: we failed to pass any health care plan; and the one we tried to pass seemed to the public to be too bureaucratic, too Rube Goldberg–like, and, to many, just another Democratic attempt to spend their money. First it was the budget and the tax increase, now health care, and later an expensive crime bill. In addition, a significant number of voters thought the Clinton plan would restrict physician choice and jeopardize the quality of care.

Majority Democrats—not insurance companies, not doctors, not powerful Washington interest groups, not Republicans—were seen as mostly responsible for its failure. Almost three times as many voters, according to one survey, blamed Congress for killing health care than blamed insurance companies and other businesses. Democrats were elected to break gridlock, but didn't. Republicans had convinced America that major change in health care was not necessary; in fact, major change was dangerous. After all, Republicans repeated, America has the best health care system in the world.

8

The Crime Bill

If you take away the guns, crazy people will find other ways
to kill large numbers of people—with gasoline and matches
or they'll use dynamite to blow people away.

—letter from a Lorain gun owner

My family and I live in government housing. We would like
this to be drug-free housing. It would be a better place to
live. It's not fair that in the summer time we can never go
outside without the cops around chasing the drug-dealers.
. . . Even the kid's swing sets behind the office is always
full of drug dealers. This is a sad situation.

—letter from a Lorain seventh grader

THE DEMOCRATS WON THE CRIME BILL. It was the best thing for the country. But it may have cost us the majority.

Over the years, each party has fallen short of finding good solutions to crime problems in America. Republican answers have been to build more prisons, lock up first-time offenders and throw away the key, and impose the death penalty more frequently. America now has more prisoners per capita than any other country in the world, and twice as many as we had twenty-five years ago. We are the only Western democracy with a death penalty, yet we have the highest murder rate in the West. And conservative Republicans reject any thought that the easy availability of guns contributes to the problem of violent crime. The bumper sticker "Those who beat their guns into plows will plow for those who don't" says it all. Clearly, Republican answers have not worked.

Democratic solutions, however, have centered largely around prevention. Favoring social programs over punishment, most Democrats believe that the environment in which young people are raised is a major cause of crime. If you want to control the deer population, hunting deer is a temporary solution; if you want to eliminate the deer population, destroy its habitat. Similarly, jailing an offender but leaving his habitat, his environment, in its same state only breeds more criminals, as others will move in and follow lives of crime. Nonetheless, Democratic answers to the crime problem—everything from full funding of Head Start to school recreation activities to drug and alcohol abuse programs—have fallen short.

The crime bill, written by the Clinton administration with the help of law enforcement officials and criminologists, combined both approaches: tougher sentencing, "federalizing" a number of crimes, applying the death penalty (which I oppose) to many of them, building more prisons, and establishing prevention programs to "destroy the habitat" of high-crime areas. It proposed, over five years, placing 100,000 more police on the streets in rural and urban areas, in suburbs and small towns. And it was already paid for: the size of the federal government had actually shrunk by a hundred thousand employees in the two years that President Clinton had been in office, so some of the money from those cuts would go toward deficit reduction and the rest toward police and paying for the crime bill.

In April 1994, the crime bill originally passed the House with sixty-five Republican votes. Republican opponents claimed that the bill was not tough enough. During the March and April debate in the House, only one Republican congressman protested the cost of the bill: Pennsylvania Republican George Gekas attacked the bill for its Great Society spending. Several law-and-order amendments were offered, mostly by Republicans, and many of them passed. The amendments played well to the crowd: to prohibit the Federal Bureau of Prisons from allowing prisoners to engage in weightlifting ("American taxpayers should not be paying for equipment that builds better thugs," said the sponsor); to deny Pell grants for inmates so all the money could go to middle-class families, many of which are now denied funding; to add death penalty provisions for a wide range of crimes.

One interesting and particularly difficult amendment required a student to be suspended automatically if he was found in school with a gun. Where does he go with his gun when he's suspended? If you vote against the amendment, you are voting against disciplining a kid in school and are against safety in school. If you support the amendment, you are voting to put a young man with a gun, and with nothing to do, on the street. Neither choice is very appealing. The amendment passed by a wide margin.

On May 5, a ban on assault weapons squeaked through the House by one vote, with thirty-five Republicans supporting it. The anger from gun owners went beyond anything I had ever seen. One NRA member in defense of the Second Amendment wrote, "I wish some of you pinheads would read your constitution. . . . It is clear to me that you are no more than another liberal in sheep's clothing. . . . The facts are that you voted against freedom and this is TREASON." Another wrote, "All tyrants and despots throughout history have tread the same path that you and the liberal, genuflect and kiss the ring of the president faction are now embarked. It is by no small coincidence that the government and some police worship the prospect of a disarmed and defenseless population that they can have their way with." And there were dozens more. "It's not the guns that cause crime. It's the criminals that cause crime. Of course, the criminals ply their foul trade now without fear of swift and sure punishment. The liberals in our judicial and political system have seen to that. Maybe you should ban liberals. . . . I know you will not respond in any meaningful way. You never do." "Criminals all over America are having champagne parties celebrating what you did. And they're laughing—at you, at Congress, and especially at guys like me, law-abiding gunowners."

At home and in response to letters, I was always careful to point out that the assault weapons ban, and for that matter the Brady Bill, was not a panacea for crime, that I believed it would only make a small difference in stopping violent crime but that it would make a difference. Former Presidents Reagan, Carter, and Ford also supported the ban. Although not a lawyer, I understand that the First Amendment, which protects freedom of speech and the right to assemble, does not protect child pornography, and a community can require a permit for people to demonstrate. Similarly, the Second Amendment, which I support, does not allow the private ownership and use of nuclear weapons or machine guns or assault weapons. An assault weapon, after all, is a gun designed to kill as many people as possible in as short a time as possible.

Three years earlier, the House had defeated the assault weapons ban by seventy votes. The intensive lobbying in 1994 by virtually every major police organization turned the tide; Houston Democratic congressman Mike Andrews, for example, voted against the ban in 1991 but for it three years later. "When law enforcement officials are outgunned, . . . we must do something [to protect them]," he said. Many members were convinced that the ban would not make a huge dent in the problem of violent crime but would save a few lives—reason enough to vote for it.

In July, the House-Senate conference committee combined the proposed crime bills with the assault weapons ban in the Omnibus Crime Bill. President Clinton, especially beleaguered before the vote, agreed to take out the very controversial racial justice provision in the conference committee. It was a provision that allowed introduction of racial discrimination factors in capital, or death penalty, cases.

Although Minority Whip Newt Gingrich said that he could support the crime bill if the racial justice provision and the assault weapons ban were taken out of it, Republican leadership and the NRA saw an opportunity. For five decades, Republicans had won elections, especially in the 1970s and 1980s, by running against communism and crime. We need to get tough, their candidates would say, on the Soviet Union and on criminals. The destruction of the Berlin Wall, the dismantling of the Soviet Union, and the collapse of European communism had taken away one of their two crucial issues; they could not let Clinton take away the other.

Gingrich understood that voting for gun control—even for the Brady Bill and the ban on assault weapons, guns very few citizens actually own—was always an unpopular and politically costly vote. Even though every major police organization in the country supported both bills, I knew they would cost me votes on election day. And even though an overwhelming majority of Americans supported both issues, a vote for them is without question a political loser. The NRA and the Gun Owners of America sent leaflets to congressional offices with the not-very-veiled threat that "gun owners are much more likely than gun control advocates to be single-issue voters. Be forewarned, there is incredible voter anger brewing outside of the Beltway!"

In the two-year debate on Brady and assault weapons, no one came up to me and said, "If you don't vote for the Brady Bill and the ban on assault weapons, I will vote for your opponent." And no one ever said, "If you vote to get rid of assault weapons, you have my vote." With few exceptions only gun owners who subscribe to the NRA's philosophy vote guns, period. Gingrich knew that his alliance with the NRA would help him build a majority in the House of Representatives.

The Republican leadership's and the National Rifle Association's plan was to oppose the bill and base its public opposition on "social spending," highlighting any waste in the bill and distorting any facts about prevention money that they could. They enlisted the *Wall Street Journal* and talk radio, always an easy task for the Republicans. Even though most of the crime bill's funding would go to police and prisons—less than a quarter was to go to prevention programs—everything said for public consumption highlighted pork and social spending; guns were not mentioned. Charlton Heston did an ad attacking social spending without mentioning guns. NRA spokespersons also criticized social spending but did not mention guns when talking to the mainstream media. Talk radio chimed in, rarely mentioning guns but always mentioning social spending and pork. A favorite—and false—statement from talk radio was that the crime bill provided two social workers for every cop.

The incessant barrage from talk radio about social spending translated into hundreds of letters and calls into my office—and thousands more to offices all over the Capitol. Talk radio, Republicans, and NRA spokespeople especially ridiculed "midnight basketball," a mostly inner-city program to give young men an alternative to late nights in crime-infested areas. When George Bush was president, he said that midnight basketball is "about providing opportunity to young adults to escape drugs and the streets and get on with their lives." Republican pollster Frank Luntz, who also worked for the NRA, called the crime bill the "Midnight Basketball Bill" and the "Social Workers' Employment Bill."

Actually, the amount of money in the bill had increased after the original bill passed the House and Senate, but mostly on more spending for prisons. The Senate originally passed the bill 95 to 5. And even though the bill was paid for by budget cuts and by slashing the size of the federal bureaucracy and was supported by all major law-enforcement groups nationally, the opposition to it intensified. A man from Chardon called me at 7:00 A.M. in my office and said: "You know those hundred thousand [additional] cops you talk about?" Yeah. "They won't really work for the city of Cleveland or for Red Simmons [Geauga County's sheriff]. They'll work for the United Nations." I don't think so. "Yeah, it's true. You gotta read the fine print."

By August the bill was in trouble. The sixty-five Republicans who had voted for the original crime bill and the thirty-five Republicans who had supported the ban on assault weapons had shrunk to less than a couple dozen. On August 9 the Republican National Committee sent copies of a resolution condemning Republicans who voted to give Bill Clinton a victory on the crime bill; implicit was the message that campaign funds would be withheld. On the morning of the vote, there were twenty committed Republican votes. Talk radio kept up their barrage; the *Wall Street Journal* editorial page, always an indicator of Republican party strategy and an enforcer of Republican party discipline, hammered on some of those—by name—who were planning to vote for the bill. Their strategy worked; the rule, which was the key vote, was defeated in the House, 210 to 225, when only eleven Republican members voted for it. They were joined by enough Democrats—including eleven members of the congressional Black Caucus who were upset at the expanded death penalties with no racial justice provision—to kill the bill . . . temporarily. The bill then went back to conference committee to be rewritten.

As the crime bill was being rewritten and debated across the country, the pressure was intense, especially from gun owners. A man from Aurora called me and said, "If you vote for this, I'll talk to all my neighbors about it. . . . Even though I almost never vote for a Democrat, if you vote your conscience and not follow the party bosses, I will consider voting for you." I told him I *was* voting my conscience. He was not impressed.

A man called our Medina office and spoke with Colin Cranston, who ran that office. Angry about my vote on the assault weapons ban he ranted and raved for about five minutes—"My rights have been violated!" "Whatever happened to the Second Amendment?"; "Why do you bastards want to take my guns?" "Law-abiding citizens don't count in this society anymore!"; and on and on. Colin told him I disagreed and was going to vote for the ban. Then the caller said, "Well then would Congressman Brown do me a favor? I just got out of prison and I'm a hunter. I can't get a hunting license because I'm an ex-con. Can you help me get a hunting license?"

At the Geauga County Fair on Labor Day weekend, a gentleman walked up to me with an idea. He obviously had been waiting for this moment. "You want to know the answer to the crime problem, and it won't cost $30 billion?" What? "Freeze 'em." Freeze 'em? "Yeah, freeze 'em." Freeze who? "All of 'em. All the murderers and rapists and armed robbers. The bleeding hearts and liberals and do-gooders wouldn't be upset because we wouldn't be killing 'em, just freezin' 'em." I never thought of it that way. "Yeah, freeze 'em and stack 'em in the cafeterias. You can store a lot of 'em that way." That would be pretty expensive, all that electricity. "Yeah, but cheaper than what we're doing now."

In the end, after several days of negotiations where some real pork was taken out of the bill (specifically, a $10 million crime center in the Judiciary Committee chairman's district) and most of the "social spending" was combined into bloc grants to be spent at the discretion of local governments and local law enforcement agencies, the rule passed with several more Republican votes, 235 to 195. The Senate followed suit when half a dozen Republicans broke with Senate Minority Leader Dole to defeat a filibuster. After six years of legislative maneuvers, Congress finally had passed a crime bill.

House leadership had asked President Clinton to take the assault weapons ban out of the bill, which would have assured passage earlier, but the president chose to fight on that issue. Many commentators and pundits said that the NRA was no longer the powerhouse that it once was, that it had been defeated. Earlier in the session, Congress had passed the Brady Bill, which required a five-day waiting period for purchasing a gun. Now, amid great pressure, Congress had voted for an assault weapon ban twice, first standing alone and second as part of the crime bill. Undoubtedly, the majority of people in the United States, according to any poll I have ever seen, support the Brady Bill and the assault weapon ban. And, for the first time, police organizations weighed in against the NRA and in support of both bills. On November 25, 1993, the *New York Times* discussed the "humiliating loss" of the NRA, which "went down with a whimper." And one prominent lawmaker bragged, "This is the first time since 1968 the NRA has been beaten on a major issue, but it won't be the last. Lawmakers will learn there is life after voting against the NRA."

Yes, the political experts said, the NRA could be defeated without reprisal or with few political repercussions. In the face of dozens of letters from gun owners pledging my defeat and angry threats at town meetings, bowling alleys, and grocery stores, some of us were not so sure.

On election night 1994 at Head's, a Washington restaurant a block away from the Cannon Building, the National Rifle Association was celebrating. Cheers went up every few minutes with the announcement that another pro–gun control Democrat went down to defeat. Several lost in Washington state, Ohio, North Carolina, Indiana, Georgia. The chairman of the Judiciary Committee, forty-two-year-incumbent Jack Brooks, in the past an NRA supporter, lost his "safe" seat after allowing the assault weapon ban to stay in the crime bill.

My support of Brady and the crime bill surely cost me 2 or 3 percent of the vote. Almost everywhere I went during the last month before the election, I was dogged by people—almost always men—who were angry with my vote. And the letters were also a warning. A man from Elyria wrote, "Do you know that it's an election year? If you vote for any assault weapons ban I will pledge my time, money, and efforts to your opponent and you will not be re-elected. What do you think about that?" And from Middlefield: "I am not registered to vote at this time, but decided to register when I saw your vote." The politics of guns are simple: without a doubt, gun owners vote guns. Others don't.

After the election, during a meeting with *Cleveland Plain Dealer* editors and reporters, President Clinton said that the gun vote cost the Democrats twenty seats and the majority in the November election. "For once the President and I agree," said Tanya Metaksa, chief NRA lobbyist. The NRA claimed it made the difference in nineteen of the twenty-four races it targeted. But damage from the crime bill was more than guns. Passage of the bill played into the image that the Democrats wanted to spend huge amounts of money and involve the federal government in local problems. The Republicans and the NRA had masterfully—and deceitfully—made the issue much bigger than guns, energizing gun owners surely, but also making the crime bill an example, similar to health care, of Democrats imposing expensive national answers on local problems.

9

The Mail, the Phones, and Other Things

A congressman's job is not to weigh the mail but to weigh
the evidence.
— Senator Hugh Scott (R-Pa.)

Throwin' strikes is a piece of cake; home plate don't move.
— Satchel Paige, first African American major league pitcher

PHONE CALLS AND LETTERS from constituents matter. They can change
a member's mind and challenge her to rethink an issue. Phone calls and
letters can let a congressional representative know that huge numbers of voters are watching her vote. Or they can add pressure in a politically threaten-
ing way.

Some people write and politely state their views. Others are a bit more
direct: "We cannot in good conscience vote for you should you choose to
act differently with respect to our views." Or, "If you don't vote with us, we
won't vote for you." Some are outright hostile: "Get the hell out of my life.
I don't need you"; or, the rather unequivocal "You make me sick."

Some have a unique way of sending a message: NAFTA opponents sent
two-by-fours with "No to NAFTA" written on each with a magic marker.
An environmental group mailed an empty prescription drug bottle with a.
message that support for the Endangered Species Act was important for
future medical research: "Please vote to strengthen the Endangered Species
Act and preserve species with proven medicinal value and those whose
medicinal value awaits future discovery. Our health and the health of our
planet depend on it."

In September 1994, opponents of a quick vote·on the General Agreement
on Tariffs and Trade sent me a pillow on which was written:

Congress' Decision Whether to Join GATT is Too Important to Rush
SLEEP ON IT

> Congress should postpone consideration of GATT until next year.
> Too much is at stake to rush.
> Sleep on this decision now, and avoid insomnia later.

At the bottom of the pillowcase was another simple message written in bold letters:

> *Warning: The World Trade Organization Could be Dangerous to Your Health.
> To fund GATT, Congress would have to raise taxes and increase the federal budget deficit weeks before election day.

A man from Illinois sent me a copy of George Orwell's *Animal Farm* with the following note: "'All animals are equal . . .' This appears to be the frightening blueprint for this administration. . . . I think that you will find that the concerned citizens of this country are not as stupid as the animals in Animal Farm." A group opposing cuts in the school lunch program sent a piece of white bread in a plastic bag, and a citizens group sent a letter about human rights with a piece of barbed wire attached.

One of the most unusual notes was in a Christmas card I received: "During this blessed holiday season, we need to thank God that Joseph, who was betrothed to Mary, did not have Jesus, our Lord and Savior, aborted through the stoning of Mary (which was Jewish law), an unwed mother. See you at the polls."

Some congressional representatives over the years have been less than tolerant of nasty letters and insulting messages. Ohio Democrat Stephen Young, who served in the Senate from 1959 to 1971, would solemnly write back to a constituent who had insulted him, "I want you to know that some lunatic has stolen your stationery, written a stupid, inane letter, and signed your name to it." A state legislator in Ohio had a special rubber stamp prepared, and he would stamp "BULLSHIT" on letters that he thought particularly nasty, ill informed, or vicious. One member received a letter from a woman in his district that asked, "Are you with God or against Him?" His response was simple: "Dear Madam: I'm with God. I sure as hell hope He's with me."

A man from Brunswick was emailing me at least once a week during the Clinton impeachment proceedings. Viciously anti-Clinton, and not much kinder to me, he closed each message with "You're lower than a tunnel rat." Then for several months we didn't hear from him. When, six months later, he wrote again—this time from Wadsworth, a community about twenty miles from Brunswick—I couldn't resist replying, "Did the tunnel rats run you out of Brunswick?" But Donna Pignatelli, my chief of staff, wouldn't let me send it. She doesn't let me have any fun. Good thing, sometimes.

Most of us, most of the time, respond politely and respectfully to all letters that we receive. And most of us know that paying attention to and responding to calls and letters is an important part of our job. Letters from the heart, or letters from experts, can make an impression on a member who does not know an issue as well as the letter writer. Congress votes on a wide variety of issues—from clean air to crime, taxes to agriculture, banking to labor law—and our mail helps to educate us. The average congressional office devotes 55 percent of its staff time to reading and answering mail. In a Western Union survey of congressional staff in 1993, 80 percent of congressional offices attach "great importance" to personal letters. Letters indicate "serious effort and thought unmatched by other, simpler (and sometimes mindless) forms of communication." Mail means everything to congressional offices. Simply put, successful members pay special attention to the mail; less successful members may not.

Former Indiana Democratic representative Lee Hamilton, chairman of the Foreign Affairs Committee during the 103d Congress, took a survey in 1967 asking his constituents how he should decide to vote. More than seven thousand people responded: 69 percent said he should vote "according to majority wishes of the district as he interprets those wishes"; 36 percent believed he should "vote according to his conscience and judgment." Obviously, a few said both.

Congressman Hamilton's questionnaire (he told me that he has not asked the question since) represents the age-old political science debate of delegate versus trustee. Should a legislator, on issue after issue, vote to satisfy her constituency's wishes? Or should conscience be her guide, as the district's voters place their trust in her as their trustee?

From a practical standpoint, every member of Congress comes out somewhere in the middle. First of all, it is virtually impossible for a congressman to know what a majority of his district thinks about an issue; issue questionnaires, town meetings, phone calls, even public surveys give a congressman an indication of district sentiment but with no real certainty. Second, it is even more difficult to measure depth of feeling or the importance of an issue to voters. For example, if 45 percent of voters support an issue rather tepidly, 40 percent oppose it passionately, and 15 percent are undecided, does a delegate-type representative vote for or against it? Or suppose

80 percent of the electorate opposes a bill but remains relatively silent, while the 10–20 percent who support it generate hundreds and hundreds of calls, letters, and postcards. How should a delegate-type legislator vote when the mail overwhelmingly states *yes* but every survey, questionnaire, and poll says *no*? Or what should a delegate-type congressman do when he receives two hundred preprinted postcards in support of an issue and twenty personal, well-written, thoughtful, analytical letters in opposition?

Some of the most effective ways that I have found to communicate with voters in my district are through phone calls that I initiate, through the occasional use of newsletters, and with issue questionnaires that I personally distribute. Some members send out three or four newsletters to their constituents each year, at about $30,000 for each districtwide mailing.

At various times during my first few years in office, we printed several thousand issue questionnaires that I handed out at shopping centers, plant gates, restaurants, downtown businesses, and in neighborhoods door to door. It was a low-cost way to communicate with people, to elicit their comments about specific issues facing Congress, and to engage people in conversation at their workplace or in the course of their day's activities. In the evenings after the House had adjourned, and from the car phone on the way home from speeches or meetings, I called a few people who had written me letters. My staff and I selected letters that were provocative or especially well written or that were from people who needed help from their government. Obviously, considering that my office receives several hundred letters each week, and sometimes thousands more postcards, we chose only relatively few.

Sometimes, though, you just can't win. One night at about 9:30, while in my Washington office, I called a man who had sent me a letter. The first thing he said was, "Is the government paying for this call?" Another man, to whom I had handed an issue questionnaire at a restaurant, wrote on it, "Another perk—and I paid 29 cents to return it."

Almost every elected official really does listen to district sentiment, yet most believe that they are entrusted by the voters to use their best judgment and, in the end, do what they believe is best for the district and the nation. At a town meeting in 1993, a Lorain County man who was angry about a vote I had cast demanded to know why I did not always vote what the district (in this case, *he*) wanted.

"First of all," I explained, "I do not always know exactly what the majority of the district wants. Second, I believe that vote was best for the nation, the Thirteenth District, and Lorain County."

That only made him angrier. "I want the budget balanced, and I want you to vote the way we tell you."

"Always? Every vote?" I asked. He said yes. "Then I will never vote for a spending cut because I have never received a majority of mail in support of any specific budget cut. People write me and tell me to balance the budget and to cut spending, but most of the letters I get on any specific program are in defense of that program and tell me not to cut it." Voters seem to want budget cuts (generally), support for their programs (specifically), a balanced budget (now), and no new taxes (ever). Voters want us to show courage and deal with almost intractable problems, yet they are often angry if we do not vote their way.

According to Roger Davidson in *The Role of the Congressman*, senior members are more likely to be "trustees" for two reasons. First they are more likely to represent "safe" seats—that is, districts solidly in support of the incumbent—and they feel more freedom to speak their minds and vote their beliefs. Second, senior members are obviously more likely to be part of House leadership and have a responsibility to carry out the platform of their national party and the platform of the majority of caucus members.

Over the years, voters' participation in government has centered around grassroots-type organizations in association with others who have similar concerns and interests: the local Democratic or Republican party, a labor union, an antihunger coalition, an environmental alliance or a student group, a local gun club, a civil rights organization, or a church group. Sometimes they'll form around one issue, such as abortion. These organizations write letters, make phone calls, make speeches, sometimes work in campaigns; they conduct traditional grassroots politics. According to the Times Mirror Center for the People and the Press, 38 percent of Americans have recently mailed in a card for interest group opinion polls or sent postcards directly to their congressperson advocating a position. The membership of the American Association of Retired Persons alone sends out fifty million pieces of mail each year.

During the last several years, "artificial" grassroots have sprung up; some call it "astro-turf lobbying." Created and managed by political consultants looking for business between elections, and paid for by corporations looking for broad public support for their political agenda, corporate grassroots have emerged as an increasingly major political force in Congress. During the health care debate, special interest groups played a major role in defeating the bill.

Beer Drinkers of America, threatened by an increase in the beer tax, activated its corporate grassroots machine funded by America's largest beer
makers; to every congressional office they sent t-shirts featuring Uncle Sam
pointing and saying "Don't Tax My Beer" as well as an 800 number. They
plastered signs on beer trucks trumpeting how much tax money was paid on
the beer that these trucks carried each year and sent out direct mail solicita-
tions and "Don't Tax My Beer" bumper stickers to hundreds of thousands
of beer drinkers (who knows where they got their lists) asking people to write
and call their congressional representative. Local chapters of Beer Drinkers
of America (which claim 190,000 members per congressional district) sent
representatives to meet with their congressmen and congresswomen. An
autoworker in Lorain—a Democrat, a union member, a supporter—visited
my office with a paid Beer Drinkers of America representative from Chicago;
he told me that any increase in a beer tax would hit his coworkers the hardest. It would punish your voters, he told me—blue-collar workers, Democrats, card-carrying union members. Implicit, of course, and reinforced by
the rather yuppie figure from Chicago, was that those voters would punish
me if I didn't see the light.

The tobacco folks were equally aggressive. Letters came from smokers
in my district stating their belief that smokers were being discriminated
against, that the government was singling them out. Tobacco companies,
secure with their tax subsidies, closed down Richmond and other "tobacco
cities" for a day, paid their workers a full day's pay, and brought several thousand employees to Capitol Hill to lobby against taxes on tobacco, for
tobacco subsidies, and against prohibitions on smoking in public places.
"Big Tobacco" also enlisted the sheet-metal workers' union to tell us that
outlawing smoking in public places would cost them jobs. Why? There
would be no more need, they told me, to install elaborate ventilation systems in restaurants, bus stations, and other public places. And for those of
us members with few tobacco workers in our district (other than tobacco
retailers and distributors), Big Tobacco sent thousands of "I Smoke and I
Vote" bumper stickers to smokers all over America.

Of course, those people who do not smoke or drink have no corporate
sponsors to underwrite any activity that advances their cause or their beliefs.
In addition, they do not have lobbyists visiting congressional offices on their
behalf, pleading their case, and leaving the congresswoman or her staff a
glossy, well-written brochure.

Occasionally, a well-organized, corporate grassroots effort does not work, or even backfires. Pharmaceutical Research, a consortium of pharmaceutical companies, sent the following form letter to thousands of their customers and asked them to mail them to their congressman:

> The free enterprise system has permitted the development of the best pharmaceutical industry in the world. Almost every new drug is invented and marketed by American firms. I see no reason why we would want to impose price controls on such an innovative industry. Prescription drugs only account for 7% of health care costs. Certainly, there are better ways to make drugs affordable than to impose price controls and risk destroying the incentives for new product development.

The letters were preaddressed, each with the salutation to the appropriate member of Congress. All the drug company customer had to do was sign the letter and mail it.

Over a two-week period, I received about five hundred of these letters. Most were simply signed; dozens of them, however, arrived with editorial comments:

> My son is a physician—and this is garbage. We need price controls on prescription drugs.
>
> This was sent to me to sign by something called Pharmaceutical Research. They picked the wrong person. . . . I disagree with this 100%.
>
> We *must* have price controls. The so-called free enterprise system has gone mad with greed. Something has to be done about the cost of adequate health services.
>
> Sock it to them.
>
> Horse hockey!!!
>
> Profit is not a dirty word. Greed is.
>
> This propaganda is bull.
>
> Our drug lords are no better than the illegal ones.
>
> I'm really upset with this letter that was sent to me. . . . I have cancer.
>
> They've milked me, I'm pill broke.
>
> I want you to get price controls on every prescription drug, and hurry it up. Please.

I think it is safe to say that pharmaceutical companies have a large number of unhappy customers. However, their efforts were very successful in helping to block major health care legislation. And they have become D.C.'s most effective lobbying organization.

The most vehement public outburst during my first term came from a different kind of group and was in reaction to an obscure and perhaps innocuous section of H.R. 6, the Elementary and Secondary Education Amendment. H.R. 6 authorized $12.7 billion for local school districts to help them achieve six national education goals, requiring states to set high achievement standards for teachers and students. The bill placed particular emphasis on poor school districts.

In February 1994, the Home School Legal Defense Association and its president, Michael Farris—an unsuccessful far-Right Virginia political candidate—noticed some slightly ambiguous language on page 218 of the 901-page H.R. 6. All students, according to that section, must be taught by teachers "certified to teach" specific subjects. It also permitted states to approve "alternative methods of teacher certification." Farris, sensing an opportunity to work his grassroots magic with his 39,000 members and many of the hundreds of thousands of home schoolers around the country, called the language "a nuclear attack upon the home schooling community." The staff attorney for the association proclaimed, "We've got telephone trees that can alert 50 percent of all home schoolers in the country."

Texas Republican Dick Armey, always looking for ways to energize the Christian Right against Democrats, immediately jumped into the fray and made it a partisan issue. Although he did nothing about the bill in committee, he wrote an amendment for the floor stating the bill did not "permit, allow, encourage or authorize any federal control over any aspect of any private, religious or home school." The Christian Right then went to work. Farris activated his home school network. Talk radio's Rush Limbaugh and his wanna-bes jumped in. So did Christian radio. On Sunday, four days after the Home School Legal Defense Association began its efforts, thousands of ministers preached against federal control of education and for the Armey amendment and exhorted their flocks to call, fax, e-mail, or visit their congressman. For the next few days, office lines were jammed—in my Washington office, in my district offices, in congressional district offices all over the country. I was answering the phones on President's Day (supposedly government offices were closed), and for several hours the calls came in steadily. One woman told me she home schooled because "I don't want my children to be exposed to all that diversity." Others simply wanted my assurances, which they got, that home schooling would not be jeopardized. Most callers explained to me that they taught their children at home "to instill integrity and Christian values." One little boy sent me a drawing that stated simply, "God bless America." The Defense Association staff attorney boasted, "We were trying to generate half a million phone calls, and I think we exceeded that." They may have. My offices received probably five hundred calls, letters, and faxes each day for four days in a row. California Democrat George Miller, who had written some of the teacher certification language, said, "In twenty years here, I never saw anything like this."

Armey and his Christian Right forces were satisfied only when, according to the *Congressional Quarterly*, "the brouhaha he started ended with [the passage of] an amendment that had his name on it" and when he and the Republicans had gained political advantage from it. The amendment passed 374 to 53. Education and Labor chairman William Ford allowed that this amendment and all that surrounded it were "an unnecessary solution to a nonexistent problem." The ranking Republican on Education and Labor called the Armey amendment more show that substance.

The grassroots effort was indeed impressive—and probably unnecessary. Ohio congressman Tom Sawyer opined that many callers were misled into thinking the language "would do something it is not intended to do." It was neither the first time nor the last time during my first two years in Congress that organizations effectively, and deceitfully, employed large numbers of volunteers to send a winning message to Congress.

Although more and more people are writing, faxing, e-mailing, and calling their representative, the early and mid-1990's saw an ever-widening gap between the government and the governed, between the congresswoman and her constituents. We came home to our districts more often, we had more town meetings, we appeared on more radio call-in shows, we wrote more letters and made more speeches, we had more listening sessions. But in the mid 1990s, the anger seems to keep growing, as evidenced in this sampling of letters and written comments I received in my first term:

A man in Wadsworth requested, "Please send me everything you know. Enclosed is a stamped, self-addressed envelope."

On a questionnaire that I had personally handed out a man in Burton wrote, "You make me sick."

"I will be 70 years old October 6. Wish I could live 70 more so I could keep voting against the Republicans," volunteered a Lorain woman.

"We're not dumb sheep out here and your practices are getting as slick as Clintons [*sic*]. Try being less of a lap dog for the administration," wrote a woman in Russell.

A man in Akron wrote, "Get the hell out of my life. I don't need you."

After the president threw out the first pitch at the Cleveland Indians' new Jacob Field ballpark on Opening Day, a woman from North Ridgeville commented, "Tell Clinton to quit going to baseball games, and start being President."

"Enjoy your present term because you won't have another one. Wish it was olden times so we could behead you," snarled "an overtaxed taxpayer" in Chardon.

"Let's face it, you don't give a damn about the citizens of this state. If you did, you would get an honest job for once, get off the public payroll, and stop filling the landfills with this garbage you distribute at my expense," wrote a Lorain couple.

But not everyone shared an anger at society and antipathy toward Congress. An Elyria man told me, "You may lose me soon as a supporter. Not in the normal way of changing views but in death. I have been diagnosed with colon cancer. . . . After reviewing the literature from the American Cancer Society and many other sources I have discovered how high the risk is in the area I have lived for so long. The environment and workplace and foods I eat have all contributed to my health and current condition. I am a single parent and I want my 12-year-old daughter to have a fighting chance in this world. The crime and violence are enough to deal with without having an increased risk of death from senseless polluting of the environment and poisoning of our foods. Please help save us all from our ignorance and abuse of this world."

And a couple of Amish farmers offered, "We are very grateful to our Heavenly father for the privilege to live in the United States and also grateful to our Government under which we live. We have many, many blessings to be thankful for, even though we have concerns and problems at times. Having our own Amish schools is a privilege that we hold quite precious and it takes the efforts of many to keep our schools running smoothly."

While the mail that members of Congress receive certainly reflects the anger and frustration of many of our constituents, it also captures the belief that Congress and representative government really can work for the people. It is the best we have.

10

Election 1994

Buck did not read the newspapers or he would've known
that trouble was brewing not alone for himself but for every
tidewater dog strong of muscle and with warm long hair
from Puget Sound to San Diego.

—Jack London, *Call of the Wild*

The artist who paints for the millions must use glaring colors.

—Anthony Trollope

IN THE EARLY FALL OF 1993, I expected, rather naively, a fairly easy race
for reelection. In September the *Cleveland Plain Dealer,* Ohio's largest
paper, had written a glowing article about my first year in office, calling me
"a feared incumbent" and "tough to beat." (Don't read your press clippings,
or at least don't believe them, a wise old politician told me years ago.) The
Plain Dealer quoted prominent Republicans saying things such as "he's
extremely popular here, even among Republicans," and "you'd have to have
the energy of three people to run against him." My seat, logic told me, would
be even safer because of the geographic expanse of this multiple-media
market district. No one, I reasoned, could run from a base of any particular
size or strength in such a far-flung gerrymandered district.

In addition, the economy seemed to be on track, the antitax furor apparently had died down, and there was little talk at that time of major Republican gains. Clinton was the first president in the last thirty years to achieve
both job growth and low inflation. The so-called "misery index"—inflation
plus unemployment—had dropped to a low of 9; under Bush it was above 11;
under Reagan it had been higher still. Thirteen months before the election,
there were no palpable signs of trouble—for me or for most Democrats.

I thought about something my brother Charlie told me many years
before. He had left law school to run my first campaign for the state legislature in 1974. The morning after we won, before he returned to school, he
told me, "I'm not doing this again. You don't need me, and I have things to

During my 1992 campaign bicycle trip across the district, we stopped at Sagamore Hills for hot apple cider, served up by some of northern Summit County's most prominent citizens. To my right is Jeff Snell, who masterminded my 1994 campaign, probably the most difficult reelection of my twenty-five-year career.

One of the most exciting days of my family's life was when my daughters, Elizabeth and Emily, held the Bible for my swearing-in as a member of Congress by Speaker of the House Thomas Foley in January 1993.

The Nestle Corporation, a Swiss company, sent each member of Congress one of their products specially decorated for NAFTA lobbying. Large multinational corporations wanted NAFTA in the worst way. In my first six years in Congress, trade issues—NAFTA, China's Most-Favored-Nation status, and Fast Track—were the most heavily lobbied issues by corporate America. CEOs did "fly-ins," parking their corporate jets at National Airport, limousining into the District, and descending on the Hill.

As one of the leaders of the NAFTA opposition, I had more than a few arguments with administration trade officials. Here, U.S. Trade Representative Mickey Kantor and I spar on the issue at a 1993 Capitol Hill meeting. Kantor argued that NAFTA meant jobs for American workers; I asserted that our trade surplus with Mexico would soon disappear and that both American and Mexican workers would be the losers.

During the 1993 auto show on the Mall in Washington, D.C., I invited President Clinton to sit in this new Thunderbird, made down the street from me in Lorain, Ohio. And he did. (I had been told by White House staff that under no circumstances would the president be allowed to get into any of the cars.) This picture was featured prominently on the front page of the *Lorain Morning Journal,* and national television picked it up as well.

In 1993 my daughters had the opportunity to meet Roslyn Carter at a luncheon in Washington. She impressed them with her humility, wit, and kindness.

Speaking to the DARE program, one of the most effective antidrug programs in the country, at Rushwood Elementary School in Sagamore Hills in 1994. School visits are part of my weekly schedule. I normally have Friday and at least most of Monday in the district to speak to students, visit businesses, and speak at noon or evening service clubs.

For this 1994 campaign shoot in Lakeview Park in Lorain, we borrowed the dog, Buttercup, from Elizabeth's friend, Mallory Donaldson. Such "warm and fuzzy" ads in which we cited my first-term accomplishments seemed to make no difference in our poll results. It was only when my opponent signed the Contract with America—thus giving me the chance to point out that the Republicans could not cut taxes on the rich, increase defense spending dramatically, *and* balance the budget without major reductions in Medicare—that I caught the district's attention.

Former civil rights leader John Lewis appeared with me on Cleveland's popular WMJI radio station. Every year John Lanigan, Jimmy Malone, Chip Kullik, and I conduct interviews and live broadcasts from the nation's capital. Lewis was one of Martin Luther King Jr.'s closest associates; he was beaten several times during the civil rights movement and jailed at least forty times during the turbulent 1960s.

Elizabeth and Emily again held the Bible for the beginning of my second term in Congress in the January 1995 swearing-in ceremony with Speaker Newt Gingrich. This was one of the few light moments between Gingrich and me. After the ceremony, Gingrich showed my daughters his dinosaur fossils, which he used as some kind of peculiar metaphor in many of his speeches.

Long active in human rights, I had the opportunity to meet the Dalai Lama in 1997 when he provided spiritual leadership to those of us opposed to granting China Most-Favored-Nation status.

I met United Nations Secretary General Kofi Annan in 1998 during his historic visit to Cleveland, where he spoke to a small group of civic leaders before addressing a community forum of more than two thousand people.

Using my Russian, I spoke in 2002 with inmates at a Siberian prison who are being cured of TB.

I played a folk dance tune for an Elyria elementary school class.

do. If you lose your reelection in two years, I'll kick your ass. But if you win with more than 65% of the vote, I'll kick your ass then too, because it means that you didn't stand up for your principles. But as 1993 wore on, more and more veteran Democrats announced their plans to retire. Some quit because a potentially difficult race loomed; others retired because Congress was not as enjoyable for them as it had once been. Many of these Democrats, especially in the South, held seats that only they as popular incumbents could retain for the Democrats. Several older members who faced competitive races told me that they no longer liked the job enough—because of more intense media scrutiny and the stricter and more complex disclosure and campaign finance rules—to work as hard as they needed to retain their seats.

The clouds began to gather late in the fall for me and other Ohio Democrats. In December, State Representative Jane Campbell (who was elected mayor of Cleveland in 2001) dropped out of the governor's race after testing the waters, leaving the field to Robert Burch, a relatively unknown state senator, to challenge Republican governor George Voinovich. That same month, under intense pressure from retiring Ohio senator Howard Metzenbaum, the Ohio AFL-CIO endorsed for the U.S. Senate Joel Hyatt, founder of Hyatt Legal Services and Metzenbaum's son-in-law.

In January the skies darkened as labor endorsed Burch and the Ohio Democratic party endorsed Hyatt for Senate and Burch for governor. Burch's Democratic primary opponent was a college professor on the political fringe, a neophyte, and a Lyndon LaRouche devotee. Burch beat him in the May primary, but not by much, and actually lost Lorain County and the Thirteenth Congressional District. Hyatt's opponent was Cuyahoga County (Cleveland) Commissioner Mary Boyle, bright and articulate but unknown to two-thirds of the state's primary voters. Boyle, who started her campaign too late, mounted an aggressive and effective campaign but came up fourteen thousand votes short (less than 2 percent) in the May 1994 primary.

In late 1993 and early 1994, Republicans were doing the best candidate recruitment in congressional races that they had done in at least a generation—in Ohio and across the country. They recruited officeholders with good name recognition and media and sports figures with even better name recognition. They also were able to convince over two dozen very wealthy candidates, many of them physicians, to run and to spend at least $100,000 of their own money. In Ohio, Republicans simply out-recruited us. Democrats left four Republicans unopposed and fielded, with few exceptions, weak challengers to Republican incumbents. Against the four first-term Democrats and one apparently vulnerable incumbent, the Republicans ran four county officials and a wealthy businessman who spent more than $500,000 of his own money. The Republican candidate in an open seat to succeed a retiring Democrat was the chairman of the Ohio Senate Finance Committee. In the three northeastern Ohio districts in the Cleveland media market, three elected county prosecutors (called "district attorneys" or "state's attorneys" in some states) were tapped to run against four-term Democrat Tom Sawyer, freshman Eric Fingerhut, and me. Crime looked to be a major issue in the 1994 election; for the first time in six years, a comprehensive crime bill was being debated in Congress, and it looked like it was going to pass. All three prosecutors opposed the crime bill, and all three opposed the ban on assault weapons; opposition to any gun control was, as the 1994 elections would show, a politically popular position. Sawyer, Fingerhut, and I later in the year voted for the crime bill and the assault weapons ban.

The Republican party was gleeful about its success in landing the prosecutors; rarely do political parties field prominent elected officials with the kind of successful electoral history that these three had achieved. In Ohio, prosecutors are often considered the most powerful elected officials in their counties and are usually very visible. Also, these candidates were in the middle of four-year terms, so they would retain their jobs even if they lost the congressional races.

My opponent, Greg White, had been Lorain County prosecutor for fourteen years. His win in 1980 was a bit of a fluke, but then he won three elections, two by relatively large margins and one when Democrats failed to field a candidate against him. White won a Silver Star as a marine in Vietnam, worked in the steel mill in Lorain while in law school, and was one of only two countywide-elected Republican officeholders. He and his chief deputy were feared by many attorneys and prominent citizens, some of whom told me privately that they could not contribute to my campaign or support me publicly because of potential legal retribution. Although the Lorain and Elyria newspapers rarely criticized him, he had been accused by political opponents of selective prosecution for political gain and for a lackluster effort in collecting delinquent child support. The criticism, though legitimate, was not widely disseminated, and almost none of it stuck.

White denied repeatedly throughout 1993 that he would run, turning down Republican pleas over and over. But in January 1994, less than six weeks before the filing deadline, the National Republican Congressional Committee (NRCC) took a poll for him, flew him to Washington, and explained to him how vulnerable I was. As they did with dozens of others all over the country, they wined and dined him—as only the Republicans can—and pointed out my political weaknesses. They gave him poll results that, while not insignificant, showed—and likely exaggerated—my vulnerabilities. The polling numbers given him by the NRCC, I was later told by two Republicans, were doctored to convince White that he was ahead in our home county of Lorain, where almost 40 percent of the vote would be cast. Our polling numbers and the November vote tally, however, showed that he was never ahead of me, or even close, in Lorain County. The NRCC predicted a big Republican sweep, perhaps not fully believing it themselves. They promised White lots and lots of campaign money and lots and lots of technical campaign assistance. And they showed him the glamour of Washington, but probably not the daily workload. He was in the race.

The local newspapers salivated over a race between two experienced, relatively young, accomplished officeholders. There had not been such a competitive congressional race in Lorain County in decades. As one reporter described it, "Brown looked as if he hadn't run a comb across his head since 1990. And White, with every hair in place, looked a little like 'the bridegroom on the wedding cake,' which is what the actress Ethel Barrymore called Thomas Dewey." It was a race, as far as the newspapers saw it, between White, the favorite son, and Brown, the interloper.

Our strategy—formulated by campaign manager Jeff Snell and political consultants Bill Burges and Jeff Rusnak and me—was to keep the message simple. Talk about the economy and fighting for jobs. Emphasize "Promises Made, Promises Kept." (Interestingly, seven months later, Newt Gingrich and the Republicans adopted the exact same slogan at the end of their Contract with America. I guess election campaigns don't qualify for copyrights.) In 1992 I had promised six specific things:

> To pay my own health care until we passed universal coverage
> To spend less money than I was budgeted
> To vote against and to reject any pay increase
> To hold regular town meetings and to refuse foreign travel at government expense
> To fight for fair trade, oppose NAFTA, and work toward an industrial policy with a strong export component
> To end corporate tax deductibility for million-dollar salaries

In the 1992 primary I dated each of the six promises and signed them. I kept all six. Keeping my word and adopting the slogan "Promises Made, Promises Kept" gave me the credibility that many short-term incumbents did not have, especially in a year like 1994.

In addition, our campaign emphasized getting Democrats out to vote and going after the Perot voters. My Washington press secretary Steve Fought said, "Where you live is where labor and Perotistas come together, especially on trade." Perot had garnered almost 30 percent of the vote in my district in 1992, his fourth-highest vote east of the Mississippi River. Perot's message during the 1992 campaign and in the ensuing two years was similar to ours: fighting the deficit and fighting for jobs. During my first term, I repeatedly argued that our biggest problems were the growing twin deficits, trade and budget. We had to aggressively fight both, and that was our message to the Perot people.

Nothing good was happening for Democrats around Ohio or the country. The Republican incumbent for governor in Ohio was spending $7 million and getting every newspaper endorsement, while his Democratic opponent could raise only about $200,000 and seemed invisible. The Democratic candidate for the Senate consistently trailed by 15 percent in the polls, and his grassroots efforts seemed nonexistent. Newspapers were writing about a potential statewide Republican sweep, and many predicted that Democrats in the Ohio House of Representatives would lose the majority for the first time in twenty-two years. Six Ohio Democrats were on the run: freshmen David Mann, Ted Strickland, Eric Fingerhut, and I; Greg DiDonato, the Democratic candidate in an eastern Ohio district, where longtime Democratic incumbent Doug Applegate was retiring; and Akron's Tom Sawyer.

Early in the campaign season, a Republican Grand Old Party Action Committee (GOPAC) seminar counseled Republican candidates to "go negative early" and "never back off." They were to find a minor negative with broad appeal, one that fueled voter outrage, and pound it home. In reaction to Republican tactics, the Democratic Congressional Campaign Committee (DCCC) warned us, "Ignore traditional wisdom of not attacking a relatively unknown opponent. The days of incumbency advantage are over. Hit hard now—don't wait for the opponent to hit you in the last two weeks. People don't like you because you are an incumbent. Therefore you need to define your opponent so they like him even less." DCCC chairman, Congressman Vic Fazio of California, told me one afternoon that, talk radio, newspapers, and others "have been running negative against you for two years." George Will, full-time Republican adviser and part-time columnist, wrote in *Newsweek*

[of ads] of an increasingly scabrous sort. These usually are 30-second snarls that preclude subtlety. Such campaigning, which is now the norm because it is effective, serves conservatism, for two reasons. First, campaigning in such

short televised bursts is survival of the briefest, and conservatism's message, distilled to its essence, often is: "No, less, stop that, cut it out." What that message lacks in poetry it makes up in concision. Second, conservatism considers distrust of government, and of people who crave political power, a virtue. Today's acidic campaigning breeds such distrust.

Consistent with Will's assertions, Republicans are more likely to start a barrage of negative ads because they typically gain more when they do. Mud usually sticks if you throw enough. I had tried otherwise in my 1990 race for Ohio secretary of state against Bob Taft. In response to his negative ads, we exhorted people to "vote against the Mud Merchants and clean up politics." We lost. Negative campaigning won. Soon after the election, Secretary-elect Taft said to Wayne West, my assistant secretary of state, "It's too bad that we had to run that kind of campaign to beat you." When both are attacking— even though one side started it and has thrown more mud—the public thinks, usually with help from the media, that they're both negative and that it's simply politics as usual. The one who started it and has thrown not only the most but the most effective mud has already gained from it. And—this is where Republicans gain—the more negative the race becomes, the lower the voter turnout is. Typically, no matter how negative the race, Republicans go to the polls and many Democrats stay home.

Voters seemed to be doing their part. When candidates talk about themselves in an ad, or advertise their accomplishments, people simply don't believe them. But when one attacks the other, people believe it. They seem to want to believe only bad things about politics and politicians. Beginning in mid-September, I ran twenty-five days of positive, substantive ads about my accomplishments, and the polls remained basically unchanged. Only when I criticized my opponent's position on several issues, especially his signing of the Contract with America, Newt Gingrich's blueprint to govern the House, did my poll numbers improve. One man said to me, when I was campaigning in front of a supermarket, "Those ads must all be true, or you guys would sue each other all the time."

Florida Democratic governor Lawton Chiles, who had never in his career run a negative advertisement, told columnist David Broder, "A couple weeks ago, my people said to me, 'You're talking about what you have done in office, but nobody is listening.'" Then Chiles began his negative ads against Jeb Bush, son of the former president. In the end, Chiles won a close race.

We all pay for negative campaigning—candidates, the voters, the political system, society. Voter turnout continues to decline; less than 40 percent showed up at the polls in 1994 and an even lower percentage in 1998, the next midterm election. The steady decline since 1960, maybe not coincidentally, since television became a national fixture in campaigns, is only half the problem; those who do vote are more cynical, more disbelieving, more likely to believe that government doesn't matter. As David Broder wrote, "It is fashionable these days to blame the politicians for everything. But cynicism is a social disease that makes politics more tawdry for the people in it and governing ever more difficult. Somehow, we have to hit the brakes on this downhill plunge—and soon."

No other profession criticizes its own the way that politicians do. Imagine Continental Airlines advertising "Don't fly Airline X, the Death Airlines." No one would fly anymore. Or what if McDonald's said that Restaurant Y sold "Cholesterol burgers" and that Restaurant Z gave its patrons trichinosis. Business at all fast-food restaurants would dry up. And in the last few years, the nasty comments that politicians make about one another are not just confined to election time. Former Appropriations chairman Dave Obey told me that Newt Gingrich, when he was in the minority, could hardly speak a paragraph about Congress without using the word "corrupt." Others don't talk about their profession that way.

An editorial on election day 1994 in Capitol Hill's *Roll Call* newspaper stated:

> The problem with toxicity on the campaign trail is that it doesn't stop on Election Day: It destroys government and the bond of trust that must exist between the people and their elected officials. . . . Running the government and running for office are elements of the same US political system. If one is poisoned, so is the other. Just look at the raw partisanship and lack of civility that's prevailed in Congress over the past few sessions, and then consider the foulness of the 1994 campaign.

For me, the campaign was a summer full of parades, festivals, county fairs, and speeches. I walked in more than a dozen parades and attended several days each of county fairs in Portage, Geauga, Medina, and Lorain Counties. Voter anger was palpable, direct, and ultimately aimed at Democrats, who controlled the White House and the Congress. Democrats thought we had a good case to make: six million private-sector jobs had been created in less than two years, twice as many as were created under President Bush in four years; the deficit was on track to decline for a third consecutive year, the first time that had occurred since the presidency of Harry Truman; we had cut the size of the federal government by more than a hundred thousand employees. The arguments made by Democrats all over the country—that the economy was better, the deficit was coming down, and the size of government was shrinking—fell on deaf ears. In fact, people simply did not believe either the president or those of us in Congress.

Nonetheless, my lead in the polls remained constant and fairly large. We held a 12- to 16-percent lead through almost the entire campaign, from after the primary to the last weekend before the election. But the undecided vote loomed dangerously large at a persistent 20 percent throughout the summer and fall. Our share of the vote never went above 44 percent; White's never above 32 percent. Two independent candidates accounted for 4–8 percent.

In September the Republicans made a fateful move, one that apparently paid off nationally but played a key role in my victory. Upward of four hundred Republican candidates and officeholders staged a signing of the Contract with America on the steps of the U.S. Capitol. Greg White did not attend the signing, but he did sign the Contract from Elyria.

Earlier in the year, Republican activists Newt Gingrich and Richard Armey had realized that they needed some sort of political document to help them nationalize the elections. Traveling the country extensively in 1993 and 1994, Gingrich knew that the public increasingly disapproved of the policies of Clinton and the Democrats, and he sensed that 1994 could actually be the year when Republicans would take control of the House of Representatives. Gingrich liked the idea of a unifying document to be unveiled in an event on the steps of the Capitol with literally hundreds of Republican incumbents and candidates together. A 1980 Capitol steps rally with candidate Ronald Reagan, Gingrich believed, had worked splendidly.

The Contract with America was drawn up, with special attention paid to the most socially conservative wing of the Republican party and the business contributors to the party. The Republican National Committee bought a $275,000 insert in *TV Guide* to give the Contract with America a distribution as wide as possible. Nationalizing the 1994 election—attempting to persuade the voters to judge their own candidates for Congress by national issues rather than local, personal characteristics—was risky, but the unpopularity of President Clinton and congressional Democrats made the risk more attractive. Besides, they had wandered in the wilderness long enough. For forty years, nothing else had worked.

Nationalizing the election also brought Republican members of Congress together. Some longtime veterans had given up on winning back a majority for their party. But most were willing to give it one last shot. By nationalizing the election and by pushing Republicans in safe seats to raise

large amounts of money, Gingrich made the difference. In 1994, according
to Ohio Republican John Boehner, 130 members of Congress raised $1.2
million to help incumbent Republicans and another $5 million for challengers.
After the election, Dick Gephardt asked Gingrich how he did it. "It's spelled
m-o-n-e-y," the Speaker-elect said. When Gephardt told the story, he added,
somewhat dejectedly, "And they wanted it more than we did. Pure and
simple."

The Contract was specifically aimed at Perot voters, those who seemed
most to demand change and were the most unhappy with Democrats for
not giving it to them. Gingrich and Armey assiduously avoided the most
controversial and divisive issues, like trade agreements, abortion, and school
prayer. Signed by 367 Republican challengers and incumbents (only three
incumbents refused; three challengers who won also did not sign), the Contract, comprised of ten bills and three resolutions, dealt with a variety of
issues that had been extensively polled, subjected to focus-group examination, and debated in Republican circles for a number of years by dozens of
candidates.

The Contract with America

H.R. 1   *Congressional Accountability Act* applies antidiscrimination laws to
Congress

H.R. 2   *Line-Item Veto Act* gives the president greater veto powers

H.R. 3   *Taking Back Our Streets Act*, an anticrime bill

H.R. 4   *Personal Responsibility Act* overhauls the nation's welfare programs

H.R. 5   *Unfunded Mandate Reform Act* cuts back on federal mandates to
states

H.R. 6   *American Dream Restoration Act* changes the tax code, reducing
some taxes, increasing others

H.R. 7   *National Security Restoration Act* increases military spending,
funding for Star Wars research

H.R. 8   *Senior Citizens' Equity Act,* Social Security reform

H.R. 9   *Job Creation/Wage Enhancement Act,* deregulates, rolls back
environmental laws

H.R. 10   *Common Sense Legal Reforms Act,* product liability and tort reform

H.R. 11   *Family Reinforcement Act,* child support, adoption reform

H.J.R. 1   *Balanced Budget Amendment,* constitutional amendment to require
a balanced budget

H.J.R. 2   *Citizen Legislature Act,* term limits—twelve years for House
members

H.J.R. 3   *Citizen Legislature Act,* term limits—six years for House members

The preelection campaign use of the Contract was very mixed. In the South, Republican challengers and incumbents were inclined to talk about it, support it, and advertise it. In many districts in the Northeast and Midwest, including mine, Democratic incumbents and challengers talked more about the Contract than the Republicans who signed it. Democrats criticized their Republican opponents for heading off lockstep to Washington to sign a document handed to them by the party bosses. Democrats also pointed out that the math simply didn't add up. Military spending increases plus tax breaks for the rich equal Medicare cuts and student loan cuts, we said.

The Contract promised a more responsive Congress, a smaller government, tax cuts, a stronger national defense, a balanced budget, and a rollback of federal regulations. Gingrich and the Republicans reprinted the Contract in *TV Guide* and urged readers to cut it out and place it on their refrigerators "so that you know we will keep our promises."

I don't think I would have won if Greg White had not signed the Contract. We defined the Contract before White did. The day before the Republicans gathered on the steps of the Capitol, I issued my own contract with the Thirteenth District that included pledges on jobs, fair trade, congressional reform, and the environment. At the same time, we used news conferences in four communities in the district to reiterate my six promises from 1992, all of which I had kept.

The national Democrats did a good job of educating national reporters and columnists about the empty promises, the major spending cuts to programs that mattered to people, and the budget-busting aspect of the Contract. According to *Plain Dealer* columnist Mary Anne Sharkey, one GOP consultant derisively described the Contract signing as "300 white guys in suits and ties standing on the steps saying, 'Trust us.'" While Newt Gingrich's hopes of nationalizing the election were realized, several Democrats across the country used the Contract to their benefit. North Dakota freshman Earl Pomeroy told me that the Contract gave his campaign an opportunity to pin his opponent down on a political philosophy that would not sell in his state. A New York Republican congressman told me that he didn't know of any Republican incumbents from the Northeast who even mentioned the Contract.

Written by insiders to be used by candidates positioning themselves as outsiders, the Contract was a collection of popular initiatives that, taken together, spelled fiscal trouble. It was criticized by former Republican senator Warren Rudman, founder of the Concord Coalition, as a fiscal disaster;

by outgoing Republican congressman Fred Grandy as "fiscal suicide"; and
by Richard Nixon's Social Security administrator Robert Ball as "a menace
to Social Security." Although it included popular issues, such as a balanced
budget amendment, defense increases, tax cuts, a line-item veto, term limits, congressional reform, and the like, it simply did not add up. It was $900
billion out of balance—$900 billion that would almost certainly have to be
made up by cutting Social Security, Medicare, and veterans' benefits.

In addition to "Promises Made, Promises Kept," my campaign was all
about the Republican Contract. Greg White was never really on the offen-
sive from that day on. When I repeatedly stated that you cannot cut taxes on
the rich, increase military spending, and balance the budget without cutting
Medicare and Social Security, he reacted angrily, emphasizing over and over
that he would oppose any cuts in Medicare or Social Security.

Aside from the Contract with America, bad news about the election in
general was all around us: an unpopular president, a perception that Congress had failed, an invisible Democratic gubernatorial nominee, a weak
Democratic Senate candidate, and the prospects of a low voter turnout,
especially among Democrats. It was hard to see why Democrats would bother
to come to the polls.

A typical day in my campaign was not much different from two years earlier: the Lorain auto plant at 5:30 A.M., followed by a plant in Elyria until
7:30; visiting several local restaurants to meet voters before they went to
work; then the rest of the day spent going door to door or campaigning at
supermarkets and discount stores or returning to campaign headquarters to
raise money over the phone. In the evening I typically campaigned at fast-
food restaurants before visiting bowling alleys, veterans' halls, and nation-
ality clubs.

Holidays were no less busy. On July 4 I walked in a parade in Chesterland, hurried to another parade at Chippewa Lake sixty miles away, played
three innings in a celebrity softball game in Avon Lake, returned to Medina
County for a 5:00 parade in Valley City, then walked in a fourth parade in
Medina at 6:00. At 7:00 we opened our Medina County campaign headquarters, and at 8:00 I directed a song with the Medina Community Band
on the square. At one parade, when I stuck out my hand to introduce myself
to a middle-aged woman, she glared at me and snorted, "I don't shake hands
with the enemy."

The other candidates and I had several debates, none of them especially
decisive. As columnist Molly Ivins said, "Political debates are sort of like

stock-car races—no one really cares who wins, they just want to see the crashes. If there aren't any crashes, everyone votes the event a total bore." There were no crashes in our debates, although perennial candidate John Michael Ryan did dress up like Paul Revere for one occasion.

By late October, during one especially long and tiring day, I thought about a candidate who, many years before, was challenging Ohio state auditor Thomas Ferguson, a longtime Democratic incumbent. The challenger, who had never before run statewide, was running a losing campaign with little money and a very small campaign staff. He was traveling alone, doing his own driving all over the state, and was quite clearly exhausted as the election drew near. As he was giving his pitch to a reporter at a small paper in western Ohio, he suddenly stopped talking. The reporter looked up from his notebook: the candidate had fallen asleep, head on the table, while he had been talking. Very kindly, the reporter turned off the lights, walked out of the conference room, and let him sleep.

Conservative groups all over the nation, especially pro-gun and antiabortion organizations, ran advertisements attacking Democrats. The messages often had nothing to do with their group's mission. For example, shortly before the election, the Independent Sportsmen of Geauga County ran full-page ads in the *Cleveland Plain Dealer,* at a cost of several thousand dollars, criticizing my support of the budget, my record as Ohio secretary of state, and my vote on a United Nations bill. They also attacked me for "carpet-bagging" and "increasing my pay 600%," a charge with no foundation. These ads, called "independent expenditures," technically are unconnected to any campaign, although their message pretty clearly parroted what Greg White was saying about my first two years in office. White's campaign did not have to disclose any information about this ad campaign. Interestingly, there was no mention of guns in these ads, and one has to wonder where this kind of group would get several thousand dollars to spend on political ads. Around the country, the National Rifle Association was spending big money on radio ads and direct mail criticizing Democrats who voted for the Brady Bill and the assault weapons ban. But they rarely mentioned guns in their ads to the general public.

My campaign raised and spent about $950,000, twice what I spent in 1992 when I was outspent two to one. When you add in the conservative independent expenditures, White spent about what I did. While incumbents around the country typically outspent their challengers, Democratic incumbents often lost much of that advantage when conservative groups poured money into anti-Democratic independent expenditures. To a lesser degree, some Republicans were targets of pro-choice independent expenditures or an occasional labor ad campaign. That year was the beginning of huge independent contributions.

Unlike many of my fellow freshmen, I did not invite cabinet members, legislative leaders, and powerful committee chairpersons into my district for big fund-raisers and highly visible public events; they only would serve as targets for the thousands of voters angry at Congress and at the Democrats. Tipper Gore, wife of the vice president, did appear at a nonpolitical event at St. Joseph's Hospital in Lorain to speak at a breast cancer program sponsored by my office. And when the president came to Cleveland two weeks before the election, I stayed in my district to campaign, as I had scheduled a speech to a class at Lorain County Community College and a number of other campaign appearances. The front page of the local newspaper featured the headline "Anybody Here See Sherrod Brown?"; but that same newspaper would have written "Brown Hobnobs with President, Ignores Lorain" if I had gone to Cleveland. Nonetheless, a number of people in Lorain and Elyria complained to me that I should not have avoided the president. My press secretary summed it up after the election: "Clinton is always welcome in Lorain. We would have loved for him to go door to door with us, or go to bingo halls and bowling alleys. But time spent in Cleveland with Clinton would have been time Brown wouldn't have been out meeting voters. Brown's goal was to meet a thousand people daily, and Clinton couldn't keep up with him."

By election day, we were confident of victory. All the local newspapers predicted that we would win, our last poll showed a comfortable lead of thirteen points (although 18 percent were still undecided), and the response I was getting from people seemed positive enough to win decisively. After I voted at a Lorain senior citizens' center in the morning, feeling good I introduced myself outside the polls to a man who was helping a Republican judicial candidate. He responded to my friendly greeting with, "I hope your opponent wins."

For the rest of the day I stood at polling places in Lorain, Brunswick, and Elyria. The feeling I had, especially in Lorain and Brunswick (both of which I won handily), was very positive. The polling places in White's hometown of Elyria, which I carried by three hundred votes, gave me more cause for concern. About fifteen minutes before the polls closed, I was leaving St. Jude's Church in Elyria, where several polling places are located, when I began experiencing the same election-night jitters almost all candidates endure. When I heard reports that exit polls across the country were showing Republicans winning almost everywhere and that they might even take control of the House, those jitters turned into full-blown anxiety. Very early in the evening, however, we were pretty certain of victory when absentee ballots came in showing us winning almost everywhere in the district. We became more certain when Lorain County numbers showed us with a substantial lead in the county that White had to win to defeat us. By 9:30 P.M. the issue was not whether we'd win, but by how much. The answer was "not by much."

In the end, we won 49 percent to White's 45.5 percent, with independents Howard Mason and John Michael Ryan splitting the rest. But as Emily said that night, "Dad, this was no fun tonight. It doesn't even seem like we won. All your friends lost." Elizabeth chimed in that 1992 was a whole lot more fun.

In Ohio Eric Fingerhut, Ted Strickland, and Daniel Mann lost. Tom Sawyer escaped by a couple percentage points. Bob Ney won the Democratic open seat. Voters were voting against government and the party of government. Democrats had controlled Congress for forty years but the White House only fourteen of those years; nonetheless, the Democrats were in charge of the House and Senate and presidency in 1993 and 1994, and the voters expressed their anger at our inability to deliver. A *Washington Post* columnist wrote, "The Democrats had it in their power to pass a package of health, welfare and political reforms. They failed utterly. No wonder the voters punished them." Editorially, the *Post* called the 1993–94 Congress the least effective in decades.

Many years ago Democratic pollster Vic Fingerhut said, "Republicans win when voters think of themselves as taxpayers. Democrats win when voters think of themselves as working people." In 1994, with the frustration that the public felt toward government, it was only natural that most people thought of themselves first as taxpayers and voted accordingly.

Ironically, first-term Democratic incumbents who campaigned in 1994 on congressional reform issues perhaps fell the hardest. Democrats did not deliver on those issues, partly because of Senate filibusters and Republican recalcitrance but also because it surely was not a top priority for Democratic leadership and the White House. Voters seem to punish those Democrats who staked their first-term accomplishments on campaign finance reform and anti-Congress themes. While voters unequivocally support congressional reform, those incumbents who talked about jobs and the economy simply did better. Voters were saying, "Yes, we support congressional reform, but please put your efforts into job creation, balancing the budget, eliminating the trade deficit."

In particular, white males, independents, and 1992 Perot voters voted against the party and the president who presented them with a health care plan that seemed too bureaucratic and took away their physician choice; who offered up a crime bill that they thought took away their guns and was loaded up with social programs and more Washington bureaucracy; who raised their taxes; and who wouldn't change the way they did business in the far-off corrupt city of Washington.

The speed at which voters had changed their views was alarming to everyone in politics, not just Democrats. In 1992, independent voters favored Democratic House candidates 54 percent to 46 percent. Two years later, they gave Republicans their votes, 56 percent to 44 percent. White males—about evenly split in 1992—overwhelmingly supported GOP congressional candidates 63–37 percent in 1994. Swing voters are especially impatient with politicians. George Bush's favorable rating plummeted from 90 percent during the Gulf War to ignominy sixteen months later. Voters were watching Washington with a remote in their hands. We're tired of Bush—ZAP! Change the channel. Maybe Perot? ZAP! Let's try Clinton. We've had enough of him. ZAP! How about Gingrich? We'll give him a year or two.

Gingrich, after the election, credited the Christian Right: "The activity engaged in by the Christian Coalition to educate and to make sure the people back home knew what was happening in Washington were a real part of why we had a revolution at the polls on November 8." At a small meeting in the majority leader's office two days after the election, Dick Gephardt told about a dozen of us that guns cost us at least ten seats. Others there put the number closer to twenty. I'm sure it cost me at least two or three percentage points, as hundreds of people approached me in the course of the election campaign and defiantly told me they were voting against me because "you want to take my guns."

Several southern Democrats said that the Democratic attacks on tobacco— no-smoking-in-public-places proposals, campaigns against youth smoking, Clinton proposals to tax tobacco to pay for his health care plan—also cost us seats in North Carolina, Georgia, Kentucky, and Tennessee. And surely racial politics and redistricting also played a role. Lyndon Johnson, when he signed the Civil Rights Act, turned to his aide Bill Moyers and lamented, "I think we delivered the South to the Republican Party for your lifetime and mine." More and more white southerners turned to the Republican party as nationally the Democrats fought for civil rights while southern politicians who opposed federal involvement were more and more likely to become Republicans. And Johnson's pronouncement did not even take into account what would happen with redistricting and the Voting Rights Act.

What happened in Georgia is instructive. Georgia was 9 to 1 Democrat before 1992 (one of the Democrats, John Lewis from Atlanta, was black); after redistricting, which the GOP supported, there were three blacks, and the partisan breakdown was 7 to 4. (Georgia got a new district because of population growth.) After the 1994 elections, the breakdown was 7 to 4 Republican. Only one white Democrat was elected, and he had always voted with Republicans; in fact, early in 1995 he switched to the Republican party, a much more comfortable place for him to be. Two white Democrats lost, both of whom were moderate and often voted with national Democrats and both of whom lost large numbers of their African American constituents in redistricting.

Redistricting surely hurt Democrats in nonsouthern states also, where lines in 1991 and 1992 were drawn by federal judges appointed by Reagan and Bush and by state legislatures that had become more Republican in the 1980s and early 1990s. California became much more difficult for Democrats as a result.

And there was the media's role. *Newsweek*'s Jonathan Alter wrote:

> Although nominal liberals still dominate the ranks of reporters, they are generally equal-opportunity character assassins (just ask the Clintons). By contrast, conservatives dominate punditry, where they hold the edge not just on radio, but among syndicated columnists and TV talking heads. So it's basically a draw. And this year the TV news magazines—aired by the hated networks—contributed directly to the GOP victory.

And the electoral message was: if you're angry with the federal government and the way they do things, vote against the Democrats because they're the ones in charge.

Democrats did not get slaughtered because we stood for the important causes and the principles for which the Democratic party is known. We didn't lose because we fought for a single-payer health care plan or stood up for the poor or advocated a fairer, more progressive tax system. We lost because of guns, gays in the military, free trade, and a Rube Goldberg–health care plan. We were in the majority. Logically, we were blamed for everything the voters did not like. Period.

PART II

When your enemy is destroying himself, don't interfere.
    —Napoleon

11

Intelligence and Surveillance

The 1994 campaign was a TRADOC [army term for Training
and Doctrine Command], theater-level campaign plan, executed
by building small-unit cohesion, delegating throughout with
mission-type orders, and designed to have real-time capability
to respond to an opponent that was changing, period. I know
it was. I have lived it.

—Newt Gingrich, at Fort Monroe, Virginia (1995)

It was with the ideal of systematically undermining the foundations, systematically destroying society and all principles;
with the idea of nonplussing everyone and making hay of
everything, and then, when society was tottering, sick and out
of joint, cynical and skeptical though filled with an intense
eagerness for self-preservation and for some guiding idea, suddenly to seize it in their hands, raising the standard of revolt
and relying on a complete network of quintets, which were
actively, meanwhile, gathering recruits and seeking out the
weak spot which could be attacked.

—Fyodor Dostoyevsky, *The Possessed*

THE CONTRACT WITH AMERICA did not spell out much of the Republican agenda in detail. After the election, committee staff began working
feverishly to draft legislation to carry out each of the items in the Contract.
Several major issues, not part of the public version, were included in the
legislation that would implement the Contract: for example, funding the
Strategic Defense Initiative (SDI, the Reagan-era "star wars"); overriding
Clinton's executive order eliminating the "gag rule," which had prohibited
physicians and other health care providers who were paid by Medicaid to
speak to a patient about the option of abortion; and a capital gains tax cut.
The revised Contract gave Republicans a document with which to govern;
it defined their agenda and provided them a vehicle for legislation, for party
discipline, and for a relatively coherent message to sell to the public.

The first Republican Speaker in forty years, Newt Gingrich calculated that for his party to take control of the House of Representatives it would, in many ways, have to destroy the institution first. The stepson of a career soldier, Gingrich, who never served in the armed forces, fashioned himself as a military leader, even telling a group of military officers in 1993, "I am in combat every day." From his early days in Congress, Gingrich traveled to military bases to study military tactics, language, and management ideas. He told military officers in 1995 that those visits "changed my life," and he told writer Elizabeth Drew that the movie *The Sands of Iwo Jima* was "the formative movie of my life."

After the Republican takeover of the House, Gingrich's ardor for all things military did not cool. The Speaker, according to *Roll Call,* privately described the Contract with America "as a basic training document for freshmen and committee chairs" to get them to do what they might not otherwise have done. In late November 1995, in the heat of the budget battles, the army, at Gingrich's request, flew about a half-dozen Republican members by helicopter from the Pentagon to Fort Monroe, Virginia, to study "the operational art of war" at the army's Training and Doctrine Command (TRADOC). These Gingrich lieutenants, under the leadership of Michigan Republican Peter Hoekstra, who had been to TRADOC before, were charged with helping the Speaker pass legislation, discipline recalcitrant Republicans, and prepare for battles on the budget. According to army notes, the seminars—which were paid for out of the Department of Defense budget, as were all travel expenses to Fort Monroe—covered "military doctrine, military staff concepts, and the operational art of war." Further, documents show that in late 1995 Gingrich asked the Pentagon for three officers to work in his office, a highly unusual practice on Capitol Hill. On January 2, 1996, air force, army, and navy officers reported to the Speaker's suite to work.

Gingrich seemed to learn well. Use words and phrases like "self-serving," "incompetent," "abuse of power," and "corrupt" when describing the Democratic majority, Gingrich said in a 1990 mailing to Republican candidates. Label Democrats "pathetic" and "sick," he advised, listing sixty-five "mix-and-matchable" characterizations of the "hypocrisy" and "bizarre, destructive" behavior of our "enemy" who has "disgraced" and "betrayed" our nation. He even blamed a South Carolina mother's killing of her two children on a society created by the permissiveness of the liberal Democrats. Elizabeth Drew recounted in her book *Showdown* an exchange between Gingrich and Vice President Al Gore during the budget negotiations at the White House: "Gingrich, replying to the President's question of where they were on the debt limit, said, 'Nowhere. How can we get somewhere when you call us extreme?' Gore responded, 'At least we didn't accuse you of killing two children before the election.'"

Gingrich did not confine his comments to the institution of Congress; as did Reagan, he wanted Americans to be contemptuous of the whole federal government and of the entire Washington establishment. "There are two realities to the current system, he claimed, "one is the government is trying to cheat you; and the second is the government is lying to you about what it's doing . . . [And] nobody would notice if you decapitated the top 12,000 bureaucrats." In 1994, as he sensed victory, he pronounced judgment on the Democratic Congress as "the enemy of ordinary Americans."

And his strategy worked. His accomplishment, however, came with a huge price for him and the Republicans and the nation. The reputation of Congress plummeted to record lows in the 1990s. And even though favorable ratings for Congress went up in the early days of the Contract with America, they soon returned to the abysmally low levels seen in other years during the decade. And now that Republicans were in charge and Gingrich was their leader, they had to contend with responsibility for an institution that was held in low regard by huge portions of the public.

To be sure, it is an American tradition to view Congress with disdain. More than 130 years ago, Artemus Ward wrote, "I venture to say that if you search the earth all over with a ten horsepower microscope, you won't be able to find such another pack of poppycock gabblers as the present Congress." Mark Twain averred that "it could probably be shown by facts and figures that there is no distinctly native American criminal class except Congress." Eugene Field tended to agree: "Some statesmen go to Congress and some go to jail. It is the same thing, after all." George Dennison Prentice claimed that "there are two periods when Congress does no business: one is before the holidays, the other after." And Will Rogers quipped, "This country has come to feel the same when Congress is in session as we do when the baby gets hold of a hammer. It's just a question of how much damage he can do with it before we can take it away from him."

But the attitude of the last decade seemed to be that government works for nobody except the most connected interest groups. Citizens' groups, trying to convince people that government does not work, want to empower people by making them angry about what government is doing *to* them.

Candidates running for Congress almost without exception position themselves as outsiders and pledge to fight business as usual in the nation's capital. Incumbents running for reelection point out that they are not like all those other congressmen and congresswomen. But once the election is over, attacks on ethics, integrity, even motive usually continue unabated.

It should be no surprise, then, that Americans participate in the political process in significantly declining numbers. Less than 5 percent of adult Americans, voting aside, participate in the political process—volunteering, contributing money, writing a letter to the editor. Fewer than one in twenty-five citizens contribute money to political campaigns. Fifteen years ago, 29 percent of taxpayers designated on their tax return that a small amount of their tax liability go to the Presidential Election Campaign Fund; that number has declined to 17 percent.

Most importantly, voter turnout is down. The last five elections provided some of the lowest turnouts in recent American political history. In the 1996 Montana Senate race, Lieutenant Governor Dennis Rehberg sent a last-minute mailing to the most likely voters for his Democratic opponent, Senator Max Baucus—Democratic women. Understanding that his chances of converting these women were very limited, Rehberg knew that his rather scurrilous mailing would raise doubts about Baucus's commitment to Democratic values, and although Rehberg was significantly outspent by Baucus, the lieutenant governor apparently believed that this was a good use of his money: Democratic female voters, he hoped, would stay home. It is usually in the interest of the Republicans to push turnout even lower; it simply helps them win elections. The 1994 Republican electoral landslide may very well have been the result of an exceptionally low turnout among women, labor union members, and minorities.

E. J. Dionne explains America's crucial role as a world leader and the only superpower in these terms: "With democracy on the march outside our borders, our first responsibility is to ensure that the United States becomes a model for what self-government should be and not an example of what happens to free nations when they lose interest in public life. A nation that hates politics will not long survive as a democracy."

12

The Coup and the Revolution

He thinks like a Tory, and talks like a Radical, and that's so
important nowadays.
— Oscar Wilde, *Lady Windermere's Fan* (1892)

I expect a kiss-my-ass-at-high-noon-in-Macy's-window loyalty.
— President Lyndon Johnson

THE 1994 ELECTION RETURNS stunned Democrats and surprised
Republicans. Most members of both parties had thought that the
Democrats were the permanent majority and Republicans the permanent
minority. While both old-time and incoming Republicans prepared for the
new session, Democrats seemed lost. Newer Democrats were obviously less
shell shocked; those in my class had little power and influence as new members of the majority and not much less as second-term members of the
minority. Committee chairs, subcommittee chairs, Democratic leaders, and
many senior Democrats, however, literally did not know what to do. In their
worst political dreams, they never expected this to happen. Some blamed
each other; many blamed Democratic leadership; others pointed fingers at
Republicans for nasty campaign tactics such as lying about the biggest tax
increase in American history; some simply blamed the gullibility of the
voters. More than a few grumbled about quitting. The job would not be fun
anymore.

Almost before the votes were counted, as Republicans nationwide celebrated their best election day in decades, Newt Gingrich began talking about
the Contract with America. He transformed this political statement, this
campaign piece, into a governing document for his new majority. The public, through the election of 230 Republicans, he told the press, had ratified
this Contract that stood for less government, lower taxes, local control. Certainly, Republicans believed, judging by the election returns, the public
wanted exactly that.

The sometimes chaotic, no-one-seems-to-be-in-charge days of the Democratic majority were out. A hierarchial, military-like style with one man in charge was in place. The once-almighty committee chairs would now answer to the Speaker. The Speaker's Advisory Group, with its military-sounding acronym, SAG, which would advise Gingrich, was to be staffed with the new Speaker's loyalists, not the chairs of the major committees with their power bases who had most of the power in the Democratic Congress. Only one committee chair, the Science Committee's Bob Walker of Pennsylvania, was in SAG, and Walker was Gingrich's best friend in Congress. The others were Dick Armey and Tom DeLay of Texas, John Boehner of Ohio, Dennis Hastert of Illinois, and Bill Paxon of New York—each far to the right on the political spectrum.

On the other side of the aisle, the mood was different. Democrats were dispirited and dejected. The day after the election, Steve Elmendorf, a top aide to the majority leader Gephardt, called me and about a dozen others to Gephardt's office to figure out what to do next. We knew we were a part of history: we represented what was left of a discredited Democratic party.

Gephardt summoned us to Washington to assist his election as minority leader. The Democratic Speaker, Tom Foley, had been defeated along with five other Democratic incumbents in Washington state, and Gephardt wanted to make sure that there was no serious challenge to his leadership position. Amazingly, there was little finger-pointing at that meeting. There was certainly no shortage of opinion about why we lost—at that meeting or in the full Democratic caucus several days later: taxes, guns, too-powerful committee chairs, unresponsive leadership, President Clinton, the health care reform debacle, failure to enact congressional and campaign finance reforms.

The first postelection Democratic caucus, held on a cold, depressing day in December, was almost pathetic. Some members were despondent; many seemed already resigned to a permanent minority status. A number of senior members still viewed the election results with incredulity. And all of us had read newspaper articles and listened to commentators predict the demise of the Democratic party. Member after member assigned blame to Clinton or guns or taxes or the health care fiasco. Few of us blamed ourselves, and fewer still were introspective. At least two dozen members had their own, unique path back to the majority: break with Clinton, move to the left, and stand for something; or, mimic the Republicans, move to the center, and stay away from social issues.

As I sat in caucus with Milwaukee Democrat Tom Barrett, one of the most decent members of the House, listening to Democratic speaker after Democratic speaker, it dawned on me how difficult the task ahead would be. Only after decades of frustration were Republicans willing to unify, submerge their own egos and individual agendas, and put their trust in one person to lead them. How long, I thought to myself as I looked around the room, would it take Democrats to do the same? How many years would it be before Democrats are even back in the game? A turnaround within the next twelve months seemed hopeless.

And then there were the immediate, practical problems the Democrats faced, for the numbers simply did not add up for members of the minority party. In the 104th Congress, Republicans would hold 52.8 percent of the seats in the House of Representatives. But, as a majority party almost always does, their ratio of seats on almost every House committee is more pronounced. The majority party does not want, for example, a 25 to 22 margin (about 53 percent majority, a reflection of the ratio of the whole House of Representatives) on a committee because of the difficulty of passing controversial legislation. A straying of two majority members could stop a bill that Republican leadership wanted. By December 1994, it became increasingly clear that not only were there no choice committee assignments for the thirteen Democratic freshmen, but several other Democratic members would be knocked off exclusive and other major committees. Republican reforms, many of them justified, plus the simple mathematics of being in the minority had decided that.

Republicans used the takeover to reduce the number of committees, reassign the jurisdiction of several panels, change the names of a number of committees, and reform the rules. They eliminated three committees — Merchant Marine and Fisheries, District of Columbia, and Post Office and Civil Service — and spread their jurisdictions among other committees. Thirty-one of 115 subcommittees were abolished. They moved Railroads out of the renamed Commerce Committee (formerly Energy and Commerce) and gave it to the also-renamed Transportation and Infrastructure Committee. This new majority made several other jurisdictional changes as well, and they renamed ten House committees, most notably (and tellingly) Education and Labor was changed to Education and Economic Opportunity.

With the elimination of three committees and a combined Democratic membership of fifty-two seats, many House Democrats felt the crunch. More significantly, committees with memberships of forty Democrats (such

as Public Works) saw the Democratic seats shrink to twenty-eight. Appropriations was a particularly difficult problem for the Democrats. Prior to the
1994 election, thirty-seven Democrats sat on the Appropriations Committee. Although five Democrats retired, ran for another office, or were
defeated, majority Republican ratios allowed the Democrats only twenty-
eight seats. Several Democrats were removed and given commitments from
both the Democratic leadership and the Democratic caucus that they would
be put back on the committee when openings occurred. They were allowed
to retain their seniority. But places had to be found for those members. The
Rules Committee and the Ways and Means Committee experienced similar
"lay offs" for minority Democrats.

In December, Minority Leader–elect Gephardt brought Commerce
Committee members to his office to ask for help in "finding" committee
slots for the thirteen freshmen and for the members who had been pushed
out of Appropriations, Ways and Means, Rules, and the three committees
that had been eliminated. Eleven of the twenty-seven Democrats on Commerce had retired, run for higher office, or been defeated. Of the remaining sixteen, some of us were asked to give up temporarily, if possible, our
seats on the committee. Representative Cardiss Collins of Chicago, ranking
Democrat on the Government Reform Committee, agreed. New Mexico
congressman Bill Richardson also stepped aside, because he already sat on
the Intelligence Committee and the Resources Committee and was now
deputy whip.

In spite of the disaster at the polls, Democrats did not seem to have much
interest in changing their leadership. The Speaker had been defeated in his
Washington state district. Richard Gephardt, majority leader under Foley,
escaped blame from most of the Democratic caucus. David Bonior, a prin-
cipled progressive from a tough Michigan district, was the third-ranked
Democrat in the 103d Congress; few blamed him, but some conservative
Democrats, mostly from the South, believed that our loss was a result of our
reputation as a liberal, tax-and-spend party, and Bonior seemed to symbol-
ize that to them. As a result, Charlie Stenholm, a moderate-to-conserva-
tive Democrat from rural Texas, was nominated to oppose Bonior for
minority whip in a race that Stenholm knew he would not win. The Stenholm challenge was good-natured but serious. Stenholm knew there were
southern Democrats who were thinking about switching parties—partly out
of ideological reasons, partly because of opportunism and a desire to serve
in the majority. But he counted himself out of that. "When people ask me,"
he told us in the House chamber in late December, "whether I would con-

sider switching parties, I tell them emphatically no. It's not easy being a Democrat where I come from. But I have always been a Democrat and will always be a Democrat. I've been married to the same woman for thirty-two years. I worship at the same church I was confirmed in. And I belong to the Democratic party." While more liberal northern and western Democrats, including me, have respect and a real fondness for Stenholm, Bonior won decisively.

This Congress looked so different. Seventy-four first-year Republicans; only thirteen incoming Democrats, most of them liberal and in safe Democratic seats. This class, so unlike the one two years earlier, was predominantly male, overwhelmingly white, and looked much like Congress of pre-1992. The seventy-three Republicans of the class of 1994 included seven women, no Latinos, and one African American. The sixty-three Democrats of the class of 1992 included twenty-three women, sixteen African Americans, and six Latinos. This class of 1994 represented more wealth than new members of Congress had in recent years and were much less likely to have held public office. Many of them were physicians or had been successful business people.

Republicans made major gains everywhere—four in North Carolina, four in Ohio, six in Washington state, dozens scattered all over the country. But there was a definite southern tinge to the new Republican majority. Republican leadership in both the House and the Senate was almost exclusively white, southern, and male. The top elected House Republicans—Speaker Newt Gingrich (Georgia), Majority Leader Richard Armey (Texas), Majority Whip Tom DeLay (Texas)—were all southern and very conservative. The chairmen of the "exclusive" and most important House committees—Thomas Bliley (Virginia) of Commerce, William Archer (Texas) of Ways and Means, Robert Livingston (Louisiana) of Appropriations—were, again, all southern and very conservative.

This Congress sounded different, too. Brimming with self-confidence, these new members talked revolution. They joined in the chorus of their leader, Newt Gingrich, when he pronounced, "I am a genuine revolutionary." Gingrich talked almost incessantly about tearing down "the decaying old order." A Republican staff person told me that they used words and phrases that "sounded like SDS [Students for a Democratic Society, a left-wing, antiwar group of the 1960s] radicals: 'revolution,' 'us versus them,' 'they're the enemy.'" The new revolutionaries made Rush Limbaugh an honorary member of the Republican freshman class. Speaker Gingrich said, "Every day, Limbaugh educates about six million people around the country who then become centers of education." Former congressman Vin Weber, a longtime confidante of Gingrich, remarked, "Rush Limbaugh is as responsible for what happened as any individual in America." The freshmen believed that it was their mission to change the world, to undo forty years of Democratic government (forgetting that during the forty years of Democratic control of the House of Representatives, Republicans had controlled the Senate for six of those years and a Republican had sat in the White House for twenty-six of those years). They believed all the loose talk and suggestions around the table at local Kiwanis Clubs ("All you gotta do in Washington is . . ."). They advocated minimalist government with power devolving back to the states. They wanted lower taxes and fewer regulations. They wanted more money for the military and less for social services for the poor. They wanted to emasculate the Environmental Protection Agency (EPA), the Occupational Safety and Health Administration (OSHA), and the Consumer Products Safety Commission (CPSC). Their desire to dismantle much of the federal government and its regulatory and social service safety net led a veteran northeastern Republican to wryly comment to me in March 1995, "The problem with the freshmen Republicans is that they don't think anything good in this country ever happened until January 1995." He then shrugged his shoulders and said, almost diffidently, "I feel like I'm still in the minority." More colorfully, one-time Republican consultant and current news analyst Kevin Phillips said, "The freshmen Republicans are like puppies; they squirm around a lot, but they don't know much."

"They thought [that their election] was the Russian Revolution," commented David Keene, a campaign strategist for Bob Dole's 1988 presidential race. Their importance, egged on by a media that loved conflict and the idea of revolution, combativeness, and confrontation, transcended anything the White House could be or the president could do. All they had to do to complete the revolution was to find a warm body, almost any prominent conservative Republican, to run for president in two years and defeat Bill Clinton.

The new Republican majority arrived in Washington amid great hope, greater promise, and the greatest expectations. Eagerly clutching their Contract with America, they chanted the mantra of "less government and no more business as usual" with revolutionary zeal, an enthusiasm not seen in Washington since, perhaps, Franklin Roosevelt's first hundred days in 1933.

They were overwhelmingly conservative, pulling an already conservative, southern-dominated Republican party further to the right and further south.

Initially more ideological than partisan, they were especially united in their antipathy to President Clinton. Some of the freshmen made an unsuccessful attempt to deny the president use of the chamber of the House of Representatives for his annual State of the Union address. Party leaders counseled their freshmen prior to the president's speech, "Please don't boo, hiss, or throw things at the president." During the speech, it was clear that most of the Republican Conference, including the new members, were taking their cues from Speaker Gingrich: when to applaud, when to stand, when to sit on their hands. Many freshmen, perhaps reminiscent (oh, how they would hate this analogy!) of another revolution on the other side of the globe, waved their little red copies of the Contract with America when President Clinton addressed the joint session of Congress.

They were also united in their loathing of Washington and all that it represented. The new members were not the first ones to run against Washington, but their public abhorrence of anything that had to do with Washington or the federal government put them in a class by themselves. They seemed almost embarrassed by the fact that they were a part of this Sodom-on-the-Potomac. A handful of first-year Republicans lived in their offices, sleeping on the sofa or on a government-supplied cot, telling people back home that they don't want to get too attached to this den of iniquity. Lewis Lapham, writing in the January 1995 edition of *Harpers,* may have exaggerated only a bit:

> The candidates new to politics put forward their ignorance of Washington as proof that they were the last people on earth likely to know how to operate the machinery of government and thus, by definition, incapable of changing even so much as a light bulb in the House of Representatives. It was as if a heart surgeon were to say that although he knew nothing of scalpels or anesthetics, and objected to the arbitrary discrimination between an artery and a vein, he was the man to perform the operation because he had adhered all his life to "Hoosier hometown values" and once had saved an Airedale from being run over by a train. Elect me, dear voter, because I am an ignorant fool. Even better, dear voter, elect me because, like you, I despise the office in pursuit of which I have already spent $24 million in promotional fees.

They were there to tear it down, and then move on.

Traditionally, Congress starts very slowly. Committees are organized, hearings are conducted, members settle into their offices, and little action on the floor takes place. The 104th Congress was different. On the first day, after

House Democratic Leader Richard Gephardt handed the gavel to Speaker Newt Gingrich, the House went to work.

"This is the first day of the revolution," the new Speaker announced. On that day, the House passed legislation to put Congress under the same set of laws as the rest of the country. (Two years earlier, as part of our limited but not insignificant reforms, we had done that in the House, but it was killed by Senate Republicans.) H.R. 1, the Congressional Accountability Act—which meant OSHA rules, sexual harassment laws, labor laws such as overtime compensation, and Equal Employment Opportunity Commission (EEOC) regulations would now apply to Congress—was passed 429 to 0. Interestingly, this first piece of legislation passed by the first Republican Congress in forty years was the first one that the same Republicans challenged in court. When Capitol Hill employees tried to form a union, Republican leaders sued to stop them, claiming that the right to organize and bargain collectively did not apply to janitors, police, and other Capitol employees. Congress should live under the same laws as everyone else, except . . . .

The first day we were in session until 2:23 A.M. Speaker Gingrich himself adjourned the House with his typical hyperbole, calling that day "one of the most productive sessions for any single day in House history."

The frenetic pace continued day after day. In addition to the Congressional Accountability Act, several parts of the Contract with America passed with little or no opposition—the Victim Restitution Act, Paperwork Reduction Act, Family Privacy Protection Act, Housing for Older Persons Act. Democrats in significant numbers joined Republicans on a variety of other issues, including term limits for the Speaker and committee chairs, securities reform, and the Unfunded Mandate Reform Act.

On several major issues, however, the partisan and ideological lines were thickly drawn. This was perhaps most obvious on H.R. 9, the Job Creation and Wage Enhancement Act. In the rush to meet their Speaker-imposed deadline, the Commerce Committee, along with, but in separate committee action, the Science Committee, moved quickly on H.R. 9. One of the major parts of the Contract with America was to reduce regulation by cutting back on laws and rules that they claimed hampered business, slowed economic growth, and cost jobs. Gingrich knew that wholesale repeal of environmental laws or a major scaling back of consumer laws or a weakening of food safety protections would meet with strong Democratic opposition in Congress, a presidential veto, and, most importantly, public antipathy. Instead, Republicans would rely on a more furtive approach, using terms like "risk assessment," "cost-benefit analysis," and "sound science."

Most Democrats agreed that some cost-benefit analysis should be applied in many cases to new health and safety rules and regulation, but cases where the public's health was immediately endangered, or when litigation brought by an affected trade association or corporation could stop almost any regulation, were a different story. Sometimes, health and safety were simply not quantifiable. The risk assessment and cost benefit language in H.R. 9 served one major purpose: to slow down and block rules from the EPA, the CPSC, or OSHA and make it as difficult as possible for federal agencies to regulate. Repealing environmental laws would not sell to the public, many GOP leaders thought. The legal murmurings of "risk assessment" were incomprehensible enough to confuse the public.

Momentum in the Commerce Committee was certainly with the Republicans. They had the votes. They had a deadline. And they were still angry enough after being in the minority for so many years that fairness, reasonableness, and deliberativeness were not important. There were only two quick hearings on the bill on consecutive days. On February 7, 1995, the bill was presented—with no advance notice and no opportunity to look at the legislation—to the Commerce Committee. Democrats quickly prepared about a dozen amendments and decided in a brief caucus who would carry which amendments. I sponsored an amendment to make an exception to the sometimes cumbersome, often litigious risk assessment in an emergency situation, when public health is in imminent danger. Commerce Committee Democrats chose me to carry the Democratic substitute, a collection of many of our amendments that would serve as an alternative bill to H.R. 9: for example, to preserve existing health, environmental, and safety laws; to require independent peer review for cost-benefit analysis; to set agency priorities based on the seriousness of risk and availability of resources. I also cosponsored with Congressman John Bryant, a gutsy, articulate Texas Democrat, an amendment to allow a federal agency to speedily remove a dangerous product from the market or immediately order the cleanup of a facility that is discharging a health-threatening toxic substance into the air or water without the cumbersome aspects of risk assessment.

Newsweek called the committee meeting "a feeding frenzy." Each of our amendments was voted down, with every Republican opposing every amendment, or a much weaker Republican amendment substituted for it. The Republicans were assisted by right-winger Billy Tauzin, a Louisiana

Democrat who switched parties later in the session and became one of the most conservative members of the Republican party. Tauzin led the charge in opposition to many of the Democratic amendments; having a nominal Democrat do the Republicans' dirty work was particularly galling to the Democrats, who were still in a dispirited and saturnine state of mind, especially since Chairman Dingell had been so solicitous of Tauzin when we were in the majority.

Democrats argued that agencies charged with protecting the public would be straitjacketed and could not act swiftly and decisively enough to protect the public. The EPA estimated that 980 new employees would need to be hired to meet congressional mandates and that it would take two years longer to act to protect the environment and public health. Attorneys for one relatively conservative environmental group predicted that H.R. 9 would repeal the ban on lead in gasoline—a government regulation that has reduced the lead in America's air by almost 98 percent over the last twenty years. Health Subcommittee ranking Democrat Henry Waxman said that H.R. 9 would require twenty-two new analytical exercises—all potential new targets for litigation. Several Democrats on the Commerce Committee labeled the risk assessment bill the "Lawyers Full Employment Act."

Republicans countered by saying that there were too many regulations already, and that any roadblocks that Congress could put in the way of federal agencies run amok would serve the public well. Besides, what could be wrong with assessing risk before promulgating a rule? What could be wrong with doing a cost-benefit analysis before writing a new regulation? And what is wrong with "sound science"?

Our singular lack of success in committee was mirrored on the floor of the House of Representatives a few days later. On February 28, 1995, Democrat George Brown, representing the Science Committee, and I, representing Commerce, attempted a substitute bill similar to ours in committee and several other amendments to the risk assessment bill. All of them failed. After the final vote was called, several of us stood at the entrances to the House chamber giving out handbills urging a "no" vote on final passage, pointing out that the bill was good for lawyers and bad for the environment. To no avail. The bill passed the House of Representatives 286 to 141. Almost all the "no" votes were Democrats.

As with much of the Contract with America, risk assessment and all of H.R. 9, which had caused such a furor in the House, died a quiet death in the Republican-controlled Senate. Senate Environment and Public Works

Committee chairman John Chafee, who had helped to write many of the nation's best environmental laws, said that the legislation went much too far.

Early in the 104th congress, Minority Leader Gephardt appointed about a dozen Democrats to help craft a message to counter the "Republican Revolution." Under the leadership of Illinois congressman Richard Durbin and Connecticut congresswoman Rosa DeLauro, the Communications Group met every morning at 8:30. We devised strategy, discussed our short-term and long-term message, planned day-to-day floor activities, and organized other House members to help us educate the public. We would choose no more than two issues each day (one of them was almost always the ethics problems of Speaker Gingrich) and line up at least ten Democratic members to speak about them. Our first big issue arrived on February 22, 1995, when Republicans on the House Education and Economic Opportunities Committee proposed a cut in the school lunch program. They voted to lump all nutrition programs into one block grant and "devolve" it, with less money, to the states. They contended that it was a reduction in the increase and that they were actually spending more money, a standard they never applied to the Defense Department budget. Democrats countered that, because of inflation, fewer children would get fewer lunches and fewer real dollars would be spent on those lunches. We also pointed out they couldn't count the cuts as a budget savings for their balanced budget plan and then deny it was a cut to children, educators, and the American public.

The Republicans had a similar group to ours, their Theme Team, run by Ohio's Martin Hoke. They coordinated their daily message in the same sort of way, sent memos to the whole Republican Conference, and recruited other Republicans to speak on the House floor. They repeated that the federal government had spent $5 *trillion,* a figure greater than the national debt, on welfare programs over the last thirty years. The levels of poverty, they asserted, continued to increase. They even argued that the federal expenditures made poverty even worse. They "forgot" to say that more than $4 trillion of the $5 trillion had been spent on Social Security, Medicare, and Medicaid, or that senior citizens, who used to be the poorest of any age group, had been lifted out of poverty by the millions because of these three programs. In 1995, as a point of reference, Social Security spent $336 billion, Medicare $160 billion, and Medicaid $115 billion.

Every day, members of our Communications Group delivered One Minutes on the House floor about "extremist Republicans" cutting school lunches. We organized one-hour Special Orders about the "Gingrich school lunch cuts." We also put together plans for local district events and suggested to other Democrats that they organize events at schools in their districts. Many of us toured school lunchrooms; met with students, teachers, and cafeteria workers; and talked to the media about the history of the school lunch program and the Republican cuts. The school lunch program was begun right after World War II when President Harry Truman was told by his generals that many (mostly rural) young men and women had failed their physicals during the war because they were malnourished.

In late March, Gephardt came to Sheffield Lake's Tennyson Elementary School in my district to highlight the Gingrich plan. In this mostly white, largely working-class and middle-class elementary school, about one-third of the school's three hundred students received free or reduced-price lunches. We ate lunch with students and parents, talked to school administrators, and spoke with the media about the importance of school lunches and school breakfasts to a child's ability to learn. Cindy Rouhier, a thirty-nine-year-old mother of five, told us that she had benefited from the reduced-fee school lunch program. Recently graduated from Lorain County Community College with a degree in nursing, she told Gephardt and me, "I won't need it next year, but I'm thankful it was available when I went back to school. I want it to be available to others who need it." Gephardt visited dozens of schools around the country and heard similar messages.

For several weeks, Democrats continued our criticism of the Republican budget. Day after day we encouraged other Democrats to go to the floor and stay "on message" about Republican plans to cut school lunches and other child-nutrition assistance to provide tax breaks mostly to the wealthy. Democrats pointed out that in the 1980s under Reagan and Bush, taxes went up for 90 percent of the population while the 10-percent-wealthiest citizens saw their taxes decline. Republicans accused Democrats of talking class warfare. We countered that GOP proposals *were* class warfare. Republicans often answered that Democrats practiced the "politics of envy."

Night after night, Democrats—usually organized and led by Connecticut's Rosa DeLauro and New Jersey's Frank Pallone—went to the floor for one-hour Special Orders to point out in more detail the extremism of the Republican agenda. Our Special Orders were certainly getting the attention of conservatives around the country. My office always cringed when I headed over to talk on the floor in the evening about the Gingrich budget cuts. Within seconds of my beginning to speak, calls—not very nice ones— would begin coming in. Woe to those in my office who had the unpleasant task of answering them! They were never from the district. I was fair game, as were any other Democrats who went to the floor on these Special Orders.

Often people would write letters to me about our Special Orders. A man from Texas wrote: "Until I heard you speak moments ago I thought the dumbest Americans in congress were Bonnie Bonior and Dickie Gephardt. Sheyyr, my boy, you put them to shame. Please, Sherrie me darling, tune in to Rush Limbaugh and listen to the truth for a change. A pox on your lying mouth." And a woman from West Virginia scolded: "It never ceases to amaze me how you Democrats can take to the floor of the house and keep a straight face while you deliberately lie about what the Republicans are attempting to do. It's too bad that your mother never taught you any better." And another one from Texas (these three were all reactions to the same speech) said, "I have never heard such a mind-numbed robot. Too bad for you, most of us are not fooled."

School lunches were only the first major budget issue that, we thought, showed the Gingrich extremist agenda. Student loans also became a major point of contention. Republicans wanted to cut the available money for student loans and grants—a reduction in the increase, they said, but it still meant fewer loans for fewer students—and wanted to end the president's Direct Loan program. Minority Leader Gephardt continued to speak out across the country against the student loan cuts and other cuts in education, and Democratic members set up events in their districts at community colleges, state universities, and private schools. In my district, we held meetings at Hiram College, the Trumbull County campus of Kent State University, Oberlin College, and Lorain County Community College to highlight the importance of student loans to middle-class and poor students and to learn what the proposed student loan cuts would mean to these students.

In spite of the negative press the Republicans were getting, and the very low poll numbers that their leader was experiencing, Republicans were winning vote after vote after vote. During the first one hundred days, every item in the Contract with America passed except term limits. In an interesting twist, Democrats tried to amend the Citizen Legislature Act to make term limits retroactive, arguing that the public was telling us that many members of Congress had already been here too long. Term limits sponsors and Republican leadership voted it down. In other words, those members who were the strongest supporters of term limits, had campaigned for them for years, and who had been members of Congress for over a decade were telling us that their term count should begin after the legislation was finally passed and ratified by the states. They should get another twelve years in addition to the sixteen or eighteen they had already served. I always thought that the public's desire for term limits was aimed at those who had been there for fifteen or twenty years; those were the politicians at whom the public's ire was directed.

As the Republicans were winning every major vote, the partisanship and rancor grew. On environmental issues, civil liberties questions, welfare reform, and product liability reform, the ideological lines between the two parties were boldly drawn. Democrats complained that these bills were rushed through committees with perfunctory hearings at best. Republicans answered that these issues had been debated for years in the public arena; besides, they had the votes—which they certainly did. The party discipline that Gingrich, Majority Leader Armey, and Whip DeLay were able to impose was nothing short of phenomenal. That kind of party cohesion—or mindless, lockstep voting, depending upon one's view of it—had not been seen in Congress since perhaps the days of Joe Cannon in the early part of the century. In Ohio, for example, twelve Ohio Republicans cast twenty-seven votes each on the Contract in the first one hundred days. One cast twenty-six votes because of an absence. Of those 350 votes cast, Ohio Republicans voted with Speaker Gingrich 347 times, or 99.1 percent of the time. Somewhat enviously, perhaps, I often cited those numbers in speeches at home and said, "Mark Twain once said that 'when two people think alike all the time, one of 'em ain't doin' much thinkin'.'"

In those early, heady days of the Republican Revolution, Gingrich's power was almost unlimited. He passed over senior members to appoint committee chairs who might be more loyal to him, more ideologically fervent, or simply more competent. He eliminated three full committees and thirty-one subcommittees. His ability to pass over others in the next session or eliminate a recalcitrant member's committee or subcommittee made him even more powerful. In September, Gingrich—again reminiscent of Speaker Cannon—had threatened Republican members of the Agricultural Committee with loss of seniority ranking on the committee, their standing on other committees, or even removal from the Agriculture Committee itself.

While the Republicans, with some justification, complained about restrictive House rules when the Democrats were in power, Newt Gingrich found a new way to manipulate the process: by simply bypassing the committee process totally and sending legislation straight to the floor of the House. After the first fifteen months of session, *Roll Call* reported that 78 percent of all legislation considered by the full membership was sent directly to the floor without committee input. The Speaker began to use task forces—on guns, Medicare, welfare, and a host of other controversial issues—to displace the work of committees. The task forces were made up of all Republicans who usually shared Gingrich's ideas on that particular issue; they would formulate ideas, sell them to the caucus, and often actually write the legislation that the full House of Representatives would consider. Gingrich's behavior caused Judiciary chair Henry Hyde to call himself "the subchairman." And in many cases the Speaker significantly rewrote legislation after the committee had marked it up. During the Medicare mark-up, I was successful in inserting an amendment in the bill on a bipartisan vote in the Commerce Committee; it was the only successful Democrat-sponsored amendment in the entire Medicare reform bill. By the time the bill reached the House floor, however, the Speaker had simply excised the amendment. It was gone, with no trace of its having ever existed. And GOP leadership rewrote the immigration reform bill to such an extent that Republican Elton Gallegly of California commented bitterly, "Why do we need committees?"

During the first one hundred days, environmental issues seemed to be shaping up as the Republicans' Achilles' heel. Democrats, newspapers, and public interest groups complained that legislation such as the Risk Assessment and Cost-Benefit Act (H.R. 1022) or the Regulatory Reform and Relief Act (H.R. 926) was written by chemical company lobbyists in the majority offices. Moderate Republicans in the Midwest and Northeast were clearly troubled by the direction their party was taking on environmental issues but, during the Contract with America, were either unwilling or unable to do anything about it.

The Republicans had a clear strategy on environmental, consumer protection, and worker safety laws. First, the GOP attempted to weaken laws protecting the environment, consumers, and people in the workplace. Second, Gingrich and his budget people cut the funding for those agencies charged with enforcing those laws still in effect: the Environmental Protection Agency, the Consumer Products Safety Commission, and the Occupational Safety and Health Administration. And third, through H.R. 10, the Common Sense Legal Reforms Act, majority Republicans tried to take away the victim's right to sue. In the end, they were unsuccessful on points one and three; budget cuts, however, did weaken the enforcement arm of several of these agencies.

Most notable, perhaps, was what happened at OSHA. Inspections at job sites, the ultimate OSHA enforcement tool, decreased significantly in 1995 and 1996. OSHA performed 24,024 on-site inspections in the fiscal year ending September 1996, a 17 percent decline from 1995, and a 43 percent drop-off from 1994, precipitated by the government shutdown and Republican budget cuts in agency enforcement.

The Republicans wanted to go significantly further on all fronts. The overriding, dominant theme of the Contract with America was "devolution," the newly coined politically correct byword of the Gingrich revolution. Devolution, defined as "the transfer of power or authority from a central government to a local government," was a pretty easy sell to the American public. In a Republican National Committee mailing, it sounded simple and noncontroversial: "moving power and money away from Washington, and back to the people and their states and communities"; "turn power back to the states"; "give local citizens control of their lives"; "government closest to the people." Thomas Jefferson believed that citizens' knowledge and capacity to understand public affairs was greatest on the local level. What works in Ohio, Republicans asserted, might not work in Maine or Mississippi or Montana. The one-size-fits-all approach from Washington was too inflexible, heavy handed, and inefficient.

But the Republican argument, as attractive as it sounded in general terms, ignored history. Before federal involvement, states did little to stop corporate polluters, regulate food safety, or protect coal miners. State and local governments were rarely strong enough to stand up to chemical companies, meat packing concerns, or coal mine operators. As history professor Newt Gingrich (!) should know, history tells us that the federal government serves as a counterweight to corporate power. *Only* the federal government has the wherewithal to face down corporate polluters, antiworker manufacturers, and wealthy interest groups.

In the eighteenth century, the Articles of Confederation were replaced, turning the loose organization of states into a more centralized constitutional system. Since then the American people have known that a strong federal government would do a better job—through national roads and canals, the Northwest Ordinance, land grant colleges, Social Security, the school lunch program, Medicare, the EPA—of addressing national concerns like fighting poverty, increasing opportunity, providing health care for the elderly, enforcing civil rights, and building an interstate highway system. That's why Abraham Lincoln at Gettysburg changed from "the United States of America *are*" to "the United States of America *is*."

As a nation, America has a long and proud history of responding to private-sector abuse of its citizens. Early this century Upton Sinclair wrote in *The Jungle* about meat-packing plants in Chicago, exposing not only the hazardous working conditions of millions of immigrant workers but also the poor and dangerous quality of our food supply. The national government—not the state of Illinois, not Cook County, not the city of Chicago—went to bat for American consumers and workers. And today, thanks to the Pure Food and Drug Act of 1906 and subsequent laws and government dicta, America has one of the safest food supplies in the world.

Another example comes from my own district. Thirty years ago, Lake Erie was a disaster—dead fish, toxic beaches, and a putrid smell. Children could no longer swim in the lake, the shallowest of the Great Lakes. The Cuyahoga River, which passes through Cleveland into Lake Erie, caught a bridge trestle on fire because of burning contaminants in the water. People literally fled northeast Ohio for the greener pastures of jobs and cleaner water in the West and South.

In the late 1960s and early 1970s, Congress passed the Clean Water Act and created the Environmental Protection Agency. Thanks to *federal* action, our children are now swimming again in Lake Erie, our drinking water again comes from the lake, and Lake Erie again plays a prominent role in commerce and recreation for citizens of northeast Ohio. The comeback of Cleveland—proclaimed an All-American City more times than any city in the nation—would simply never have happened without the action of our national legislature. Cleanup of Lake Erie was done not by the state of Ohio or the Cleveland City Health Department but by the power, the resources, and the authority of the federal government.

The consensus that an overwhelming number of Americans built and now support high standards for food safety, clean drinking water, and safe consumer products was being challenged and dismantled by this 104th Congress. This devolution of power to the states would pit one state's worker safety laws against another, leading to an inexorable race to the bottom. If the state of Indiana wants to convince a major Ohio industrial plant to move to Indianapolis, what better way than to offer weaker worker safety laws? Or lower environmental standards? Or perhaps cut Medicaid health services for poor children so that the corporate tax rate can be reduced? This race to the bottom—where states compete for the title of most corporate-friendly business atmosphere—will inevitably leave us with more worker deaths, higher rates of cancer, and a torn safety net for our least advantaged citizens.

A few years ago, Congress passed legislation requiring competitive bidding for infant formula for the Women, Infants, Children (WIC) program, a program that provides food to pregnant women and infants. The Government Accounting Office estimated that the competitive bidding process saved the government over $1 billion, enabling WIC to feed 1.6 million more women and children. Under the Gingrich devolutionary bloc grant program, Congress would give WIC to the states and eliminate the requirement for competitive bidding. Infant formula manufacturers would benefit. Poor children would not.

Or take a look at Medicaid, the program begun in the 1960s during the Great Society. The federal government requires, with the federal dollars sent to the states, that each state meet certain criteria: safety standards in nursing homes, individual choice for nursing home patients, guarantees of coverage for poor children, mandatory coverage for mammograms and other breast cancer services, and other standards and benefits.

Medicaid was begun because many states were not providing nursing home care for the elderly or prenatal and well-baby care for the poor or support for severely injured children. Years later, in reaction to reports that some nursing homes around the country were oversedating and restraining patients, President Reagan and the Democratic Congress passed legislation setting up standards for nursing homes. Simply put, the federal government stepped in because many states were not providing for their people. And now, under Gingrich's devolutionary bloc grant program, there was to be even less money available for the Medicaid program overall. Federal requirements for nursing home standards, patient or family choice for nursing home care, breast cancer services, and health care coverage for poor children would be eliminated. Instead, we would see fifty state bureaucracies directed by fifty state legislatures responding to the most effective interest groups demanding money from a shrinking pie. Nursing homes would likely win; but, again, poor children would lose.

While citizens are more likely to know personally some of their municipal, county, or school officials (at least in smaller communities), voters are much more aware of what the national government does. Twice as many people typically vote in national elections, especially in presidential years, than in municipal or school elections. The political pundits in Washington, talk radio shows, and national general-circulation news magazines all talk about national issues. Citizens who benefit from the discourse of an articulate, well-informed national policy analyst rarely find a similar voice on the state or local level. Fewer stories about lobbyists' influence in state legislatures, fewer articles about state bureaucracies, fewer shows about local government waste all point to citizens who are less informed about state and local government than about Washington goings-on. The devolution of power to the states could mean less information, more secrecy, and more corruption.

With the exception of the welfare bill, signed by President Clinton in the summer of 1996, Republicans were not successful in accomplishing their "devolution agenda." Risk assessment, Medicaid reform, the Job Creation and Wage Enhancement Act all passed the House but never made it to the president's desk. House Republicans could, however, rightly claim credit for passing almost every item in their Contract with America within the first one hundred days. The public, though, didn't seem all that impressed. The two issues most visible to the public and, according to public opinion polls, with the greatest public support—term limits and the balanced budget amendment—had both been defeated. Term limits lost in the House; the balanced budget amendment lost in the Senate. Other issues made barely a blip on the public screen. Even at the ceremony celebrating "Promises Made, Promises Kept," storm clouds began to gather. Some Republican House members did not show up for the event. The Senate seemed little interested in several aspects of the Contract. The president had threatened vetoes against other parts. The promises of the Contract seemed to many an exercise in futility, simply because few of the items would become law. And, months later, the public would clearly be more interested in student loans, school lunches, Medicare, and the environment than in some of the reforms that one house of their national legislature had passed.

After disgruntled voters had unceremoniously rejected Bush, Perot, and Clinton, Gingrich seemed perilously close to being the next victim. It was becoming more and more clear that Gingrich had misread the 1994 election results. In spite of his leadership skills and his unchallenged power in the Republican Conference, Gingrich had traveled a rough road since November. Before the public had gotten to know this history professor from Georgia, he had signed a book deal with HarperCollins for a $4.5 million advance, an absolutely unprecedented move and sum for a sitting elected official. He was already a powerful political figure—perhaps for a time the most powerful person in the nation—before the country knew anything about him. Election night and the ensuing week served as the first introduction to Newt Gingrich for most of America. Then he signed the book deal with a company owned by Rupert Murdoch, one of the world's wealthiest people and a man who could stand to gain immensely from a personal relationship with the new Speaker. Democrats took particular delight in the Speaker's defensiveness because it was Gingrich who led the charge on a book deal that resulted in the resignation of Speaker Jim Wright. In the end, Gingrich turned down the advance.

On January 18, 1995, Florida second-term Democrat Carrie Meek, the granddaughter of a slave, took to the House floor to talk about the "perception of impropriety" and the "potential of conflict of interest" surrounding the Gingrich-Murdoch book deal. "How hard," she asked, will Rupert Murdoch's firm "work to hawk this book?" Gingrich's best friend in the House, Pennsylvania's Bob Walker, attempted to protect the Speaker by moving to "take down" Meeks's words, a parliamentary maneuver to strike the offending words from the record. The words are repeated for examination by the whole House and read again before a vote is taken to uphold the ruling of the chair. In the age of C-SPAN and an electronic press corps that revels in conflict and confrontation, "taking down the words" of a member of Congress only serves to amplify the comments.

Not surprisingly, Republican efforts to silence Meek backfired. Network news ran the story, replaying the story of the book deal, the Democrats' interest in talking about it, and the Republicans' effort to silence the Democrats. The incident woke up some of the Democratic party's sleeping giants, like John Dingell, who took to the floor to protest: "This is not the Duma. This is not the Reichstag. This is the house of the people." Other Democrats, especially Harold Volkmer, a heretofore quiet backbencher from Missouri, came to the floor regularly to challenge Gingrich's ethics and to protect other members whom Republicans tried to silence. Congressman Bill Hefner, commenting about Volkmer's coming into his own after a quiet eighteen-year career in the House, said that "watching Harold Volkmer on the House floor is like watching a baby discover his hands." The 104th Congress was never the same.

Other ethics charges swirled around Gingrich in the first one hundred days, especially concerning GOPAC and the Speaker's fundraising activities. Articles about Gingrich's divorce, the private funding of his college course, and his use of the House floor to promote his nongovernment activities appeared in abundance in newspapers and magazines.

As 1995 wore on, House Democrats were buoyed by the support we seemed to be generating in our defense of student loans, school lunches, and Medicare. Town meetings at home were upbeat, with people encouraging us to keep fighting Gingrich's policies. The mail in my office, despite the organized efforts by the far Right, affirmed what we were doing. Polls indicated that the public thought the Gingrich agenda "extreme," that Republicans were "going too far." Our spirits would dampen, though, when pollsters who came in front of our caucus would remind us that, yes, the voters are unhappy with Republicans, but they don't much like Democrats either; they're not ready to turn the place back over to the Democrats yet.

We experienced psychological setbacks too. During 1995 five southern Democrats announced that they were switching parties: second-termer Nathan Deal of Georgia switched first, on April 10; Greg Laughlin, in his fourth term from Texas, changed parties on June 26; fifteen-year veteran Billy Tauzin from Louisiana switched on August 6; Mike Parker, in his fourth term from Mississippi, announced his change on November 10; and Louisiana's fifth-term congressman Jimmy Hays announced he was switching on the first day of December. Deal, Tauzin, Hays, and Parker had been consistently voting with the Republicans, almost without exception, for years. But losing one after another was clearly a blow to the Democrats.

We viewed the party switching with mixed feelings, to be sure. We were troubled by the fact that the hill we had to climb in order to retake the majority looked measurably steeper than it once had. Yet most Democrats were glad to be rid of them: Tauzin, even though he had been given the ranking Democrat slot on his Commerce subcommittee and former chairman John Dingell had always gone out of his way to work with him, had regularly done the Republicans' bidding on the Commerce Committee; Hays, a bright but disengaged member who was an excellent orator when he wanted to be, did not seem to make much of an impression on anyone; Laughlin, the most moderate of the group, was the biggest surprise; Parker, a funeral director whose personality fit his profession, had not voted for Gephardt in January 1995 and had taunted party leaders to "throw me out of the Democratic Party"; and Deal, the first one to switch after Democrats had assiduously worked with him and accommodated him on the welfare bill, forgot that he had publicly promised that if he ever switched parties he would immediately resign and run again.

And for Gingrich, there was a price. Following Tauzin's switch he told Gephardt, "Understand, Dick, I'll do anything, ANYTHING, to get one of yours to become one of mine." Tauzin, who was given his seniority and vaulted over twenty-three Republicans, including an unamused Mike Oxley, was promised a subcommittee chairmanship in the next session if Republicans kept control. Oxley, a Republican who represents my mother in Mansfield, Ohio, had labored in the minority for fourteen years and in 1997 was in line for the chairmanship he had always dreamed of, the Telecommunications and Securities Subcommittee, if Republicans retained their majority. Here comes Billy Tauzin—a majority Democrat for fifteen years and now in the majority again—with all his seniority. To Oxley, it did not seem fair. In the next session after the 1996 election, Gingrich split the subcommittee, presumably to no one's satisfaction, and gave part of it to Tauzin and part of it to Oxley. In early 1996, I said to Oxley, whom I have known and liked for twenty years, that I could get him a chairmanship if he switched parties. He smiled. Sort of. The deal was completed in 2001 when Republican leadership installed Tauzin as the chairman of the Energy and Commerce Committee and Oxley as the Chairman of Financial Services, a committee on which he had never sat. In doing so, Republicans pushed aside Marge Roukema, the only female committee chair they would have had.

Gingrich gave Laughlin a seat on Ways and Means, a plum he had sought for several terms; to his fellow Georgian Deal a spot on Commerce, with seniority intact; and to Hays a Ways and Means seat. It was unclear, at least to me, what Parker was given. He said publicly that he did not want anything. It is highly unusual to add members to exclusive committees in the middle of a term, but the majority can do whatever it chooses. It writes the rules.

The five party switchers met with mixed success in the 1996 elections. Hays ran for the Senate in Louisiana as a Republican and finished a single-digit fourth. Tauzin won handily, as did Deal. Parker, who may have switched in part because his 35-percent African American district would likely have ousted him in a primary someday, won easily. He then announced in early 1998 that he would not seek another term. In spite of significant help from Gingrich and dozens of fellow House Republicans, Laughlin lost in the Republican primary. Not surprisingly, the most active and loyal Republicans in his Texas district had been voting against him in general elections for years. More than half of them could not see their way—Gingrich's and Armey's pleas notwithstanding—to vote for him now in a Republican primary.

The 1990s were bad years for Democrats in the South. In 1982 Democrats held 71 percent of House seats in the South; by the end of the decade we had less than one-half. It remained to be seen whether our strength in the South would cost us in other areas of the nation, such as New England and the West Coast. History would suggest, at least in presidential elections, that strength in the South spells difficulty in much of the rest of the country. From 1868 to 1928, the Democrats had an almost unbreakable lock on the South in electoral votes and in our congressional delegations, yet Republicans won twelve of sixteen presidential elections. And now that Republicans enjoy a majority of southern-state congressional delegations, their success in presidential races has begun to falter.

It is much about culture and much about issues. In the 104th Congress the ten highest-ranked Republican House and Senate leaders—all southern, all male, all white—were very conservative. They were all pro-life, while other areas of the country were much more likely to be pro-choice. And all had lined up in support of cutting social spending and weakening environmental protection. The conservatism of southern Republican elected officials has become even more pronounced. According to *U.S. News and World Report,* the Christian Coalition is now responsible for one-third of the vote in southern Republican primaries, pushing Republican officeholders, especially on social issues, farther to the Right.

Most of the country outside the South sees things differently. Labor issues, environment, education, and a host of other issues paint a vivid line between what appeals to southern voters and to voters elsewhere. Especially among women. The ever-growing gender gap is even more pronounced between the South and the rest of the country. Even back to the fight over the passage of the Equal Rights Amendment in the 1970s, the differences were stark. The great majority of states in New England, the Great Lakes region, and the West ratified it. The South defeated it.

On the eve of the completion of the Contract with America, an NBC/*Wall Street Journal* poll showed Gingrich with a 27–39 percent favorable/unfavorable rating with the American public. His daily press briefings—though not unprecedented for a Speaker of the House, but he was the first to allow television cameras at the sessions—showed him often vitriolic, usually testy, and almost always attacking Democrats and the media. His friends repeatedly told him he was overexposed.

Soon after the Contract with America was completed, the Christian Coalition stepped forward with its Contract with the American Family. On May 17, with Newt Gingrich at their sides, leaders of the Christian Coalition held a news conference in Washington to announce their plan to restore the American family—a ten-point document that would, among other things, restrict abortion, eliminate the Department of Education and the Corporation for Public Broadcasting, and cut substantially the Legal Services Corporation. Moderate Republicans were displeased. Many of them had voted for parts of the Contract with America that had troubled them, especially on environmental protection, civil liberties, and children's issues. They thought that they had paid their dues and that the Republican leadership should move the party more to the center, where they believed the vast majority of their constituents were. They sensed they were in more trouble at home, especially those members from New England, where this brand of conservatism was looked at with so much suspicion.

Conservatives wanted to keep their revolution going, especially on social issues. Republican leadership knew they needed to pay back the Christian Right, whom many credited with taking the House in the first place. Besides, the Christian Coalition and the Christian Right had dutifully supported the Contract with America, lobbied intensively for it, and patiently awaited their turn. The Christian Coalition had committed to, according to its executive director in a speech to the Detroit Economic Club, "the largest single lobbying effort in our history . . . to mobilize our 1.5 million members . . . to deluge Capitol Hill with phone calls, faxes, and telegrams."

While Republican leaders knew that social issues were divisive, they also understood that those issues played well to the GOP base, that they energized their restless and ideological freshman class, and that these issues were especially important to their growing southern constituency. They hoped— and history said they were usually right—that these issues would take public attention away from the cuts in education and Medicare and the weakening of environmental regulations that Republicans had proposed.

The four most visible issues that Republicans chose—a constitutional amendment to ban flag burning, the outlaw of late-term abortions, a prohibition on same-sex marriage, legislation making English the official language—were surely divisive. They divided Congress and the American public along lines of race, religion, culture, and gender. Some Democrats argued that these were all solutions looking for nonexistent problems. Many Democrats were asking: How often are flags burned? How many late-term abortions are there? When did you hear about a same-sex marriage? What's the problem with English? And why is Congress spending time on these issues? In some ways, the Republican strategy worked. The questions I was asked most frequently in my reelection campaign were about my votes against the Defense of Marriage Act and against a prohibition on certain late-term abortions.

Three of the four bills were named and timed for maximum political effect. The Language of Government Act, which passed the House in August 1996, died in the Senate. The presidential veto of the Partial Birth Abortion Ban Act, which took place almost six months earlier, was overridden on September 19, 1996. According to Donna Pignatelli (who had served as chief of staff for a Massachusetts congressman in the late 1970s and then left the Hill for several years before joining me as chief of staff in September 1995), the Republicans held it to maximize its electoral effect, and the Senate sustained the veto. Only the Defense of Marriage Act became law, passing the House in the summer of 1996. It was signed late at night on September 21, six weeks before the election. Only sixty-seven House members and fourteen senators voted against it. Columnist Robert Reno wrote in *Newsday* on October 2: "The quaintly named Defense of Marriage Act, rammed through by the most heavily divorced congressional leadership in history, might count as one of the 104th great achievements—if it could be proved that it achieved a single marriage or prevented a single divorce."

The majority of Republicans in Congress believed that these hot-button issues—anti-abortion, anti–gay rights, anti-immigrant—were the way to energize their conservative base and turn out the vote in November.

13

Storming the Palace:
The Government Shutdown

They were careless people. . . . They smashed up things and creatures and then retreated back into their money or their vast carelessness, or whatever it was that kept them together, and let other people clean up the mess they had made.

—F. Scott Fitzgerald, *The Great Gatsby*

The right wing won't let them [Republicans] be sensible, and the country won't let them be extremist.

—Congressman Barney Frank (D-Mass.)

THE WORK ON THE CONTRACT WITH AMERICA pushed aside much of the work that Congress usually does in the first half of the year. As the cherry blossoms came and went, little had been done in the House of Representatives to enact a budget to run the government. The president's budget, introduced in February 1995, was generally ignored. The budget process, usually begun in the first quarter of the calendar year, was delayed. Appropriations bills, normally discussed and debated early in the spring, were set aside.

Running the government requires the passage of thirteen separate appropriations bills: Agriculture; Commerce, Justice, State; Defense; District of Columbia; Energy and Water Development; Foreign Operations; Interior; Labor, Health and Human Services, Education; Legislative Branch; Military Construction; Transportation; Treasury, Postal Service, General Government; and Veterans Affairs, Housing and Urban Development, Independent Agencies. Each operates its section of the government from October 1 to September 30 of the following year. Over the years, Congress would occasionally fail to pass and get to the president's desk one or two of the thirteen by the October 1 deadline. More often than not, the House and Senate would pass a Continuing Resolution (CR), whereby all the unpassed appropriations bills would be lumped together—controversial items eliminated, differences compromised—and passed to keep the government running for the next week or two until the separate appropriations bills could each be resolved.

There had been seven brief government shutdowns in the last decade, but they were of little consequence. The public hardly noticed them because of their brevity and because the affected agencies had little direct and immediate impact on the public. But 1995 was different. Republicans were inexperienced at running the Congress and may have been unaware of the complexities of negotiating and passing these thirteen appropriations bills. The Contract with America had eaten up valuable time. There were major, unresolved differences between the revolutionary, very conservative House and the more deliberate, relatively moderate Senate.

House Republicans also attempted to add riders to many of the appropriations bills, making passage much more difficult. While this was probably a violation of House rules, leadership could always find a way around the prohibition. Speaker Gingrich, Majority Whip DeLay, and other Republican leaders saw the appropriations process as the best way to accomplish their revolution. Legislation that would be very difficult to push through the House on an up-or-down vote with the attendant media scrutiny could be slipped into an appropriations bill with little fanfare. The bill could then pass unnoticed by much of the Congress, the media, and the public.

Some of the amendments were clearly related to appropriations: Republicans phased out the Legal Services Corporation, a program they particularly despised; made huge cuts in the Labor Relations Board, another agency Republican rank-and-file members loved to hate; cut worker safety enforcement dollars by almost half; and eliminated an agency that enforced parts of the Endangered Species Act.

Majority Republicans also included other riders in their appropriations bills, many of which had nothing to do with appropriations. Freshman Mark Neumann, a wealthy Republican homebuilder from Wisconsin, reversed an OSHA regulation that the American Homebuilders Association had wanted overturned. Other amendments, pushed by the Christian Coalition, attempted to stop embryo medical research and prohibited not-for-profits that receive federal money from lobbying the government. Gingrich referred to this amendment, sponsored by Representative Ernest Istook (R-Okla.), as "defunding the Left," although "the Left" included the Girl Scouts, the American Association of Retired Persons, and the Red Cross.

Democrats on the Appropriations Committee countered with an amendment to cut off funding for defense firms and others who lobby the government for multimillion-dollar contracts. Wisconsin Democrat David Obey suggested that the lobbying prohibition "should apply to the big boys, not just the groups that Mr. Istook doesn't like." The Democratic amendment, of course, failed.

Republican Whip DeLay's favorite, and perhaps the most notable, amendments were the antienvironmental riders added to the Veterans Affairs, Housing and Urban Development, Independent Agencies Appropriations Bill (VA/HUD), H.R. 2099. These seventeen riders would have dramatically rolled back major parts of environmental law passed, often bipartisanly, in the last several sessions of Congress. The riders cut EPA funding for enforcement of environmental laws by one-half; the Clean Air Act was decimated; wetlands enforcement was eliminated. The fingerprints of all kinds of special interest groups—pesticide manufacturers, cement kilns, oil refineries—could be found all over the DeLay riders.

On Friday, July 28, an amendment on the floor to remove the riders, offered by Ohio Democrat Louis Stokes, passed 212 to 206; it was Speaker Gingrich's first major loss, handed to him by a coalition of environmental groups, Democrats, and fifty-one Republicans, mostly from the Northeast. DeLay, the owner of a pesticide company, did not give up easily. He wore proudly and defiantly his reputation as "enemy number one of the environmental movement." And DeLay, who during the debate on the Stokes amendment called the EPA the "Gestapo of government agencies," was not about to give up in his fight against the "environmental extremists."

The following Monday evening, Gingrich and DeLay, noticing that there were fourteen absent Democrats, most of whom had voted for the Stokes amendment on Friday, decided to bring the vote up again. The scoreboard on the wall of the House chamber, and the accompanying printout, lists all members and their votes on each issue, so it is simple to figure attendance. While DeLay was unable to change the minds or votes of any of the fifty-one Republicans who supported the Stokes amendment, the absent Democrats would mean that they could likely defeat the amendment on a revote. He was right; the amendment was defeated 210 to 210. (Amendments are defeated when they tie.) Although DeLay's antienvironment language was still in the appropriations bill, his insistence on this revote may have cost him the seat of one of his members. Ohio's Martin Hoke, whose support of the Stokes amendment was his first major vote against his party's leadership, was absent on Monday. He was holding a fund-raiser with Speaker Gingrich in Cleveland that day. A cardinal rule of politics is "don't miss an important vote when the outcome is close." A cardinal rule of politics *in the 1990s* was "never attend a fund-raiser and miss a vote." Another cardinal rule in 1995, according to another Ohio Republican, was "don't get your picture taken with Newt Gingrich." The combination for Martin Hoke was explosive. He lost fourteen months later by 2 percent of the vote.

But Stokes, the environmental community, and a handful of moderate Republicans were not about to give up. In early November, Stokes offered a motion to instruct House conferees to delete the seventeen riders. The motion, which was nonbinding on the conference committee, passed 227 to 194. My legislative assistant Don Hoppert, who handled environmental issues, told me that the severe cut in funding for EPA enforcement was at least as damaging as the DeLay riders. It was for that reason that Clinton vetoed the bill.

The president and the Congress were far apart on both individual appropriations measures and general spending priorities. Spending for the Department of Defense was a good example. Although the president actually supported an increase in military spending, the Republicans wanted much more, $6 billion more than even the Pentagon requested. In a September letter to Minority Leader Gephardt, Alice Rivlin, the director of the Office of Management and Budget, stated that the changes in the conference committee to the fiscal year 1996 defense appropriations bill still "do not address the Administration's fundamental concerns about spending priorities. . . . For this reason, in the absence of an agreement between the Administration and Congress resolving these important issues, the President would veto this bill."

As the October 1 deadline approached, Congress had simply not done its work. Not one appropriations bill was sent to the president's desk for a signature prior to October 1. The Military Construction Appropriations bill was actually signed on October 3. The other twelve were awaiting Senate action or were in conference committees or were being held up for some other reason by Congress. And some Republicans—especially a large number of the new members—were itching for confrontation with the Democrats and a showdown with the president.

They seemed to be walking off the cliff together—new members especially, but veterans too; the far-right wing of the Republican party in particular, but moderates as well. As Gingrich's public support fell to historic

lows throughout the summer and fall of 1995, Republicans were still optimistic about public reaction and future elections. A few Republicans understood the risk to their reelection and political future, but most saw political
rewards in shutting down the government to force a balanced budget on the
president—a balanced budget exactly on their terms. They read polls that
showed that the public wanted a balanced budget, smaller government,
fewer bureaucrats. Surveys and common sense told them that people wanted
lower taxes. And town meetings, focus groups, and conservative columnists
reinforced their notion that power should be "devolved"—taken from the
federal government and handed to the states and local governments.

Gingrich misread the public on its feelings about Medicare also. In his
first month as Speaker, he made a statement to a conservative foundation
in Washington that this Congress would "transform Medicare." Few people
seemed to even notice. He later reiterated his plans to not only cut Medicare
but to make major programmatic changes.

Later in the year, it became obvious that Republican budget cuts—school
lunches, student loans, and especially Medicare—were costing their members at home. In October, as a few of us in the House gym were watching
CNN's story on Speaker Gingrich and his declining public support, I commented to Republican Majority Whip DeLay that Gingrich reminds me of
a teacher I once had: "The more he talked, the less we liked him." Gingrich's
public favorability rating had dropped to 27 percent. DeLay responded, "As
long as it doesn't drop below 18 percent, I'm happy. Engler was at 18 percent." He repeatedly cited Michigan governor John Engler's exceptionally
low standing in the polls in 1991 as historical evidence that Republicans
could drastically cut services and still survive at the polls. Elected in 1990 in
an upset, Engler had cut welfare sharply soon after he became governor. He
withstood a ferocious public assault and even a recall effort. Three years later,
Engler battled back with an astoundingly large reelection victory in 1994.
Stand firm against initial public criticism, Engler's experience told House
Republicans, and the political kingdom will be yours.

However, DeLay forgot to mention—to me, or more importantly, to his
fellow Republicans, who were about to shut down the government—a few
differences:

1. Engler cut general relief, a program benefiting the poor that had limited
public support. Gingrich was cutting Medicare and student loans, programs
with large middle-class constituencies.

2. Engler's cuts did not get the attention that Gingrich's cuts did. He was also not as personally disliked as Gingrich.

3. Even the 18 percent figure was misleading. Gingrich's ratings were in response to the question, "Do you have a favorable or unfavorable opinion of Speaker Newt Gingrich?" Unfavorable won consistently in poll after poll by a two-to-one margin. Michigan pollsters queried, "If the election for governor were held today, would you vote for Governor Engler, or would you prefer someone else?" Even popular elected officials who are virtually assured of reelection do not score very well on that one; there is always somebody better.

4. Election day for Engler was three years away. He had a political eternity to recover and rebuild his reputation. Gingrich and the Republicans had one year.

5. Election Day 1994, when Engler won his landslide, was nationally the best day for Republicans in decades. For Republicans, 1996 did not look so fortuitous.

Republican leadership did something else. Believing so deeply that the public would see it their way by 1996, or simply wanting desperately to get their agenda enacted, they "bucked up" their members, especially their freshmen. National Republican chair Haley Barbour seconded the motion, telling new members that if they took the tough votes early, the voters would reward them as they had rewarded "courageous governors." Conservative columnists went to work. Talk radio and letter-writing campaigns were organized. *Our* balanced budget at any cost. It's what the public wants. If people suffer when the government is shut down, so be it.

Barbour and Republican leaders thought moving too slowly was politically more dangerous than doing too much too fast. History would judge the Republican Congress by its accomplishments and the direction it took the country, they thought, and there was little time to waste. "Promises Made, Promises Kept," the slogan Republicans used to commemorate the completion of their Contract with America, confirmed Republican efforts to move quickly and decisively and to sell it to the American public.

When it became clear that most of the thirteen appropriations bills would not be anywhere near enactment by October 1, the White House, Gingrich, and Dole prepared a tepid Continuing Resolution to keep the government from shutting down. We passed the CR, which kept the government operating until November 13. But the two-week respite gave little comfort to budget negotiators, who were almost certain that all thirteen of the bills could not be passed and signed by the president by that date. At the same time, Republican leadership was working on the reconciliation bill, which

they had labeled the Balanced Budget Act. The reconciliation bill, the legislation that "reconciled" spending and revenue, included all budget items
outside the thirteen appropriations bills. Medicare and tax cuts—the two
most important parts of the reconciliation bill—were the major points of
contention.

Early in the summer, Democrat leaders taunted Gingrich about reconciliation, asserting that he should pass the bill before we went home for the
August work period; all he had to do, we suggested over and over on the
House floor, was remove his "huge tax breaks for the rich" and "keep his
hands off Medicare." As it was, Gingrich was not going to back off the tax
cuts; even if he wanted to—and he didn't—the seventy-three freshmen would
never let him. And he needed Medicare cuts to pay for them; it was the only
way to come up with the hundreds of billions of dollars that he was demanding. He had to figure out a way to sell the Medicare cuts to the public.

On October 19 the House passed, with only six Republican dissenters,
their Medicare reform bill. According to Gingrich, they wanted to pass it
separately to show the country that it had nothing to do with a tax cut; it
would stand alone. That, of course, did not stop us from saying that it had
everything to do with their tax cut. The only way to pay for their $245 billion
tax break was by taking a large part of the money from Medicare and Medicaid. Several Democrats stood on the floor denouncing Republican plans
to privatize Medicare through their medical savings accounts proposals.
Other Democrats, myself included, reminded our colleagues and C-SPAN
viewers of the longtime hostility that Republican leaders had felt toward
Medicare; now, we emphasized, Republicans say they want to "preserve it."
Democratic Whip David Bonior, emphasizing that dollar amounts were
only part of the differences between the Gingrich plan and Democratic plans
for Medicare reform, said, "For thirty years, they have waited for this
moment to dismantle the system."

One week later, the House passed the reconciliation bill, with Medicare
in it, by a vote of 227 to 203. Ten Republicans voted "no" because of a provision to open the Arctic National Wildlife Refuge in Alaska to oil explo-
ration. Gingrich, who loved to compare the first one hundred days of the
104th Congress to the first one hundred days of Franklin Roosevelt's presidency, called passage of this budget the "most decisive vote" in changing the
direction of the government since 1933.

On November 9, both houses passed and sent to the president the debt
limit increase and the CR. Dick Durbin, the Illinois Democrat who chaired

the Communications Group, said on the floor, "The Speaker wants to shut the government down so he can raise Medicare premiums." The next day, President Clinton said, "Last night, Republicans in Congress raised Medicare premiums, cut education, and [rolled back] bipartisan environmental safeguards." Three days later, when the president vetoed the CR, the government shut down, and 800,000 federal workers were furloughed.

The Republicans learned too well the lesson that President Clinton inadvertently taught them: when a comprehensive and complicated health care plan lays open to public scrutiny, public opposition crystallizes and can ultimately defeat the legislation. They went to the other extreme. Republicans developed their Medicare plan in secrecy, refused Democratic and senior citizen groups' calls to reveal their plan, delayed its introduction again and again, then submitted it less than twenty-four hours before giving it only one hearing.

The Republicans tried to remake the Medicare health care system—in which the government spends about $180 billion each year—in a day. And it was a day that Commerce chairman Thomas Bliley will regret for a long time. In September 1995, Speaker Gingrich brought his Medicare reform bill to the House Commerce Committee with instructions to hold no hearings, mark up the bill, and pass it the same day. The bill contained $270 billion in cuts to Medicare, roughly the same number of dollars, Democrats liked to point out, that Republicans wanted to give in tax cuts, mostly to the wealthy. As the committee meeting began, a senior citizen from Falls Church, Virginia, walked forward, said she would like to testify, and was gaveled out of order by Chairman Bliley. She refused to quit talking as other senior citizens walked forward with her. The lights in the committee room were then shut off. Finally, a visibly angry Bliley ordered the Capitol Hill police to arrest her and the other protesters. As the senior citizens were taken out of the committee room, four of us on the committee—Democrats Ron Klink of Pennsylvania, Bobby Rush from Chicago, Bart Stupak of Michigan, and I—went with the dozen or so seniors whom the police arrested. (On the way to the paddywagons and police cruisers, Senate Majority Leader Bob Dole was leaving the Rayburn House Office Building with his entourage. A reporter asked what we were doing as we walked past Dole, who grumbled, "It's a bunch of senior citizens mounting a phony protest because the liberal Democrats told them to.")

I rode to the police station in the back of a cruiser with Rush, who had been a member of the Black Panthers in the 1960s. Touching the metal screen separating us from the officer in the front seat, Bobby said, "I assume I've spent more time in the back of one of these than you have." Although the elderly protesters were not treated rudely or roughly by an embarrassed and reluctant group of Capitol Hill police officers, the "lawbreakers" were handcuffed and taken to a D.C. jail. When we all arrived, the officials, still acting under orders from Chairman Bliley, fingerprinted the protesters. Two hours later, Bliley, finally understanding how all of this looked, ordered their release.

In the Ways and Means Committee, it was not much different. Gingrich told Chairman Bill Archer to have one hearing and then mark the bill up, defeat all Democrat amendments, and offer none of their own. Archer, of course, complied.

Democrats responded to the majority's unwillingness to hold hearings on Medicare by holding hearings on our own—outside the Capitol because we were denied a hearing room inside the Capitol. Democrats pointed out that there had been fifty-nine days of hearings on Whitewater, twelve days of hearings on Waco, and fourteen days of hearings on Ruby Ridge, but not one on Medicare, perhaps the most important governmental program in this nation's history. From senior citizens to small business owners to labor organizations to consumer groups to economists, witnesses told us that the Republican plan would likely mean a doubling of premiums, an increase of four hundred dollars a year, and an increase in co-payments and deductibles.

Starting in the summer of 1995, Gingrich thought he could pass his Medicare reform to pay for his "crown jewel" of the Contract with America—the tax cut—by doing two things: neutralize opposition by affected groups with carrots and sticks, with promises and threats; and sell the cuts as reforming Medicare and saving the system.

The first worked pretty well. The American Association of Retired Persons (AARP) was given a carrot; they stayed on the sidelines because the Republicans had promised them that the largest share of the cuts would be borne by providers—hospitals and doctors. They were also threatened with a stick. Senator Alan Simpson (R-Wyo.) launched a highly public investigation of the AARP. Ernest Istook (R-Okla.) was attempting to place in any legislative vehicle that came along his amendment to restrict lobbying by not-for-profits. Opponents of the Gingrich Medicare plan got the message. If you want to have a role in this Congress in determining health care policy, if you want to have any input in our decisions, stay quiet about your opposition to our Medicare plan.

Hospitals were shown a stick. They did not squawk too much because, according to health care lobbyists, they were threatened with a loss of access to Republican leadership if they mounted a campaign protesting the cuts. When the hospital association ran advertisements critical of the GOP plan, Republican Conference leader John Boehner of Ohio replied by complaining of their attacks and their contributions to Democrats and letting them know they would be unwelcome on the Republican side until they shaped up. At least one ad was shelved by the association as a result.

In a deal struck in the middle of the night in the Speaker's office, the American Medical Association (AMA) was given a whole bunch of carrots; it supported the Republican plan because members were given assurances that Congress would address their malpractice concerns and that antitrust restrictions against physicians wanting to form health maintenance organizations (HMOs) would be lifted. Thus, reimbursement cuts were also scaled back. Thirty years earlier, the AMA had led the opposition to the creation of Medicare, so Gingrich had little trouble coming to an agreement with them. Although tens of thousands of doctors had become rich on Medicare, some in the AMA still thought it "socialist."

Another physician group, however, clearly did not like the Republican plan but was torn on whether the political price for public opposition was too high to pay. At its meeting in the early fall of 1995, the American College of Physicians, one of the few physician groups to support the Clinton health plan two years earlier, decided, at least for a while, to stay on the sidelines. They stayed officially neutral through the whole session on the Gingrich Medicare plan, but they did send an open letter to the president and to Speaker Gingrich opposing the cuts, saying they were too deep and that they "would not help long-term solvency" of Medicare.

The second part of the Gingrich strategy came out of the Medicare Communications Group of the House Republican Conference. Republican pollster Frank Luntz wrote in a June 1995 memo to the group, "If we can't prove that Medicare is going bankrupt, we'll never be able to sell our solutions." The Republicans cited the 1995 Trustees Report for the Hospital Insurance Trust Fund that predicted that by 2002 Medicare would pay out more in Part A hospital benefits than it actually brought in through taxes. Medicare, according to Luntz and other Republican gurus, would go bankrupt unless they saved it!

Republican pollster Linda DiVall told Republicans in May that they should never use the word "cut"; use words like "preserve" and "save," and tell voters that the Gingrich plan provides "more options" to America's senior citizens. The "more options" phrase that Republicans used was curious. Focus groups and polls had, in all likelihood, tested the phrase and found that voters responded well to it. It's hard, though, to imagine that the Republican medical savings accounts or health maintenance organizations could mean more choice than traditional fee-for-service Medicare with absolute choice of provider.

Medicare provides health care to America's elderly in two ways. Part A, the Hospital Insurance Trust Fund, is funded by a payroll tax on all working people. Part B, funded by premiums (about $55 per person per month), deductibles (about $250 per year), and co-payments (usually $10 per physician visit), pays for physician services. The bulk of Part B comes from the general fund.

Democrats were arguing that Republican cuts were severe and that Medicare should not be cut to pay for tax breaks for people who did not need them. The $283 billion cuts over seven years would add $1,060 to the out-of-pocket costs to Medicare beneficiaries in 2000, totaling about $3,500 over the seven years. But in the end the Medicare fight was about much more than money and the dollar differences between the Clinton plan and the Gingrich plan. The programmatic changes in Medicare that the Republicans proposed would, contended Democrats, end Medicare as we know it; it would privatize the government-run Medicare system. The most notable of the Republican proposals would set up medical savings accounts (MSAs), which would allow Medicare beneficiaries to take the roughly 4,500 Medicare dollars allocated to them, buy private catastrophic insurance with some part of it, and keep the rest. As the healthiest Medicare beneficiaries do that, the universal insurance pool that Medicare has created would be fractured. Only the sickest and oldest would remain in Medicare, costs for the government would increase sharply, and Medicare would no longer exist. Interestingly, those people who choose MSAs when they are sixty-eight and healthy, and who are able to pocket some of the $4,500 because their health care costs are low, will likely choose to reenter traditional Medicare when they get older and their health begins to decline.

On another track, the Republican rush toward full privatization of Medicare continues unabated. One-sixth of Medicare beneficiaries—generally the healthiest and youngest—are currently enrolled in HMOs run mostly by for-profit private insurance companies. As HMOs "skim off" the healthiest beneficiaries and leave behind the most expensive Medicare beneficiaries, the fiscal health of Medicare continues to decline.

The GOP consistently shifted the focus to the Medicare Trust Fund, always hiding its antipathy toward the government-run health program called Medicare. Another Republican memo from later in the year, as the debate was getting away from the Republicans, implored Republican members to say, "If we don't act today, the Medicare Trust Fund will be bankrupt. We cannot wait until the system goes bankrupt before we solve the problem. . . . Millions of seniors rely on Medicare for their basic health care and we must protect them from the impending bankruptcy of the system." Much of the press seemed to support the Republican attempts to reform Medicare, citing the Trustees Report and mentioning that the trustees were mostly Clinton appointees. Democrats answered by pointing out that, every year since 1970, the Trustees Report made similar findings, and Congress would always respond by making minor adjustments in reimbursement, benefits, or taxes. Besides, Republican after Republican said, "we're not really cutting Medicare; we are increasing Medicare 7 percent." "Only in Washington," they said, "could an increase be called a cut."

But Democrats seemed to be winning the Medicare debate with the public. Beginning in early May 1995, long before President Clinton threatened a veto, House Democrats took to the floor day and night to talk about Republican Medicare cuts in order to pay for tax breaks for the wealthy. House Democrats organized a petition drive, where several dozen of us circulated petitions in our districts, asking senior citizens to sign if they opposed the Medicare cuts in order to give tax breaks to the wealthiest people in society.

Democrats had repeated their mantra month after month until finally President Clinton, ignoring the advice of his chief political adviser, Dick Morris, took on the issue that thus far defined both his presidency and his 1996 campaign. Then, on October 24, 1995, Speaker Gingrich and Senator Dole, to different groups on the same day, revealed their true feelings and views about Medicare. In an address to insurance company executives, most of whom would benefit handsomely from the privatization of Medicare, Gingrich proclaimed, "Now, we didn't get rid of it in round one because we don't think that that's politically smart and we don't think that's the right way to go through a transition. But we believe it's going to wither on the vine." Senator Dole, speaking to the American Conservative Union, a group he knew was especially important to him in winning the Republican nomination for president, said, "I was there, fighting the fight, one of twelve, voting against Medicare because in 1965 we knew it wouldn't work." The Democratic party and organized labor went on the air with television ads showing the videotape of Gingrich and Dole speaking their minds about Medicare.

The president's opposition to Republican Medicare cuts, the Dole and Gingrich affirmation of the Democrats' contention that Republicans have no real interest in saving Medicare, and Democratic House members' continued assault to the Republican budget sent Republican poll numbers plummeting. Congressional Democrats continued to pile on: One Minute speeches in the mornings, one-hour Special Orders at night, and attempts at any other time we could to remind the public that Republicans wanted to privatize Medicare.

On November 14, after the first government shutdown, California Democratic congressman Pete Stark, representing the Ways and Means Committee, and I, representing the Commerce Committee, went to the floor on a simple, noncontroversial bill repealing "an unnecessary medical device reporting requirement." H.R. 2366 amended a section of the Social Security Act (42 U.S.C. 1395y) that included Medicare provisions. The Republican sponsor, Nevada Republican Barbara Vucanovich, had brought the bill to the floor under the Speaker's special Corrections Calendar. She was joined by Florida Republican Michael Bilirakis, representing Commerce Committee Republicans. Unlike many in his party, Bilirakis really does believe in Medicare. Neither Vucanovich nor Bilirakis expected more than five or ten minutes of friendly, uneventful discussion or anything other than a unanimous vote. Under the rules, each side—Bilirakis representing the Republicans, I the Democrats—was given thirty minutes for its presentation.

Prefacing our remarks by pointing out that Republicans had allowed virtually no debate time on the floor on their Medicare plan and only cursory hearings in the Commerce and Ways and Means Committees, we used our time to discuss the Gingrich Medicare plan. I yielded time to Stark, who talked about fifteen minutes on the real need for corrections: that their Medicaid and Medicare plan would increase the number of uninsured Americans from forty million to sixty-six million in seven years; that antifraud provisions aimed at providers would be diluted in the Gingrich plan; that disabled people would be excluded from Medicaid coverage. Stark demanded of the

Republicans, "When you are cutting $450 billion out of a budget to pay for tax cuts for the rich, can you not find enough to require that governors under these bloc grants keep disabled people in the Medicaid plan?" After repeated pleas—or exhortations—from Bilirakis to confine our remarks precisely to the bill at hand, I rose to remind C-SPAN viewers of Republican attempts to privatize Medicare and pointed out Gingrich's and Dole's statements the month before about their opposition to Medicare.

The hypocrisy that so many Democrats believed they saw among conservative Republicans brought new passion to the Medicare debate. Republicans claimed to be saving Medicare, to want to preserve it for future generations. Yet their party opposed its very creation for decades, aligning themselves with conservative southern Democrats to kill President Truman's 1948 attempts to create a health care program for the elderly, opposing it with wealthy physician groups throughout the 1950s, doing all they could to stop its passage in 1965, when it was finally enacted. Republicans had refused to supply a single vote in the House or Senate when Congress responded to the 1993 Medicare Trust Fund recommendation to adjust and fix it.

The comments about Medicare from prominent Republicans, Democrats thought, again showed Republicans' true attitude toward the program. California congressman William Thomas called it "socialized medicine." Majority Leader Dick Armey said that Medicare "is a program I would have no part of in a free world." To make himself more clear, Armey added, "Hundreds of thousands of seniors rely on Medicare. I'm sorry they do, but they do." And, of course, Gingrich said it would "wither on the vine" under his proposal, and Dole bragged about his opposition to it, saying he knew it wouldn't work. Many years ago, as a House Republican leader, Gerald Ford had said, "We are going to find our aged bewildered by a multiheaded bureaucratic maze of confusion over what program covers what and who is on first base." To Democrats, Republican comments about preserving Medicare simply did not ring true.

As I continued to speak in the House chamber that day about Medicare and the Republicans' plans to privatize it, a parade of Republican members—Robert Ehrlich of Maryland, Joe Barton of Texas, and Vucanovich—tried to get Stark and me ruled out of order. Our side was joined by freshman Mike Ward of Kentucky and second-termer Gene Green from Texas, who sits with me on the Health and Environment subcommittee and is one of my best friends in Congress. Each made the case about Republicans shutting down debate and resisted attempts by the majority party to declare us out of order. North Carolina's Sue Myrick happened to be in the chair, serving that day as Speaker pro tempore. Intermittently, as I was interrupted perhaps a half-dozen times by Republicans trying to rule my comments out of order, she would either ask me to confine my remarks specifically to the bill or appeal to the parliamentarian on whether she could silence me. The parliamentarian ruled that my comments were in order, that the subject of the bill was a section of the Social Security (and Medicare) law, and that I could proceed. An exasperated and unamused Myrick stated, "The chair finds that the most recent debate maintains the proper nexus to the bill. The gentleman may proceed." At one point, Republicans were planning to appeal to the entire House for a recorded vote to stop the debate, but they realized that would only make the issue bigger, would only highlight their legislative leaders' statements about Medicare, and would remind viewers that there was only one hearing on Medicare. And it might mean that the day's proceeding would be on the six o'clock news and cause even more controversy to swirl around their Medicare plan.

A few days later, a strange and extraordinary incident occurred. During a rare Saturday session that was especially acrimonious and rancorous, the Republicans abruptly adjourned and left the floor at about 3:00 P.M. Some one hundred Democrats stayed on or near the floor wondering what to do. Republicans had turned off the microphones even as Democratic leaders were preparing to speak (the majority controls the House floor even when we are not in session). John Lewis, the acknowledged conscience of the Congress, started it off. Unaided by a microphone, but assisted with excellent acoustics, Lewis preached to us as he walked up and down the aisles. He talked about his days as a poor boy feeding chickens on an Alabama farm. He talked about civil rights and how he was beaten up by southern police. He talked about the Republican budget that rewarded the rich and punished the poor. "I stood up to Bull Connor in Birmingham," he thundered. "I stood up to George Wallace in Alabama. I'm not going to run from Newt Gingrich."

There were no more than fifty tourists in the visitors' gallery. There were few reporters in the press gallery. The cameras on the floor were turned off, and no one's words were broadcast on C-SPAN. There was not even a complete record of what was said. It was just us, talking to one another. Member after member stepped forward to talk about why they ran for office, what attracted them to public service, why the Gingrich budget was a betrayal of

American values. José Serrano, a New York Democrat who represents one of America's poorest congressional districts, paced back and forth, attacking the Gingrich revolution. "A revolution usually helps people on the bottom. . . . This revolution attacks children." After a couple of hours, with most of the one hundred Democrats still in their seats, we knew why this budget fight was so important.

At around the same time, a story broke that may have done more to damage Speaker Gingrich's credibility than the government shutdown. After the November 4 assassination of Israeli prime minister Yitzhak Rabin, an official U.S. government delegation accompanied the president on Air Force One to the funeral. Gingrich complained to the American press when he got home that the president had snubbed him on the plane and he had been made to get off the back of the plane when disembarking in Tel Aviv. (Gingrich was the only official to have a spouse on the plane, having complained when told there was not room for spouses.) A couple of days later, I was sitting in my office working, only half paying attention to C-SPAN, when I heard perhaps the funniest speech of the 104th Congress. Illinois Democrat Luis Gutierrez, mocking the Speaker's "juvenile behavior," said: "I had a traumatic experience on an airplane Monday. I asked for an aisle seat and they gave me a window. The pilot never came back to say hello, and when we landed, I, a Member of Congress, had to walk out with all the rest of the passengers. So I drafted a bill to shut down the Government until the airline apologizes to me."

Six days later, after the president agreed to a balanced budget in seven years with Congressional Budget Office scoring of the budget figures, the House and Senate passed and the president signed a new CR—without including their Medicare reforms—that would keep the government open until December 15. Those parts of the government for which appropriations had not passed would be funded at the level of the House-passed, Senate-passed, or prior-year appropriation, whichever was lowest. Those agencies slated to be abolished would be funded at 75 percent of the previous year's appropriations.

But the budget stalemate continued. On December 6 Clinton vetoed the Republican Balanced Budget Act, symbolically using the pen that President Johnson had used to sign the bill creating Medicare in 1965. As December 15 approached, Republicans were unwilling, by that point, to keep the government open if there were not significant signs of progress in the budget negotiations. When the government closed on that day, 280,000 workers were furloughed, while some went to work but were not allowed to spend any money to do their job (buy gas, supplies, and the like).

The budget negotiations over Christmas and New Year's between the congressional Republicans and the White House were fruitless. Six of the thirteen appropriations bills had still not become law. The president had vetoed three of them. Two of them were in conference committees because Republican House and Senate members could not come to agreement. And one was held up by Senate Democrats because of an antistriker replacement provision. During one of the marathon negotiation sessions, a tired and frustrated Bob Dole, who was more impatient with Gingrich and the freshmen Republicans than he was with the White House, turned to Gephardt and muttered, "Dick, I wanna get outta here. I gotta go to New Hampshire." Dole never had much use for the young revolutionary from Georgia. The feelings were reciprocated by Gingrich, who thought Dole an agent of the established order. During the Bush budget stalemate, Gingrich called Dole the "tax collector for the welfare state." It had to be especially galling to Dole that the Democrats linked Dole and Gingrich during the presidential campaign, showing footage of the two legislators together in numerous Clinton ads.

On January 6, in light of opinion polls showing that twice as many voters were blaming Republicans as Democrats, the shutdown ended. The White House declared victory with language that protected Medicare, Medicaid, education, and the environment. After talks broke off permanently, and it was clear that the government would run on a series of CRs, Clinton savored his victory again. On January 23, in his State of the Union address, he turned toward the Republican side of the chamber and scolded, "Never, ever shut the federal government down again." The president instead might have reminded the Republicans—whose entire revolution revolved around balancing the federal budget, Congressional Budget Office estimates, and deficits—of Willie Stark in Robert Penn Warren's *All the King's Men,* the classic fictional account of Louisiana's Huey Long: "Folks don't listen to you when your voice is low and patient and you stop them in the hot sun and make them do arithmetic."

Richard Darman, budget director to President George Bush, recalls a meeting at the White House with Georgia congressman Newt Gingrich: "In his cheerful, confident, radical, professorial way, Gingrich explained that to do what he wanted, government first had to be completely discredited—ethically, programmatically, managerially, philosophically." While his strategy may have worked (certainly it played a major role in bringing down the Democrats and capturing the House for the Republicans), Gingrich did not stop when he was in power. As October 1—the first day of the new fiscal year, the day when government activities would actually cease—approached, an outspoken Gingrich continued to assert that a government shutdown would underscore to the public that government is corrupt. The ultimate way to discredit government, the Speaker's actions suggested, was to shut down a government that people would probably not miss anyway.

He had help. The seventy-three-member-strong freshman class was urging the Speaker on, believing, too, that their constituents would applaud a Congress that stood up to the president, the bureaucrats, and a government Sodom and Gomorrah that had run amok. They were still revolutionaries; they wanted decisive action, not incremental change that accomplished little and was noticed by almost nobody.

Even when Gingrich began to see the potential political damage building for Republicans, especially after the first government shutdown, the freshmen would not let Gingrich negotiate a reasonable budget deal with the president. To be fair, many Democratic members, buttressed by a small handful of presidential advisers in the Clinton White House, did all they could to prevent the president from negotiating a budget deal with the Speaker. And some freshmen were already grumbling about their leaders. Ultraconservative Republican Todd Tiahrt from Kansas complained that their leadership—especially Gingrich and Armey, who both taught college before they were elected to Congress—was getting snookered: "What I see are college professors negotiating for us. They don't have a lot of experience in this kind of thing."

The Republicans failed in the budget battles for a number of reasons. Their attempt to remake the federal government through the budget had left Republicans demoralized. They believed that they could roll over a president whom they saw as weak, unsure of himself, and prone to change his mind. Clinton had seemed to capitulate to Republicans several times in his first two years: the stimulus package and the BTU tax in 1993, several of his appointees to major administrative positions in 1993 and 1994, health care in 1994. His statement to wealthy contributors in Houston in mid-October that he should not have raised their taxes so much encouraged the Republican belief that this president would not stand and fight.

Their self-righteousness and moral certainty (remember the statement from the senior Republican that the freshmen "don't think anything good in this country ever happened until January 1995") led them to believe that the country believed the same things that they did, that their mission—to repeal, in effect, the New Deal—had broad public support. They talked among themselves, they listened to Rush Limbaugh, they read their own press clippings; after all, they had won a big election in 1994. The country ratified what they said they wanted to do.

Republicans, especially the far-right wing of the party, failed to understand that Americans do not hate government. Americans like Medicare and national parks. They believe in strong environmental laws and worker safety regulations. They appreciate Social Security and pure food laws. When the American people came to realize that this new crowd in Congress did not just want to shrink government, they wanted to dismantle it, the revolution was over. Republicans were dead wrong when they thought the public would not care that the government was shut down.

After the talks broke off for the last time, and the principals on both sides realized that the next election must dictate the budget agreement, the president's position seemed to hold. The government shutdown had obscured what Republicans thought was the most important issue of the entire 104th Congress, balancing the budget. The shutdown, believed by most voters to have been caused by the GOP, was emblazoned in the public mind. Public opinion polls showed that a large majority of voters thought that deep Republican Medicare cuts were to be used to give lavish tax breaks for the rich, and Republicans seemed to be willing to shut down the federal government for that. And President Clinton had convinced the public that he had blocked the Republican extremists from doing just that.

14

The Counteroffensive: M2E2

How far can we push the revolution, and bring back a
majority of our members?
    —John Boehner (R-Ohio)

Should any political party attempt to abolish Social Security
and unemployment insurance and eliminate labor laws and
farm programs, you would not hear of that party again in
our political history.
    —Dwight Eisenhower

UNTIL NOVEMBER, the president was not having a good 1995. He was
fairly and unfairly criticized for things he did and things he did not do.
He seemed disengaged. Republicans in Congress were passing item after
item on the Contract with America. Newt Gingrich was the new national
media star. Clearly still bothered from the disastrous 1994 midterm elections,
a frustrated Bill Clinton actually said, "The president is relevant here." His
own pollster, Stanley Greenberg, wrote in a memo that Clinton was "fun-
damentally mispositioned" for the 1996 presidential race.

During the first hundred days, and continuing through the first half of
1995, House Democrats believed that we were on our own. We were getting
little help from the president in fighting the most objectionable parts of the
Contract with America. He had not yet used his veto, although, in fairness,
he had little opportunity since most of the substantive and controversial
Contract items had died in the Senate. The president, most House Democrats thought, was not weighing in on this marathon fight. At a Democratic
caucus in late February, President Clinton came to the Capitol to meet with
still-dispirited Democrats. Only about 60 percent of Democratic members
bothered to show up. We met in a sterile, windowless room in the basement
of the Capitol (the majority party, which controls all rooms and scheduling
in the Capitol, told us that no other room was available for the president's

visit). The occasion had neither the festiveness that this president usually brought to such a gathering nor the sober importance that a presidential visit could generate. Usually a politician under siege speaking to politicians of his own party has the camaraderie of a foxhole: We're in this together; let's make the most of it. His presentation seemed more like a speech to the Elyria Rotary, listing accomplishments and achievements to a generally friendly crowd but one where people are a bit skeptical of motives and performance. He spoke a bit too long and people grew restless—again, as often happens at the Elyria Rotary. In the end, he did not connect with the members who were there—and I *know* that happens at the Elyria Rotary.

Nothing much changed. Sensing the resentment building from Capitol Hill, the White House set up a series of regional meetings between Democratic members of Congress and the president. On April 6 several Democratic members from the Southwest met with the president. There was visible anger directed at Clinton from some who wanted a veto of a health care bill that included two riders: one, likely inserted by Gingrich, to provide huge tax breaks to Rupert Murdoch and another that gave major tax advantages to extraordinarily wealthy Americans who renounce their citizenship. One hundred thirty-nine Democrats had signed a letter asking the president to veto the bill. Others were critical of other omissions or commissions by the president. Lloyd Doggett, an outspoken and articulate freshman Democrat from Austin, Texas, complained to President Clinton that he did not stand up and fight for what he believed in. "That's bullshit," shot back the president. The hostility and anger dissipated . . . only very slowly.

For some reason, the White House never got around to setting up a meeting with my region of the country, perhaps as a result of the tensions in the April 6 meeting. As a freshman in the majority in 1993–94, I was invited to the White House and saw and spoke with the president many times. During my second term, the White House congressional picnic and the White House Christmas party were about our only meetings. Republican rank and file, the new majority, made the trip up Pennsylvania Avenue much more often.

Not only did we Democrats believe that we were on our own, but we often thought that the president had undercut us. We wanted him to lead, to be sure; but if he wasn't advocating the principles we all stood for, we wanted him to let us lead. In mid-May Democrats started to focus on the issues that illustrated with a bold, black line the difference between the Gingrich Republicans and the national Democrats.

There were occasional signs that the president was facing down the Republicans and challenging them when their behavior was particularly outrageous. On May 16, 1995, the House passed legislation repealing major parts of the Clean Water Act of 1972. That legislation was especially important for my district and the rest of northern Ohio. Written partly as a response to a railroad trestle catching fire from chemicals in the Cuyahoga River in Cleveland, the Clean Water Act was responsible for the cleanup of Lake Erie, and ultimately, I believe, the comeback of Cleveland. The bill to repeal large parts of the Clean Water Act was opposed by a strong majority of Democrats and thirty moderate Republicans. The president, in a heartening performance that House Democrats widely applauded, chose a picturesque site in Rock Creek Park in Washington to accuse the Republican Congress of turning over the writing of environmental law to developers, chemical companies, and agribusinesses. He pledged to fight the "Dirty Water Act" with all his might, an action that thrilled most of us in the House.

Unfortunately, this event was an exception. The president did not seem to weigh in on the budget that passed May 17, and as Republicans moved toward a balanced budget at any cost, Democrats were powerless to fight back. And so the Gingrich balanced budget—with $288 billion in Medicare cuts, $67 billion in defense increases, an increase in taxes for twelve million families making less than $28,000, and $353 billion in tax cuts—passed 238 to 193. Democrats began the mantra of "no cuts in Medicare and student loans to pay for tax breaks for the rich." Gingrich responded by ridiculing our "primal screaming." The Democrats' tax-and-spend days and their era of big government, he said, were drawing to an end.

The seeds of a victory strategy were being planted as Democrats attempted to shift the debate from the Leviathan of big government to whether the American public wants a wholesale dismantling of government and the total destruction of most nondefense government programs. The Medicare message, according to a *Los Angeles Times* survey, was beginning to make an impression on the American public. Minority Whip David Bonior had made repeated and personal requests of Clinton and others at the White House to incorporate the Medicare and student loan message in the president's message, but to no avail. Many of us in the House made similar, unsuccessful requests to other presidential advisers. But then in late May, the bottom dropped out. The president, in a very short statement on national television from the Oval Office, threw his support to a balanced budget, including sizable Medicare cuts. Congressional Democrats didn't even know it was

coming. Democrats were already angry at Clinton for a little campaign
finance love-in he had had at a senior center in New Hampshire the week
before with Newt Gingrich. And now this. He seemed to be following the
advice of a new bipartisan political adviser named Dick Morris, who recommended a new policy of triangulation. Clinton should separate himself
from Democrats and Republicans, Morris argued, and govern as a con-
venient Independent. Many of us in Congress had never even heard of
Dick Morris. Most of us had never seen him. Yet the president was listening
to a consultant who had advised Republican senator Jesse Helms to run a
racist television ad against an African American candidate, a man who, only a
few months earlier, had counseled Trent Lott, who was destined to be Bob
Dole's successor as Senate majority leader. Later in the summer, when it
became clearer and clearer that Morris had the ear of the president, he became
bolder. Not only was Morris advising Clinton, he was talking to and giving
information directly to his former client, Lott, a highly unusual situation
rarely, if ever, found in the annals of modern-day government.

The birth of triangulation came with great labor pains. Democrats were
angry about the president's snuggling up to Gingrich, whom Democrats
thought we had on the run. We were unhappy about the White House's failure to tell us of the president's plan. Democrats were especially livid about
the $125 billion in Medicare cuts. Our message linking Medicare with tax
breaks for the rich was working. We were criticizing the Republicans for cutting Medicare to pay for tax breaks and then the president proposes smaller
cuts, but cuts nonetheless. We were regularly pointing out the ethics cloud
hanging over Gingrich's head and then the president cozies up to him in
New Hampshire. At the Communications Group meeting the morning that
Clinton proposed his Medicare cuts, Democrats used terms like "betrayal,"
"sold out," and "deceit." We were angry and disrespectful. During the meeting, I suggested in jest, to what I thought was a group of people who would
keep it in confidence, that "maybe we should think about reopening Pennsylvania Avenue," a not-very-wise reference to the area of Pennsylvania
Avenue in front of the White House that had been closed following the
Oklahoma City bombing. Thanks to a fellow Democrat in the meeting who
gave my comments to a reporter, the *New York Post,* then Rush Limbaugh,
then a bunch of Ohio newspapers and radio shows picked it up. Right-wing
talk radio used it to show how unhappy Clinton's own party was with his
presidency; local reporters used it to say that I should simply shut up. But I

was not the only tart-tongued Democrat. Wisconsin's David Obey, the top-ranked Democrat on Appropriations who never minces words, was unhappy with the president's change of position. He sent a release to the press that said succinctly, "I think most of us learned some time ago, if you don't like the President's position on a particular issue, you simply need to wait a few weeks." Several veteran Democrats said that they had never heard such talk about a president from members of his party as they had that morning in the caucus and in the Communications Group.

Senator Dole and Speaker Gingrich issued a statement applauding the president and welcoming him to their side with his new proposal: that a balanced budget is necessary and achievable, that cuts in Medicare are necessary, and that taxes should be cut. But, only a few days later, when newspapers and Republicans began to question the president's economic growth assumptions, Republican leaders quickly dismissed the Clinton balanced budget proposal. Republicans now saw the Clinton budget not as a serious document but as a concession—on Medicare, tax cuts, and defense. It was only the beginning of negotiations, and Gingrich thought he had won a key battle in a perhaps protracted war. House Democrats, still smarting from what many of us saw as, at best, bad judgment from the White House, were beginning to realize that we could continue to talk about Medicare and student loans. The president, once the Republicans wrote off his budget, was starting to speak out against Republican Medicare cuts and extremist Republicans. Perhaps the president's budget proposal, and our reaction to it in Congress, was only a tempest in a teapot. It was forgotten by both the media and the American public, if it was ever heard at all. House Democrats could resume their mantra: "No Medicare and student loan cuts to pay for tax breaks for the rich."

And Republicans went back to work. Republicans were cutting Medicare by $270 billion in order to give a $245 billion tax break to the rich. Their reconciliation bill, which they termed the Balanced Budget Act, was making it easy for the Democrats on Capitol Hill and on Pennsylvania Avenue: a $245 billion tax cut and a $270 billion cut in Medicare. The symmetry of the numbers made it almost too easy for the Democrats. The Democratic counteroffensive was on.

On November 15, 1995, two days after Clinton had vetoed the temporary spending bill and the debt limit bill, and the day after the government had shut down, I was waiting tables at a charitable dinner sponsored by my friend

Rick Diegel and the International Brotherhood of Electrical Workers. A hotel employee told me that the White House was calling for me. Since this was the first time that the president had personally lobbied me on an issue, I was obviously excited to return the call. Using the phone at the hotel's front desk, I asked the White House switchboard operator to connect me with the president. After no more than ninety seconds, a familiar voice came on the phone. "I need your help, Sherrod," he told me after we exchanged pleasantries. He was calling to ask for my support on his budget veto, knowing that I had voted for the Balanced Budget Amendment. I assured him that I was with him, adding that "you're doing the right thing for the country and the right thing politically for the Democratic party." He said nothing in response but went on as if I had not even spoken. That happened two or three more times, creating what seemed from my end a rather disjointed conversation.

Walking the several blocks back to my Longworth Building office at about 9:00 that night, it occurred to me that he had to be on guard about anything he said on the phone, and even about any response he made to anyone else. Someone could have been listening on my end. I could have had a local reporter with me, for example, who would have loved to write a story about the local congressman's conversation with the president about the budget. Even a hint of acknowledgment that what he was doing was good politics might have been a national story, albeit a potentially damaging one. He could never acknowledge politics or personalities or partisanship.

Something less obvious had happened—beyond Gingrich's bad polling numbers, the public disapproval of the student loan and Medicare cuts, and the extremist label that more and more people were attaching to the Republican Congress. In 1994 the Republicans had won the election on the question of shrinking the size of the federal government. I remember my opponent that year saying at the end of every speech, "If you believe that government can solve all your problems, and that big government is the answer, then vote for Sherrod Brown. But if you believe that people can take care of themselves and solve their own problems, and that government is too big, then you should vote for Greg White." That sentiment was echoed all over the country by almost every Republican in almost every race. The Democrats simply did not fight back very well on that issue.

But the Republicans, driven mostly by the new members, had shifted the debate to the issue of dismantling the federal government, eliminating popular programs, and cutting agencies with broad public support. They were soon to find out that was an issue they could not win. Comments about revolution, that Washington was some alien place, and that federal bureaucrats were enemies of the American people dug a deeper hole for House Republicans and their agenda.

But it was more than the new Republican members. Majority Leader Dick Armey, the former college professor, wrote, "Between our New Deals and New Frontiers and Great Societies you will find, with a difference only in power and nerve, the same sort of person who gave the world its Five Year Plans and Great Leaps Forward—the Soviet and Chinese counterparts." To Armey, government programs—Medicare or school lunches, Social Security or OSHA, the EPA or the FDA—had no legitimacy in a free and capitalist society; those programs smacked of totalitarianism. Intrusive government, which told businesses what to pay their workers, what they could discharge into the air and water, and how to protect their safety, compromised capitalism and took away freedom. There was no place, Armey repeated, "for Medicare in a free society." The advocates for these agencies, the employees of these agencies, the clients and customers of these agencies had no legitimate role in either our society or our nation.

Then, on April 19, 1995, a bomb exploded in the Alfred Murrah Federal Building in Oklahoma City, killing 168 federal employees, children of federal workers, and clients. Two members of a militia group—a part of society that most Americans did not know even existed—were fingered as the culprits. Republican antigovernment rhetoric took a different tone and was heard in a different way by mainstream America. Republicans in Congress, a huge proportion of whom had been elected with substantial National Rifle Association support, were in the very awkward position of explaining or even defending the militia. One member of Congress, Republican freshman Steve Stockman of Texas, had a connection to militia groups and had spoken with some of their members only minutes after the bombing. Stockman, an interesting character, had gone to Texas from Michigan without a job back in the late 1970s. He was homeless for a time and lived out of a station wagon. In 1994, after unsuccessful attempts in 1990 and 1992, he upset the forty-two-year incumbent Judiciary chairman Jack Brooks after Brooks dropped his long-standing opposition to gun control and let the assault weapons ban out of his Judiciary Committee. Stockman was defeated in a 1996 run-off by Democrat Nick Lampson.

As the public got to know more about the militias and the most extreme of the gun fanatics, Republicans had to spend valuable time and resources to separate themselves from those groups. Republicans were further ridiculed when they continued to insist on repealing the assault weapons ban. Newspapers, Democrats, and some Republicans made clear that the vote to repeal the assault weapons ban, which passed comfortably, was a payback to the NRA for their support in the 1994 election.

The bombing of the federal building in Oklahoma City did cause Republicans in the House and Senate to pause in their rush to pass the repeal. The Senate had planned to bring it up right around the time of the bombing. After waiting for several months, the presidential elections came into play and, amid taunts from the White House, Senator Dole decided it would be wise to indefinitely postpone a repeal vote. Presidential election politics played little or no role in the House. After waiting a politically safe number of months after the Oklahoma City bombing, the House passed the repeal 239 to 173 on March 22, 1996.

The gun control debate may have been the most interesting issue of the 1994 and 1996 elections. After the 1994 election, most political analysts and prominent political figures—including Bill Clinton, Newt Gingrich, and Dick Gephardt—credited the National Rifle Association with making the difference for the Republicans in ten to twenty seats. Gun control of any kind, the commentators purred, would not be on the agenda at any time in the foreseeable future, regardless of which party was in power. But after Oklahoma City, the "discovery" of the militias, the stories about political payoffs by the NRA, and the general reputation of the Gingrich Congress as "extremist," the gun issue and the public reaction to it underwent a huge shift. To be sure, the only voters who seemed to vote "guns only" on election day were very pro-gun. But they already knew who their friends in Congress were. The push to repeal the ban on assault weapons and to repeal the Brady Bill caused large numbers of moderate suburbanites—both Republicans and women—to believe that Gingrich and the new Republican members really were extremist and out of touch with mainstream America.

That did not mean that the NRA went into hiding. After the Oklahoma City bombing, and before Republican leaders made clear that a quick vote on the repeal of the assault weapons ban would be politically too difficult, the National Rifle Association had kicked their grassroots efforts into gear. In June I was scheduled to have a town meeting—specifically to talk about Medicare—at the Elyria Methodist Home, a senior citizens' home in the second largest city in my district. Three days before, the NRA sent to its members an alert:

Members are urged to attend and take this opportunity to remind him to vote for H.R. 1488 (the repeal of the Clinton gun ban) when it comes up for a vote in the House of Representatives this summer.

Please dress appropriately; suits and/or ties make a better impression than sports or outdoor wear.

Unlike town meetings leading up to the original vote on the assault weapons ban in 1993, there were few, if any, NRA members who came to the Methodist Home; none spoke up about guns.

The president, who knew he had almost no electoral support from gun enthusiasts, continued to brand opponents of Brady and the assault weapons ban as extremists, a label that seemed to stick to a party that also seemed out of touch on Medicare, education, and the environment. The president's and the Democrats' position on crime—community policing, the Brady Bill and the assault weapons ban, the COPS program—was attracting significant support and major endorsements from police organizations all over the country. Endorsements from the Fraternal Order of Police and the National Chiefs of Police, which in past elections had usually backed Republicans, further isolated Republicans and their NRA supporters.

Democrats were now finding receptive audiences to discuss the proper role of government, and the relevance of government to people's everyday lives: pure food laws, environmental protection, Medicare, education, worker safety, minimum wage. It was no longer a debate on Republican terms: "Is government too big?" It was now an argument on Democratic terms: "Should government be dismantled or should we protect important programs like Medicare, Medicaid, education, and the environment?" House Democrats began to make the case for a government that protects those things that are important to people. And a year later the president joined the battle; he was masterful at making the case for the legitimate role of government in our lives.

In most countries in the world through most of history, governments were controlled by the wealthiest people in the country for the benefit of the wealthiest people in the country. Government was an ally of the rich and the powerful and was often made up of and usually controlled by those same people. It was rarely on the side of the poor or the working class and rarely protected workers against exploitation. Government rarely stood with the oppressed against the oppressor.

The American government, at its best, took the side of the less powerful. Government in the United States, in its best times, has protected workers and the environment, often at the expense of the rich and the powerful. In its proud moments, it has stood with the oppressed against discrimination or for a minimum wage or for justice. E. J. Dionne, in *They Only Look Dead: Why Progressives Will Dominate the Next Political Era,* discussed "the use of government to give men and women the tools needed for positive liberty, beginning with free elementary and secondary education and moving in the Depression and postwar era to Social Security, unemployment compensation, and access to college and to health insurance." Government in twentieth-century Russia and eighteenth-century France oppressed their people. Government in twentieth-century America in many cases provided liberty and opportunity: student loans and minimum wage, free public education and workplace safety, cleaner air and purer food.

On my suit coat I wear a lapel pin that depicts a canary in a birdcage. In the early days of the twentieth century, when every year more than 2,000 U.S. coalminers were killed in U.S. mines, workers took canaries into the mines to warn them of toxic gases or lack of oxygen: if the canary died they knew they had to get out of the mine quickly. Any protection the miners had they had to provide it themselves—no mine safety laws, no worker protections, no trade unions, no real support from their elected officials or their government. A baby born at the beginning of the twentieth century had a life expectancy of about forty-seven years. Today, thanks to progressive government and an aggressive labor movement, Americans can expect to live about three decades longer. It has been a hundred-year battle between the privileged and ordinary people—battling oil and chemical companies to enact clean air and safe drinking water laws; the automobile industry to pass auto safety rules; the American Medical Association to establish Medicare for senior citizens; Wall Street bankers to enact Social Security; entrenched business interests in enacting women's and civil rights, protections for the disabled, and prohibitions on child labor. Virtually every bit of progress made in the fight for economic and social justice came against the opposition of society's most privileged and most advantaged and was won by ordinary, working families. The canary signifies that the struggle continues today—against the powerful interest groups that too often control our government.

A once-dispirited Democratic party was fighting back in defense of a government that the American people wanted. Democrat George Miller, a twenty-one-year veteran from California, told the House on May 3, 1995, "The Republicans have now come to face the fact that they cannot give tax cuts to the wealthy, balance the budget and preserve Medicare, so now they are devising a plan by which they can make the cuts in Medicare to provide for the tax cuts for the wealthy." Other Democrats followed, adding student loans, Medicaid, the environment, and education.

More than a dozen of us in the House—led by Connecticut's Rosa DeLauro and New Jersey's Frank Pallone—repeated this message night after night, day after day, Special Order after Special Order, One Minute after One Minute. Columnist Mark Shields wrote, "With no encouragement from the president and with the unconcealed contempt of the president's minions, congressional Democrats repeated the charge and, in the process, changed political history."

In June 1995, voters over sixty-five were consistently the most supportive of the Republican agenda of any age group, according to a *Wall Street Journal*/NBC News poll. Thirteen months later, as the president began to talk about M2E2 (the political shorthand for Medicare, Medicaid, education, and the environment), while other voters' party identification had remained statistically unchanged, 20 percent of voters over sixty-five had swung from Republican to Democrat.

By the spring of 1996, President Clinton was much less interested in reaching a budget compromise and a Medicare compromise with the Republicans. To the delight of most Democrats in the House, he had rejected, apparently, the advice of his conservative, let's-make-a-deal adviser Dickie Morris. Many of the national commentators credited Morris with the president's political comeback because he advised Clinton to move to the right, talk more about values and school uniforms and less about health care, sign the welfare bill, and generally out-Republican the Republicans. Most of us in the House—joined by Mark Shields and several other political analysts— saw that Clinton's poll ratings began to go up when he held the line on Medicare, stood up and fought, and made the differences between himself and Gingrich clear. We knew that the president, when facing political or electoral turbulence, had always returned to the core values of the Democratic party. The right thing to do, and the politically smart thing to do, was to draw a line between the two parties and let the voters choose which philosophy about government should direct the country into the next century. The debate over government's role in our lives had been joined. The 1996 election was in full swing.

15

The Truce

It all ended up in one total mess. People are legitimately mad.
 —Newt Gingrich, *USA Today* (February 26, 1996)

Congress' approval ratings are back to autumn 1994 contempt
levels. The notions of a reform Congress are right up there with
Tinkerbell and the Tooth Fairy.
 —Kevin Phillips (February 7, 1996)

AFTER THE GOVERNMENT SHUTDOWN, large numbers of Republican-
elected officials—inside and outside Congress—understood that the
revolution had gone too far and that electoral problems were on the hori-
zon. Their most visible leader, Newt Gingrich, was the most unpopular
politician in America. Their Contract with America was mostly unpassed by
the Senate, unsigned by the president, and unappreciated by the American
public. "People wanted change," New York senator Alfonse d'Amato told a
group of fellow Republicans. "But they did not want a so-called counter-
revolution that threatened our very foundations."

Senator Dole and Speaker Gingrich had contemplated an aggressive strategy, one advocated by a number of freshman House Republicans, which
entailed passing several major, poll-driven, mostly social issues that would
put the president on the defensive in the last few months before the election,
forcing him to veto popular legislation opposed by his Democratic base. But
after their sobering experience with the government shutdown, Republican
leaders rejected this strategy. Gingrich was not the only one who knew he
needed to take something home in 1996. The Speaker, obviously, had a dis-
mal 1995, especially during the last six months: his book deal, ethics charges,
abysmally low poll ratings, government shutdowns. Clinton had fought his
way out of feeling he had to assert his relevance as president early in the year
and, as 1995 drew to a close, was now being heralded as the protector of the

middle class, the elderly, and students. Clinton had very effectively played defense against the "Gingrich extremists" on Capitol Hill. But he needed something more.

As 1996 wore on, it became clear to House Democrats that our electoral interests did not always coincide with the Democratic president's. His proposed Medicare cuts in June 1995, his October 1995 comment in Houston that Congress pushed him to raise taxes too much in 1993, and his triangulation strategy did not sit well with most of us in the House Democratic caucus. With each incident it became more apparent that his reelection strategy might not necessarily help us regain the majority. It did not come as a terrific surprise, therefore, when the evidence began to accumulate that the president might really sign the Republican welfare bill, which most Democrats thought a disaster as well as an abandonment of Democratic principles.

In September 1995, while the Senate debated and passed the welfare bill overwhelmingly, it came to light that the Department of Health and Human Services was sitting on a report that showed that the Senate welfare bill would disqualify about one million children who were now receiving public assistance. And yet the Senate bill was markedly more moderate than the House bill.

During the Contract with America in early 1995, House Democrats had cobbled together a bill that dramatically changed welfare. *Every* House Democrat—northern liberals, southern conservatives, urban African Americans, suburban whites, rural Latinos—voted for the alternative to the "extremist" Republican bill. I remember asking several senior Democrats on the floor of the House if they had ever seen that kind of Democratic unity— *unanimity*—on any controversial bill. Never, they replied. Losing gets one's attention.

More than a few of us wondered why we did not do this when we were in the majority, especially since so many commentators had averred that, if the Democrats had passed a welfare bill instead of putting so many eggs in the health care reform basket, we would still be in control of the House. Being outnumbered focuses the mind, and being in the minority enforces discipline. Liberals and conservatives alike admitted, in moments of candor, that they could not have agreed on a controversial bill of this magnitude if they were actually writing the law.

Although Democrats had failed to pass a serious and comprehensive welfare reform bill by a vote of only 205 to 228, we all believed we could argue in the 1996 election that we had voted for real welfare reform, even if we voted against passage of the "punitive, extremist" bill that the Republicans would ultimately pass. We were convinced that, in most cases, Democratic votes against the Gingrich bill would not cause significant electoral problems.

Many of us argued that welfare reform was not about saving money—initially. Real welfare reform, with job training and job creation and child and health care, would at first cost more money. But in the end, with former welfare recipients in the workforce paying taxes, much more money would be saved. Republicans were using "welfare reform" as a cover, we asserted, simply to cut the budget; their plan would result in more poor children and more poverty. It would not reform welfare to make it work better for the poor or help the poor find jobs. But it would save $55 billion to be used for defense or deficit reduction or tax breaks for the rich or something else. One out of four American children under the age of six is poor—a number higher than in any other major Western democracy. Sixty-two percent of those poor children are sons and daughters of parents with jobs. The supplemental benefits and assistance that many of these families were receiving would also be cut under the Republican welfare plan.

In the past, conservative Republicans opposed welfare and expenditures on all kinds of services to the poor by saying taxpayers should not be forced to pay taxes to help people who refuse to work. Ronald Reagan built a career on public resentment of welfare cheaters, or "welfare queens," as he referred to them. Now, in an interesting twist, Republicans suggested that their major interest was helping the poor, that the system was creating more poverty and more poor people, that the system was trapping them, and that they—the Republicans—wanted to help. Their welfare bill would be *good* for the poor.

Anecdotes say one thing. Facts say something else. The Center on Budget and Policy Priorities, one of the few liberal think tanks in Washington, wrote that "federal and state anti-poverty programs have lifted millions of children and disabled and elderly people out of poverty." The poverty rate among the elderly in 1995 was 9 percent. Without Social Security and Medicare, the poverty rate among the elderly would have been 50 percent, and safety-net programs such as Aid to Families with Dependent Children and food stamps "reduced the child poverty rate from 24% before benefits to 16%." There would have been 57.6 million people in poverty in 1995 without the government safety net. But with "food stamps, housing assistance, school lunch support and benefits provided through the earned-income tax credit, the number of poor people drops to 30.3 million."

What happens without the safety net? States with historically low support for the poor have had, logically enough, an especially high number of indigent people. Texas, which has the distinction of providing the least to its citizens in Aid for Dependent Children, announced soon after the welfare bill was signed that the state would privatize the welfare delivery system. Officials in Texas (which, interestingly, has the second-highest adolescent birthrate in the nation while providing the lowest dollar amount per child) believed that the profit motive would allow Texas to take care of its poor just as well as they had in the past, and spend less money doing it. The state built into its bid process financial incentives for the private concern that wins the bid to spend less than Texas spent the previous year.

Democrats in the House thought a Clinton veto would not only be sustained in the House but also could be politically defended. Disabled children would be denied benefits; there were no provisions in the GOP bill for job creation and little funding for job and skills training; and one million children would be thrown off government assistance. The bill was another example, we contended, of Gingrich extremism.

In the original House-passed welfare bill, Republicans had moved toward repeal of the Earned Income Tax Credit (EITC), a tax break that saved about a thousand dollars in taxes for a family of four earning about $28,000 a year. Begun during the Nixon administration and expanded by President Ronald Reagan, who loved the idea and spoke glowingly of it, EITC to conservative Republicans seemed no longer to be of any use.

Republican hypocrisy on welfare and taxes, many of us asserted on the House floor, was especially grating. Cutting taxes on the wealthy (the average person making $200,000 a year would see their taxes reduced by about $12,000) while increasing taxes on the working poor (the average family earning $20,000 a year would pay an additional $500) was immoral. And they bragged about it!

In the summer of 1996, before the House voted on it a second time, and fifteen months after it passed the House the first time, President Clinton announced he would sign the welfare bill. He had vetoed two welfare bills that were significantly worse than this one. He had negotiated out the draconian EITC measures and some other profoundly egregious sections. A few days later, almost every Republican voted for it. Almost one hundred Democrats, half the caucus, voted for it, though many reluctantly because they had lost the president's "cover." Quite simply, voting "no" was very difficult to explain to a public that wanted welfare reform, especially when a

Democratic president signed it and spoke positively about it. Two Republicans voted against the bill.

When President Clinton signed the bill on July 31, 1996, he cited his 1992 campaign promise to "end welfare as we know it" and said the legislation was a good start. Congress in the next session, he said, would fix what was wrong with the bill. The statement was disingenuous. A conservative Congress wanted the punitive measures in the bill, and they were certainly not going to repeal what the president thought were its worst features. Veto the bill, children's advocates said, then agree to sign it after those parts are fixed. After the president signed the Republican welfare legislation, three high-ranking presidential appointees at the Department of Health and Human Services—Mary Jo Bane, assistant secretary for Children and Families; Wendell Primus, deputy assistant secretary for Human Services Policy; and Peter Edelman, assistant secretary for Planning and Evaluation, and a long-time friend of President and Mrs. Clinton—resigned.

Gingrich had won his biggest legislative victory! He had the accomplishment he wanted in 1996. With one stroke of the presidential pen, it had become immensely more difficult to convince the public that the Gingrich Republicans were extremists. After all, a Democratic president had said that Gingrich's bill was a good start.

That was only half the story. As 1996 wore on, the planets aligned themselves in such an unexpected and unpredictable way that Congress passed incremental health care reform, the Safe Drinking Water Act, and an increase in the minimum wage. An increase in the minimum wage? The Democrats had not done that in 1993–94. Majority Leader Armey said in early 1995 that he would fight a minimum wage "with every fiber of my being," and that it would "pass over my dead body." And some Republican freshmen publicly, vociferously, and unapologetically called for a repeal of the whole idea of a minimum wage. In March 1996, Republicans successfully blocked House consideration of the minimum wage bill; only seven Republicans voted with the Democrats to bring the legislation to the floor for a vote. Yet two days later, Clinton chided Republican lawmakers in his weekly radio address: "You need to know that a member of Congress who refuses to allow the minimum wage to come up for a vote made more money during last year's one-month government shutdown than a minimum wage–worker makes in a year."

As the year wore on, moderate Republicans were warning their leadership that Republicans needed to move more into the political mainstream.

And so eventually, Republican moderates and pragmatists were able to convince their conference to bring the minimum wage bill to the floor for a vote. To be sure, Democrats supported these bills—health care, safe drinking water, and minimum wage—in significantly higher numbers than did Republicans, but the Republicans were in the majority when those bills passed. And so they got at least some of the credit.

Gingrich's poll ratings were part of the reason. So was organized labor. Labor was targeting districts represented by vulnerable Republicans, mostly freshmen. Many of those districts had high union membership. The AFL-CIO ads, mostly about the minimum wage, accomplished three things: they built public support for the minimum wage, even in districts where the ads were not run; they weakened Republican incumbents, most of whom were already seen as vulnerable; and they made clear that labor was again a force to be reckoned with. The labor ads were effective enough that several Republicans, including Cleveland's Martin Hoke, cast their votes for the minimum wage increase even though, months before, they had taken a public position in opposition to it.

What really moved these bills were members' weekend trips home to our districts. Quit the silly political games and work together, we were told. Stop the partisanship and get something done. Republicans were hearing about Gingrich's unpopularity and the popularity of and general support for the minimum wage and about Medicare, the environment, and education. But what Republicans wanted least of all was to be labeled a "do-nothing Congress."

On August 2 an increase in the minimum wage passed the House, in spite of opposition by *all* the top GOP leadership. While Speaker Gingrich did not vote (Speakers abstain on most votes), Majority Leader Armey, Whip DeLay, Conference Chairman Boehner, and Ways and Means Chairman Archer all voted against it. One hundred sixty Republicans joined 193 Democrats (two Democrats, Ralph Hall and Pete Geren, both from Texas, voted against it) to enact the higher minimum wage.

The 354 to 72 vote did not come easy. The debate was lively. Conservative Republicans called it a payoff by Democrats to organized labor. They did not say why the 160 Republicans, most of whom labor was opposing in the November election, were voting for it. Many freshman Republicans were livid with their colleagues who voted for it. As I walked up the steps and into the House chamber to vote that day, I overheard several of the most conservative new Republicans talking to one another. "Get the names of the

Republican 'yeses'; we especially want the freshmen," one of them bitterly said. What might have fueled their anger was the fact that, with election day drawing nearer and freshmen always the most electorally vulnerable members of the House, a commanding majority of these new Republicans voted for the minimum wage increase, 43 to 27. That turnabout might have been the most remarkable and unexpected of all.

Health care reform also passed the House in the fall of 1996 and was enacted into law. While the legislation did not even approach the 1993 Clinton goal of providing universal health care coverage, the Kennedy-Kassebaum bill did make several important reforms: it provided for portability of health insurance so people could switch jobs and keep their insurance intact; it prohibited the denial of care based on a preexisting condition, thereby providing care to hundreds of thousands of Americans who were without health care coverage; it expanded deductibility to 40 percent (and ultimately, in ten years, to 80 percent) of health insurance premiums for self-employed people; and it placed volunteer health care providers under the employ (for malpractice insurance purposes only) of the United States Public Health Service. That was particularly important for the Lorain free clinic in my hometown. Several physicians and volunteers in my church, First Lutheran Church in Lorain, work at the Free Clinic, which over the years has had difficulties with legal protection for its health care providers. In addition, Congress passed and the president signed legislation that stops insurance companies from forcing new mothers out of maternity wards within twenty-four hours of delivery. Insurance companies, acclaimed by Gingrich as the GOP's most important source for money, were powerless to stop this new regulation, so in the end they did not even mount a significant effort against it.

Democrats and other moderate Republicans were pushing Republican leadership on the environmental front also. The Safe Drinking Water Act had not yet been reauthorized, and environmental groups, municipal water systems, and public health organizations were telling members of Congress of its importance.

So far, this Congress had, according to environmental groups, the worst environmental record of any Congress in memory. Environmentalists had been critical of the Democratic 103d (1993–94) Congress also, not for what it had done, but for what it had failed to do. Its accomplishments were too modest. This 104th Congress had literally no positive environmental achievements, its environmental critics contended, and a whole host of environmental debacles: partial repeal of the Clean Water Act, the antienvironmental riders on appropriations bills, cutbacks in EPA enforcement, risk assessment, regulatory reform. The League of Conservation Voters gave this Congress the lowest rating it had ever given any Congress in its twenty-five-year history. Like Armey and DeLay, Gingrich, throughout his eighteen-year career in the House, had been very close to the major polluters and had received lots of money from them.

In the late 1970s, my brother Charlie, then a young lawyer at the Federal Trade Commission, was visiting a friend in his D.C. neighborhood. He met a youngish, gregarious southerner who was running for Congress for the third time. Characterizing himself as a Rockefeller Republican, he had lost twice to a very conservative southern Democrat who had made the "Dirty Dozen" list, a group of twelve members of Congress chosen by the Sierra Club as having the worst records on environmental issues. Convinced he was a friend of the environment, Charlie wished the young candidate well.

The young candidate, Newt Gingrich, did not remain a Rockefeller Republican after that successful election. Nor did environmental groups long consider him an ally. But now, as Speaker, Gingrich knew that his party was in trouble on environmental issues. It was no accident that President Clinton, in almost every speech he made, mentioned the environment. Poll numbers showed an overwhelming public support for strengthening environmental laws and an increasingly negative public attitude toward Republicans for their position on environmental policies. Republican pollster Linda DiVall told the Republican conference that 55 percent of Republicans did not trust their own party to protect the environment (72 percent of Democrats trusted their party, she added). In late March 1996, Speaker Gingrich told CNN in an interview, "I think you're going to see us make a real effort to have a positive environmental message." His days of referring to the EPA as a "jobs-killing agency" were, at least for the time being, over. For Earth Day 1996, Gingrich instructed his members to "plant a tree" or visit a zoo or speak to a school or start a recycling project. *Time* ran a picture of Gingrich with a snake around his neck at the Columbus (Ohio) Zoo.

The deepest fissures in the Republican conference were caused by environmental issues. While as many as fifty of the less conservative members of the Republican conference would sometimes vote for environmental issues, others were proudly and defiantly "antienvironmentalist." Alaska

Republican Don Young, who was chairman of the Interior Committee, labeled environmentalists a "waffle-stomping, Harvard-graduating, intellectual bunch of idiots that don't understand they're leading this country into environmental disaster." Gingrich realized his party had a problem. The moderates realized it. Even Tom DeLay realized it, although he thought the bad press and the negative public reaction to Republican environmental policy were a result of media bias and the inability of Republicans to explain themselves better.

One of American politics' greatest myths is the conservative belief that there exists a monolithic "liberal media." Nominal liberals may still dominate among work-a-day reporters, at least in large newspapers, but most of these reporters bend over backward to hide any liberal leanings they may have—perhaps even going overboard from time to time in criticizing Democrats so they cannot be accused of bias. It is their responsibility to be fair, objective, and nonpartisan. Editors and publishers, however, have no such constraints. They are more likely to be conservative Republicans (especially the publishers who own the papers, which are large, profitable corporations) and are expected to state their positions on the issues of the day. Newspaper endorsements are overwhelmingly Republican in presidential and congressional races. In this century, only twice has a Democratic candidate for president received a majority of newspaper endorsements: Johnson in 1964 and Clinton in 1992. In other words, the liberals at the paper are charged with being objective. The conservatives are supposed to show their conservatism. By contrast, conservatives sit behind the microphones on almost all the talk radio shows and the Washington television shows, and they are frequently newspaper columnists.

So it seemed that Gingrich was listening to his moderate members on public reaction to the Republicans' stance on the environment. The Safe Drinking Water Act was awaiting action in the Commerce Committee. In 1994, Democrats, then in the majority, had crafted a strong, bipartisan bill with Dingell and Bliley as cosponsors, but the legislation had died when Congress adjourned. In 1995, Democrats, now in the minority, had been pushing majority Republicans to adopt legislation similar to the 1994 bipartisan bill. There was little response from Republicans.

Safe Drinking Water was the issue that Gingrich thought would best answer his environmental critics. Bliley was faced with the prospect of either convening his committee to take action on a moderate, bipartisan bill or seeing the House pass something resembling the generally pro-environment, bipartisan Senate bill without input from the House Commerce Committee. If there were no action from Bliley, Gingrich threatened to go directly to the floor of the House of Representatives.

Bliley had seen this before. Medicare was given to him with orders to pass it quickly with no amendments. Telecommunications was changed dramatically on the floor after a huge amount of work was done in committee on a balanced bill. In several other cases, the Commerce Committee (or other committees on other bills) was simply ignored by a very powerful Speaker who could get away with exercising his power that way. Bliley decided to pursue compromise legislation on Safe Drinking Water in the summer of 1996. Once that happened, the House moved forward quickly on the legislation, in a bipartisan way.

I had an amendment dealing with breast cancer that I thought would be difficult to get into the legislation, expecting some kind of partisan opposition. Kevin Brennan, my legislative director, approached the committee staff to discuss it, and Chairman Bliley accepted the amendment in the chairman's mark. (The chairman's mark is the substitute bill that the chairman brings to the committee to use as the vehicle to discuss the bill and mark it up. If language is included in the chairman's mark, the chances of its remaining as part of the bill are very good.) The amendment, written by Bart Stupak (D-Mich.) and me, required the Environmental Protection Agency to screen and test for estrogenic substances and other endocrine disruptors that may cause the immune system to malfunction, leading to cancer and genetic abnormalities. Many medical researchers believe these estrogenic substances are a major cause of breast cancer. Northeast Ohio has a particularly high incidence of breast and prostate cancers. The amendment stayed in the bill without opposition. The Safe Drinking Water Act, with our amendment attached to it, passed out of committee unanimously and passed the House by voice vote right before the August recess.

The last important issue Congress dealt with was the education budget. Many House Republicans, spearheaded by the most conservative of the conservative freshmen, wanted to reengage the budget battles. A May 8 memo from the House Republican conference, entitled "Talking Points: Republicans Unveil Balanced Budget," egged them on. Using such rhetoric as "failed, Washington-dictated Medicaid reform" and the "disastrous Washington status quo," the memo exhorted House Republicans to reject Clinton's budget "gimmicks," "accounting tricks," and "tax increases." They wanted to stand fast, even if it meant another showdown with the president.

But Republicans in the Senate had other ideas. Although criticized by House Republicans for caving in too quickly to President Clinton's and congressional Democrats' demands, Senate leader Trent Lott approved and pushed his House and Senate colleagues to support $6.5 billion in additional spending for education. Lott did not want to risk a presidential veto on the funding of education within six or seven weeks of the election. Education funding for the coming fiscal year, in this Republican, antieducation Congress, had been increased! Student loans, Head Start, the Drug-Free Schools program, Title I—all had gotten increases in their budget.

If graded by the goals that its leaders hoped to achieve at the beginning of the session, this Congress would rate as a failure. To be fair, though, its success at passing bipartisan legislation that affects people's lives was significant. It was no small irony that Congress's accomplishments of 1996 saved the Republican majority and that these accomplishments seemed to be mostly Democratic issues: an increase in the minimum wage; forcing insurance companies to allow new mothers to stay in hospitals for more than twenty-four hours; updating and strengthening the Safe Drinking Water Act; and forcing insurance companies to allow portability in their health care plans. Although these issues all passed with stronger Democratic than Republican support, the Gingrich majority was given some or much of the credit. The "extremist" label pinned adroitly by the Democrats on the Republicans in 1995 seemed to loosen and practically fall off by Election Day 1996.

It is interesting to contrast the Republicans' two years in the majority with the Democrats' last two years in the majority. The Democrats had a pretty good 1993 but an awful congressional session in 1994, the election year. The Republicans, to their great satisfaction, had, by and large, the reverse: a not particularly good 1995 but a pretty good 1996. It was not the revolution that the conservatives had promised, but bipartisan, incremental change for the better. The public seemed satisfied. For a few weeks, Republicans had acted like Democrats. And they had dodged the bullet.

16

The Campaign

It takes a lot of money to even get beat nowadays.
　—Will Rogers

Half the money you spend in a campaign is wasted. You just
don't know which half.
　—Courthouse politician, Mansfield, Ohio

You gotta stand for something or you'll fall for anything.
　—John Mellencamp

IT WAS A LONG WAY BACK FROM 1994. The Republicans, the commentators told the American people, were the new majority party, not just in Congress and the statehouses but in neighborhoods and small towns and suburbs and farm communities. *U.S. News and World Report* carried a cover story in November 1995 about the demise of the Democratic party under the headline "The Democrats: Is the Party Over?" "They know they're in trouble," the magazine said. "And it's even worse than they think." Five House Democrats became House Republicans in 1995. Even a book about the Democrats' coming back, written by E. J. Dionne, perhaps the best political analyst in Washington, was titled *They Only Look Dead*. There was a certain resignation among some of my Democratic colleagues, and a palpable euphoria among Republican members of Congress, that Democrats were a permanent minority.

Yet the Democrats *just* missed in 1996. Counting the Texas run-off elections, where Democrat Nick Lampson beat incumbent freshman Steve Stockman, House Democrats picked up ten seats, half the margin needed to win back the House. A switch of just twelve thousand votes apportioned in close races around the country would have meant a Democratic majority in the House. The articles about the demise of the Democratic party were forgotten.

Democrats had been optimistic throughout 1996, since the second government shutdown. Democratic caucuses were better attended than caucuses the year before. Members were enthusiastic about retaking the House. Poll numbers about both Gingrich and Democratic fortunes continued to look good throughout the year. Fundraising for individual members and for the Democratic Congressional Campaign Committee had improved significantly.

At almost every caucus, Minority Leader Gephardt would exhort us to stay on message. We were to remind voters of the government shutdown and Gingrich's complicity in it, of Medicare cuts to pay for tax breaks for the rich, and of cuts in student loans, education, and the environment. Immediately after the government shutdown and reopening, Gephardt told the caucus, "Return to our mantra," no Medicare cuts to pay for tax breaks for the rich. Gephardt or Democratic caucus chairman Vic Fazio, an eight-termer from California, often showed us poll numbers about how far we had come and historical facts and figures illustrating why we had a very good chance to win back the majority. In February the leadership prepared a series of charts under the heading "Building a Democratic Majority" and presented them at the caucus. Pointing out that Democrats needed a net gain of twenty seats to take back the House, party leaders outlined these facts:

Since 1946 the average swing per election cycle is twenty-four seats.

One party has gained twenty or more seats in twelve out of the twenty-five elections since World War II.

Landslide elections such as the 1994 midterm are regularly followed by an "adjustment," where the losing party one cycle reverses these losses in the next election.

Forty-two seats were won in 1994 by less than 5 percent of the vote.

Eighty-five seats were won in 1994 by less than 10 percent of the vote.

Republicans hold seventy-seven seats that Clinton carried in 1992.

Thirty-three Republican freshmen represent districts that Clinton carried; twenty-nine of these thirty-three were elected with 55 percent or less of the vote.

Gingrich's disapproval is higher than Nixon's when he resigned.

August 1974 — 66 percent Nixon; January 1996 — 70 percent Gingrich [Harris poll statistics]

The country has more confidence in Democrats on Key Issues [*Wall Street Journal* poll, December 1995]

Medicare (44%–24%)   Education (35%–25%)
Environment (45%–13%)   Protecting Middle Class (43%–24%)

Texas Democrat Martin Frost, the chairman of the Democratic Congressional Campaign Committee, talked to us about candidate recruitment, campaign research and planning, communications, and fundraising. At that point, Democrats had "a strong candidate in forty-eight of our top fifty-one races." In the two hundred congressional districts where the filing deadline had passed, there were Democratic candidates in all but three of them.

Frost told us that while Republicans had outraised us by millions of dollars, Democrats were doing better than ever before. Groups that refused to help Democrats in 1995 were changing their strategy as they saw the unpopularity of the Gingrich Congress. The DCCC had 68,000 more small contributors on file than twelve months earlier. More members of Congress had contributed to the DCCC by far than at any time in its history. What Democratic members must do, Gephardt explained, was what Republicans did when they were in the minority: raise money for their Republican challengers. Ranking members of committees and subcommittees had in 1994 been expected to raise the most, followed by members of exclusive committees—Appropriations, Ways and Means, and Commerce. All other Republicans, especially those in safe seats, were expected to give and raise several thousand dollars each.

Beginning as early as summer 1995, Democratic allies were engaged and energized for the first time in a long time. All the groups that were big losers under the Republican Congress were preparing for 1996. Senior citizens' groups were fighting back; many organized protests at congressional offices and spoke out at senior citizens' meetings. Environmental groups were mobilizing their members and their resources; they had been successful in grassroots lobbying in the Senate to stop the most egregious and far-reaching legislation. House Republicans' environmental agenda had stimulated an increase in the membership of groups like the Sierra Club, Friends of the Earth, and the Environmental Defense Fund. National civil rights organizations were rebuilding at the local levels, promising better voter registration efforts than ever before. And under the vigorous new leadership of the Service Employees International Union's John Sweeney, labor, which may have had the most at stake in 1996, was energized and enthusiastic. Sweeney was the first international AFL-CIO president to come from a service industry union; the first to come from a union with large numbers of public employees; and also the first to come from a union with a majority of female members—indications of the changes in the economy and the labor movement.

The foundation was laid for labor's involvement in House campaigns more than a year before the election. In the spring of 1995, as Congress's work on the Contract with America was drawing to a close, county labor federations, the umbrella organizations for local labor unions, invited their members of Congress—Democrats and Republicans—to one of their meetings. In Lorain County, the federation president, John Gallo, and others in the county's AFL-CIO asked me a series of questions about my voting record and how I stood on issues that might come in front of Congress in the months ahead: OSHA reform, minimum wage, health care, pension reform, Medicare, education. The thirty or so union activists at the meeting, each representing steelworkers or the American Federation of State, County and Municipal Employees (AFSCME) or the United Food and Commercial Workers (UFCW) or other locals, were involved, educated about the issues, and enthusiastic. They wrote down my answers and reported them to AFL-CIO political organizers in Washington.

The international unions in Washington, under Sweeney's leadership, went to work. It had been years since organized labor was recognized as a major political force and a feared opponent by such groups as the Chamber of Commerce and the National Association of Manufacturers. Sweeney's goal was to recapture the House and replace the antilabor Republican Congress with members more disposed to the positions of organized labor. Sweeney and organized labor pledged to spend $35 million in several dozen districts around the country to defeat incumbents who were unfriendly to labor. They announced that they would use grassroots organizers and paid television and radio primarily aimed at the most vulnerable House Republican freshmen and a smaller number of second-termers and veteran members of Congress. In their ads, the AFL-CIO encouraged viewers and listeners to call their congressional representative and express their displeasure with the member's vote or position on that issue. The first ad, which may have attracted more media attention than was actually spent on the media buy, warned the voters about the Republican cuts in Medicare and Medicaid. Later ads centered around the minimum wage, education, and pension reform.

Republicans were livid. They claimed the ads were distortions and lies. There was a concerted effort by Republican leadership in Washington to encourage each targeted member to go to local television stations and ask them not to run the ads. A few stations backed down and pulled the ads. It was one of the first times in American political history that a group of incumbents were subjected to concerted, organized criticism this far before an election. First-year Republicans were returning home each weekend to the negative environment that television advertising can create.

As Labor Day—the traditional kick-off for American political campaigns—came and went, Republicans remained concerned. Polls showed a persistent double-digit lead for Clinton-Gore. The generic congressional polls gave Democrats consistent leads as high as eight or nine points. Democratic activists—labor, minorities, environmentalists, women's groups—were energized. Although Dole's campaign spokespeople promised a stronger campaign and a November victory, and New York Republican Bill Paxon, the National Republican Congressional Committee (NRCC) chairman, predicted at least a fourteen-seat GOP gain, no one much believed them. There was little excitement from Dole's campaign, the enthusiasm from the Republican party faithful was tepid, and many Republican officeholders were starting to run from their presidential nominee.

On September 11, with one day's notice, Dole and running mate Jack Kemp came to Capitol Hill for a pep rally with Republican members of the House and Senate. Party officials knew that congressional Republicans were drifting away from the Dole effort, and Dole needed to bring them back. Meeting in the ornate Ways and Means hearing room in the Longworth House Office building, Dole recounted how he overcame adversity when he fought back after his World War II injury. He would fight back now with the same perseverance and prove the naysayers wrong. We're going to stick to the economic message, Dole reminded the Republican lawmakers; the 15 percent across-the-board tax cut is very popular with the American people, he insisted.

The response was less than overwhelming. *Washington Post* columnist Mary McGrory judged that the GOP pep rally "had little pep and less rally." Fewer than 120 (out of approximately 290) Republican senators and congressmen and congresswomen bothered to show up. A Republican colleague told me, "Everyone in the room was thinking about their own survival," no longer really concerned about propping up a presidential candidate who seemed to be going nowhere.

As election day approached, Republicans were especially troubled about voter turnout. They knew that a low turnout of Democrats in 1994 caused the Democrats to lose control of the House. Although turnout was almost always more of a problem for the Democrats than the Republicans, polls were showing that more self-identified Republicans were going to stay home than self-identified Democrats. To compound their turnout problems, Republicans in Congress were hearing that the Dole campaign was pulling out of key congressional states such as California, New Jersey, and Ohio. Although the denials were immediate and vehement, Republicans remembered the 1992 decision by George Bush's campaign to pull out of California, which may have cost the Republicans two or three seats in Congress that year. Dole's writing off the nation's largest state would mean a weaker grassroots effort on behalf of all Republicans, fewer presidential candidate and surrogate visits and the attendant free media, and less paid television time promoting the Republican message. Even though Dole did not "pull out" of any of the three states, the damage was done. In Ohio, Democrats donned Gingrich and Dole masks and threw a going-away party—complete with champagne and balloons—for Dole and his campaign.

Dispirited Republicans, and the turnout problems that a somnolent and lethargic presidential campaign brought, did not, however, necessarily translate into positive things for House Democrats. Presidential coattails did not seem to be as prominent as they had in earlier elections (almost every state has outlawed voter machines where voters could, with one lever, cast a vote for every Democrat or Republican on the ballot). Many House Democrats believed, at least until very late in the fall campaign, that Clinton was indifferent to electing a Democratic House. Others thought he wanted a Democratic House but that he believed that his triangulation strategy—in a sense, running against Republicans and Democrats in Congress—helped him win, and he was unwilling to alter that strategy. Still others grumbled that the president actually wanted a Republican Congress; after all, his comeback and newly found electoral strength came from confrontation with Gingrich and the conservative House of Representatives.

Before October, the president had given and raised relatively little money for House Democrats. Moreover, many Democrats thought that his strategy of signing the welfare bill and pursuing a bipartisan legislative agenda in the summer of 1996 undermined our chances of retaking the House. In caucus after caucus, Democrats of all political stripes were asking why the president was not helping.

But by mid-October, Bill Clinton began helping Democrats—with money, campaign appearances, and the grassroots "coordinated campaign." More cynical House members believed that his sudden interest in helping was that a Democratic House and Senate would be easier on him in a second term; Republican committee chairpersons would continue to hold hearings on Whitewater and any other potential political or legal problems. A high voter turnout, especially if it were coupled with a fairly low Republican turnout at the polls, would likely mean substantial gains in House seats and an easy takeover of the House by the Democrats. In the last two weeks before the election, the president came to the Cleveland area twice—partly for himself, partly for Democratic challengers Dennis Kucinich (who defeated second-termer Martin Hoke) and Tom Coyne (who lost to freshman Steve LaTourette), and partly for fundraising, but mostly for voter turnout.

Senator Dole was trying to pump up voter turnout, too. He went on a ninety-six-hour marathon campaign swing into more than a dozen states with big electoral votes and numerous close congressional races. His more-or-less sleepless full-court press on the campaign's last four days seemed to energize Republican faithfuls in many key Senate and House races. Republican congressional candidates, including incumbents, seemed more willing—even eager—to appear on stage with their rejuvenated nominee.

Thirty days before the election, Democrats' chances of winning control of the House looked strong. Poll numbers showed large numbers of freshmen and vulnerable second-term Republicans with less than 50 percent of the vote. (In answer to the question "If the election for Congress were today, would you vote for John Smith, the Republican, or Jane Jones, the Democrat?" poll numbers indicated that less than 50 percent was a danger sign for incumbents. Unlike previous years, undecideds in the 1990s seemed to break in overwhelming numbers, sometimes five or six to one, against the incumbent. When my 1994 poll numbers consistently showed me at about 43 percent to 29 percent, I sensed, as did the national Republicans who were polling, that I was in trouble. Most incumbents who were in that situation lost.) Clinton's double-digit lead was holding steady, and Democratic challengers, while being outspent, seemed to be holding their own on television with at least adequate buys. The generic poll question was consistently giving Democrats a four- to eight-point lead. It appeared that Democrats had succeeded in "nationalizing" the elections almost as well as the Republicans had in 1994.

Republican interest groups—the NRA, the Christian Coalition, National Right to Life—were not as organized or active as they had been two years earlier. The one big exception to that may have been the National Federation of Independent Businesses. In my race in 1994, my opponent announced with great fanfare an endorsement of the NFIB, an organization of 600,000 business people. It gave him credibility, mailing lists, and some money. Until the fall of 1994, most politicians thought of it as a politically inert organization that served its membership well but engaged in little electoral activity. That changed in 1994. And then in 1996 an even more active NFIB chose 250 candidates to assist. With a campaign war chest of some $3.5 million, the NFIB contributed $5,000 to many of them, provided campaign training to NFIB members in targeted districts, sent letters to the approximately fifteen hundred NFIB members in the district, and helped organize get-out-the-vote efforts. My 1996 opponent, one of those they helped, was head of the NFIB in Ohio. Because of his leadership in small business issues, I had appointed him to the White House Conference on Small Business in 1994.

My campaign actually began in the fall of 1995. For less than $15,000, I ran a couple of weeks of cable television ads about Republican efforts to privatize Medicare. I also wanted to remind voters that I kept my promises in my first term and was doing the same this term. In my 1994 race, our "Promises Made, Promises Kept" theme recalled the specific commitments from 1992. I promised to continue to fight Republican budget priorities—which included increased military spending, cuts to Medicare and student loans, tax cuts for the wealthy—in the next Congress. The unspoken message to a potential opponent (the deadline for filing for declaration of candidacy was in January) was that if you think the "Medicare and education cuts to pay for tax breaks for the rich" was a major theme in 1994, you ain't seen nothing yet. A prospective opponent could not help but notice that my campaign had more than a quarter of a million dollars in the bank. We also targeted various constituencies in a variety of ways, aiming especially at potential opponents.

No doubt I was on the Republican target list. My naivete of 1993, tempered by the election of 1994, had hardened into the reality of 1995. Only half a dozen Democrats won in 1994 with less than 50 percent of the vote, surely not a sign of impervious electoral strength and political invincibility.

National Republicans began their recruiting early, again asking my 1994 opponent Greg White to try again. No thank you, he said. His county prosecutor term was up, and he would have to give up his office to run this time. They asked, without success, Geauga County prosecutor David Joyce, a friendly, popular Republican who told me two years earlier, "How can I come from here in Geauga County and beat you when I have to spot you twenty-five or thirty thousand votes in Lorain County?" They also spoke with State Representative Diane Grendell, also from Geauga County, who would have had to give up her seat in the Ohio General Assembly to run. She declined also. In the end, the NRCC recruited no one. So often, an election is decided before the filing deadline. Four Republicans did step forward, though none was taken especially seriously by the NRCC. Each was on his own in the primary. None of the four candidates—a retired policeman, a manufacturers representative who ran against me as an independent in 1994 and got 4 percent of the vote, the owner of a trucking company, and a Perot organizer—had ever held partisan elected office. None raised more than $20,000 in the primary. At least one newspaper, the *Elyria Chronicle-Telegram,* then a down-the-line Republican newspaper, refused to endorse any of the four in the primary. Eight months later, and for the first time in my career, the *Chronicle-Telegram* endorsed me. It was one of those we-don't-much-like-Brown-but-we-guess-he's-better-than-the-other-guy kinds of endorsements.

The winner of the Republican primary was Kenneth Blair, who owned a trucking company in Newbury, a small community in Geauga County. He had served on the elected board of education in Newbury for twenty-four years and had just helped to settle a difficult labor-management situation and avoid a strike in that school system. Although Blair had a debt from the primary and was apparently not getting much help from the NRCC, I ran a full-blown campaign, hiring two full-time staff people and organizing a large-scale grassroots effort. We worked closely with the Clinton-Gore coordinated campaign, renting a headquarters jointly. We had volunteer coordinators in the district's seven counties and ran Lorain County's effort out of our Lorain city campaign headquarters. Our coordinators—Alex Kish and Kathie Johnson in Trumbull County, Gary Pierce in Portage County, Jill Adam in Cuyahoga County, and Anne Eisenhower (the grandniece of the president!) in Medina County—handed out campaign literature at football games, worked on parades, organized door-to-door efforts, made speeches at events I could not attend, put up yard signs, and did all the other activities that a grassroots effort suggests. We also piggybacked with several local candidates, including Prosecutor Dean Holman in Medina, Mike Ross in Lorain, Sheriff Red Simmons and Joanna Davison in Geauga, and Jeff Snell (my campaign manager in 1994) in Summit.

We pulled back our network television buy at the last minute, after we were sure that my opponent was not in a position to purchase any appreciable amount of television. My political consultant who bought our media,

Bill Burges, checked regularly with Cleveland's television stations to make sure that Blair had not surprised us with a large network buy. My campaign did purchase a fair number of cable television and radio spots. On the entire campaign we spent about $300,000. The final returns showed me with 60 percent, Blair with 36 percent, and David Kluter, the Natural Law party candidate, with 3 percent.

The last two or three weeks spelled trouble for the Democrats nationally, as the president's fundraising practices became the focus of hundreds of news stories. Kevin Phillips wrote in *Time* after the election, "Until President Clinton handed his opponents a windfall of October campaign finance scandals, the Democrats seemed headed toward re-claiming the House." The issues that had dominated the campaign were pushed aside by stories about campaign finance. Democrats running for Congress were forced to share the bad publicity that washed over all Democrats. Equally important, the momentum Democrats were enjoying seemed to dissipate.

While Clinton's and the Democratic National Committee's fundraising captured the media's attention, Republicans actually outraised the Democrats by a significant margin in the 1995–96 election cycle, $399 million to $242 million. A president's fund-raising almost always attracts more attention than does his challengers', and this president's alleged use of the White House especially piqued the media's attention. The pressure on the DNC to raise huge amounts of money was increased when Clinton directed it to spend $2.5 million to air two television ads on crime in key states in June 1995, almost certainly earlier than any presidential candidate in history. The ads were run only a couple of months after the president was stressing his "relevance."

Later in the year, the party spent $15 million on an ad campaign on the budget, defending Democratic positions on Medicare and education. That ad campaign, greeted with enthusiasm on Capitol Hill, buttressed the Democrats during the government shutdown and undoubtedly played a role in strengthening the president and Democrats in Congress as election year 1996 began.

Democrats believed they needed to spend money early to set the tone of the debate and to define the political agenda for the election. Although the National Education Association (the nation's largest teachers' organization) and AFL-CIO spent considerable amounts in key races in the last couple of weeks, they had to spend much of their money early to weaken Republican incumbents. Corporations, however, outspent labor unions by an almost seven-to-one margin: $242 million to $35 million. The Republican National Committee funneled millions of dollars to various interest groups that were ideological soul mates. One group, Americans for Tax Reform, received from the RNC some $4.5 million, using it for mailings, phone banks, and other grassroots activities in support of the Republican message. And ads warning of an unshackled Clinton with a liberal Democratic Congress played over and over. They reminded voters how bad the Democrats were in the past and painted a tax-and-spend picture of the future. Conservative newspapers ran stories about the "ultra-liberal" chairmen that Democrats would select. Democrats would increase taxes, cut national defense, and undo welfare reform. The liberals in the Democratic leadership, their radio ads told us, would bring back health care reform, perhaps a bureaucratic, single-payer system. One Republican National Committee mailing asked, "What would a Democratic Congress look like? Look LEFT." Republican mailings and ads cited the liberal credentials of Gephardt, Bonior, Obey, and Rangel, and the *Wall Street Journal* editorial page followed suit. Or maybe the *Wall Street Journal* cited the Democratic leaders' liberal credentials, and Republican mailings followed suit. The heir apparent Democratic Ways and Means chairman Charlie Rangel felt compelled to respond in October: "It is impossible [that we] could even contemplate putting tax increases on the boards."

In an unprecedented move, the national Republicans spent $200,000 to run radio ads in eight West Coast and Rocky Mountain states on election day (even as late as afternoon drive-time!) encouraging ticket splitting: "Some say the early returns back East mean we don't need to vote today. But we have too much at stake to let easterners decide our state's elections. . . . Don't let the media stop you from voting, and don't hand Bill Clinton a blank check." An especially bad election for the Republicans in the eastern time zone—Democrats picked up seats in Maine, Massachusetts (two seats), Connecticut, New York, New Jersey, North Carolina (two), Ohio (two), and Michigan, while losing only one, in Kentucky—was in part reversed in the West.

The last two weeks made the difference, even more than they usually do in an election. Voters who made up their minds more than a month in advance, according to exit polls, supported Democrats in congressional races 51 percent to 47 percent. Voters who decided in the last two to four weeks voted for Democrats 51 percent to 48 percent. Those who made up their minds in the last week favored Republicans 53 percent to 44 percent, and those in the last three days went for Republicans 55 percent to 41 percent. Two weeks before the election, Democrats and Republicans polled even on the question of ethics; on election day, Republicans were ahead by fifteen percentage points. On personal responsibility, Republicans gained 7 percent in the last two weeks. The actual vote on election day was split almost evenly between Republicans and Democrats.

Retirements badly hurt the Democrats as well. Of the thirteen previously Democratic House seats that elected Republicans in 1995, ten were contests to fill the seat of a retiring Democrat, mostly from the South. The Democratic incumbent would likely have held onto almost all of them.

In the end, voter turnout was abysmal, probably worse for Democrats than Republicans. Among a few groups, it was higher than in 1992. Hispanic turnout was higher, which helped oust California Republican Bob Dornan, who was defeated by Latina Loretta Sanchez. Labor turnout was up, which was crucial in Dennis Kucinich's defeat of Martin Hoke in Ohio. And of the new voters from 1994 to 1996, 78 percent never went to college and 72 percent made less than $50,000 a year; House Democrats won that group by 17 percent. Overall, only 49 percent of eligible Americans went to the polls, a drop of 6 percent from 1992.

Labor obviously fell short of its goal. Branded as one of the big losers in the 1996 elections by much of the "chattering class," the political pundits and commentators on the Washington talk-show circuit, labor failed in its mission of defeating an antilabor Congress. But its defenders argue that labor could not have done much more. Most of the defeats of Republican incumbents were in large part attributable to organized labor's early television ads, grassroots efforts, and get-out-the-vote programs. Without concerted targeting by the AFL-CIO, Democrats would probably not have gained any seats.

By election day, the unions' most concerted efforts had been aimed at forty-five Republican incumbents; they succeeded in defeating nineteen of them. Dennis Kucinich and Ted Strickland, Ohio Democrats who beat Republican incumbents, both told me that they would not have won without the early media efforts of the AFL-CIO. The ads, run for several months before the election, "softened up" Republican incumbents, exposing their votes and records on pension reform, Medicare, and minimum wage. So while Kucinich's opponent, Congressman Martin Hoke, and Strickland's opponent, Congressman Frank Cremeans, outspent the Democratic challengers by at least a factor of two, labor spending gave the challengers an opportunity to run competitively.

In addition, the Congress of 1996 was so different from the Congress of 1995 in large part because of labor's involvement. The minimum wage bill passed Congress and was signed by the president, something no one could have predicted would happen following the 1994 elections. Health care was reformed, albeit incrementally, but the new laws governing preexisting conditions and portability made a difference in the lives of several million people. And improving education became a part of the congressional agenda. The year after the GOP slashed education funding, vulnerable Republicans were hammered on television and at town meetings about those cuts. As a result, Congress appropriated a $6-billion increase in education funding just before we adjourned for the 1996 election campaign. Not only did labor help set the congressional table for some of its issues to be enacted, but many of labor's issues became part of the 1996 presidential and congressional campaigns.

Finally, the Washington political establishment now took notice of organized labor. Labor's decline in membership, its calcified leadership, its inability to turn out its vote for endorsed candidates all enabled Republicans and the media to write off the trade union movement, in most areas of the country, as a force in American electoral politics. When Republican National Committee chairman Haley Barbour and executives at the U.S. Chamber of Commerce and the National Association of Manufacturers lambasted the "labor bosses" and accused them of trying to buy the elections, it warmed labor leaders' hearts. Unions now believed they could again compete with the big boys in Washington.

Even though they were outspent by corporate America by as much as seven to one, labor won nineteen of their forty-five targeted races, a percentage much better, AFL-CIO political director Steve Rosenthal argued, than the typical 10 percent success rate that challengers usually experience against incumbent members of Congress. Labor's voter turnout was higher, and labor union members voted more Democratic. In 1992 union households represented 19 percent of the electorate; in 1994 that number declined to only 14 percent; but in 1996, with labor's media advertisements and grassroots efforts, labor union households represented 22 percent of voters. And in this election, labor union members voted 62 percent to 35 percent for the Democratic candidate, while the rest of the electorate voted 53 percent to 45 percent Republican.

Among white males, the core of the Republican party, the numbers were even more pronounced: nonunion white men voted Republican for Congress 64 percent to 36 percent; white men who belonged to unions voted for the Democrat for Congress 61 percent to 39 percent (taking out the small percentage of independents in each case). Those results show the success, both that year and years past, of labor's efforts to educate and politicize its members. Republican anger toward labor's involvement and their threats of legislative retribution underscore one thing: Republicans fear a rejuvenated labor movement with the resources, expertise, desire, and track record to win elections. As Clarence Monin, international president of the Brotherhood of Locomotive Engineers, told me on a plane from Washington to Cleveland in December 1996, "We're going to do more next time."

But in the end, labor was unable to change the Congress that they believed was the most antilabor in recent political history. They tried to overthrow the leader, Newt Gingrich, whom they had demonized. And as Ralph Waldo Emerson said, "If you are going to attack the king, you better kill him." There would be a price to pay by this reelected Republican Congress. Even moderate Republicans with significant labor constituencies in their districts warned after the election that labor would be a target in the 105th Congress. Labor already thought it had been.

The most surprising numbers from the 1996 election returns came from voters over sixty years of age. In 1994, the most Republican year in at least a couple of generations, older Americans voted for Republican candidates for Congress by only two percentage points, 51 percent to 49 percent (if one takes out independent votes). Two years later, after months and months of talk about Medicare and Medicaid, Republicans again won among voters sixty and over, 51 percent to 49 percent. Democratic gains, which enabled us to pick up ten seats, came from younger voters, especially eighteen to thirty year olds. Democrats had actually led among elderly voters in polls earlier in the year by as much as sixteen percentage points. So what happened?

First, Medicare was never the major thrust of the president's message; in most of his speeches it was lumped in with Medicaid, education, and the environment. The presidential standard-bearer normally carries the party's message, not the three or four hundred cacophonous voices of congressional candidates, no matter how hard we are trying to stay on message. In the spring of 1996, noticing that poll results showed our lead among the elderly slipping to the low single digits, I asked Minority Leader Gephardt why. "They're not hearing it. You're not saying it. We've got to say it every day. They have to hear it every day." Pretty clearly, America's elderly did not hear it every day.

The president's campaign finance problems, with the accusations of Indonesian and Chinese money in his campaign, pushed the Democratic message off the front pages and off the six o'clock news during the last two weeks of the campaign. When my daughters and I attended a presidential rally in Cleveland on the day before the election—the first joint appearance, I believe, since the Democratic Convention, of the president, vice president, the First Lady, and Mrs. Gore—Clinton continued to emphasize the same message of Medicare, Medicaid, education, and the environment. But the media were more interested, as they were everywhere else around the country, in the Indonesian money issue. The message about Medicare was not being heard in the closing days of the campaign.

Second, many editorial writers, as usual, were endorsing mostly Republican candidates, siding with the GOP on the Medicare debate, and accusing Democrats of demagoguing the issue. They ignored the fact that today's self-proclaimed saviors of Medicare were opposed to its very existence for most of the past three decades: Gerald Ford and Bob Dole in the 1960s, and Bob Dole bragging about it thirty years later; the chairman of the Health Subcommittee of Ways and Means and the House majority leader saying in this session of Congress that Medicare is socialism and unnecessary in a free society. Even some papers with moderately liberal reputations, like the *Washington Post,* had been critical of Democrats on Medicare, calling Democrats' opposition to the Gingrich plan "Mediscare." Some newspapers concentrated on the dollar differences between the Clinton and Gingrich plans, calling them minimal or inconsequential, seemingly unaware of Republican long-term attempts to privatize a system that has worked to insure thirty-seven million mostly low- and moderate-income senior citizens. More conservative papers, such as the *Cleveland Plain Dealer,* were worse. Their editorial writers regurgitated a report from "nonpartisan and partisan experts" (whoever they were, since the paper did not identify them) that Medicare shortfalls would amount to as much as "$2.7 trillion—that's *trillion*—a year." Now *that's* "Mediscare."

Third, most voters over sixty could not fathom that any elected official would dare touch their Medicare. They were already on Medicare. Who would possibly take it away from them? Others figured Clinton had saved the program during the government shutdown. It was of more concern, though, to voters in their fifties. Watching the debate, they were less sure that Medicare would be there for them when they retired.

Fourth, Republicans effectively confused the issue. Ohio Republican Frank Cremeans filmed a commercial of his very elderly, frail father with his freshman congressman son asking, "Would I vote to cut my dad's Medicare?" Republicans ran ads informing the voters that they had increased spending on Medicare, citing dollar amounts but ignoring medical inflation and the increasing number of patients over sixty-five years of age. The issue was further—and very purposely and purposefully—clouded by several front groups the Republicans established to "help protect Medicare." These groups, funded by ultraconservative think tanks, foundations, and insurance companies, rated members of Congress on their votes to "protect and preserve" Medicare. Typically, Republican congressmen and congresswomen were rated 100 percent, while Democrats usually earned a big fat zero. At least two of these groups—the United Senior Association (USA), directed by David Keene, who was chairman of the American Conservative Union; and the Seniors Coalition, chaired by former Idaho Republican senator Steven Symms, who was one of the Senate's most conservative members and who had never in his Senate career shown any special affinity for Medicare— each had enough money to mail extensively to senior citizens, showing those voters that it was the Republicans who want to save Medicare. Democrats were using "Mediscare tactics" to get votes, they advised. And dozens of Republicans were presented with "Guardians of Medicare" awards for their "work in protecting and preserving Medicare," with photographs and news releases sent to local papers in the congressman's district replete with glowing comments from national senior citizen leaders.

In the end, older Americans mainly cast their votes based on other issues. The clash of accusations, ratings, and television ads apparently confused voters enough that Medicare meant little on election day.

The Republicans held onto the House majority with little room to spare. After the Texas special elections in December, where the Democrats picked up one more seat, the GOP controlled the House of Representatives 225 to 209, the smallest congressional majority for any party in over six decades; one independent, Bernie Sanders from Vermont, almost always lined up with the Democrats. Leaders in both parties extolled the virtues of bipartisan cooperation, heralding a new era of American government. We'll be able to work together, gushed almost everyone, just like we did in the summer of 1996. Voters, after all, asked for a bipartisan government. Clinton was rehired, the chattering class told us, to check the Republican extremists in the House. Republicans in the House and Senate were reelected to curb the "liberal impulses" of a second Clinton term.

A closer analysis of the election returns casts an interesting light on their meaning. According to exit polls, only one out of seven voters went into the voting booths and chose to do what we all, in the aggregate, actually did: vote for Clinton as president and a Republican for Congress. Clinton voters cast ballots overwhelmingly for Democrats for Congress. Dole voters chose Republicans for Congress by huge percentages. Perot voters divided their votes but gave Republicans an edge. Most voters, it is clear from those numbers, want their views, their party, and their philosophy represented in all branches of government. A relatively small number of people kept it from happening. The hortatory comments of the Republican National Committee changed few minds, and the radio ads warning of total Democratic control persuaded few independents to cast a vote for Clinton for president and a Republican for Congress.

Before the ink was dry on the Texas run-off election ballots, ethics problems again began to swirl around Newt Gingrich. The Speaker, already weakened by his unpopularity in the great majority of congressional districts around the country, was weakened further by his admission of guilt to the bipartisan Ethics Committee. He had previously been cited for six other violations, something that had never happened to a sitting Speaker of the House in the history of the United States Congress. He was hit with an unprecedented $300,000 penalty, further eroding his reputation with the public and his stature with his colleagues. While still a big draw on the fundraising and rubber chicken circuit, Gingrich would no longer have total control of the Republican message and agenda.

Republican committee chairs were already sitting up to take notice. At no time since Speaker Joseph Cannon had a Speaker wielded the kind of power over his committee chairmen as Gingrich did. In 1995, much important legislation simply bypassed committee debate and went straight to the floor. Other legislation was significantly changed—unilaterally by the Speaker and his advisory group—after a committee passed it. Some legislation, unchanged by amendments, was passed in committee under direct and strict orders from the Speaker. Even more irksome to committee chairs in the 104th Congress, task forces had been formed perhaps to someday replace the committee structure.

Those days were over. Too many Republicans had lost or barely won because they had been too closely identified with Newt Gingrich. With the Speaker hobbled with bad polls and ethics problems, committee chairs began to assert themselves. Most of the task forces would be abolished. The committees would again write their own bills. Committees would no longer be bypassed for immediate floor votes. When the leadership would try, threats of defeating the bill on the floor sent the Speaker a message. Committee chairs would be able to resist orders from the leadership. The Speaker's power was further diminished when a number of House Republicans, led by Majority Whip Tom DeLay and GOP boy wonder Bill Paxon, tried unsuccessfully to depose him. At Washington's National Airport, DeLay's celebration of victory was a bit premature. Hanging up the phone in the Continental Airline's President's Club on the evening of the coup after he thought he had overthrown the Speaker, he gave high-fives to his staff. Later that evening, he found out he was on the wrong side of history.

The 105th Congress would be more of a group effort. It is unlikely that a majority party will entrust their Speaker with the kind of power that Newt Gingrich had in 1995 for a long, long time—if ever again.

17

The 105th Congress

I am a genuine revolutionary. If you are a bureaucrat in the welfare state, or you're a trial lawyer, or you're a genuine left-winger, or you're a professional Democrat, I am your opponent. Of course you don't like me.

—Newt Gingrich

THE NEW 105TH REPUBLICAN CONGRESS, more chastened than its revolutionary predecessor, convened in January 1997 with significantly more modest goals. Many of its members, including Speaker Gingrich, had learned the sobering lessons taught them during election year 1996: don't overreach, don't propose weakening environmental laws, don't tear apart the social service safety net, do support public education, do work with the president. GOP leaders and committee chairs understood that to remain in power, the zeal and extreme ideology of the Republican far Right had to be checked and tempered. But many others, especially the most rabid of the 1994 freshmen Republicans, saw something very different. Only a handful of their classmates had lost their bids for reelection; their intense dislike of President Clinton had not abated; and in their districts their exaggerated antigovernment rhetoric still was received with enthusiasm by their partisan audiences.

To this group, the performance of the Republican Congress in 1996 was pathetic; their leaders and many of their GOP colleagues had caved in to environmentalists, teachers, labor unions, and social service advocates. Congressional passage of a higher minimum wage, increased funding for schools, legislation to provide health insurance for five million poor children, and patient protections had infuriated House conservatives. They wanted less government involvement, not more. And their colleagues' refusal to provide major tax cuts for the wealthiest taxpayers and repeal environmental and worker safety laws was unforgivable.

As far as the extremists were concerned, 1997 was a loss, too. Congress passed, bipartisanly and with a presidential signature, a balanced budget agreement that was too full of compromises. The Senate approved a chemical weapons treaty. Congress named a government office building in New York for the late commerce secretary Ron Brown. And a Republican Congress had renewed authorization for the National Endowment for the Arts. But voters seemed relatively happy that some things they liked were getting done: the balanced budget, increased aid to education, modest health care reform. And some things the public didn't like were stopped: elimination of the Department of Education, weakening of environmental laws, major cuts in Medicare.

In my subcommittee—the Commerce Committee's Health and Environment subcommittee, of which I had been elected ranking Democrat in January 1997—we passed some important legislation, most notably a bill to extend health care coverage to several million uninsured poor and working-class children, on which freshman Colorado Democrat Diana DeGette did yeoman's work. But the 150 or so hard-line GOP conservatives were angry. In their districts, which were mostly very conservative and overwhelmingly Republican, they believed that the revolution was not really over. They had decidedly and collectively misread the national electorate. The anti-Washington, anti-Democrat, anti-incumbent fervor had been building up long before the 1994 elections. The peak of support for conservative Republican policies had been reached somewhere between November 1994 and the government shutdown a year later. The wave had crested, and support for extreme Republican antigovernment ideas had waned. The public had tired of the GOP mantra of tax cuts, smaller government, higher defense spending, and devolution to the states.

However, the Democratic president, weakened by another sex scandal, had offered the country a host of ideas, programs, and policies, taking the country in the direction that he and congressional Democrats thought the country should go: a raise in the minimum wage, a patients' bill of rights, Medicare expansion, and proposals on education and child care. Democrats needed to get back to their core values.

In his 1998 State of the Union speech—particularly difficult because of the latest sex scandal—President Clinton reached back to recount the successes of his five-year presidency. The budget, passed in 1993 with, as he pointed out, no Republican votes, set the stage for five years of uninterrupted economic growth: 14 million new jobs; the lowest unemployment rate in twenty-four years; a deficit shrinking from $290 billion to near zero; inflation at its lowest level in thirty years. One need only look back to the big issues of the Congress of 1993–94, during President Clinton's first two years in office, to see where the country had moved. All four issues discussed in earlier chapters—the budget, crime, NAFTA, and health care—played a major role in the Republican takeover of Congress. In 1998 all four were still very much in play, both in terms of public policy and in the struggle for control of the House.

The president's 1993 budget, by almost any measure, was a success. The good things—employment, jobs, economic growth—were up; the bad things—inflation, unemployment, poverty, the budget deficit—were down. And the stock market had continued its upward spiral throughout his presidency. Republican critics like Texan Dick Armey had warned the nation that the Clinton budget "is a job killer. . . . The economy will sputter along. . . . It will be a disaster for the performance of the economy." Echoing his leader's words about jobs, Ohio Republican John Kasich chastised House Democrats, "Do you know what? This is your package. We will come back here next year and try to help you when this puts the economy in the gutter. . . . This plan will not work. If it was to work, then I'd have to become a Democrat." Republicans, none of whom voted for the Clinton budget in either house, were considerably less vocal five years later.

The president's health care initiative had fallen flat in the 1993–94 Congress. Critics, especially health insurance companies, had warned that the government health care plan would set up huge health care bureaucracies, take away physician choice, cause administrative costs to balloon, and interfere with the patient-doctor relationship. Their words were prescient. Only it was not the government but the health insurance companies themselves that created these huge bureaucracies and interfered in the doctor-patient relationship. And the number of uninsured Americans continued to increase, from about thirty-seven million in 1993 to forty-one million in 1998. Congress had taken small steps since 1994 to address some of the problems of access to health care services. Legislation passed prohibiting "drive-through deliveries" for new mothers and infants. (Soon after I was elected as ranking Democrat on the Health and Environment subcommittee, I told an Ohio reporter that I was going to introduce legislation to prohibit "drive-through mastectomies" to stop HMOs from prematurely discharging women who have undergone radical breast surgery. His story read: "Ohio Democratic Congressman Sherrod Brown, the new ranking Democrat on the

Health and Environment Subcommittee, plans to introduce legislation to prohibit drive-by vasectomies." Several callers to our office that day suggested that vasectomies could be done on an outpatient basis but that obviously Brown has never had one.) The Children's Health initiative provided health care coverage to those children, most in working families, who had none before. And the president, Congressman Pete Stark (D-Calif.), and I were suggesting the expansion of Medicare in a voluntary, pay-for-itself program for people between the ages of fifty-five and sixty-five. But we had fallen far short of the goal of covering those millions of uninsured.

Crime was down in every major category. It surely had something to do with an improving economy and lower unemployment and because of crime-fighting efforts in state and local governments. The president's Crime Bill of 1994, always a bit oversold, undoubtedly had some impact. The assault weapons ban, the prevention aspects of the bill, and the community policing provisions all contributed to the lower national crime rate. The community policing program, part of the president's proposal to put 100,000 police on the streets, surely made a difference in my district as well as in hundreds of others around the country.

The North American Free Trade Agreement, passed by Congress in a close vote in 1993, was the first time that a president had to fight hard in Congress for a trade initiative. For decades, Congress and the American people were not engaged in trade debates; typically, a few members of Congress on the Ways and Means Committee, major corporate law firms in Washington, and the administration's trade officials would negotiate trade agreements and shepherd them through Congress with little opposition from the public or Congress. Few took much notice.

Perhaps the most notable and newsworthy achievement of the 105th Congress was a nonachievement: the derailing of the president's Fast Track trade legislation. After many delays, Speaker Gingrich scheduled a vote on legislation to extend NAFTA to other nations in Latin America in early November 1997. Virtually all of America's economic elite had lined up with Gingrich and Clinton to enact Fast Track: almost all of America's largest newspapers, virtually every major corporate leader, former presidents, Ways and Means Chairman Archer, Senate Majority Leader Lott. Yet 80 percent of House Democrats and about one-third of House Republicans said "no," a stunning and unprecedented defeat for America's economic elite. From now on, the American people would be involved in major trade issues.

A month before the vote, I had flown with a couple of friends to McAllen, Texas, rented a car, and driven to Reynosa, Mexico, to gaze into the face of the new global economy. What I saw told me more about free trade than all the testimony and lobbying from trade experts and economists.

Rafael and Felicia Espinosa (not their real names) of Reynosa dream of an education for their children, more secure jobs, and a nicer house. They work for General Motors in Mexico's maquiladora, the area along the U.S.-Mexico border where American companies get special tax treatment by the Mexican government and special tariff treatment by the United States. Rafael and Felicia each work forty-five hours per week, and each earns ninety cents an hour. I sat with them in their tiny house, which had no electricity or running water and had a leaky roof that they only had scrap materials to repair it with, as they told me they'd done many times before. Their children, happy as most children are when they have loving parents, ran barefoot on the dirt floors.

Mexican law requires that companies distribute 10 percent of their profits to their workers. Rafael and Felicia have yet to see a peso of those profits. Their employer, General Motors, the largest private employer in Mexico, claims it has no profits in its Mexico operations, an amazing assertion for a company with several modern plants there and that pays its skilled workers forty dollars a week. As one analyst calculated, if General Motors and other U.S. companies paid their workers the one-tenth of profits owed them, their forty-dollar-a-week pay would double.

Joe Ramos of Laredo, Texas, was also doing the best he could. An able and articulate man of about forty, he was the lone U.S. Department of Transportation inspector at the Laredo–Nuevo Laredo border. More than twenty-five hundred trucks enter the United States here every day, the busiest U.S. port of entry for trucks. Agent Ramos examines about ten trucks each day and pulls all of them out of service. The Texas Department of Public Service under Governor George W. Bush, has been of little help in these truck inspections. The truck scales have been broken for a month, and Joe does not know when the state will fix them.

Juanita Gonzalez doesn't know where to turn. For years she worked at Envisions, an American company in Mexico that prints labels for American mail-order firms. On a Monday morning a couple of months earlier, she and her 350 coworkers found a note on the door informing them that the plant had closed. The workers were given no notice of the shutdown and received

no severance pay, both clear violations of Mexican law. Even though
NAFTA requires it, neither the Mexican nor the American government
seemed much interested in pursuing company executives to make them
comply with the law and pay their workers what is owed them. '

Rita Torres works at General Electric, one of the largest corporations in
the world. The Reynosa plant pays about a dollar an hour. Out of her forty-
dollar-a-week paycheck, her employer deducts nine dollars for a very small
stove, which she proudly showed me. For fifty-two weeks, nearly one-quarter
of her paycheck goes toward a stove that probably costs no more than $250
in the United States. While she is lucky enough to have electricity, she and
her husband live in a little hut with dirt floors and no running water. Their
son plays alongside a small ditch that oozes an unidentifiable liquid.

The titanic struggles that will take place in Congress during the next
decade over trade agreements and how we write them will affect the lives
of Rita, Joe, Rafael, Felicia, and Juanita. Will we include strong environmental laws similar to those we have in the United States? Will trade agreements protect worker safety the way we do in the United States? Will we
build a floor under wages with an international minimum wage so that
exorbitant profits are not taken out of the community and impoverished
workers left behind? Or, as we negotiate trade agreements around the world,
will our failure to include safety and health rules for all nations hasten the
dismantling of our environment, food quality, and worker safety laws?
Deregulating the world economy so that environmental and worker safety
laws are diluted while wages stagnate will accelerate the race to the bottom
for most of the world's citizens.

The Clinton-Gingrich effort to deregulate the international economy and
apply trickle-down economic principles to the global economy took a similar tack in our nation's government-run health care system. The media and
conservative pundits and politicians wrote and spoken incessantly about the
impending bankruptcy of Medicare, the government health program for
forty million Americans over the age of sixty-five. The real crisis in Medicare
is the plan to privatize perhaps the best government program in American
history. One-sixth of Medicare beneficiaries—generally the healthiest and
youngest—are currently enrolled in HMOs run mostly by private insurance
companies. Several hundred thousand more Medicare patients belong to
provider service organizations (PSOs), managed care networks typically
owned and managed by physicians. Republicans are now proposing that half
a million beneficiaries join medical savings accounts plans, private high-

deductible health insurance policies that cover catastrophic illness. Senate Republicans, at the behest of the American Medical Association, are pushing legislation to allow physicians, in the name of patient choice, to charge Medicare patients whatever rate they want outside of Medicare.

GOP efforts to privatize Medicare are proceeding apace. The most expensive 10 percent of Medicare beneficiaries cost taxpayers an average of $37,000 per person per year. The other 90 percent of beneficiaries cost Medicare about $1,400 per year. The government pays managed care companies about $5,000 for each Medicare beneficiary they enroll. At $5,000 each, managed care companies can shower their members with eyeglasses, prescription drugs, and in some cases even health club memberships. And there are piles of money left over—for huge profits, exorbitant executive salaries, and sophisticated lobbying and marketing campaigns.

In Cleveland, managed care companies launched extravagantly expensive campaigns to urge the healthiest people to reject traditional fee-for-service Medicare and instead to join them. Managed care companies spend millions (a full-page ad in the Sunday *Plain Dealer* costs upward of $20,000) to attract the most affluent, the healthiest, and the youngest seniors. Some companies sponsor recruiting dances, and some locate their offices on the second floor of buildings without elevators in order to discourage the less able-bodied.

Marketing costs, excessive profits, huge executive salaries, and perks unknown in the not-for-profit health care system drain money from patient care. Nonprofit HMOs still spend about 90 percent of their revenues on patients. In contrast, Health Net, the California-based HMO that provided a golden parachute of almost $20 million for its departing CEO, spends only about sixty-eight cents of every premium dollar on health care. The CEO of a New Hampshire–based HMO was rewarded with $15.5 million for one year's work.

As seniors enrolled in managed care plans age and become sicker and more expensive to insure, a funny thing happens. Obstacles erected to deny and discourage care push them back into traditional fee-for-service Medicare, effectively disenrolling them from the managed care plan. The cost to the government in the first year after a beneficiary disenrolls is approximately 160 percent that of a typical Medicare beneficiary. The HMO takes care of you when you're well; Uncle Sam takes care of you when you're not.

Republicans call HMOs, PSOs, and MSAs more choice for senior citizens. But such talk is a smoke screen for the eventual privatization of Medicare. Privatizing Medicare gives Americans a two-tiered health care system with excellent, high-quality care for the affluent and lower quality, impersonal, welfare-type health care for the rest of the country. Ever higher premiums for wealthier beneficiaries will encourage the healthy among them to abandon Medicare. Enrolling affluent, healthy, and younger beneficiaries in private health insurance programs saps money from America's most successful government health program and diverts it to nonhealth uses. And as more insurance companies and their managed care affiliates enter Medicare, fewer dollars go into caring for patients. That's the crisis in Medicare.

The issues of health care reform, the budget, crime, and trade—all central to the U.S. economy and to our lives—will continue to occupy the Congress. Whichever party is in control—and it is very possible that it will change hands several times in the next decade or so—Congress will probably not make significant changes in any of these four major areas. It is simply too difficult to pass comprehensive and controversial legislation when the majority party has a slim governing majority. And it is very likely that neither party will dominate Congress in the foreseeable future. The anti-incumbent fervor seems to have abated. The public does not seem to be crying out for major change.

18

Election 1998 and the 106th Congress

A population becomes distracted by trivia, when cultural life
is redefined as a perpetual round of entertainments, when
serious conversation becomes a form of baby talk, when in
short, a people become an audience and their public business
a vaudeville act.

—Aldous Huxley, *Brave New World*

They have such refined and delicate palates that they can
discover no one worthy of their ballots, and then when
someone terrible gets elected they say, "There, that's just
what I expected."

—Ogden Nash

I confess that I went out of a thoughtless curiosity to see
how the Chief Magistrate bore himself under these untoward
circumstances, but I did not enjoy the visit.

—Mark Twain, reporter for the *Hartford Courant*,
about his visit to the White House after President
Andrew Johnson's impeachment

THE 1998 ELECTIONS were a major loss for the national Republican
party. GOP Senate leaders had predicted a five- or six-seat pickup, giving
their party sixty votes and thus the ability to cut off Democratic filibusters.
Two Republican incumbents lost, one Democratic incumbent was defeated,
two open seats held by Democrats were won by Republicans, and one open
Republican seat was captured by a Democrat. The predicted five-seat GOP
gain never materialized, meaning that there was no net loss for either party.

On the House side, Republican campaign officials forecasted gains of
approximately twenty seats. The fourth-ranked Republican in the House

pronounced on the morning of the election that his party would gain fifteen seats. Speaker Newt Gingrich foresaw a forty-seat gain by the GOP. And like birds flying off a telephone wire, just about every media pundit inside the Beltway also predicted huge Republican gains. After all, they pointed out omnisciently, the president's party always loses seats in an off-year election (only in 1934 when FDR was president did the party out of power lose seats). Columnist Tony Snow, formerly a Bush speechwriter and now a Republican cheerleader on Fox Television, wrote that Democrats will "count it a victory if they lose only a dozen seats in the House."

The five-seat gain by *Democrats* on November 3, 1998, shocked and angered rank-and-file Republicans and made the GOP leadership tremble. Three days after the election, class-of-1994er Steve Largent (R-Okla.), in announcing his challenge to Majority Leader Dick Armey, said, "On November 3, the Republican party hit an iceberg," and now it's time to change the crew of the *Titanic.* Two hours later, Bob Livingston of Louisiana kicked off his campaign to unseat Speaker Gingrich. And still later that same day, Gingrich announced his intention to step down not only from his Speakership but from his congressional seat.

Livingston immediately cleared the field and was unanimously elected Speaker by the Republican Conference in a December meeting. Congressman Armey survived challenges from Largent, Jennifer Dunn (Wash.), and Dennis Hastert (Ill.), who finished fourth with eighteen votes. But neither Speaker Gingrich nor Speaker-designate Livingston was willing to preside over the House impeachment debate in mid-December, so Congressman Ray LaHood, a little-known but respected representative from downstate Illinois, was chosen to preside.

But in a stunning turn of events, on December 18, as *Hustler* magazine publisher Larry Flynt prepared to go to press with the names and stories of members of Congress whom he claimed had had extramarital affairs, Bob Livingston announced to the Republican Conference that he had committed adultery. The two hundred or so Republicans in the room gave him a standing ovation, many commenting that he had never lied under oath about it, that he had not had a relationship with anyone in his office, that he had confessed to his wrongdoings. The next morning, on the day of the impeachment vote, Livingston announced on the House floor that, because he "had strayed from his marriage," he was leaving the Congress and would not allow his name to be submitted to the House for the Speakership. He then called on the president to resign also. And so in early January, Dennis

Hastert, a member of the Commerce Committee and a protégé of Majority Whip Tom Delay, was uanimously selected Speaker by the Republican Conference.

Gingrich and the Republicans had assumed that historical trends and the president's problems would combine to score huge gains for Republicans in the House elections. There was no need for ideas, proposals, or, for that matter, legislative accomplishments. Once they agreed on the strategy, as Tony Snow said, "they busied themselves with doing as little as possible. They scheduled just eighty-nine days of legislative work. They proposed nothing big. They watched the economy head upward and the Monica story spiral sewerward, and they smiled." In reality, Gingrich had used the Monica Lewinsky affair to cover up the fact that the 105th Congress had enacted fewer laws than any Congress in more than three decades.

While Democrats did very well in open seats, Republicans were saved perhaps by the fact that there were not many retirements in either party, meaning that there were not many hotly contested races. In contrast to the congressional elections in the early nineties, when term limits was a big issue, 98.5 percent of incumbents—395 out of 401—were reelected; only five Republicans and one Democrat were defeated.

The major loser in the fall of 1998, however, was the electorate as a whole. The 1998 elections continued the inexorable trend toward big money, negative campaigning, and depressed voter turnout. Larry Makinson, director of the nonpartisan Center for Responsive Politics, told USA Today that 94 percent of Senate races and 95 percent of House races were won by the candidate who spent the most money. "These are the highest percentages we've ever seen of people winning based on the money." Most races—all but two in Ohio, for example—were decided long before the November election because of the strengths of incumbency, the partisan makeup of the districts, and the huge money advantage that most incumbents enjoy.

Distressingly, voter turnout was abysmally low. Only 36.1 percent of eligible voters went to the polls, the lowest turnout in a midterm election since 1942, when America was in the midst of war. In Ohio there were fifty thousand fewer voters than in 1994, which was considered at the time a very low turnout election. Editorial writers piously bemoaned low voter turnout with their obligatory election-year columns, demanding to know why politicians do not talk about issues. Yet at the same time news conferences about Medicare or the environment get little attention from those same large newspapers and television stations. (By way of example, news directors sent their television cameras to Cleveland Hopkins Airport to interview me and other local congressmen returning from Washington about the Starr Report and the Clinton tapes, but rarely does television cover a story about congressional decisions that affect peoples' everyday lives.)

Throughout the fall, newspapers predicted record-low voter turnout. Prior to the elections some reporters and columnists referred to 1998 as "the Year of Apathy"; others, in calling on the president to resign, said that there is no reason to vote this year because politics is so rotten. The Lewinsky affair, the media told us, would depress turnout. The negative ads, the media told us, would depress turnout. The huge amount of soft money spent by interest groups, the media told us, would depress turnout. The expensive television ads run by the candidates, the media told us, would depress turnout. And, indeed, turnout was depressed.

But this did not happen by accident. The Republicans devised a strategy for the 1998 elections, one that almost always worked for them: launch the first negative ad that scores a direct hit and drives the opponent's negatives up. The public complains, rightly, of negative campaigning without knowing whom to blame, and the newspapers give little guidance about whose responsibility the ads are, other than pointing out that too many politicians run negative ads. And, in the end, voters stay home—especially Democratic voters.

What happened in Ohio, probably the Republicans' "best state" in the 1998 elections, serves as a good example of this strategy.

In the state's gubernatorial race, Republican Robert Taft, with a family name well known to Ohio voters, was leading by a dozen or so points throughout the spring and summer. As the fall campaign evolved, Democrat Lee Fisher cut Taft's lead to single digits. Once the race began tightening, Taft ran the first negative television ads of the campaign. Largely inaccurate, they nevertheless hit hard. Fisher's momentum came to a halt, and Taft's lead began to swell again. Fisher then began responding with criticisms of Taft, and the attacks and counterattacks multiplied, and people complained about the negative campaigns both candidates were running.

The Taft ads, however, were so negative that the Ohio Elections Commission—a bipartisan state agency remade and reformed by legislation that Secretary of State Taft himself proposed—found Taft guilty of knowingly lying in his ads. It was the first time in the twenty-five-year history of the Ohio Elections Commission that a gubernatorial candidate had been found guilty of campaign violations. Fisher attempted to point out that Taft had been found guilty by the Elections Commission, but meanwhile Taft ran ads saying that Fisher was a bigger liar. "Lie. Lee. Lose," blared Taft's television ads. To further muddy the waters, Taft filed an Elections Commission complaint against Fisher, but it was dismissed.

Most of the state's major newspapers, feeling no obligation to clear up the confusion, simply bemoaned the fact that political campaigns were nasty, negative, and too often without substance. Confused voters, generally unaware that Taft started the negatives, that he ran more negative ads, and that he was found guilty by a bipartisan state commission, collectively shrugged their shoulders with a pox-on-both-your-houses attitude.

In race after race in Ohio, Republican party operatives poured huge amounts of money into television and direct mail, lied about their opponents, and were found guilty of election law violations by the bipartisan Ohio Elections Commission.

In Lorain, Democrat Ron Nabakowski, a former state senator and Ohio Lottery director with a good record of public service, was opposed by the former mayor of North Ridgeville and former losing candidate for the state senate, Jeff Armbruster. Nabakowski was accused by Armbruster of "corruption, backroom deals, and payoffs." When confronted by a teacher who thought the attacks unfair, Armbruster said that the ads were not his, that they had been produced and paid for by the Ohio Republican Senate campaign committee, and that he had nothing to do with them. Interestingly, however, similar ads were run later with Armbruster's campaign committee's disclaimer on them.

Nabakowski filed a complaint against Armbruster with the Ohio Elections Commission. And, in good Republican form, Armbruster filed a complaint against Nabakowski, further muddying the waters and making it difficult for the voters to figure out who was slinging the mud and who was getting hit in the face with it. While the Elections Commission found probable cause to go ahead with Nabakowski's complaint against Armbuster (but election day came before there was time for a hearing), Armbruster's complaint was dismissed without probable cause. But the tactic worked: the voters were confused. In addition, Armbruster was the beneficiary of a lot of money (he and the Republicans spent as much as $800,000 on his campaign, while Nabakowski and the Democrats spent barely $100,000), very effective negative ads, a lower voter turnout brought about by negative television, and a confusion among the voters about the truth of the ads and who started the nasty campaigning.

Newspapers were critical of the tone of both campaigns, decrying nega-tive advertising and the paucity of real issues in the campaign. Yet seldom did they mention that the negatives were very one-sided, that the Ohio Elections Commission prejudged Armbruster's ads as being untrue, that Nabakowski's ads were not in violation of the rules, that Armbruster had simply lied. Armbruster won by 600 votes out of 120,000 cast.

This same statewide formula and the same Republican strategy were used, though with a different electoral outcome in Mansfield, my old state legislative seat. Democratic incumbent Bill Harnett, appointed to the seat when a fifteen-year incumbent retired for medical reasons, had retired as a school superintendent fourteen years earlier, and, with a modest amount of money, he was conducting a traditional campaign. The Ohio House Repub-lican campaign committee spent hundreds of thousands of dollars claiming Harnett had accepted a big pay increase in 1984 while the schools were deeply in debt and forced to borrow money from the state loan fund. Their facts were completely wrong. In typical fashion, the Republican candidate, Sally DeVito Houk, said she did not like negative campaigning, claimed the ads were not really hers, and asked her state party to withdraw them. Also in typical fashion, the ads continued to run.

But this time the scenario played out differently. The *Mansfield News Journal*, surely not a Democratic paper, took on the Republicans in this race by telling the truth and asking the voters to punish those who do not. Edi-tor Tom Brennan directed his reporters to write articles questioning the veracity of Houk's ads. He editorialized twice against Houk, saying she should not have agreed to the ads, or, if she had not, she should have been able to stop them. Either way, the *News Journal* wrote, Houk and the state GOP "owe the voters an apology." This time the Democrat won. The news-paper's coverage and their exhortation to the electorate turned the tables on a strategy that is becoming too commonplace in Republican party circles.

But the dynamic of 1998 was a bit different. The Republican-led drive toward removal of the president clearly offended large numbers of inde-pendent voters, as did the post-election hearings and the largely party-line vote on impeachment. By the time of the Senate trial, huge majorities of Americans—according to virtually every public opinion poll taken—wanted the year-long odyssey to end. Pundits began to predict Democratic takeovers in the House and Senate, Republican governors were counseling their brethren in the Senate to end the trial, and Republican senators in marginal seats scurried for the darkest corner they could find.

They were angry. They hated his tactics. They were furious with his behavior. And many congressional Republicans detested President Clinton personally. But they couldn't beat him.

After their takeover of Congress in 1995, the Republicans thought that any prominent Republican could defeat this weakened president. But he had outmaneuvered them legislatively at almost every turn and had repeatedly defeated them in the court of public opinion—from the government shutdown to the Democratic gains in the 1998 congressional elections. And he was much more popular than they were. How could that be? Why didn't the public see him the way they did? Congressional Republicans were incredulous that the public not only did not want this president removed from office but seemed to resent those who tried to do so.

President Clinton had a pretty impressive record to which he could point: uninterrupted economic growth, a falling crime rate, low inflation, improvements in environmental quality, a rapidly shrinking federal budget deficit. Republican leaders said that all the country's good fortune came about in spite of this president, not because of him. But the country did not see it that way. For better or worse, presidents are usually blamed for bad economic times or credited with good ones.

Then on December 19, 1998—against the backdrop of a good economy and with a generally satisfied and optimistic public and an angry GOP leadership—the United States House of Representatives, mostly along party lines, voted two articles of impeachment against William Jefferson Clinton. He was the first president since Andrew Johnson to be impeached and the first since Richard Nixon who faced the serious possibility of removal from office.

Nixon's case was, in fact, very different. The House Judiciary Committee held extensive hearings in 1974 to determine whether the president had committed impeachable offenses. Public opinion turned strongly against Nixon as the hearings wore on that summer: before the Watergate hearings, the public was 2-1 against the president's removal from office; by August 1974, as the Judiciary Committee completed its work, public sentiment was 2-1 in favor of his impeachment or resignation. Nonetheless, the Judiciary Committee voted for three impeachment articles and against two others, bipartisanly contending that tax evasion was a personal crime, not a "high crime or misdemeanor" where Nixon used the powers of the office to commit a crime against the government.

In August 1974, after the articles of impeachment were approved by the Judiciary Committee, House Minority Leader John Rhodes and Arizona senator Barry Goldwater went to the White House to urge Nixon to resign. They told him that it was in the best interests of his party, the presidency, and the nation that he step down. On August 9, 1974, Richard Nixon became the first American president to resign from office.

But 1998 was a very different story. Many Americans viewed the impeachment process as partisan, unfair, and unnecessary. *New York Times* reporter Adam Clymer called it "the House's party-line lynching." Some congressional Democrats believed impeachment efforts were a payback for their investigations into Watergate and into Reagan's Iran-Contra scandal. Other Democrats ascribed it as a vendetta against a president whom Republicans (especially those elected in 1994) despised. To be sure, most of us believed President Clinton had acted badly, embarrassed the country and himself, and deserved censure in some form. Removal from office, however, was a step reserved for the most extraordinary misuse of power. Few constitutional scholars believed that Clinton's deeds fell into this category, and the public, as I heard over and over, even from Republicans in my district, thought that impeachment proceedings had ended with the Democrats picking up seats in the November 1998 congressional elections.

After the House voted the two articles of impeachment on December 19, Minority Leader Richard Gephardt led well over half the Democratic caucus to the White House to urge President Clinton to fight the articles in the Senate. Contrasted with Goldwater's 1974 visit to Nixon, Gephardt wanted the message to be that congressional members of the president's party believed that he should not resign. Most believed it was in the best interests of the nation, the presidency, and the Democratic party that Clinton stay and fight. Clearly the embattled president did not need to be convinced.

Initially, I had little interest in visiting the White House to urge to stay the course a president with whom most of us in the House were not especially happy. My chief of staff, Donna Pignatelli, and I talked about whether we wanted to go; in the end, we decided to do so, for the simple reason that the next day we would surely be sorry to have missed such an important historical moment.

The scene at the White House was surreal. We gathered in the East Room to await the arrival of the president, the first lady, the vice-president, and Mrs. Gore. The atmosphere was more upbeat than it had any business being. When the president entered, the cheers were too enthusiastic. The hand-shaking was too vigorous. The comments were too supportive. It felt like a pep rally. While the Republicans were clearly out of touch with the national sentiment in forcing the impeachment vote, I feared that the public would not like our response either: America wanted this sordid chapter of American history closed.

Even the first day of the 106th Congress, in January 1999, seemed to be different. The irenic atmosphere of a new Congress—when people celebrate their return to the House, and families and friends fete the new members— this time seemed less celebratory. Impeachment had infected two Congresses, the 105th and the 106th, and after the president survived the February 1999 impeachment trial in the Senate (by a wide margin), a shadow of incivility, partisanship, and rancor fell over the Congress for most of the year.

There was much activity on Capitol Hill in 1999, but little was accomplished. What was left undone—prescription drug coverage, a tax bill, the Patients Bill of Rights, campaign finance reform, a minimum wage increase—was far more impressive than what was actually done. Many commentators, and certainly most lobbyists, said that the most significant accomplishment of the first session of the 106th Congress was the enactment of a banking bill that allowed banks, insurance companies, and securities firms to compete on each other's turf. More important, at least to many of us in the House and I believe to most of the country, the president and House Democrats were successful in getting into the Labor, Health, and Human Services and Education appropriations measure $1.3 billion for 100,000 teachers to reduce class size in grades one through three.

On other issues, there seemed to be much ado . . . and then nothing. A minimum wage bill died in committee. A strong bipartisan campaign finance bill passed the House but was killed in the Senate by Majority Leader Trent Lott. A gun safety bill designed to closed gun show loopholes passed the Senate but was emasculated by Tom DeLay and Republican leaders in the House. The House overwhelmingly, with near unanimous Democratic support and almost half of the House Republicans, passed legislation to allow the president to limit steel imports for three years, using quotas and tariffs; the much more pro–free trade Senate defeated it narrowly. A strong patient's bill of rights passed the House with a solid bipartisan majority, but Trent Lott told the insurance industry to "get off your wallets" and help him defeat it in the Senate. They did, and he did.

Republicans had no better luck with their priorities, which really was one big priority: originally an $864 billion tax cut aimed mostly at upper-income taxpayers, those who Republicans say pay most of the taxes so should be awarded most of the tax breaks. Tax cuts are probably the most unifying issue in the increasingly fractious House Republican Conference. Divisions, often brought about by issues like the minimum wage, the patient protection bill, and campaign finance reform, had developed quickly in the Republican House ranks—problems the party could ill afford, given its slimmest congressional majority in decades. And that slim margin shrank to five when Republican Michael Forbes of New York became Democrat Michael Forbes of New York. It was a turnabout not seen in a few years.

Rather than trying to broker a deal with the president on modest tax cuts, Republican leadership believed a massive tax cut of almost a trillion dollars would bring Republicans together, rally the country around them, and label their recalcitrant, obstructionist opponents as "tax-and-spend Democrats." But something else happened. It unified Democrats. Even conservative Democrats agreed that their plan's capital gains reductions and inheritance tax elimination gave too much to the rich. Besides, as Alan Greenspan and the budget-conscious Concord Coalition asserted, it was bad economics— we finally had the budget under control and now this. Also, the tax cut was scaled down to $792 billion to meet some Republican objections that money had to be set aside for deficit reduction. And Democrats convinced many in the country that a tax cut of this magnitude—whether $864 billion or $792 billion—could inflict major damage on the growing economy as well as rob social security and other programs, like education, defense, and Medicare, of needed dollars.

The president's veto was done almost gleefully, hardly a reaction he would have had to a popular initiative. Almost no one—from my district's conservative Geauga Countians to its business leaders in Medina—told me that they wanted this huge tax cut, especially if it might jeopardize a very strong economy and a much improved federal budget situation.

And while Republicans' domestic policy seemed out of step, a disturbing isolationism on the international scene was growing among their leadership and its conservative rank-and-file. The Senate defeated a ratification of the Comprehensive Test Ban Treaty, even as India and Pakistan were openly testing nuclear weapons. It was the first defeat of an international nuclear treaty in the nation's history. The president also had great difficulty persuading Congress to agree to pay the United States's back dues to the United Nations. And five weeks after the bombing began in Kosovo, Republicans in the House, for the first time in memory, defeated a resolution 213-213 (a tie vote means a resolution or amendment fails) endorsing a military action that had already commenced. Interestingly, Speaker Dennis Hastert, in one of his first tests of leadership, voted for the resolution—quietly, almost apologetically—while Majority Whip DeLay twisted arms on the House floor, instructing his minions "not to take ownership of an incompetent administration's policy." The Speaker, in suffering a defeat while aligning with a president whom he did not much like, had walked on the floor very late, almost meekly casting his vote, perhaps hoping no one noticed, a rather peculiar act by a Speaker of the House.

And all the while, the money chase was on. Big money, the constant pursuit of campaign cash, and the political issue of campaign finance reform cast a shadow over the entire institution. House members delivered passionate speeches, but in the end Congress did nothing. Yet leadership in both parties bragged about the money they—and we—raised. The competition was fierce. The Democratic Congressional Campaign Committee, through the first half of 1999, had accomplished something that had not happened since the GOP gained the majority: Democrats actually had more cash on hand than the National Republican Congressional Committee. Under the leadership of Congressman Patrick Kennedy, the Democrats had raised $17 million, a 150-percent increase over the same period in 1997. By year end, the DCCC had raised more money than any time in its history, and this was not an election year.

No one in Washington missed that story. In 1995, when many observers thought Republicans would be in control of Congress for a decade or more, business was ecstatic. In the first half of that year, the Republicans outraised Democrats by a 3-1 margin. The 1995–96 election cycle saw business give 64 percent of its money to Republicans. During the 1997–98 cycle, business gave 63 percent of its congressional contributions to the House Republicans. But in 1999, business split its contributions almost 50-50, sending shivers along Republican spines. Big business surely prefers Republicans; but, more than that, it wants to be on the winning side, and business believed that Democrats were in the hunt to take back the majority. One top GOP lobbyist who represents several Fortune 100 companies opined to a *Washington Post* reporter that "this could go either way. We better make sure our interests are protected no matter who's in control."

The effect of these huge sums of money on the political process is insidious. Campaign money from insurance companies makes passage of a national health care plan exceedingly more difficult. Money from the National Rifle

Association helps stop gun safety legislation. And big dollars from the drug companies seem to have stopped prescription drug legislation dead in its tracks.

The difficulty outsiders have in raising money hurts the entire process. Many young people who would like to pursue a career in government service give up before they start when they find out the amount of money it takes to run for a seat in the state legislature, let alone in Congress. During a question-and-answer session in January 2000 in Lorain, Sharon Soucy, who works at a joint vocational school in Oberlin, entreated me, as her representative, to do something, because people like her "thirty-year-old sons want to work to change the world. But how could people like them ever run for office when it costs so much?"

The work coming out of the Health and Environment subcommittee, of which I am the ranking Democrat, was mixed. When Republican leadership allowed Chairman Michael Bilirakis and me to work together, we could deliver. But too often—from prescription drugs to modernization of Medicare—our work was stifled. We did succeed—quietly, cooperatively, and bipartisanly—on several less visible issues. We reauthorized the Agency for Healthcare Research and Quality, helping children's hospitals with their physician training programs, and passed legislation to stop nursing homes from dumping less profitable Medicaid patients. Our most important success was the Work Incentives Act, probably the disabled community's number-one priority since the 1990 passage of the Americans with Disabilities Act. While our subcommittee passed the bill expeditiously, the House Ways and Means Committee scaled the bill back significantly.

On December 17, my daughter Emily, home from Swarthmore College for the holidays, attended the bill signing with me at the Franklin Delano Roosevelt Memorial. Joining President Clinton on the podium were Senators Edward Kennedy, who had also played a major role in the ADA bill a decade earlier, and James Jeffords (R-Vt.) and three prominent activists in the disabled community, including Donna McNamee from northeastern Ohio; Congressman Rick Lazio (R-N.Y.) and I were in the audience—senators almost always get higher billing than representatives, no matter the accomplishment. It was a joyous occasion, as the president announced that this would be "the last bill which I sign in the twentieth century." He used a different pen to sign each of the letters in his name—W-i-l-l-i-a-m J-e-f-f-e-r-s-o-n C-l-i-n-t-o-n—and then distributed the pens to each of the most active participants. It was my first.

Our biggest failure as a subcommittee and as a Congress was our inability to do much of anything to deal with the problem of the increasing numbers of Americans without health care coverage. In 1994, when Congress failed to pass the Clinton health care plan, 40 million Americans had no health insurance; by 1998, 44.3 million people were without coverage. Even though, by most measures, the economy was booming, more and more people were without health insurance, which makes more troubling the specter of an economic downturn and what that will mean for American families who are unlucky enough to suffer major illnesses.

Wendy Johnson, a bilingual Cleveland inner-city family practice physician, explained what the health care crisis really is for many Americans and for those treating the poor:

> There are no residencies for this "specialty." Many of us trained to do internal medicine, family practice, pediatrics. We found residencies in inner cities and rural areas so we could learn the combination of social work, advocacy, and medicine needed to care for patients in a terribly flawed system. We know which antibiotics and blood pressure medications are the cheapest, and often prescribe drugs because we are thinking of cost rather than more medically respectable grounds like efficacy or side-effect profiles. We learn to pare down to the essentials, narrowing our diagnostic studies to a vital few. We practice at public hospitals or community health centers which attempt to provide "charity care" to the uninsured—at least those lucky enough to live near such increasingly rare institutions. We do have a cobbled-together network of hospitals and clinics serving the uninsured, but people still fall through the cracks. Some live too far away, some are immigrants—with and without papers—we allow to do our hardest labor while denying them basic health care services. Some have problems like drug addiction or mental illness for which accessible treatments are even scarcer than for other medical problems.
>
> Of course, I don't like to practice medicine this way—spending an hour on the phone to find mental health services for a patient, begging for free samples from drug company representatives, calling specialists to find one who will let patients pay off their bill $10 a month. It certainly isn't what I was taught in medical school. But because of the growing recognition of our two-tiered practice of medicine, we now even have our own professional society, the Association of Clinicians of the Underserved. Demand for our services is growing as the nation's policy makers show little interest in taking on the lobbyists who represent the private HMOs and insurance companies.

Several ideas have been offered in Congress: single-payer (a sort of Medicare for the entire population), where the government serves as the insurance company, everyone is covered, and providers are actually paid by, but do not work for, the governnment; tax incentives, where in exchange for the tax credit people are required to buy at least basic coverage for themselves; medical savings accounts, in which people are provided with a set amount of money that is deposited into a personal account to be used for purchasing health services; a federalist model, where states are given money by the federal government and the states will be required to provide universal coverage with a federally determined minimal benefit package for their citizens. None of these plans went anywhere in our subcommittee, in Ways and Means, or in the House or Senate.

One idea, introduced in previous Congresses by California Democrat Pete Stark and me, extended Medicare voluntarily to people aged fifty-five to sixty-four. On March 17, 1998, in the House Ways and Means Committee hearing room in the Longworth House Office Building, Senator Moynihan (D-N.Y.), Senator Kennedy, President Clinton, Congressman Stark, and I announced our legislation to allow people aged fifty-five to sixty-four to buy into Medicare at a significantly higher rate, which would make that part of the program budget-neutral. As more and more Americans in their late fifties and early sixties lose their jobs when companies downsize, or when Americans of that age see their health care benefits scaled down or eliminated, and as Americans of that age begin to experience more health problems as they grow older, the need for expanding Medicare becomes greater.

We knew that Medicare was perhaps America's most successful and popular government program. At the time of its creation in 1965, the American Medical Association (representing well over half of America's physicians then, but far fewer than half today) and conservatives, including Congressman Bob Dole, labeled this new program "socialized medicine." With almost 97 percent of America's senior citizens now receiving Medicare benefits, few call it that anymore. My mail and my conversations at town meetings during my first term taught me that many Americans do not even think of Medicare as a government program; several elderly critics of the Clinton health plan reminded me that we should keep government out of our health care: "I have to wait two years for Medicare. I don't know what I'm going to do. But I'm against Clinton's plan; I don't want the government doing it." Medicare is so immensely popular that it has become part of our country's heritage. What better way to move toward universal coverage than to extend Medicare to people aged fifty-five to sixty-four, and then to children under eighteen, and then to the rest of the population? At a 1992 news conference in support of a different universal health care idea, Senator Kennedy said, "Ask any senior citizen whether they think Medicare is socialized medicine. We won that battle for health care for the elderly a generation ago, and the time has come to win it now for every other American."

On a personal note, that kick-off ceremony on St. Patrick's Day for the Medicare buy-in bill was one of the highlights of my congressional service. Stark spoke and then introduced Moynihan, who spoke and then introduced me. At the conclusion of my remarks, I introduced Ted Kennedy, who spoke and then introduced President Clinton. After our remarks, I complimented Kennedy on the performance of his son Patrick, a second-term House Democrat from Rhode Island. The senator responded, "Sometimes Patrick pinches himself because he can't believe that he is a member of the House." I answered, "I'm pinching myself right now because I can't believe I am standing between Senator Kennedy and the president of the United States." Kennedy laughed appreciatively.

We were growing increasingly frustrated with the minority party's inability to set the agenda on a day-to-day basis. While the issues that received the most attention were by most accounts "Democratic" issues—minimum wage, campaign finance reform, the patient's bill of rights, education, for example—Republican leadership had blocked, in one chamber or another, enactment of these bills. (And, as we saw in previous sessions, with the Kennedy-Kassenbaum health bill and the increase in the minimum wage, election years have a way of pushing Congress to do things that its leaders may oppose—but never without a huge fight.) In the end, the majority party decides the issues we debate, calls the committee hearings, and schedules the floor votes. One particularly maddening example of the power play was my imploring of Chairman Bilirakis, a decent and cooperative man, to hold hearings and to mark up legislation on presciption drug coverage and pricing, which went absolutely nowhere. Late in the year we had one perfunctory hearing that had no impact either on legislation or on the national debate, but we did have numerous lengthy hearings on Medicare Y2K compatibility, as if these federal agencies were not aware of potential problems in 2000.

As 1999 came to a close, an event took place that had a huge impact on Congress and ultimately on the American people. On November 30 the debate on trade changed. Thirty thousand mostly middle-aged steelworkers and autoworkers and machinists and Teamsters joined ten thousand college students, environmentalists, antiwar activists, and human rights advocates to walk together through the streets of Seattle—peaceful in their belief that direct, nonviolent action might indeed wake up the country to what they perceived as trade injustices and passionate in their opposition to a World Trade Organization (WTO) that operates in secret and fails to consider labor rights and environmental standards.

There were a few hundred demonstrators who turned violent and caught the media's most direct attention, informing the public that something big—not really seen in this country in over two decades—was happening in Seattle, the home of huge export businesses like Microsoft and Boeing and the site of America's only workers' general strike in 1919.

The demonstrators— environmentalists, trade union members, students, food safety advocates—wanted a WTO that is more democratic, more transparent, and less beholden to the largest multinational corporations. Representatives of 134 countries had convened in Seattle to launch a new round of official trade talks. The Uruguay Round, kicked off in Montevideo in 1986, had concluded with the passage of the General Agreement of Tariffs and Trade (GATT) by the United States Congress and other nations in 1994 and with the creation of the World Trade Organization in 1995. The WTO was formed to serve as a vehicle to open up trade, liberalize trade laws, and arbitrate trade disputes brought by one member against another. Although GATT passed a lame-duck Congress with many votes to spare, warning signals were sent about its secrecy, potential power, and refusal to address human rights, labor standards, or environmental and food safety rules.

Fears that the WTO would operate in secret with little public accountability were quickly realized. By its very nature, the World Trade Organization is an undemocratic organization that is staffed exclusively by unelected bureaucrats. Its three-judge panels, typically consisting of trade lawyers not accountable to the public, rule on issues of public health and safety, environmental laws, and other trade disputes. The panel's decisions, with no public input allowed from health or environmental organizations, are announced to the public, but the panels do not reveal the process surrounding the outcome. Any appeals by those contesting WTO decisions are also secret, being decided by a different three-judge panel. The process is exceedingly slow and laborious. Dr. Jeff Sachs, a Harvard economist, said after Seattle that "international institutions like IMF [International Monetary Fund] and WTO have a deep democratic deficit." William Greider, who has written extensively about trade, called the WTO "a private club for deal-making among the most powerful interests, portrayed as a public institution searching for international 'consensus.' . . . The WTO aspires, in effect, to create a bill of rights for capital, crafted one case at a time by the corporate lawyers filing their confidential pleadings in Geneva. It is not hyperbole when critics say the system defends property rights but dismisses human rights and common social concerns as irrelevant to trade."

Three important things happened in Seattle. First, the depth of passion and breadth of support for enforceable labor and environmental standards surprised the delegates. Few finance ministers and trade officials knew of the strong beliefs of the protestors and the millions of workers they represented in the United States and around the world. The delegates expected some opposition, to be sure, but mostly from people on the fringe, not from middle-class, middle-aged workers. And when President Clinton flew to Seattle and delivered a message that labor standards—enforced with sanctions against those countries that do not abide by International Labor Organizations standards—should be included in the core agreements of the WTO, their surprise turned to shock . . . and anger. Shock that he, too, was supportive of enforceable labor standards. Anger that negotiations with the United States were going to be appreciably more difficult.

The media was equally surprised by the passion and support for labor standards they witnessed in Seattle. Ferocious attacks by the free-trade-at-all-costs pundit class—Charles Krauthammer, George Will, Thomas Friedman, people who really do not believe in labor standards even in the United States, much less in developing countries—confirmed by their intensity that more and more Americans were questioning the unregulated global commerce central to our trade policy. Newspapers like the *New York Times* and the *Washington Post* were editorializing that labor rights should in fact be considered as part of trade agreements into which the nation enters.

The most important result of the protests in Seattle was a heightened interest among the public in U.S. trade policy, which until the 1990s was largely the province of a few corporate lawyers, Wall Street bankers, and a small number of mostly appointed government officials at the State Department, Commerce Department, and on the House Ways and Means Committee. The Congress simply ratified these arcane agreements.

The debate in 1993 on the North American Free Trade Agreement engaged, to some degree, the public, especially labor union members and Ross Perot devotees. Then, in the second half of the decade, Congress defeated or blocked several trade issues: the Caribbean Basin Initiative, the Africa trade bill, and the Multilateral Agreement on Investment. In 1997, in

the biggest setback of the last half-century for free trade advocates, the legislation granting the president Fast Track negotiating authority was taken off
the House calendar by a frustrated and angry Newt Gingrich, who knew the
legislation faced certain defeat. Many members of Congress saw Fast Track
as an international counterpart of Speaker Gingrich's Contract with America, a sort of "trickle-down" economic model on a global scale. The public
and opponents in Congress saw the Fast Track vote as a referendum on
NAFTA, a reasonable interpretation since the authority granted by Fast
Track was requested to assist Trade Representative Charlene Barshefsky in
negotiating an agreement with Chile and extending NAFTA-type agreements to most of the rest of Latin America. And then the following year, not
long before the November 1998 election, the House of Representatives overwhelmingly defeated Fast Track legislation. The public was uneasy with
trade legislation written for the global economy by unelected representatives
who seemed to be answerable to nobody.

Indeed, the public began to notice that global trade rules were being written by faceless foreign finance ministers, unknown trade officials from the
United States, and nameless corporate leaders of the world's largest companies. They noticed that the promises made about trade were not being
kept. And the more the public learned about U.S. trade policy, the less they
liked it. They were finding out that our clean air laws were weakened when
the WTO sided with the state-run Venezuelan oil company's contention that
U.S. regulations against gasoline contaminants were too stringent. They
were learning that our endangered species and animal protection laws were
compromised when foreign tuna and shrimp interests brought actions
against the United States in the World Trade Organization. They were hearing that our Great Lakes water may one day be treated as any other com-
modity and be available for sale to any country wanting water. And they suspected that our antidumping laws, which keep subsidized steel and other
goods from flooding U.S. markets, could be legally challenged in the WTO.
Some of the European Union's most important food safety laws were challenged on behalf of the beef industry and overturned by our government
and the WTO. The Canadian government, at the behest of Canada's
asbestos industry, filed a WTO action against France and nine other countries in the EU that banned the use of asbestos, one of the most recognized
carcinogens in the world. In fact, as delegates gathered in Seattle and as the
WTO approached its fifth anniversary, it had a perfect streak: every democratically attained environmental and public health rule or law challenged in

the WTO had been overturned. Every single one. These public health laws were erected by democratically elected governments to protect the well-being of their citizens. Yet, under the rules and guidelines of the World Trade Organization, these laws were all considered nontariff barriers to trade, illegal trade barriers that must be eliminated or changed under WTO rules.

The public became increasingly aware that our clean air and water regulations and our food safety laws are increasingly subject to the whims of the unelected and unaccountable trade lawyers in Geneva. The marchers in Seattle believed that if trade laws protect intellectual property rights, they should also protect the environment. If our trade laws protect patents, they should protect our food safety. If our trade laws protect Hollywood movies, they should protect worker rights. The delegates inside and the public outside the meetings—and I was part of both—heard the cry of support for enforceable standards to help workers and to protect the environment and for a trade policy as interested in American values of fairness as in corporate profits.

Leading up to and in Seattle, I met with religious groups that were opposed to the way China persecutes Muslims and Christians and condones forced abortions. I marched with men and women in labor unions who were competing against a flood of imports made by children in factories with padlocked doors and by political prisoners in labor camps. I shared a cup of coffee with veterans who do not want our nation to trade with a country like China, which organizes riots against our embassy and steals our nuclear secrets. And I met with the Malaysian trade minister and listened to his fears that low-wage workers in neighboring Indonesia would rob his country of desperately needed investment.

The "Battle in Seattle" reminded many Americans that we had been here before. The WTO represents a replay of the struggles we have had in this country throughout the last century: the massive shift of power from democratically elected governments to private interests. The American people—as played out in Upton Sinclair's 1906 book *The Jungle*—fought for food safety laws against large food-processing companies and their allies in government. And the American people won. We now have the world's safest food supply. American workers, many suffering from the violence inflicted upon them by Pinkertons, fought for the right to organize and to be paid a livable wage. And the American people won. We now have solid workers' rights, safer workplaces, and a strong middle class. In our lifetimes, the American people have fought for strong environmental laws against powerful

American industrialists who wanted no part of government regulation. And the American people won. Just look at Lake Erie and the Cuyahoga River and the air over northeast Ohio to see how far we have come.

And in 1999 Americans were beginning to understand that the rules of international trade shift power dramatically from elected governments to private interests. One WTO bureaucrat told the *Financial Times,* "The World Trade Organization is the place where governments collude in private against their domestic pressure groups." This is why it is so important to get worker and environmental standards at the core of the World Trade Organization.

Because WTO rules protecting worker rights, the environment, and food safety are as yet unwritten, permitting China to accede to the WTO was a grave mistake. China is a nation of 1.2 billion people ruled by an authoritarian government with a demonstrated aversion to environmental and labor standards and human rights. Letting China join the WTO amidst the negotiations for worker rights and the environment can only pull down the standards that we hope we can convince the WTO to adopt.

The Clinton administration touted the creation of its working group on labor and the environment as a major breakthrough for the World Trade Organization. It is envisioned that in the next decade the group will finalize a set of recommendations on how best to incorporate things like clean air, food safety standards, and labor rights. Given the snail-like pace of reform inherent in large bureaucracies, the fight to incorporate real standards will be a difficult one. This fight will require a president and a Congress determined to extend the same protections to the rest of the world that we have in this country.

Trade, like capitalism, can create great wealth for the world's people. The economic benefits of trade, unfortunately, have not trickled down to the world's poorest people. The massive wealth that has been generated by trade has not enabled them to afford or receive medical care. It has not provided them a decent education or the chance to actually earn enough money to buy any of our exports. In 1960, before globalization, the most affluent 20 percent of the world's population were thirty times richer than the poorest 20 percent. In 1997, at the height of globalization, the most fortunate were seventy-four times richer than the world's poorest. The combined fortunes of the four hundred richest people in the world equals more than the annual income of the poorest 50 percent of the world's people.

The sad reality is that there is no real mechanism in our trade laws to help the developing countries share the wealth that is being generated by trade. In 1998 the Nike Corporation paid Michael Jordan as much ($25 million) to endorse its shoes as it paid 35,000 Vietnamese to make them. In Mexico, workers living in the shadow of the some of the world's greatest companies for which they work, creating great wealth for American and Asian investors, live in *colonias,* makeshift cardboard shacks with no electricity and no running water.

Since the end of the second world war, successive administrations have pressured other countries to accept our ideas on intellectual property rights, the deregulation of financial markets, and the privatization of state-run services. Why should we not try to sell and promote around the world our *whole* economic package? If we protect intellectual property rights, Hollywood movies, patents, and CD-ROMS, why not protect the environment, worker rights, and food safety? We need to protect basic human rights for workers around the world—freedom from child labor, forced labor, and discrimination, freedom to join together with others in a union to have a voice at work. We are so proud of our success at exporting our products around the world, let us work with equal pride in exporting our democratic values of human rights, labor rights, and environmental standards. After all, a global economy that fails to lift the standard of living and to honor the values of working men and women will not work for working people. If it does not work for those who work with their hands, and if it does not work for those who create the world's products and the world's wealth, then it will not work at all, for any of us.

I had a personal decision to make leading up to the 2000 elections. The Ohio press corps had declared Ohio Republican senator Mike DeWine vulnerable to a strong challenge. Although as a member of the Senate Judiciary Committee he stepped up to the plate on impeachment, appearing on several national television programs and speaking out about the president's removal from office, DeWine had very few significant legislative accomplishments, was almost invisible in Washington, and had little presence in Ohio. With this in mind, Senate Minority Leader Tom Daschle and Democratic Senatorial Campaign Committee (DSCC) chairman Bob Torricelli invited me and my chief of staff, Donna Pignatelli, to the leader's office, where they told me that I was their first choice to run against DeWine in

2000. They promised significant financial support and any other services that the DSCC could offer. In the ethereal, rarified atmosphere adjacent to the Senate chamber, these two men were very persuasive.

I thought seriously about it, listing the advantages of serving in the United States Senate—where an individual can absolutely make a difference, the six-year term, no potential redistricting problems, the opportunity to serve as a senator from a large state, membership in the most exclusive club in the world, and greater access to the national media.

But after conversations with family and friends and supporters in Ohio, I declined. In so many ways, serving in the House of Representatives is the best job in the world. Few have the opportunity to make such a difference in the lives of so many people. Further, the Democrats in the House had an excellent chance of recapturing the majority in the 2000 elections, in which case I was in line to chair the Subcommittee on Health and the Environment, considered one of the best subcommittees in the entire Congress. The opportunity to work on issues about which I care so passionately—Medicare, prescription drugs, food safety, tuberculosis, clean air and water, universal health care coverage—was too great to pass up.

Besides, as Speaker Sam Rayburn once said to a House member who was contemplating a run for the Senate, "Why would you do that? You're already in Washington."

PART III

By assiduous flattery the hedonistic philosopher Aristippus had won himself a comfortable sinecure at the court of Dionysius, tyrant of Syracuse. One day, observing Diogenes preparing some lentils for a meager meal, Aristippus offered some worldly wisdom to his fellow sage: "If you would only learn to compliment Dionysius, you wouldn't have to live on lentils." Diogenes retorted, "If you would only learn to live on lentils, you wouldn't have to flatter Dionysius."

Pray for the dead and fight like hell for the living.
— Mary Harris (Mother Jones)

Against economic tyranny, the American citizen could only appeal to the organized power of government.
— Franklin Delano Roosevelt

The consciousness of being at war, and therefore in danger, makes the handing over of all power to a small caste seem the natural, unavoidable condition of survival.
— George Orwell, *Nineteen Eighty-Four*

19

Florida 2000, Class Warfare, and a Missed Opportunity

Class warfare? That's all over. The rich have won.
—Mark Shields

If a journalist had been present at the Sermon on the Mount, the caption in the morning papers would have read, "Cleric Sees Take-over By Meek."
—John Gardner, *Personal Journals* [published book?]

M Y DAUGHTER EMILY and I had never seen anything like it. Neither, of course, had America. Home from Swarthmore College for her Thanksgiving recess, she went with me to Florida to observe the infamous recount of the 2000 presidential race. Although 539,898 more people across the country voted for Al Gore than for George Bush, the outcome of the election hinged on the Florida recount, and the Democratic National Committee had asked me, as Ohio's former secretary of state and chief elections official, to observe the recount and talk to the media in Palm Beach, Miami-Dade, and Broward Counties. As we stepped off the plane in Fort Lauderdale, we knew we were in the eye of a Florida storm.

By then, three weeks after the election, we knew something about what led us to this place. During the summer of 1999 Florida secretary of state Katherine Harris, with the consent and support of Governor Jeb Bush, hired a Texas firm, Database Technologies, to clean up its voter registration rolls. The State of Florida paid this firm $4 million to "purge" its rolls. In most states elections officials, usually the secretary of state, are required to clean up the voter rolls by removing, or "purging," the names of people who are no longer eligible to vote, a generally cumbersome and laborious process. But few, if any, states turn to outside consultants. Names are deleted from the rolls for a variety of reasons, most notably failure to vote over a specific time (usually two or four consecutive general elections). A death certificate, a notification from a court of a felony conviction and sentencing, a change-of-address card sent in by a voter who has moved out of the county are other common reasons to invalidate a voter's registration. When I was Ohio secretary of state and the state's chief elections official in the 1980s, we were always extremely careful in removing names, giving the prospective voter the benefit of the doubt. I insisted, as did almost all my Republican and Democratic colleagues in other states, on the sanctity of the vote. When we were purging the rolls, we mailed a nonforwardable postcard to the home of any voter who had failed to vote for four consecutive years. If the postcard came back to the county board of elections as undeliverable, only then did we remove the name. If the voter still lived at the address, she could send us the form requesting to remain on the rolls.

After the process had been completed by Harris and Database Technologies, more than 57,000 Florida citizens were removed from the voter rolls, a number that, to say the least, would have raised eyebrows in Ohio when I was secretary of state. One person, Thomas Cooper, as pointed out by investigative reporter Greg Palast, was stricken from the rolls because Harris's office noted that he had been convicted of a felony in 2007 [*sic*]. Even the Data Technologies's CEO was surprised with the aggressiveness and zeal of Florida's secretary of state in removing names from the voter rolls. It was later shown that thousands of those citizens who had been stricken from the rolls had never committed a crime and should have remained legal voters.

What Emily and I saw in West Palm Beach was telling. Republicans had more star power, were better organized, and were more assertive than their Democratic counterparts. They stayed on script—even when the script had little familiarity with the truth. Dutiful party men, Governor Gilmor of Virginia, Governor Pataki of New York, Senator Lugar of Indiana, and Governor Racicot of Montana were there to do the GOP's heavy lifting. Some wanted a job with the Bush administration, and they did everything possible to ensure that there would be a Republican president. Their discipline was impressive. Every couple of hours they would disappear, returning forty-five minutes or so later looking like the Chicago Bears coming out for the second half. They were disciplined. They were enthusiastic. The crowds cheered them on. The press gathered around each as they fanned out over the compound. These politicans were scripted, on-message, and self-assured—an altogether impressive show. Except they made a lot of it up.

Governor Pataki, perhaps the most brazen and straight-faced of the lot, delivered his lines without flinching. "How many times does Al Gore want to count the ballots? He has already had four recounts," he thundered. "How many recounts does he need? Does he want to keep counting until he wins?" Pataki had to know that there had so far been not one single statewide recount and that the Republicans were trying to stop even a full recount in Palm Beach County. But the media never asked him to explain what he meant; they never demanded an explanation from Pataki of his statement. In the finest he-said/she-said journalism, the gaggle of perhaps a dozen reporters turned to me, the closest Democrat, to get "the Democrats' side." I said that there had not been four recounts, that the hand count is accepted practice all over the country, and that we should all stop obstructing the recount and get on with it. They broadcast his statement and my statement with no real explanation of the truth and no tough questioning for either of us. The governor of New York. A four-term congressman from the Midwest. Whom are you to believe? And later in the day Senator Lugar, a man of great decency and integrity, who was sorely misled by the Bush handlers, decreed that "we use punch-card voting in Indiana and we never—in fact it is illegal—hand count our ballots." A nearby Gore staffer called on a cell phone and found out that in Indiana hand counting *is* legal, has been done in close races on many occasions, and is believed by elections officials in both parties to yield the most accurate results. I pointed that out to a dwindling and visibly uninterested press corps, but nothing came of it. The five-term senator from Indiana. A largely unknown congressman from Ohio. Whom are you going to believe?

Conventional wisdom, as the *Washington Monthly* pointed out, holds that Republicans were more motivated during the Florida recount; that may have been the difference in the portrayal by the national media of the process. To be sure, many of their more prominent elected officials—and lots of potential job seekers—were there arguing the case. As it turned out, at least fifty of the Florida "GOP ground troops"—people carrying signs that read "Sore Loserman"; clean-cut Hill staffers who pounded on the doors of the Miami-Dade Elections Department and actually forced a cessation of the vote recount in that county; Republican operatives who chanted whenever there were live shots from West Palm Beach election headquarters—were later appointed to top jobs in the Bush administration: John Bolton, undersecretary of state for arms control; Matt Schlapp, special assistant to the president; Sue Cobb, U.S. ambassador to Jamaica; Jeanie Mamo, a White

House spokeswoman; T. Ted Cruz, director of policy and planning at the Federal Trade Commission; at least five lawyers in the White House counsel's office; and three general counsels to cabinet secretaries.

As we observed the recount inside the emergency shelter in Palm Beach County, my thoughts went back to Al Gore and his first debate with George Bush. While the media (and the Republicans) downplayed expectations for Bush's performance, Gore was the one who underperformed. Certainly Bush was not impressive, but he was good enough when voters compared him to Gore's much-less-than-expected performance. During the campaign Gore was mediocre at best. Most Democrats thought he should have won the election by ten percentage points. He had a strong economy on which to campaign. He had experience that Bush could not touch. (He would have been only the third person in American history—joining Richard Nixon and Lyndon Johnson—to hold all four elected offices: representative, senator, vice president, president.) And he was without a doubt much more knowledgeable about the issues

At lunch on a September day with several Democrats at the Capitol, I was wondering aloud what Gore's problem was, why he was not holding a decisive lead, why he was not connecting with the voters. George Miller, a gutsy Democrat from California, offered, "Even when I am angry with Clinton, when I'm done talking with him, I forget why I was pissed off. After talking to Gore, I'm even more pissed off." Back in my district the voters were also disenchanted with Gore. On one occasion, in October 2000, I was drinking coffee with several autoworkers in the cafeteria at the Ford plant in Avon Lake and discussing the presidential election. All but one of the men said they were voting for the UAW-endorsed Gore. The lone dissenter announced he was voting for Bush, even though he knew the Republican was hostile to organized labor and working-class concerns, because "Gore wants to take my gun." A Gore supporter seated next to me retorted, "Well, Sherrod has the same position that Gore does." "Yeah," the Bush voter responded, "but at least Brown is fighting for stuff I care about."

The acme of Gore's campaign was when he was "fighting for stuff" people cared about. When Gore talked about "the people versus the powerful," when he attacked "big tobacco, big oil, the big polluters, the pharmaceutical companies, the HMOs" his rise in the polls was sharp, definite, and measurable. Before that, he was down 48-38; afterward he moved ahead 49-38, and his gains looked sustainable. But some leading Democrats, far too easily cowed and urged on by a generally conservative corporate media and a running mate who was uncomfortable with any criticism of business, backed Gore away from his populist agenda. Some reporters said that there was a disconnect developing between Gore and the average voter. The fear, according to journalist/pundit Carl Bernstein, was that "Gore's populist manifesto amounts to class warfare," as if voters disagreed with the vice president's criticism of HMOs, oil companies, and big pharmaceutical companies. In fact, Gore's twenty-one-point net gain in the polls could be attributed to nothing else. Few things that reporters write, or corporate PR flacks and Republicans say, are more grating than accusing liberal or populist Democrats—which I obviously am—of class warfare. Many Democrats retreat when accused of such bestiality, but some of us turn up the volume, repeat our words, and continue.

Over lunch one day in late 2002 with political pundit Mark Shields, I shared with him my frustration about Democrats' reluctance to point out Republicans' single-minded mission to help the rich. They started class warfare when they cut taxes for the most privileged people in our society, I said. "Class warfare?" Shields said. "Class warfare's over. The rich have already won." Shields was right. Look at what has happened. As recounted by Kevin Phillips and by Molly Ivins, the very rich have gained fabulous new wealth while the income and net worth of most of society have shrunk. CEO pay was 25 times that of hourly production workers in 1960. In 1970 it was 30 to 1; now it is 458 to 1. In the last decade wages were stagnant while America's top executives of America's largest corporations saw compensation increases of 481 percent. The income of the richest 5 percent of Americans has risen 54 percent in the last twenty years, while the income of the bottom 20 percent has increased only 1.5 percent. The effective tax rate (income and FICA, the Medicare and social security tax) for the top 1 percent of families fell from 69 percent in 1970 to 40 percent in 1993. The tax rate for the median family increased from 16 percent to 25 percent. Between 1950 and 2000 corporate taxes as a percentage of total tax receipts fell from 27 to 10 percent while FICA jumped from 7 percent to 31 percent. The top 20 percent of households own 83 percent of our nation's wealth. The bottom 60 percent owns less than 5 percent of the wealth, and the bottom 40 percent owns less than 1 percent of this country's wealth.

From 1990 to 2000 the average work year had expanded by 184 hours, according to the Bureau of Labor Statistics; the average American worked 350 hours annually more than the average European. And in 1999 the after-tax average income of the middle 60 percent of Americans was actually lower than in 1977. But the four hundred richest Americans between 1982 and 1999 increased their average net worth from $230 million to $2.6 billion, a more than 500 percent increase in constant dollars. From 1980 to 1999 the five hundred largest U.S. corporations tripled their assets and their profits, and enlarged their market value eightfold, as measured by stock prices. During the same period, those same corporations eliminated 5,000,000 jobs.

Yet, as if that is not enough, Republicans continue to practice class warfare almost every day: cuts in programs for the poor so we can afford tax cuts for the most privileged; weakening environmental laws on behalf of corporate interests; scaling back OSHA enforcement at the request of big manufacturers; a bankruptcy bill that takes care of Ken Lay and screws the working single mother with a sick kid and no health insurance. Perhaps most tellingly, the frequency of audits of low-income taxpayers—especially those who are eligible for the Earned Income Tax Credit (EITC)—have increased sharply, while the number of audits of higher income taxpayers has precipitously dropped. And even though audits of taxpayers earning more than $100,000 annually yield almost $5,000 to the government on average, and audits of lower income taxpayers yield less than half of that, the wrath of the Internal Revenue Service is most often reserved for those who are claiming the EITC. An individual earning more than $100,000 a year has a 1 in 208 chance of being audited; a low-income taxpayer's chance of an audit is 1 in 50.

The first thing that President Bush did upon assuming office in 2001 was push through a tax cut that went overwhelmingly to the wealthiest 1 percent of Americans. President Bush, the ultimate practitioner of class warfare, has since turned over environmental policy to the chemical companies, energy policy to the oil companies, Medicare policy to the insurance and prescription drug industry, Social Security privatization to Wall Street, and public health policy to the tobacco companies. He has appointed food company executives to food safety positions in the Department of Agriculture and then weakened food safety rules and regulations. He has scaled back worker safety and environmental laws, opened loopholes for corporations to move to Bermuda and other offshore havens to avoid paying U.S. taxes and still be eligible for government contracts, and cut taxes for the richest Americans while sending working class kids to fight in Afghanistan and Iraq.

And we who point this out and occasionally rail against it are practicing class warfare?! While the GOP wages class warfare in their everyday machinations of governing, they are very quick to accuse Democrats of "engaging in class warfare." The best defense, Republican operatives will privately say, is a good, aggressive offense. They know that when populist Democrats criticize the oil companies and the big pharmaceutical firms, it resonates with the voters. And Republicans know that most voters believe that their party is far too close to large corporate interests.

Sitting on the House floor one day, I imagined a very different Washington. On December 11, 2001, I spoke on the House of Representatives about a government of which we as a nation could be very proud.

> Three months ago today, as we all know, was September 11. The great, great majority of people in this country came together. They put out their flags, they gave blood, they volunteered. Some went to New York to volunteer, others went to the Pentagon to volunteer, and schoolchildren all over the country collected pennies, nickels, and dimes to send to the victims and their families.
>
> My dad used to talk about World War II and shared sacrifice, about war bonds and WAVES and WACS and victory gardens and scrap metal drives. Imagine if the president and the Republican Congress called on us—like in World War II—for shared sacrifice. Imagine if the president called on young patriotic Americans to enlist in the army or the Peace Corps, to enlist in the navy or AmeriCorps, to enlist in the air force or Teach for America. That is what waving the American flag is all about.
>
> Imagine if the president said to his friends, and the Republican leadership said to their friends in the drug industry, "No more special favors; we are not going to allow them to charge American consumers and America's elderly more for prescription drugs than anywhere else in the world." That is what waving the American flag is all about.
>
> Imagine if the president called on Americans to volunteer for Meals on Wheels or for cleaning up the neighborhood or tutoring children that are having difficulty keeping up. That is what waving the American flag is all about.
>
> Imagine if the president would say to his friends in the oil business, "We are going to wean ourselves off Middle Eastern oil. We are going to find a way to help Americans conserve and get better gas mileage and turn their thermostats down" and all the things the president could do to appeal to Americans, to appeal to his friends in the corporate boardrooms and the oil companies. That is what waving the American flag is all about.
>
> Instead of this Republican president and Republican leadership bestowing tax cuts on the wealthiest Americans, imagine if we helped those who needed help the most. And instead of the president and the Republican leadership bestowing tax cuts on the largest corporations in the world in this country, imagine instead if they appealed to the best in America. Imagine.

20

September 11 and the 107th Congress

Sometimes, tragedy also presents opportunities for those who are alert.

— U.S. Trade Representative Robert Zoellick, October 2001

This tragedy will only be magnified if it is exploited for political gain. Politicians who wrap themselves in the flag while relentlessly pursuing their usual partisan agenda are not true patriots, and history will not forgive them.

— Paul Krugman, *New York Times* columnist

SIX DECADES AGO millions of Americans reacted as one to the tragedy of December 7, 1941, when Pearl Harbor, Hawaii, was attacked by the Japanese. A stunned nation listened to the reassuring words of its leader, President Franklin Delano Roosevelt, as he called on citizens to fight for democracy and rally around the war effort. In a display of bipartisanship, he appointed prominent Republicans to help lead the war effort, most notably Henry Stimson as secretary of the war and Frank Knox as secretary of the navy. President Roosevelt talked of "shared sacrifice" and the country responded. Millions of men and women stepped forward to volunteer for the armed services, and hundreds of thousands of women went to work in industrial plants to fuel the war machine. Taxes were raised on the wealthiest citizens to fund the war effort, and people bought war bonds, set up victory gardens, organized scrap metal drives. In Great Britain, Prime Minister Winston Churchill, a Tory who had become that nation's leader in 1940, chose as his deputy prime minister the leader of the Labour Party, Clement Atlee. Their bipartisan coordination of the war helped bring the British people together.

To us in the twenty-first century, the gruesome September 11 terrorist attacks on two American symbols—the World Trade Center and the Pentagon—seemed much like the Japanese assault on Pearl Harbor. Thousands died. The attack was vicious and the damage unimaginable. It appeared to have been planned for months. The response to both tragedies seemed similar. President George W. Bush asked for support and unity from the American people in this global fight against terrorism. Americans rallied around him and the war effort. Young men and women called their local enlistment offices. Millions of Americans put up flags at their homes, in their workplaces, on their SUVs. Hundreds of thousands of Americans donated blood, many for the first time in their lives. Tens of thousands volunteered to help rescue efforts at the Pentagon, at Ground Zero in New York where the buildings had stood, and in their communities. Thousands of schoolchildren collected pennies and nickels and dimes to send to the victims and their families. And Americans by the millions honored those who lost their lives, especially police and firefighters who performed some of the greatest acts of heroism that our nation has ever seen.

But this unity looked very different inside the Washington Beltway. It was not long after the terrorist attacks on the World Trade Center and the Pentagon that the wartime political profiteering began. Administration officials called on Congress to immediately pass the stalled and generally accepted-as-unworkable National Missile Defense program (as if that would have stopped or deterred the airplane attacks on our nation). Less than forty-eight hours after the attack, Republican Ways and Means chairman Bill Thomas of California tried to railroad through Congress a major cut in the capital gains tax; fully 80 percent of the benefits would have gone to 2 percent of taxpayers, the 2 percent at the top of the economic ladder.

Within days Congress, at the insistence of President Bush, gave the airlines $5 billion—no strings attached—with no sacrifice from executives, no assistance for their 100,000 laid-off employees, and no attention paid to airport security. House Republican leadership insisted on a continued privatized airport security system, where checkers and screeners were typically paid no more than seven dollars an hour with no benefits and little training; only later did they yield to public opinion and federalize the system. House Republicans also quickly passed a stimulus package that would retroactively (back to 1986) eliminate the minimum taxes that America's largest corporations have paid. Under the GOP plan IBM would get a check from Washington for $1.4 billion, Ford for $1 billion, General Motors for $800 million, Enron for $250 million. More than a dozen other large U.S. companies would receive refunds of at least $100 million for fifteen years of corporate taxes. American Airlines and United Airlines, back in the soup line, were each expected to receive a check for several hundred million dollars. All this was in the name of stimulating the economy. New Jersey Democrat Frank Pallone grumbled, "All you have to do is mention September 11 to get your way around here."

In early October 2001 the Bush administration joined with the U.S. Chamber of Commerce to come to the aid of the nation's largest tobacco companies, which had tried to insert language into antiterrorism legislation to protect them from a spate of pending civil Racketeer Influenced and Corrupt Organizations Act (RICO) lawsuits filed by foreign governments in U.S. courts. They were successful in placing language in the House-passed USA PATRIOT Act, which would have taken away foreign governments' ability to bring federal racketeering charges against American tobacco companies that had laundered money in their countries. Despite White House lobbying efforts on behalf of the tobacco companies, Senate Democrats dropped the pro-tobacco language.

Then came Fast Track—now renamed, in Bush administration "newspeak," Trade Promotion Authority (TPA). Fast Track legislation had been so discredited in the eyes of Congress and the public that the administration thought it needed a new label. This TPA legislation would give the president the ability to negotiate trade agreements with no labor or environmental safeguards and with little congressional input. The final, negotiated product would then be presented to Congress, with no possibility of amendments or change, for a simple up-or-down vote. President Bush planned to use TPA first, and most importantly, to pass NAFTA-like agreements for all of Latin America.

U.S. Trade Representative Robert Zoellick almost immediately linked the president's need for TPA to the fight against terrorism: "America's trade leadership can build a coalition of countries that cherish liberty in all its aspects." In this difficult time our country needs TPA, he said, "as a cornerstone of international leadership." Calling failure to pass the president's plan in this international time of crisis "a mistake of historical magnitude," Zoellick even compared those who opposed TPA to Gavrilo Princip, the fanatic who is credited with igniting World War I by assassinating Austrian Archduke Franz Ferdinand, implying that Balkan-like "tirades of hate and invective" by TPA opponents could lead to the same kind of "dangerous 'isms'—protectionism, isolationism, authoritarianism"—that Princip's murderous act precipitated. Republican Majority Leader Dick Armey chimed in, echoing Zoellick's words and pointing out "the national security dimension of fast track." So did former Mexican president Ernesto Zedillo, by then a board member of the multinational corporation Procter and Gamble, proclaiming that environmental, labor, and civic protestors have "an unexpected alliance" with terrorists. David Hartridge, an influential senior official at the WTO Secretariat, openly declared that the September 11 terrorists and activists against corporate-driven globalization shared a propensity for "violent behavior."

Charles Rangel, the senior Democrat on the House Ways and Means Committee and a veteran of combat in the Korean War, angrily responded to Zoellick's efforts to "wrap a trade promotion authority bill in the flag. . . . To appeal to patriotism in an effort to force Congress to move on Fast Track by claiming it is needed to fight terrorism would be laughable if it weren't so serious." Joining Rangel was veteran Ways and Means Democrat Robert Matsui of California, who had voted for every trade agreement since he had come to Congress in 1979. Matsui had been rebuffed in trying to work out a more moderate bill with Thomas that protected labor and environmental standards and preserved more congressional oversight and input into trade negotiations. Leo Gerard, president of the United Steelworkers of America, said, "Fast Track will not foster national security, nor defend us against other acts of terrorism. Fast Track will not find the perpetrators. Fast Track will not help those unemployed by the attack or provide an immediate stimulus for the economy."

Fast Track—the 2001 version—had been in deep trouble prior to September 11. Despite regular predictions by the White House and Republican congressional leaders that they were going to bring it to a vote in July, then August, then right after Labor Day, it was clear that pro–free trade forces were at least a couple dozen votes short. In the weeks after the terrorist attacks, labor and environmental groups, the core of the opposition to Fast Track, were slow to resume their opposition. Most of us thought it unseemly to press our case with the media, other members of Congress, and the public in the ensuing weeks after our country's tragedy. But others had a very different view. As the president spoke of national unity and called on Congress to put aside partisan differences, his man on the Ways and Means Committee, Chairman Thomas, led the profiteering by pushing through his TPA bill on a mostly party-line vote and with no consultation with Democratic leaders on that committee.

While many in the Bush administration and in Congress were using the events of September 11 to argue for their pre-attack agenda, the government was moving ahead to meet real terrorism threats. Lines were longer at the nation's airports, even though fewer people were flying, as the still-private airport security firms asked more questions of passengers and looked more closely at their carry-on luggage. Local governments, with little funding from the federal government, beefed up security at public buildings and municipal water facilities: municipal electric authorities hired police officers to guard their power plants.

Many of us in Congress who believed our government had starved public health in the United States called for a rebuilding of our public health infrastructure. We knew that as a nation we did too little to combat foodborne illness, to practice preventive medicine, to deter antibiotic resistance. We wanted more funding for the Centers for Disease Control and Prevention (CDC) and for local and state public health departments—the first line of defense against bioterrorism and the more common, nagging, persistent public health problems like the flu, low birthweight babies, lead poisoning, and the growing disparities in health outcomes based on race and class.

Others who have had little interest in the past in funding the CDC, the nation's (and the world's) preeminent public health organization, discovered that the agency had an important role in public health. Unfortunately, their interest in public health seemed to begin and end with bioterrorism. They were willing to increase the funding for CDC, and for local and state health departments around the country, at least to respond to anthrax scares. And although the Bush administration proposed cutting the CDC's budget prior to September 11, they were now willing to buy (albeit at too high a price, allowing the politically influential prescription drug companies to profiteer a bit) huge quantities of Cipro, an antibiotic used against anthrax, and smallpox vaccines for hundreds of millions of dollars.

As President Bush was assembling the multinational coalition in September 2001 to fight terrorism, 80,000 people died that month around the world from malaria, including one child under the age of five every forty seconds. During the week of October 7, 2002, when the U.S. began its bombing campaign in Afghanistan, 30,000 Africans died from HIV/AIDS. On October 17, 2001, the day that anthrax shut down the United States House of Representatives and Speaker Hastert told members of Congress to leave the Capitol, 1,100 people in India alone died from tuberculosis.

Trade figures prominently in the spread of infectious disease. As coffee refugees in Nicaragua lose their farms in part because of World Bank–induced plummeting coffee prices, they flock to refugee camps and urban areas, dramatically increasing their chances of contracting tuberculosis or HIV or hepatitis. As the World Bank forces on some of the poorest nations structural adjustment programs—which mandates that developing countries cut funding on education and health care in order to pay foreign debt and to develop an export economy so that they will export more—the cuts in public health spending devastate an already exceedingly inadequate and fragile health care infrastructure.

As administration lobbyists were unsuccessful in their efforts to link expanded trade and terrorism, Trade Representative Zoellick told Congress that the United States would be embarrassed if the new round of trade talks, the ministerial in Qatar, would find the U.S. government unable to empower their trade negotiators with Fast Track. But Zoellick's and Thomas's pleas for TPA fell on deaf congressional ears. Whether in the name of antiterrorism or to protect the position of the United States as the world's leading trading nation, the Bush administration simply could not round up the votes before the WTO's November meeting in Qatar.

As usual, you didn't need a scorecard to identify the players on each side. In support of Trade Promotion Authority/Fast Track were the president, Republican leadership, CEOs of America's most powerful and wealthiest corporations, and almost every major newspaper publisher and editor in the country. In opposition were House Democratic leaders, labor unions, environmental organizations, human rights groups, and—according to every major published poll—a strong majority of the public. With the power and influence arrayed against us, as on every trade bill, those of us in opposition knew that we had our work cut out for us.

We used the familiar arguments with other members, in news conferences, on talk shows, and in speeches at home: the trade deficit had swelled from $182 billion when NAFTA took effect in 1994 to $439 billion in 2000. According to the first President Bush and his economic formula and calculations, this growth in the U.S. trade deficit translates into 5,100,000 mostly good-paying, industrial jobs. The U.S. economy was experiencing the longest decline in industrial output activity since the Great Depression levels of 1932. We lost more than one million manufacturing jobs in the first ten months of the George W. Bush administration.

In the developing world, things were much worse. The income gap between the fifth of the world's people living in the riches countries and the fifth living in the poorest doubled between 1960 and 1990, from a 30-1 ratio to 60-1. By 1998 it had ballooned to 78-1, the United Nations' *Human Development Report* announced, with 100 million more poor people in the developing world today than ten years earlier.

Before Thanksgiving 2001 Republican Majority Leader Dick Armey announced that the vote on TPA would take place on December 6, giving both sides a day at which to aim their lobbying efforts. As the vote drew nearer, the appeals to patriotism and to "do this for the president" became more frequent. President Bush himself called or personally met with more than three dozen representatives, asserting that he needed members of Congress, especially Republicans, to fight this war on terrorism. Two Florida Republicans were invited on Air Force One so the president would have an opportunity to lobby them, meet their objections, and cut a (likely protectionist) deal. Secretary of Commerce Don Evans said he met with more than a hundred members to try to convince them to support TPA. In a series of meetings at the White House, the president promised House Republicans, in a free trade bill, protection for textiles, citrus, apparel, and specialty crops. But mostly the president's pitch was patriotism. Ultraconservative Bob Barr, a Georgia Republican who lost a primary election in August 2002, said that Bush told him, "As president, I need your vote for our nation's security." Speaker Dennis Hastert, an Illinois Republican, also chimed in. "Support our president who is fighting a courageous war on terrorism," he intoned solemnly.

Matsui, Rangel, and Michigan's Sandy Levin, the senior Democrat on the Ways and Means subcommittee on Trade, suggested language that would have provided substantive labor and environmental standards, not as mere window dressing but as real protections in the core agreement. "It's no longer whether you are for or against trade," Matsui said, "it's how you manage trade."

I organized a meeting with major environmental groups in Democratic Whip David Bonior's office, with leading environmental members of Congress, including George Miller, Peter DeFazio, Mike Capuano, Jan Schakowsky, Lynn Woolsey, and Lloyd Doggett. Prior to this vote on trade promotion authority, the environmental movement as a whole had never fought against a trade bill. During the NAFTA debate in 1993, President Clinton in his first year as president strong-armed several unsure environmental groups (almost all of whom had supported his campaign) to support his trade bill. This year things were different. Environmentalists saw in George Bush the most antienvironmental president in decades. In a letter to House members, the League of Conservation Voters announced that it would likely include this vote on its environmental scorecard, an important consideration at election time for many members who proudly point to their proenvironment voting record.

The weekly trade whip meetings to count votes and organize our forces began in mid-October. Almost from the start, we knew that we had at least 160 Democratic votes in opposition to trade promotion authority. Only seven Democrats were publicly committed to vote for this bill. We also knew that another five to ten would be exceedingly difficult to hold. And Bonior, Matsui, and I, who led the whip effort, knew that we had to keep the Democratic losses under about twenty. Too many Republicans would wilt under pressure from the president. Amazingly, we could find no Republican to organize a whip effort in opposition to the Trade Promotion Authority legislation even though fifty-eight Republican members who were still in Congress had voted against granting Fast Track authority to President Clinton. The ability of Republican leadership to enforce discipline on its members was nothing short of remarkable. It was clear that at least half of those Republicans who had established themselves as opponents of free trade would drop their opposition because the appeal came from a Republican president. It was an easy vote for them when Bill Clinton was president. We also knew that a call from President Bush, especially with an appeal to patriotism, would cause many Republicans to drop their long-held opposition to TPA.

Thousands of calls, perhaps tens of thousands of calls, came into the offices of the thirty to forty undecided Republican and Democratic members. They came from business lobbyists, their corporate clients, and their executives; on the other side came significantly more calls from labor union members, environmental activists, and human rights advocates. As Georgia congressman John Lewis said, "Passion is on our side on these trade issues; money is on their side." Other efforts continued around the country. Both sides ran radio and television ads in the districts of undecided members. Democratic Majority Leader Gephardt met with small groups of undecided members to try to persuade them to oppose TPA. Ohio Democrat Marcy Kaptur and other agriculture experts and farm state opponents to TPA buttonholed their colleagues on the deleterious effects of trade agreements on agriculture. Freshmen Hilda Solis (D-Calif.) and Stephen Lynch (D-Mass.) were earning their spurs on this vote, as they dutifully took names at Whip meetings and talked with members whom they were getting to know. Lloyd Doggett, Tom Allen, and I spoke with a couple dozen Republicans about a provision inserted into TPA by America's drug companies that would have given them a greater ability to negotiate even higher prescription drug prices.

On the day of the vote, we knew that the Republicans were a few votes short. We were going to lose around twenty Democrats (we hoped to keep it under that number), but we thought we had a chance to get as many as twenty-seven or twenty-eight Republicans. There was some speculation that Republican leaders, strong TPA advocates to the person, might pull the bill off the floor because they were not sure that they were going to win. But they decided to roll the dice.

After the debate, the roll call began. Usually lasting the fifteen minutes on the scoreboard clock, plus another couple of minutes to make sure that everyone has a chance to vote, this roll call was surely going to last a lot longer. It was clear that the Republican leadership was still a handful of votes short, perhaps as many as five. But after the seventeen minutes turned into twenty-five, thirty, and then thirty-five, and we were still ahead (by a vote of 210-214), political cynicism kicked in.

South Carolina Republican Jim DeMint—who represents a textile area, who had publicly opposed Fast Track, and who actually already cast a "no" vote—yielded to the pressure tactics of Republican leadership. He secured a letter promising assistance in protecting in a *free trade* agreement textile companies in South Carolina. DeMint went down to the well of the House chamber, in view of everyone, and switched his vote, to the cheers of rank-and-file Republicans and the jeers of many Democrats. (Most members of the House have seen letters like the one DeMint was given, with promises from presidents to address specific, parochial, or district concerns; we have also seen the promises inevitably evaporate after the vote is cast. Indeed, within days of DeMint's switch the evaporation process had already begun. Thomas, the Republican Ways and Means Chairman from California, told people privately the next day that he was determined to "break the promise" that Speaker Hastert and Whip DeLay had made to DeMint.) After DeMint brandished his letter—and the roll call by then had been held open for twenty extra minutes—four other Republicans came down to the well to cast their votes in support. One of them, Representative Robin Hayes, who was actually whipping against Fast Track during the first minutes of the roll call vote, had tears in his eyes as he succumbed to the pressure of Majority Whip Tom DeLay and GOP leadership. The *Wall Street Journal,* an enforcer of Republican party discipline and the nation's chief cheerleader for free trade, said that Hayes was "visibly shaken" by his vote switch. Lindsay Graham, a gutsy South Carolina Republican who was later elected to the Senate and who actually stands for something, opposed granting Fast Track to Clinton and again opposed giving it to Bush. The morning after the vote, he ruefully told me, "Several Republicans lost their jobs last night."

Fully 90 percent of House Democrats opposed TPA, a testament to the work of an energized labor and environmental movement, David Bonior and the Democratic whip operation, and the work of Bob Matsui, the California Democrat who had supported every trade agreement during his twenty-three-year congressional career. All six members from northeast Ohio voted no—Tubbs Jones, Kucinich, Regula, Sawyer, LaTourette, and I—clearly a victory for the organizational efforts of Barbara Janis, John Ryan, Linda Romanik, Dave Prentice, and others in Cleveland, Akron, and Lorain.

The passage of TPA was assured, however, because of the huge number of Republicans supporting the bill. No less than 194 Republicans voted for the bill; only twenty-three opposed it. Two-thirds of the 58 Republicans who voted against Fast Track for President Clinton turned around and supported granting that same authority to President Bush. Several Republican members were disappointments because of the economic devastation suffered in their home districts due to the damage to the steel industry brought on from foreign imports. Others, who represented textile areas, which may have experienced even more disastrous economic woes than steel, were equally disappointing. But the biggest disappointments of all were those members who dutifully trooped to the House floor night after night in 1993 during the NAFTA debate and in 1997 and 1998 when Congress considered granting Fast Track authority to President Clinton. They seemed to put party above their fair trade principles, responding instead to President Bush's call to party loyalty.

Respected long-time *Washington Post* columnist David Broder called the 215-214 passage of Trade Promotion Authority "a nakedly partisan vote." It broke, he said, the bipartisanship that had generally characterized the trade debates and trade policy in the past. Few issues were this partisan in Congress, with about 90 percent of each party going one way; and trade in the past had never been. Broder blamed Republican leadership, especially fingering Republican Whip Tom DeLay as the main culprit. Martin Tolchin, publisher of the Capital Hill newspaper *The Hill,* wrote of the unprecedented twenty-three-minute delay in keeping the vote open and the "frantic last-minute arm-twisting, horse trading and blatant political bribery" by Republican leaders on the House floor. Tom Donahue, president of the U.S. Chamber of Commerce, said simply, "A one-vote margin was all we could afford."

Much was at stake, as it always is on trade votes. Columnist Broder said that there were more lobbyists lined up outside the House chamber and on the sidewalk to the Capitol than he had seen in his several decades of covering the Congress. Republicans—almost 90 percent of them—rallied around the Republican president and came to the aid of their corporate allies, many of whom contributed large sums of money to the National Republican

Congressional Committee and to individual members. Democrats, in even higher percentages, supported their traditional labor and environment and human rights allies. In the end, most Democrats just did not trust a president who had, in less than a year in office, fought so hard to weaken environmental and labor standards in the domestic economy. Why would we expect him to enforce or strengthen those standards in a globalized economy?

While much of the work of the 107th Congress centered around the fight against terrorism, much of its activity was taken up with what a number of Democrats might call "class warfare legislation." From weakening environmental laws to tax cuts that overwhelmingly benefited the most privileged, from cutting back on financial regulation to passing trade promotion authority, President Bush was asking us to do it all. And, unfortunately, Congress all too often complied. Whatever the corporate agenda, the president and Republican congressional leadership enthusiastically supported it.

Through most of the first half of 2002, things looked good for President Bush and the Republican majority in the House. The president's ratings were high after September 11; the public seemed satisfied with the nation's political leadership, and voters were optimistic about the future. In the aftermath of September, heroic firefighters, the president, and Congress responded aggressively to our national tragedy. Fully two-thirds of Americans, the polls said then, thought the country was "on the right track."

That began to change rapidly as the summer of 2002 wore on. Enron. Arthur Andersen. WorldCom. Tyco. Adelphia. Then Stanley Works, a company known for its high quality of American workmanship, announced that its shareholders had approved a plan to change its place of incorporation from Connecticut to Bermuda, thus saving about $30 million in federal taxes annually. All Stanley Works had to do was to file articles of incorporation in Bermuda, open a post office box there, and hold an annual meeting there. Nothing else changed for the company: they still qualified for state and local tax abatement; they could still stamp "Made in USA" on their products; they were still eligible for federal government contracts.

Republicans, who were confident that they would pick up House seats in the November midterm elections, were increasingly nervous. Political poll after poll showed the "right track/wrong track" numbers going in the wrong direction. Even columnists like George Will, Cal Thomas, and Bob Novak, all cheerleaders for Republican orthodoxy and enforcers of Republican party discipline, were opining that the corporate scandals could cost the GOP control of the House of Representatives. On the last night of the summer session, Connecticut congresswoman Rosa DeLauro offered an amendment to the Homeland Security legislation that caused panic among Republican rank-and-file members. It was straightforward and simple: no company that moved offshore to avoid U.S. taxes would be eligible for government contracts. DeLauro said, "These are corporate traitors. We should not be willing to do business, as the U.S. government, with those who want the benefits of U.S. citizenship without the responsibilities that go with it." Majority Leader Dick Armey spoke for the Republicans: "Mr. Speaker, let me appreciate the concern that the gentlewoman expresses over the burden of our taxes that make American corporations undertake regrettable action. Mr. Speaker, that is just one of the burdens of our current Tax Code that would be corrected by the flat tax." The fact that corporate taxes as a percent of federal revenues has declined from 23.2 percent in 1960 to 12.5 percent in 1980 to 10.1 percent in 2000 did not cool Armey's distaste for what he liked to call the excessive burden of corporate taxes. Nor did it seem to bother him that the tax burden in the United States had been shifted mostly to middle-class families. Armey was only mouthing the words that the *Wall Street Journal* had already written: "Why it's patriotic to avoid paying high tax rates." Enron, for instance, had 881 "subsidiaries" abroad, helping it shed much of its federal tax burden, or tax responsibilities, depending on how you look at it. Halliburton, Vice President Cheney's former company (and which is still paying him $13,000 each month), had only nine subsidiaries incorporated in offshore tax havens when he became CEO in 1995; five years later it had forty-four, enabling it to cut its taxes from $302 million to less than zero. Halliburton, which did huge amounts of business with the government, actually received an $85 million rebate.

Offshore "reincorporation," Democrats pointed out, cost the U.S. Treasury $70 billion in tax receipts annually. The $70 billion dollars would have to be made up by less affluent taxpayers or by cuts in services like student loans and health care or by adding to the national debt. Congressman Maloney (D-Conn.) may have said it best when he pointed out: "It is unpatriotic and immoral for companies to do this in time of war, when we have brave American men and women in harm's way. The people of America deserve better."

When the vote was taken, all but one Democrat voted for the motion. As the clock ticked down to zero time, and the roll was left open for the few who had not yet voted, only eight Republicans—all in very tough races in the fall—had voted for it. But then something peculiar, and exceedingly rare, happened. When it was clear that the DeLauro motion was going to pass, albeit by a very narrow margin, dozens of Republicans decided that they did not want to be on record as having opposed such a popular initiative in an election year. As the Speaker Pro Tempore bellowed, "Anyone want to change their vote?" Republican members lined up, jostling for position, more than 100 of them, some of them a bit embarrassed, in the well of the House, picking up a green card from the box on the table in front of the clerk and changing their votes. By the time the Speaker gaveled the amendment, it had passed 318-110, with 109 Republicans joining 207 Democrats and two independents in support.

Although political profiteering became more difficult for those to whom allegiance to corporate interests was their highest calling, the week of July 22 illustrated Congress's addiction to corporate money and its inability (or unwillingness) to wean itself from the "mother's milk of politics," as California Assembly Speaker Jess Unruh termed political contributions. Under enormous pressure from defrauded investors, the Republican leadership finally, though reluctantly, agreed to bring a relatively strong accounting reform bill to the floor. The bill made America's corporations more accountable to shareholders and would begin to restore investor faith in our markets. But, as *The American Prospect* said, "It's corporate reform Thursday, corporate cave-in Friday." Indeed, on the very next day the Republican-dominated House was poised to turn around and give corporate America its two most desired prizes: bankruptcy reform and Fast Track (Trade Promotion Authority). TPA, which had passed the House by one vote seven months earlier, was emerging from a House-Senate conference committee. Democrats, perhaps a bit cynically, thought that Republican efforts would ease some of the pain that Republican contributors might have felt in Congress's rush to discipline corporate America. The bankruptcy bill, pushed by the credit card companies and some of the nation's largest banks to make it more difficult for Americans of modest means to discharge their credit card debt, made no allowance for Americans who lost jobs and life savings from WorldCom and Enron collapses, who had suffered major illness, who had been victimized by bad luck. Nor did congressional consideration of the bill lessen credit card solicitation.

But organized business—in particular the National Federation of Independent Business, the U.S. Chamber of Commerce, and the National Association of Manufacturers—still had enough clout to move the trade legislation. The House-Senate conference committee had moved quickly. A Senate staffer who watched the conference committee summed it up: "The news wasn't good; a bad Senate bill was conferenced with a terrible House bill, and the result was predictably awful." Members had no time to read the bill. The debate began late in the evening. Ohio Representative Marcy Kaptur told the House that the president and Republican leadership "want to debate it in the middle of the night while most people are sleeping." A few hours earlier as we were debating the legislation to create the Office of Homeland Defense, members of Congress had received in their offices an email notification that we could review the 304-page legislation on the congressional website. Then, before the bill could be taken up, in the middle of the night, Congress had to invoke Martial Law, an unusual procedure that waives the requirement that members be given at least one day to review legislation before voting on it.

This time we were pretty sure that we were going to lose. President Bush had made a rare visit to Capitol Hill to speak to the Republican Conference on the day of the vote to put even more pressure on wavering Republicans. We knew that it would be difficult to get the twenty-eight or twenty-nine Republicans we would need. When Democratic Leader Gephardt on the House floor asked me, as probably the House member most familiar with the Democratic count, how many Democrats we would lose, I told him twenty-six or twenty-seven.

Speaking to the House, Representative David Bonior said, "This night will be remembered as one of the largest surrenders of constitutional authority in American history." In the end, at 3:18 in the morning on July 27, twenty-five Democrats joined 190 Republicans and voted for Fast Track; twenty-seven Republicans and 183 Democrats voted no, along with two independents. The margin was slightly larger than December, but still razor thin: 215-212. Two Republicans, Californians Duncan Hunter and Dana Rohrbacher, had told the president back in December that they would give him "one vote"; this time each voted no. Robin Hayes, the embattled North Carolina Republican who had cried on the House floor in December when GOP leadership strong-armed him into a yes vote, cast his vote "no" after he saw the scoreboard and knew that the legislation would pass without him.

The next week the Senate easily passed the legislation giving the president Trade Promotion Authority. The huge disappointment experienced by House Democrats was aimed in large part at Montana Democrat Max Baucus, the chairman of the Senate finance Committee. Baucus had pushed

Democratic Majority Leader Tom Daschle for a quick vote (most of us in
the House thought he wanted a bill-signing photo-op with the president to
show back home during his reelection campaign). Flanked by fellow Republicans Trent Lott, Trade Representative Robert Zoellick, and Commerce Secretary Donald Evans, Iowa Republican Charles Grassley presented the Montana Democrat with a t-shirt that read "TPA Works for America." The t-shirt
was made in Mexico.

Earlier the same evening that the TPA bill was taken up, Congress had
another duty to fulfill. After several weeks of investigation, several days of
hearings, and five hours of rebuttal from Congressman James Traficant, the
Standards and Ethics Committee had recommended unanimously that the
Youngstown, Ohio, congressman be expelled. On April 10, 2002, Traficant,
an eighteen-year veteran of the House, had been convicted by a jury in a
Cleveland federal court on ten counts, including bribery, racketeering, and
tax evasion. A Democrat who shared Trumbull County with me, Traficant
had for all intents and purposes become a Republican when he voted for
Dennis Hastert for Speaker in 2001 and then voted with the Republican
majority on almost every vote in the last three or four years.

My first encounter with Sheriff James Traficant, after he won the 1984
Democratic primary for Congress, was when, as Ohio's secretary of state, I
attended a Democratic fundraiser in Youngstown. When I introduced myself
to him and congratulated him on his resounding primary victory, he said in
a loud voice, "I kicked their ass, didn't I?" He later attended my Columbus
fundraiser when he was running as "a favorite son" candidate for president
of the United States. And four years later, as we sat next to each other on
folding chairs on a flatbed truck at a Trumbull County Democratic rally, he
suddenly reached over, took me in a headlock, and gave me a noogie. He was
a colorful character, to say the least. That night, I thought about all of that.

The mood was somber. Members of Congress were subdued. A few
minutes before the proceedings began, the embattled congressman entered
the chamber on the Republican side and took a seat on the front row next
to Ohio Republican Bob Ney. A motion from Traficant's old friend Steve
LaTourette (R-Ohio) to delay the expulsion for six weeks was defeated handily. The expulsion procedure was about to begin. The Ethics Committee
accusers faced their congressional colleague accused. Most of the four hundred or so jurors sat quietly, marking the historical moment, planning to
vote to expel a colleague who disgusted some, embarrassed many, and dis-

tracted all of us. Congressman James Traficant was given forty-five minutes to make his case, to defend himself. Initially appearing uncharacteristically humble and also looking a bit larger than life, Traficant stood behind the lectern in the well of the House, the same lectern from which he delivered his daily One-Minutes, his diatribes and harangues against President Clinton, the IRS, immigration, trade agreements, Democrats. His presentation was rambling and unfocused, but in some ways it was loud and clear.

It could have been Huey Long, or perhaps Father Coughlin or Ezra Pound or Tom Watson. As he has done for most of his career, he spoke to a vein of American society that probably represents 20 percent of our country: anti-immigrant, antigovernment, with occasional threats of violence, laced with derogatory comments about Jews and Chinese and Mexicans. Punctuated with his trademark rhetoric—like "I love my country. I hate my government"—he showed little contrition and an abundance of defiance. "I'll go to jail before I'll resign for something I didn't do," and "I'm prepared to lose everything. I'm prepared to go to jail. You can expel me."

In the history of the House of Representatives, only four members had ever been expelled: three during the Civil War because of treason and one as a result of the ABSCAM scandal in 1980. By a vote of 430-1, James Traficant had become the fifth. By 9:00 that night, his office website—featuring an animated graphic of the congressman swinging a stick, "banging away in DC"—was gone and the sign was removed from the office door. In late July he was sentenced to seven and a half years in prison. After a night in the Summit County jail, former Congressman Traficant was taken to federal prison in White Deer, Pennsylvania. In November 2002, while sitting in prison in Allenwood Federal Correctional Institution, Traficant received 15 percent of the vote as an independent candidate running for Congress. In his redistricted seat, more than 20 percent of his former constituents voted for him.

21

Redistricting

If there is a member of Congress walking around with a
target on his head, it is Brown.
            —"Cook's Call," *The Almanac of American Politics*, March 2001

I belong to the Democratic wing of the Democratic Party.
            —Senator Paul Wellstone

While addressing a political rally, Australian prime minister
Robert Gordon Menzies was interrupted by a heckler shout-
ing, "I wouldn't vote for you if you were the Archangel
Gabriel!" Menzies shot back, "Madam, if I were the
Archangel Gabriel, you would not be in my district."

WE KNEW IT WOULD NOT be pretty. The Republicans controlled the
Ohio House of Representatives and the Ohio Senate and were the
majority on the Ohio Supreme Court. Governor Robert A. Taft, who had
defeated me in my 1990 reelection for Ohio Secretary of State, boasted a
Republican pedigree that went back almost to Lincoln and the founding of
the Republican party. Due to the sluggish population growth in the Midwest and Northeast, the Census Bureau determined that Ohio was slated
to lose one congressional seat prior to the 2002 congressional elections.
Ohio, which once had twenty-four congressional districts, was to drop to
eighteen seats, taking it down to its smallest number of representatives in
Congress in 150 years. The waning influence of New York (which lost ten
seats in the last three censuses), Pennsylvania (which cast thirty-seven electoral votes for Franklin Roosevelt in 1944 and thirty-two electoral votes for
John F. Kennedy in 1960 but will cast only twenty-one in 2004), Michigan,
Ohio, and Illinois was all too apparent. These five states had lost almost fifty
seats in the last half-century, while California had picked up thirty seats since
World War II.

We heard that the White House and the Republican National Committee were eyeing Michigan, Ohio, and Pennsylvania as huge redistricting opportunities to more than offset potential Democratic gains in California and Georgia. They were looking to eliminate Democratic seats, force Democratic incumbents to run against one another, and create—even as the states lost districts—new Republican-dominated seats. It was a pretty tall order, but the right political climate, helped by outrageously huge amounts of money, was likely to spell disaster to Democrats in those states. Republicans were gleefully predicting a pickup of at least eight to ten seats from redistricting alone, with almost the entire net gain in these three Great Lakes states. Most political pundits in Ohio and Washington were predicting that Republicans would gain three or four seats in Ohio and that my district would probably be the first to go, partly because of its shape and location and partly because I am the least favorite Democrat among state Republicans and within the Ohio delegation in Washington—a mantle I wear rather proudly.

Immediately after the 2000 elections, when my chief of staff Donna Pignatelli, a few friends, and I sat down to map out a strategy (every member of Congress should have a redistricting strategy, although amazingly many do not), we knew we had a few things working for us. We also knew that those few advantages would not be nearly enough to protect us or other Ohio Democrats unless we developed them and figured out how to take full advantage of them. First, I had well over $1 million in my campaign account, Friends of Sherrod Brown, having raised several hundred thousand dollars more than we spent in each of the last three (generally weakly contested) reelections. We knew, too, that my leadership on health care issues and my position as the ranking Democrat on the Health subcommittee were valuable to the state, especially in northeast Ohio, which is a nationally known health care and health research center. That, we hoped, might translate into some help from influential Republicans prominent in the health care industry. Also, we had the state court system, which was highly partisan, and the possibility of taking our case to the federal court, which gave us some, but not much, hope. We knew, too, that if redistricting did not work out, I had the option of running for governor or another statewide office. Republicans had controlled nearly all of state government for twelve years, and we thought that voters were perhaps ready for a change.

In December 2000, working with national Democrats, I filed, alleging underrepresentation, lawsuits in federal district court in Cleveland and in

state court in Cuyahoga County (also Cleveland). My staff and I were counseled by Democratic National Committee lawyers to present our case in the
most Democratic jurisdiction we could find, which meant filing first in
Cleveland before the Republicans filed a suit in the more Republican areas
of Columbus or Cincinnati. In the end, several months later, both suits were
thrown out.

We then formed kitchen cabinets in Washington and in Ohio, recruiting
friends and political allies who would serve as eyes and ears for us, advise
us on redistricting strategy, and make our case in redistricting among political types in D.C. and Columbus. The Ohio kitchen cabinet organized a petition drive led by teacher-activist David Bruening. The goal was to put pressure on the mostly Republican state legislators in Lorain County, arguing
that this county of almost 300,000 people should be kept together and not
be split among three or four different congressional districts. Friends wrote
letters to the editors of local newspapers, and at the same time we encouraged the two daily Lorain County newspapers, the *Morning Journal* in
Lorain and the *Chronicle Telegram* in Elyria, to editorialize in support of that
effort. They each did, twice. Our state legislators, one Democratic and two
Republican state representatives and a Republican state senator, promised
publicly to work to keep Lorain County in one district. If we could keep
Lorain County—my home and political base with a population equal to
almost one-half of a congressional district and a county that I had carried by
margins of 30,000, 37,000, and 46,000 votes in the last three elections—
together in one district, it would be very hard to draw a district I could not
win. The Washington kitchen cabinet, which was as well connected nationally as the state cabinet was in northeast Ohio, kept us up-to-date on what
Republican House members were doing and what interest groups were
involved. They gave me and my staff their ideas about how to influence
Republican plans. To newspapers and to other politicians, especially to Republicans, they discussed my message about my role in health care issues,
about how my seniority is helpful to the state, about my desire to stay in
Congress.

Both kitchen cabinets helped plan and set up speeches around the state,
especially in areas surrounding my present congressional district. The word
was out—although I really had no plans to do it—that I would consider
moving if the district lines were drawn in such a way that I could not have
won in my present district. But the speeches I made in contiguous counties
to the presently constituted Thirteenth District sent a message that I was

prepared to run against Paul Gillmor, a Republican who borders my district and shares some of Lorain County, and perhaps other Republicans in other parts of Ohio. Then in Columbus one day in February 2001, a newspaper article quoted me as saying, "If Lorain County is divided into three or four districts, I will run for governor, auditor, or some other statewide office." In the midst of my formal visits to prominent Republican and Democratic elected officials to tell them of my interest in retaining my seat, I ran into Republican Attorney General Betty Montgomery, who because of term limits was planning to run for state auditor. She greeted me with, "Sure hope we can get you a district, Congressman."

The strategy was set. Our best opportunity, it dawned on us, was something that nobody had been thinking much about. We knew that Governor Taft, and perhaps other statewide Republican officials, were potentially vulnerable to a well-financed, aggressive Democrat. The only sitting Democratic elected official in Ohio who had won a statewide race, I figured that Taft saw me as a potential opponent, and apparently so did at least a few others. In my obligatory visits to officeholders and political activists, I heard more and more that my comments to newspapers about running statewide were causing some concerns. But we knew we had to do more. The governor, especially, had to know that I was serious: if he and the legislature eliminated my district or cut up Lorain County or drew me into an unwinnable situation, then the governor's race was a *real* possibility.

In January 2001 I had written a letter to Governor Taft asking that Ohio participate in a federal program—which came out of a bill that I cosponsored and helped to pass through the Health subcommittee in 2000—that provided the states a 70-percent match to pay for breast and cervical cancer treatment for low-income, uninsured women, almost all of whom worked in low-wage jobs and were therefore not eligible for Medicaid. But by early spring it was clear that the governor was not going to participate. The state said it could not afford it, he said. Besides, the governor's office told us, these women all get treatment eventually because doctors and hospitals will provide charity care. But the governor's office did not tell us why, then, women with breast cancer *without* insurance are 40 percent more likely to die than women with breast cancer *with* insurance.

Joined by the Breast Cancer Coalition of Cincinnati, Liz Schulte of the Breast Cancer Coalition of Northeast Ohio, and public health officials, I went on the road and held news conferences in Cleveland and Youngstown and Steubenville and Dayton and Cincinnati and Columbus and Lorain all to put pressure on the governor to spend the $300,000–$400,000 it would take to attract the federal dollars to fund the program and to take care of these several dozen women. I called newspaper editors and columnists, asking them to support state funding of this program, arguing against the cruelty of diagnosing someone with cancer and then telling her she is on her own, asserting that it is mostly federal money that Ohio is not receiving, and reminding them that Ohio was one of only a few states that was not participating. Several editors and columnists jumped on the issue, giving us a louder voice across the state. And breast cancer survivors wrote moving editorials and letters to the editors. We organized state legislators (mostly Democrats, but a few Republicans joined us) to support state funding. Legislation was introduced and several members promised to try to amend the state budget. Representatives and senators—Ed Jerse from Euclid, Dale Miller from Cleveland, Joyce Beatty from Columbus, and others—joined us at our news conferences. Finally the governor capitulated and agreed to fund the program.

Other groups, too, saw a more responsive governor on the eve of an election year and were emboldened by our coalition's ability to push a generally very conservative and very recalcitrant and tight-fisted legislature to move on women's health legislation. Planned Parenthood, led by Carol Rogers in Columbus, Roberta Aber in Akron, and Karen Hackenberry in Youngstown, succeeded in pushing a heretofore reluctant governor to support non-abortion-related family planning money. A couple months later the Diabetes Association of Greater Cleveland and the Central Ohio Diabetes Association, observing our success and knowing of my interest in health issues, enlisted my help in pushing the legislature to make Ohio the forty-seventh state to require that diabetes (including insulin and oral medication) be covered by all health insurance policies. Joined by Republican state representative Michelle Schneider and Democratic state representative Joyce Beatty, we urged legislative action in several media markets around the state. Although the bill passed the Ohio House with bipartisan support, the Senate's Republican leadership philosophically opposed health insurance regulation of any kind. Another group that spoke up were the veterans organizations, who were angry that the governor had failed to apply for federal dollars to hire veterans to counsel and train other veterans who were out of work, also joined in. Newspapers carried stories outlining the hundreds of thousands of dollars in job training money that Ohio turned back unused to the federal government.

Now the governor's political people were seeing almost weekly that I was organizing groups around popular issues, traveling the state frequently, attracting news coverage, and pressuring a change in state government's policies. But we knew we needed to do more. Our fundraising kicked into high gear in 2001. With a balance of more than $1 million dollars after the 2000 election, we went to work to put together the biggest event I had ever held. Approaching almost everyone I knew in northeastern Ohio and around the state who I thought could afford to contribute at least several hundred dollars, I discussed my strategy of sending a message to the Republicans that I was serious about this race, that I had strong support from Democrats and Republicans alike (especially in the health care community), and that I would have significant support for a governor's race (or other statewide office) if the Thirteenth District were eliminated. Connie Krauss and my campaign staff put together an event in Cleveland headlined by Democratic Minority Leader Dick Gephardt that raised nearly $300,000, almost three times what I had ever raised in one event in my career. By the time that the legislature got around to drawing the lines in early 2002, I had significantly more money in my campaign account than any other member in either party of the Ohio delegation.

While my office and my campaign were organizing news events, pushing for legislation and for action from the governor on health and jobs issues, and raising money, the state legislature seemed to be in no hurry to draw the new districts. There was no action and little public discussion in the summer of 2001. September came and went as the country focused on one of our nation's great tragedies. October passed, the month that I thought was the target for the Republican legislature to act, then November and December. All the while Republican friends of mine across the state—from health care activists to lawyers, corporate leaders to hospital administrators, physicians to Republican elected officials—were weighing in and asking legislative leaders to keep Lorain County together. Finally, in January, we began to see maps drawn up by different groups and individuals: Republican elected officials, the Ohio Republican congressional delegation in Washington, Republican state headquarters in Columbus.

There was still pressure on state legislators—from the White House, from some at state Republican headquarters, and from the National Republican Congressional Committee—to draw a map that would allow Republicans to pick up three or four seats in Ohio, most likely done by eliminating the much more Republican Tony Hall's Dayton seat (many thought the twenty-two-year veteran was about to announce his retirement to join the Bush administration); Ted Strickland's southern Ohio district; Tom Sawyer's Akron district; Jim Traficant's Youngstown seat; and my district.

But suddenly the Republicans in the legislature realized they had waited too long. The deadline for filing for the primary elections in Ohio was in late February. The Ohio Constitution requires that a new law does not take effect for ninety days (unless passed by a supermajority, a two-thirds vote). Even if it did pass a bill by mid-January (now an almost impossible task), the legislature was facing the possibility of two primaries, one with a filing deadline in February for a May primary for state and local races and one for a later filing deadline at least ninety days after the redistricting bill was signed by the governor and a statutory primary seventy-five days later, likely some time in August.

Even as Republican as most of them are, Ohio's newspapers expressed outrage. Lee Leonard, probably the most thoughtful and experienced reporter in the Statehouse, wrote in the *Columbus Dispatch*, "It'll cost about $7 million to reopen the polls in August, but what's another $7 million in a two-year budget of $45 billion?" The *Akron Beacon-Journal* opined, "How irritating that a party having just demanded that agency after agency tighten its belt would dip into state coffers for $6 million to gain an edge it doesn't need. That verges on an arrogance usually worn by juntas. It suggests the mighty have become too powerful." With the state's budget situation deteriorating almost daily—college tuition rising as much as 20 percent, cuts in health departments, the closing of prisons, the inability of the legislature to honor the state supreme court's order on school funding—the Republicans knew they had only one choice: to bring in enough Democrats in each house of the legislature to reach the two-thirds supermajority of votes necessary so that a bill becomes effective immediately, a so-called emergency clause. Democrats in Columbus, who had been told nothing about redistricting for several months, who had absolutely no input on the district lines, and who were seen as irrelevant to their Republican colleagues, now had a seat at the table!

With a unified caucus behind them, Democratic Senate leader Leigh Herington and Democratic House leader Dean DePiero skillfully negotiated a plan where every unindicted Democrat had a seat that was at least as Democratic as it had been the last ten years. The exception was Dayton's Third District, which, because of suburban population growth in a very Republican part of Ohio, now leaned more to the Republicans.

Interestingly, there had been no maps from the governor's office. We were told repeatedly that the governor had only one request: create a district that Brown can win and one that includes his home in Lorain. At one small meeting of leading Senate and House Republicans, one senator grumbled, "The governor has only one request: leave Sherrod Brown alone." Republicans in Washington were incredulous. The evening before the final map was introduced in the Ohio General Assembly, Ohio's Republican congressional delegation and Republican state legislative leaders were awaiting the tardy arrival of Governor Taft. A northern Ohio congressman quipped, "Is Taft meeting with Brown first to get his approval for the map?"

While I never had a conversation with the governor, I was satisfied with my district and with what the plan meant to Ohio: Congressman Strickland would have no trouble keeping his seat; Marcy Kaptur had a more Democratic district; the two Cleveland Democratic members were safe; the combined Sawyer-Traficant district had a Democratic performance of almost 64 percent. Brent Larkin of the *Cleveland Plain Dealer* chimed in: "Republicans spent more than $100 million over the last decade to capture every constitutional statewide office and huge majorities in both houses of the legislature. This huge investment was made, in part, to guarantee that Republicans would draw new districts that favor Republicans. Instead, Ohio is on the brink of passing a redistricting bill that protects Democrats."

In many states where control of the redistricting process is shared by each of the major parties incumbent protection measures were passed. In New York one incumbent in each party retired to avoid a primary race against a colleague. In Illinois, which lost one seat due to census numbers, an incumbent Republican faced off against an incumbent Democrat; everyone else was protected. In California, where Democrats enjoyed a 32-20 advantage by virtue of a four-seat pickup in 2000 and controlled the entire process, the state assembly protected all thirty-two incumbents and drew one additional Democratic seat. At the time it seemed that Democrats were hurt badly in Michigan and Pennsylvania, and Republicans were to suffer a similar fate in Georgia and, to a lesser degree, in Iowa, New Mexico, Arizona, and North Carolina. But redistricting had by and large become an incumbent-protection exercise, even more than in previous decades.

By the time redistricting was completed in all the states, it was apparent that neither party had particularly benefited, although Republicans had predicted a year earlier that they would gain eight to ten seats in the process. The *National Journal*'s "Congress Daily," a newsletter that goes to members of Congress, congressional staff, and lobbyists on Capitol Hill, said: "The biggest opportunity in redistricting might have been in Ohio, where Republicans controlled the entire redistricting process. GOP Gov. Bob Taft backed away from plans to draw a more aggressive map favorable to the GOP, after

Democratic Rep. Sherrod Brown threatened to challenge Taft if Republicans targeted his district in redistricting. When Taft signed the map into law, the Ohio GOP chairman noted the White House's disappointment." And Fred Barnes, writing for the ultraconservative *Weekly Standard,* wrote, "In Ohio, Republicans were in charge and could have made Rep. Sherrod Brown and several other Democrats vulnerable. But Gov. Robert Taft feared Brown might run against him for governor and so his district was protected. Instead of picking up four seats in Ohio, Republicans now will settle for a gain of one."

Later in the year, not long before the November 2002 elections, I was speaking to Ohio Republicans John Boehner and David Hobson on the House floor. Hobson asked me, "Have you endorsed Bob Taft yet?" Boehner laughed and said, "Yeah, after all he did for you."

Even before the ink was dry on the ballots, some interesting things began to happen. As Republicans were celebrating their takeover of the U.S. Senate and the pick-up of a handful of seats in the House of Representatives, other Republicans were preparing frenetically for the next two years.

Two weeks after the election, Senate Republican Leader Trent Lott convened a meeting of about a dozen corporate trade associations in his office to thank them for their support and their loyalty to the Republican party and tell them his plans for their future. In no uncertain terms, he let them—and, indirectly, the rest of Washington's lobbying community—know that those groups who helped Democrats would not be welcomed in his office. A Lott loyalist, a lobbyist for the Business-Industry Political Action Committee, told *Roll Call,* "Obviously certain people weren't invited, and they know who they are." One Republican lobbyist said about the Republican leader, "He's making a list, and he's checking it twice." Two of Lott's favorite groups that did so much to make him Majority Leader were present: United Seniors Association (USA) and the Pharmaceutical Research and Manufacturers of America (PhRMA). PhRMA contributed more than 95 percent of its campaign dollars to Republicans, and millions more to USA, which mostly served as a front group for PhRMA.

It's not much of a stretch to see the connection between the mid-November meeting in Lott's office and the actions of the House and Senate conference committees in the next few days. Working with lobbyists and executives from Eli-Lilly, Lott and Tennessee Senator Bill Frist were successful in inserting the provision in the Homeland Security bill the provision that saved the Indianapolis drugmaker literally hundreds of millions of dollars by limiting the right to sue by the parents of autistic children.

Lott had had a good November. Along with Frist, who ran the National Republican Senatorial Committee (NRSC), Lott was credited by his colleagues with gaining two seats in the November elections and with making the Republicans the majority party in the Senate. Some Republicans had blamed Lott for "losing the Senate" in 2001 when Vermont's James Jeffords left the Republican party, calling it extreme and out-of-touch. Jefford's switch gave Democrats the majority and elevated Tom Daschle to majority leader. That was mostly forgotten when Republican senators voted unanimously to make Lott the new majority leader.

But December was a different story. On Thursday, December 5, at a 100th birthday party for outgoing Senator Strom Thurmond, Lott said to the assembled crowd, which included almost every GOP senator, "I want to say this about my state: When Strom Thurmond ran for president, we voted for him. We're proud of it. And if the rest of the country had followed our lead, we wouldn't have had all these problems over all these years, either." The mostly partisan—"Republican," no longer "Dixiecrat"—audience laughed and clapped at the first part and mostly sat in stunned silence upon hearing the second.

Initially there was little attention paid to Lott's comments. The majority leader's racist past and his callous treatment of civil rights issues as a congressman and a senator was a dirty little secret that most in the media knew but, for whatever reason, did not want to write about or broadcast. But by Sunday, Washington was abuzz with discussions of Lott's remarks, his earlier comments about race, and his behavior toward minorities throughout his Senate and House career.

In mid-December I phoned twenty African American leaders in Akron—elected officials, ministers, community activists. We held a rally/news conference at the Maple Valley library, where U.S. Poet Laureate Rita Dove had worked during high school. The assembled leaders and I launched a petition drive aimed at Ohio Republican Senators George Voinovich and Mike DeWine, who were supporting Lott, asking them to change their minds and vote against him as their leader. The next day, we held a similar event in Lorain.

By Christmas Lott was gone—still in the Senate but relegated to the back bench by President Bush, who, after waiting several days, finally spoke out against Lott. The same fifty-one Republicans who elected Trent Lott unanimously in November selected unanimously in December Bill Frist, who has an almost identical voting record as the ousted Mississippi leader.

22

A Case Study of the Drug Industry and Its Political Power in the Halls of Congress

> There is no corporate investment with a higher return on capital than political contributions.
>
> —John Bogle, founder, Vanguard Group

> What is called sound economics is very often what mirrors the needs of the respectably affluent.
>
> —John Kenneth Galbraith

IT WAS COLLEGIAL and it was partisan. There was sportsmanship and there was anger. And there were hundreds of billions of dollars on the table in a high-stakes poker game.

The prescription drug issue is one of Congress's most interesting. Few things have united and ignited the public as the behavior of pharmaceutical manufacturers. Congressman Henry Waxman, the California Democrat who had preceded me as the ranking Democrat on the Health and Environment subcommittee, issued reports through his Government Operations Committee on prescription drug pricing in a handful of districts, including mine, around the country. We found that drug companies charge individual Americans, mostly senior citizens, twice what they charge insurance companies, large hospitals, the Veterans Administration, and Health Maintenance Organizations. We also found that Canadians pay about 60 percent less than Americans for the same dosage of the same drug. For example, a month's supply of Tamoxifin, a breast cancer drug, costs $156 in the United States but only $12 in Canada. We learned that some identical drugs that are sold for animals are priced signficantly higher when sold for people. And Congressman Pete Stark issued a report that illustrated that drug companies' effective tax rate is 40 percent less than other industries, and their profit margin three times higher.

Yet drug companies are the most profitable industry in America—by far. According to *Fortune* magazine, pharmaceutical manufacturers in 1998 made $22 billion, 5 percent more than any other industry. Among Fortune 500 companies, they ranked first in return on revenues, first in return on equity, and first in return on assets. The twenty-five highest paid executives in the twelve largest drug firms in the United States were paid $545 million in 1998, not including stock options. Pharmaceutical manufacturers spent more money lobbying Congress than any other industry in America and ranked near the top in campaign contributions to congressional candidates.

Drug companies claim that they need these huge profits to pay for their very expensive research, which they say costs $500 million per drug. But they have never provided the American people with the information to prove it. They spent $30 million on television ads in 1999 to tell the American public that "government should stay out of your medicine cabinet." They also spent $35 million in 2000, an election year.

The drug companies forget to tell the public one big thing. They do only half the research and development for new drugs in this country. We taxpayers do most of the rest, through the National Institutes of Health: 42 percent of research and development expenditures are made by the federal government, and another 10 percent is funded by not-for-profit foundations. Furthermore, drug companies receive tax breaks for the research that they actually do. For example, Taxol, a very effective cancer-fighting drug, was developed entirely by the National Institutes of Health and then "given" to Bristol, Myers, Squibb because the government is not in the business of manufacturing, marketing, and selling drugs. BMS enjoyed sales of $1 billion of Taxol in 1998, signficantly more in 1999 and 2000, and the government doesn't get a single penny for research royalties. Also, Americans pay more for Taxol than do German or Japanese or Israeli or Canadian citizens. American drug companies—or European drug companies, for that matter—charge Americans almost any price they want because there is often no competitive product available.

Almost every member of Congress has heard from constituents—some angry, some desperate, some resigned—about the high cost of prescription drugs. A woman in Elyria told me that she receives $800 a month from social security and spends $350 a month on prescription drugs. She often cuts her daily dosage in half so that her prescription lasts twice as long. Hers is a story repeated in probably every community across the country. The president has built a strong case that Medicare should offer a prescription drug benefit;

after all, when Medicare was signed by President Lyndon Johnson in 1965, prescription drugs were not an especially important part of our health care system. Medicare was passed to cover doctor visits and hospital stays. To modernize Medicare in the year 2000, we need to cover the cost of prescription drugs, the president rightly argues, and several of us in Congress have taken further approaches to dealing with the high cost of medication. A bill I proposed would permit competitors to enter the market for drugs that are unreasonably priced, whether the drug's patent has expired or not. The patent holder would receive royalties for being the first on the market, and Americans would receive a price break fueled by competition. The bill would also require drug companies to publicly disclose audited financial information justifying the prices they charge.

The Energy and Commerce Committee mark-up of the prescription drug bill—perhaps, next to the president's tax cut and the corporate reform legislation, the most important domestic issue of the 107th Congress—began on a Wednesday morning in June 2002. The Republican proposal subsidized insurance companies to cover the costs of prescription drugs for Medicare beneficiaries. Even though "drug only" insurance exists in theory only (and in one failed experiment in Nevada), Republicans argued that tens of billions of dollars in public money would create a vibrant market and that the health insurance industry would then underwrite drug coverage. Energy and Commerce chairman W. J. "Billy" Tauzin, a Louisiana Republican, informed us that we would end our day's work at 5:00 P.M. because of "an important meeting" that many of the committee members would need to attend.

The "important meeting," it turned out, was a Republican fundraising gala the likes of which even Washington had not seen. President George W. Bush headlined the event. Vice President Richard Cheney was there. The party raised at least $30 million for Republican coffers. Underwritten by the pharmaceutical industry, the event's chairman, Robert A. Ingram, was the CEO of British drug company GlaxoSmithKline, which contributed $250,000 to the GOP, and the prescription drug industry's trade association, Pharmaceutical Research and Manufacturing Association (PhRMA), donated another $250,000. Other drug companies chipped in contributions of $50,000, $100,000, and $250,000, bringing the total from PhRMA members alone to almost $3 million. That evening President Bush was so appreciative that he personally thanked Ingram during his speech to the more than 6,000 guests.

The next day our committee continued the mark-up. The lines were drawn and the election year knives were out. Democrats offered amendment after amendment, each opposed by the pharmaceutical industry, each voted down by committee Republicans in a party-line vote. Representative Frank Pallone, a New Jersey Democrat noted for his courage in standing up to the drug companies, many of which are headquartered in his state, and I repeatedly reminded the Republicans, the lobbyists and reporters in the hearing room, and the C-Span audience that there might be a connection between Republican votes on the amendments and the drug company contributions of the night before. As we began our mark-up the morning after the fundraising gala, another prescription drug meeting was convening not far from the Capitol. Eighteen top PhRMA executives gathered for their monthly strategy session and to discuss how to have maximum impact on *our* committee meeting that was affecting *their* industry. The industry had already largely succeeded.

PhRMA, under the very able direction of Alan Holmer, had in a few short years built itself into a powerhouse and was perhaps the most effective lobbying organization in Washington. In 1996, when Holmer joined PhRMA, there were only two lobbyists on the federal staff; today there are seventeen. In addition, they had enlisted the services of some of the most effective, most expensive, and best-connected hired guns in the city. According to a study by Public Citizen, the entire drug industry—PhRMA and all its member companies—had 623 lobbyists on their payroll in 2001 (that was *before* the drug debate really heated up!), including twenty-three former members of Congress, and had spent over $70 million lobbying Capitol Hill in the 107th Congress alone. They also bought at least $40 million of television, radio, and print ads to persuade voters to influence lawmakers. And in the five years before the 2002 election season, they donated more than $50 million directly to political campaigns, more than four-fifths of it going to Republicans. Unfortunately, the significant amount that went to Democrats seemed to have an impact too.

The pharmaceutical companies' effectiveness can perhaps best be described by the fact that, in my ten years in Washington, the drug industry has never lost a major issue in Congress. Although it is probably the most disliked and unpopular business in the United States, it has for each of the last twenty years been the most profitable. And even though it is the target of intense wrath and anger, especially from senior citizens, it continues to enjoy the lowest tax burden of any other industry in the country. And while most Americans know that prices for the same medicine in the same dosage are one-half or one-third that price in other countries, the industry still enjoys the political and economic success in Congress that only an incredibly lavishly financed and well-tuned lobbying machine can deliver. (Since 1998 five or six times a year my campaign charters a bus to take a group of Ohioans, mostly senior citizens, to Canada to buy prescription drugs. The first trip was organized in response to the calls our office was getting and the pleas from seniors to do something—anything—about the high cost of medicine. Our destination was Windsor, Ontario, a three-hour drive. Before each trip the constituents send us their prescriptions; we then check with the Canadian pharmacist to see how much money they would save and then arrange for a Canadian doctor to co-sign the prescription. A typical savings for one of our bus riders has been about $500. Over the years, we estimate, our bus trips have resulted in savings of more than $250,000.)

I had seen them push through the Health subcommittee and the full Energy and Commerce Committee legislation—almost unamended, with no dissenting Republicans and with the support of almost a quarter of the Democrats—that gave incentive to drug makers to perform prescription drug testing on children, adding hundreds of millions, perhaps billions, of dollars to their annual profit statements. While the goal was admirable—so that pediatricians would know with more certainty the optimal dosage for children—it was accomplished at a huge cost to consumers and became a great windfall for the drug industry.

I had seen their influence with the Bush-appointed Food and Drug Administration as well. In an amazing display of indifference to drug safety and of unbridled enthusiasm for drug company profits, FDA officials made a presentation to Democratic Health subcommittee members that their proudest accomplishments at the FDA in the last couple of years was that the U.S. drug industry market share had increased significantly. Some of us emphasized that the FDA is charged with guaranteeing drug safety and efficacy, not industry market share, but the enthusiasm did not wane. The turnaround in market share for the U.S. drug industry, Deputy Commissioner Lester Crawford told the subcommittee, is "nothing short of remarkable. . . . The European share of the world pharmaceutical market fell from 32 to 22 percent over the past ten years while U.S. market share rose from 31 to 43 percent." On the other side of the Capitol, former commissioner Jane Henney told the Senate that the FDA has helped to "enhance U.S. competitiveness in global markets . . . and strengthen the domestic economy as a whole by inviting increased foreign investment." The pharmaceutical industry influence on the 2002 Food and Drug Administration was nothing short of remarkable.

I had watched them manipulate the prescription drug bill. They had opened up a loophole in the generic drug law and driven a multibillion-dollar Brink's truck through it. They convinced the president to oppose bipartisan efforts to close those loopholes and, perhaps most importantly, littered the Bush administration with a number of key drug company executives. Mitch Daniels, who was an Eli Lilly vice president, was appointed by President Bush to be the head of the Office of Management and Budget. Linda Arey Skladany, a former lobbyist for at least four different drug companies, was selected as deputy commissioner for External Affairs at the Food and Drug Administration. Ann-Marie Lynch, who was vice president of Policy for PhRMA, was appointed deputy assistant secretary at Health and Human Services. (In her government job, Lynch was perhaps best known for a widely circulated study that her office conducted that warned that a drug benefit delivered through Medicare would devastate research and development and harm seniors—a conclusion identical to, and in language not much different from, a report on the PhRMA website.) And Sidney Taurel, Eli Lilly's chairman, president, and CEO, was appointed to a coveted seat on the president's Homeland Security Advisory Council. Interestingly, after the 2002 elections, under the almost literal cover of night, Republicans inserted into the bill to create a Department of Homeland Security a provision to protect Eli Lilly and a few other big pharmaceutical outfits from lawsuits by parents who believe their children were harmed by thimerosal, an additive to vaccines that some think may cause autism in children, a provision that will certainly save the drug company hundreds of millions of dollars.

The industry's effectiveness, of course, reaches well beyond the influence it directly wields in Congress and within the Bush administration. During the previous election cycle, obviously aware of the push that the Clinton administration was making to provide a drug benefit, pharmaceutical firms spent $65 million through an organization that it had formed and funded called Citizens for Better Medicare. Most of that money was used for television ads to keep Congress from moving forward on legislation to provide a prescription drug benefit. In the year 2000 the group spent almost $3 billion on consumer advertising alone. While drug companies claim that their advertising is an educational tool, only 1 percent of its 10,000 drugs available to patients are advertised; 95 percent of all advertising was spent on just fifty drugs, and those fifty drugs accounted for half of the $21 billion increase in drug sales from 1999 to 2000. The industry's research dollars, markedly fewer than their marketing dollars, mostly go for copycat versions of already profitable drugs, not breakthrough drugs that save lives.

In the last decade or so drug makers have doubled their number of pharmaceutical representatives, the mostly clean-cut, young sales and marketing people who visit doctors' offices, clinics, and hospitals distributing gifts, athletic event tickets, and meals to medical professionals they want to influence. And most recently the industry has paid dozens of celebrities—from Rob Lowe to Kathleen Turner to Lauren Bacall—to mention drugs by name in interviews or on television shows. Bacall, for example, mentioned the drug Visudyne and was "compensated for her time," according to a medical affairs director at Navartis, maker of the drug.

Nor has the drug industry ignored America's younger consumers. Wyeth, a large New Jersey–based pharmaceutical firm, launched in late 2002 an education campaign about depression on college campuses. Marketing its antidepressant Effexor, Wyeth hired MTV star Cara Kahn to draw students to its campus events. Providing free screenings for depression, the firm's representatives aimed to convince large numbers of college students that there is always a drug available to solve life's problems. A Wyeth spokesman told *Boston Globe* columnist Alex Beam, "We refer to it as an educational campaign, not a promotion." At about the time that Wyeth kicked off its campus tour, the *Wall Street Journal* reported on drug makers' attempts to open up the Japanese market. Trying to sell antidepressants in a culture that was resistant to its efforts, Western pharmaceutical firms were attempting to substitute the Japanese word for "depression" with a word translated roughly as "the soul catching a cold."

While the drug industry rarely misses an opportunity to market its products, its lobbying machine seems to be changing course. After fighting a prescription drug benefit for the last several years, PhRMA in 2002 commented that it supported a drug benefit—as long as it was done their way. According to *National Journal,* drug industry lobbyist Peter Teeley of Amgen said the drug makers wanted a bill "that provides some kind of public protection for the industry." And that's just what the Republicans were doing in the Energy and Commerce Committee mark-up.

Halfway through the mark-up, the committee again recessed, this time for the traditional congressional baseball game where House and Senate

Republicans play hardball against House and Senate Democrats at a Class AA baseball stadium in Bowie, Maryland. We all wear the uniform of our favorite major or minor league team or a university or college located in our districts. I wore a Cleveland Indians uniform and, unfortunately, played no better than my boyhood idols. The contentiousness of the committee work evolved into the competitiveness and bragging rights of a bunch of mostly men in their thirties and forties playing a game that they loved and one at which some had excelled in high school and college. After the Republicans won the game, we shook hands in the middle of the ball diamond in the time-honored tradition we all learned in Little League and then gathered in a large suite above home plate to eat, talk baseball, congratulate each other, and generally get along. (I was reminded of the collegial nature of *this* game when, after making a bad play in center field I was sitting dejectedly in the dugout, feeling sorry for myself, Jay Inslee, a Democrat from Seattle, told me, "Two years ago you and your daughter were almost killed in a car accident. At least you can run around the outfield. Get over it!" Well said.)

At about 10:30 that Thursday evening, baseball players and other Energy and Commerce members returned to the work at hand (after, of course, the rehashing of baseball exploits and a bit of earned gloating by a couple of senior Republicans who had played on inferior GOP teams in the early-1990s, when we Democrats won). The chairman told us that if we all introduced what we had planned, there would be some sixty amendments to be considered. Democrats had good, solid proconsumer amendments: pooling forty million Medicare beneficiaries to extract major discounts from the drug companies; ending pharmaceutical company gaming of the patent system that cost seniors, employers, and taxpayers tens of billions of dollars; filling the hole of $2,500 in out-of-pocket costs in the Republican plan. We had amendments that underscored the vulnerabilities of Republicans in difficult reelection fights: rural health care; community pharmacists' participation in the Medicare plan; coverage for veterans, widows, and Alzheimers patients. We had amendments that exposed hypocrisy in Republican rhetoric: proponents of the GOP drug plan said that seniors deserved a prescription drug benefit as good as members of Congress received, so we offered an amendment to require just that.

All these amendments, and some fifty others, were voted down, all but a couple on a straight party-line vote. On almost every one of these amendments, several vulnerable Republicans in tough reelection fights—John Shimkus of Illinois, Charles Pickering of Mississippi, Charles Bass of New

Hampshire, Heather Wilson of New Mexico—stuck with their party leadership . . . and with the drug industry.

In committee tempers flared, but civility always won out. There are few workplaces in America like it. We get along because most politicians are likable and because we have a general respect for one another, a camaraderie born of a belief in our profession and from an understanding that we all fought similar battles to get here and to stay here. We get along because we need to. But we argue passionately because most of us care about what government does and because we believe that what we do matters in peoples' lives. We argue angrily because we believe that our views and positions are right and those of our opponents are wrong.

Republicans believe that Democrats want to spend money, that we think every problem can be solved with a government program, that we revere a Medicare system badly in need of a fix. Democrats believe that Republicans are water boys (and, in a few isolated cases in their male-dominated party, water girls) for the rich, that their tax cuts give too much to the most privileged and make it impossible to afford an adequate prescription drug benefit for the nation's seniors, and that the GOP has never really supported and wants to privatize the Medicare system. We attack each other because there is an election coming up and we think—no, we know—that the country will be much better off if our side wins. But both sides agree that the election is about values. The Republicans tell us that people can spend their own money better than Washington can, while Democrats argue that spending money on a public purpose—Medicare, food safety, environment, Head Start, national defense—is one of our nation's most important values. Republicans say that they want to strengthen, preserve, and modernize Medicare. (Their pollsters caution them to avoid the word "privatize.") At election time they go on television, look into the camera, and tell their constituents that Medicare is important to their mother and that they would never do anything to jeopardize it. Between elections, however, they shower Health Maintenance Organizations (HMOs) with more and more public dollars, trying to lure—or force—seniors out of traditional Medicare and into a privatized insurance scheme. They say that Medicare is "inflexible," "worn-out," "hopelessly out-of-date."

Around 2:00 Friday morning, as members were tired and emotions were raw and after the television crews had gone home, a Democratic amendment was offered that would have stopped Republican efforts to privatize, as one committee Democrat put it, "the system that you have never supported any-way." We argued that Republican efforts to "strengthen and preserve" Medi-care were disingenuous, that Republican officeholders have never believed in a government health program like Medicare—from 1965 when it was cre-ated, and when most Republicans voted against this "socialist new program," until today's attempts to privatize it. A number of us reminded our small audience, and one another, of some Republican views of Medicare.

At this point Steve Buyer, a Republican from Indiana, had had enough. He announced to his colleagues that he had done some research and that in 1965, when Congress was considering the Medicare bill, Republicans had in fact voted for its passage. The vote, he informed us, was 79 yes, 78 no, 2 abstained (actually still not a majority, as Congressman Tom Barrett of Wisconsin pointed out in committee). Buyer's claims notwithstanding, a majority of Republicans in 1965 in the House and in the Senate voted against passage of the Medicare bill; in the House 248 Democrats supported its passage, and only 42 Democrats (40 of them from the South) opposed it. One typical Republican comment in opposition (notable only because he was my parents' congressman) came from Jackson Betts from Findlay, Ohio: "Until now this Committee (Ways and Means) has been a bulwark which millions of people have relied on to stem the tide against oppressive increases of payroll taxes. Now that is over, and most of my constituents are fearful of the future" (April 8, 1965, debate prior to the passage of Medicare). And House Republican leaders and future president Gerald Ford predicted, "We are going to find our aged bewildered by a multiheaded bureaucratic maze of confusion over what program covers what and who is on first base." The key vote on a motion to recommit the bill and turn it into a voluntary pro-gram (not much different from today's privatization scheme) was supported by House Republicans 128-10. Then, as now, many Republicans did not want to be seen as opposing what became "perhaps the best government program in American history." Members of Congress who don't like to cast politically unpopular votes; they support weakening amendments, motions to recommit, support of an often transparent substitute, and, if they all fail, they vote reluctantly for final passage.

Bob Dole, as he was running for president in 1995, bragged to a cheer-ing group of conservatives that "in a free society, we wouldn't have Medi-care." Also at about that time Speaker Newt Gingrich said, "We don't get rid of Medicare in Round One because we don't think it's politically smart," predicting and hoping that Medicare "would wither on the vine." And Republicans did savagely cut the program repeatedly during the 1990s, proposing one $250 billion cut and several others.

Nonetheless, the Democrats' Stop Privatization amendment—supported by consumer and senior groups and opposed by the pharmaceutical and insurance companies—was voted down in committee on a party-line vote. At about 9:00 that Friday morning, after an eighteen-hour marathon mark-up session, the Energy and Commerce Committee completed its work and passed the bill the drug companies wanted.

But the drug industry's work was far from complete. The following week the bill passed the House mostly along party lines. The Republican leadership allowed no amendments to be offered; we were not allowed even to offer an alternative. Eight Democrats voted for the bill; most of them were afraid to go home and be accused of voting against a prescription drug benefit. The eight Republicans who voted no were mostly critical of the bill's failure to do anything about prescription drug prices.

Then the drug industry's political consultants stepped up. The pharmaceutical companies, which had spent $12 million on issue ads during the first seventeen months of the Bush administration, working through conservative groups such as United Seniors Association (USA) and Sixty Plus, spent $2 million in advertisements in the next two weeks in support of their bill in twenty-nine selected districts around the country, benefiting those members who had voted for the legislation. Already USA was the biggest "issue advertiser" of the 107th Congress. Millions of dollars were contributed by drug companies directly to candidates, mostly Republicans, and to political parties, again overwhelmingly to Republicans. And drug companies purchased tens of millions of dollars for issue ads almost exclusively for Republicans in tough races, always with disclaimers that the ads were paid for by United Seniors Association, Sixty Plus, and Citizens for Better Medicare. There was no hint of the fact that the campaign was funded by the pharmaceutical industry.

The drug industry wrote the legislation for the House Republicans. The pharmaceutical firms gave the GOP campaigns millions of dollars as the bill wound its way through the House of Representatives. Their allies in Congress passed the bill, and the industry congratulated them for helping the nation's seniors. And from the looks of the election returns on November 5, 2002, the public bought it. Republicans Shimkus, Bass, Wilson, and Pickering won, as did all but two Republicans who voted in lockstep with the drug industry on the House floor and, coincidentally, were the beneficiaries of millions of pharmaceutical dollars and thank-you campaigns. Karen Thurman, an articulate Democratic opponent of the drug industry, lost her Florida district after five terms as Republicans and their allies spent almost $10 million dollars to defeat her, much of that money coming from the pharmaceutical companies, and $4 million dollars buried John Norris in Iowa. In the final count, the prescription drug industry spent more than $95 million to keep Republicans in power in the House of Representatives in 2002. As far as the drug industry's bottom line was concerned, it was money well spent.

The contrast between President Clinton's administration and that of President Bush was stark. During the Clinton years scores of Labor Department appointments, for example, came out of the labor movement and worked passionately for worker rights. Dozens of Interior Department appointees went from working for environmental groups to fighting—now from *inside* the government—for stronger environmental rules and regulations. And consumer advocates were working throughout the Clinton executive branch—in the Food and Drug Administration and the Department of Agriculture, in Health and Human Services and the Consumer Products Safety Commission.

Not so in the Bush administration. Hundreds of Bush appointees came from industry—in many cases from the industry they were hired to regulate. In July 2000 the National Labor Committee (the organization that exposed the sweatshop origins of Kathy Lee Gifford's line of clothing and turned a spotlight on the textile and apparel industries' exploitation of child labor and mistreatment of workers all over the world) asked me to go to Nicaragua on behalf of several hundred apparel workers. The workers, mostly young women, earn about 35 cents an hour. Every day they join 26,000 other workers in the Nicaraguan Free Trade Zone working for companies mostly owned by Taiwanese, Koreans, and Americans. Gloria and the other union leaders whom I met at a small hotel near the airport had lost their jobs after they declared a one-hour work stoppage when they asked that they receive an additional thirteen cents for every pair of jeans they sewed. The company, insisting that twenty-three cents per pair of jeans was enough, fired the dozen union leaders. On my return to Washington from my two-day trip to Managua, I called the Department of Labor. Although I thought President Clinton's trade policies to be wrongheaded and was disappointed that he had not attempted to raise workers' living standards around the world, his Department of Labor went to work on this issue. And they made a difference; several months later, the workers were rehired, and their wages were increased.

The difference between a Clinton administration and a Bush administration lies in conflicting philosophies of government. A Republican government is procorporation. A Democratic government is not. It is as simple as that.

23

Tuberculosis: How an Issue Gets on the Public Agenda

This is what I signed up for.
—Dr. Jim Kim, Partners in Health

The Russian prison system acts as an epidemiological pump, releasing into society tens of thousands of active TB cases and hundreds of thousands of infected individuals every year.
—Public Health Research Institute

EVERY DAY 1,100 people in India die from tuberculosis. Two million people die around the globe each year from TB. Two billion—fully one-third of the world's population—carry the TB bacteria, awaiting a compromised immune system to emerge into full-blown active tuberculosis; 10 to 15 million of them are Americans. In Africa almost 40 percent of deaths attributed to HIV/AIDS are actually from TB.

Five years ago I knew about tuberculosis only that it was a disease of yesteryear, called "consumption" in those years, a more or less (at least to me) mysterious killer that laid waste to some of the world's great figures: Eleanor Roosevelt, Charlotte Bronte, John Wesley, George Orwell, Dr. B. F. Goodrich, Frederic Chopin, Francis of Assisi, Fyodor Dostoyevsky, John Keats. In 1970, as a senior in high school in Mansfield, Ohio, my dad and I were driving past the Beatty Clinic, which was about to close its doors. He explained to me that the clinic, formerly a TB sanatorium and then a treatment center, was no longer necessary, "Tuberculosis isn't a problem here anymore, son."

But it never really went away. While easily treatable since the development of antibiotics in the late 1940s, TB has continued to attack millions in the world's poorest nations. Not much of society really noticed. The media didn't cover it. Washington didn't think it important enough to respond. But America's public health community was alarmed.

The outbreak in New York City in the 1990s, mostly springing from prisons like Rikers Island, caught a complacent federal government, Congress, and local officials flat footed. In 1992 New York City had almost 4,000 cases of tuberculosis, 441 of them multidrug-resistant tuberculosis (MDR-TB). And while that epidemic was finally controlled and contained, several hundred people—mostly those with the deadly combination of HIV and TB—died. One-third of those with TB were found to be resistant to one or more antibiotics, a fact recognized relatively quickly by NYC Health Commissioner Margaret Hamburg. The scrimping on preventive care (Congress did away with funding for TB control and elimination and replaced it with block grants) had cost taxpayers dearly in the end. The TB epidemic in New York cost more than $1 billion.

One of the great gifts of serving in the United States Congress in the twenty-first century is the opportunity to look at the world's most interesting menu, see where you can make a difference, and sink your teeth into almost any issue you want to try to change the world.

At 5:30 in the morning in late August 2002, our Siberian Airlines plane landed in Tomsk, a city of half a million in south central Russia. The four-hour overnight flight from Moscow brought me and my fellow travelers to this four hundred-year-old city, one of the first settlements in Siberia. In the nineteenth century Tomsk was a place of exile; fully one-fifth of its residents had been sent there, mostly as political prisoners, by the tsar. Many of the Russian empire's most famous political prisoners—anarchists, socialist revolutionaries, and Communists—were exiled to Tomsk: M. A. Bakunin, A. A. Kropotkin, A. I. Rykov, Y. M. Sverdlov, Joseph Stalin. And years later, Stalin, perhaps mindful of his time in this faraway city, followed the lead of his political oppressor ancestors and sent tens of thousands of political opponents into exile in Tomsk in the 1930s, 1940s, and early 1950s. Perhaps paradoxically, perhaps not, since so many intellectuals were exiled to this Siberian city, Tomsk was the site of the first Siberian university, in 1888, and is home today of a larger percentage of professors and scientists than any other city in Russia.

Jim Hong Kim, a physician and anthropologist; Donna Barry, a nurse practitioner and fluent speaker of Russian; and Joanne Carter, a veterinarian-turned-activist, had been involved in combating TB and other infectious diseases for several years. Jim and Donna were part of Partners in Health (PIH), which Jim and Dr. Paul Farmer founded. PIH has a major presence in Haiti, home of one of the world's best AIDS clinics, and Peru, where they have perhaps the best TB program on earth. Jim and Donna wanted to show Joanne and me how U.S. tax dollars were being spent in helping a nation where TB was reaching epidemic proportions. Joanne, the legislative director of RESULTS, an amazingly effective grassroots public interest group in Washington, had come to me five years earlier because of my interest in international health with an idea—and an amendment. Even with the very serious outbreak of MDR-TB in New York City in the early 1990s, Congress had ignored the exploding tuberculosis crisis in the world. The amendment we discussed, and which ultimately passed, began to direct some U.S. aid to treat TB in developing countries.

The day before we left for Siberia, we visited a detention center where prisoners who had not yet been charged were living in small cells with little ventilation. Some could expect to be detained for years in this hundred-year-old prison not far from the center of Moscow. We entered the wing of the prison where tuberculosis patients were housed. Seven prisoners ranging in age from nineteen to about fifty-five were squeezed in a room no larger than a typical American bedroom, perhaps 15 feet by 10 feet. Two small windows provided a bit of ventilation, although in the long Russian winter with the ventilation came the bitter nordic cold. All seven were being treated for TB. Some might have had the worst kind of tuberculosis, a drug-resistant variation that is rarely cured in Russia because of a shortage of second-line drugs. The lab facilities, while being built in this center by a very dedicated and professional staff, were inadequate here and nonexistent in most of the Russian prison system. Among the world's most common and lethal infectious diseases, TB is uncommonly slow to diagnose: its bacteria culture grows and multiplies at such a rate that it takes as long as eight weeks to determine drug resistance. Therefore a course of treatment, while very inexpensive for most, is not always easily determined.

After our time in Moscow's detention facility, we visited a "shooting gallery" just outside of Moscow in the small town of Mytyshi. (Coincidentally, twenty-nine years ago I had gone to a rock concert of sorts in Mytyshi, where some Russian and American friends and I, with my guitar, went up on stage to play and sing "Please Please Me" and "Yellow Submarine" in front of 500 Russians.) The shooting gallery was nothing more than a van parked just outside the city limits; needle exchange is illegal inside Moscow. While our presence surely discouraged their clients from approaching the van, we talked to several volunteers—themselves perhaps former drug addicts or commercial sex workers—who befriended, counseled, provided clean needles, and gave out condoms. Some of the commercial sex workers came from as far away as Moldova and Ukraine and sent money home to their families. Russia's HIV rate is increasing faster than that of anywhere else on earth. In the small city of Ryazan, for example, a hundred miles or so south of Moscow, new HIV cases went from fewer than a dozen a year through most of the 1990s to 300 in 1999 and 508 in 2000. Most of the transmission, it is believed, was from prostitution and reusing dirty needles. And high HIV rates, coupled with tuberculosis, especially drug-resistant TB, is a lethal time bomb waiting impatiently to explode.

We met with the First Vice Minister of Health and the Chief of the Russian Prison system (whom Jim referred to as "the gulag-meister"). The United States and Russia have the highest per capita inmate population in the world. Russia, where most of its prisoners are confined because of property crimes, has decided to do a major amnesty for nonviolent offenders, reducing its prison population from about one million to some 600,000 by 2004. Unfortunately, at least 10 percent of those released prisoners have tuberculosis, and some 20 to 30 percent of those have drug-resistant tuberculosis. It is only a matter of time until MDR-TB reaches our shores, and in alarming numbers.

Once in Siberia we began with a visit to the Tomsk TB Dispensary, where TB patients come for their medicine and a couple of hot meals six days a week. When talking to TB patients who were in the midst of their six-month or two-year treatment for MDR-TB, as I did in the detention center in Moscow, I donned a mask. (When Jim, however, entered the room with the contagious patients without a mask, I was surprised. "That's what I signed up for in medical school," he smiled.) After four or five minutes of exchanges, my college Russian vocabulary had been exhausted, and I relied on a translator to continue the conversations. Many of these patients—knowing of the deadliness of TB, the condition of the Russian health care system, and the unavailability of antibiotics—had expected only a few months earlier to die. Most by now were on their way to recovery.

But none of this prepared me for the Tomsk Prison. Built in 1947 when Stalin again revved up his forced labor machine, the prison colony is located on the edge of town next to several high-rise apartment buildings. Greeted at the prison gates by Warden Nicholai Kostolov, I told him that Dr. Kim said that this was perhaps the best prison colony in all of Russia. "A golden cage," the warden said, "is still a cage." Also there was Colonel Balkovnik, a tough military man missing two fingers who ran the entire prison system in that part of Siberia. He told me, as we walked through the prison colony, that all of the prisons he administered were as humane and well run as this one. He wanted a livable prison where "his men" would be cured. The colony had a pigsty with at least one hundred pigs and there was a huge garden with row after row of beets, carrots, and other vegetables. Kostolov had set up a bakery. To provide the resources to run the prison, prisoners built log cabins in the courtyard of the colony that were disassembled and sold outside the prison and also sold crafts and artwork. Best of all, this prison colony, which was home to 1,000 TB patients who had been brought from other prisons in the Tomsk region, was curing its inmates of TB. In 1996 sixty-five of its prisoners died of that disease; in 1999 forty died; in 2000 twelve succumbed to TB. As of our visit in late August, not one had died in 2002.

About a dozen inmates marched out of their barracks to talk to us. Standing at attention, they told us their stories. All had MDR-TB. All thought they were going to die. All weathered the gruesome side effects of the first months of their antibiotic regimen. And all now believed that they were going to be completely cured. And they probably will be. But there was still a shortage of second-line antibiotics. Behind a fence near one end of the compound stood a dozen men quarantined from the rest. They were all seriously ill with a strain of MDR-TB, and they had to wait their turn because the prison colony simply did not have enough money for their medicine. Their time might come, or it might not. It was partly dependent on a bankrupt Russian government in Moscow or perhaps on the generosity of the international relief community . . . or maybe on the U.S. Congress.

When we left the country, disappointment followed me home. While groups like RESULTS and Partners in Health and members of Congress like Connie Morella and Nancy Pelosi have helped us increase U.S. assistance to fight TB from $12 million in 1999 to $75 million today, this short excursion to Tomsk showed me that far too little of our money is going to the purchase of diagnostic equipment and second-line drugs for tuberculosis patients. We had work to do. During the appropriations cycle, Joanne Carter, Fran DuMelle of the American Lung Association, and other public health organizations sent emails and letters to congressional offices, made phone calls to newspapers, wrote letters to the editor, and visited their local congressmen in an attempt to increase the allocation in the Foreign Operations appropriations bill. Arlan Fuller, my staff assistant, and I spent hours talking with the major players on the Appropriations Committee and on the

Foreign Operations subcommittee, and on the House floor I gathered signatures of sympathetic colleagues on both sides of the aisle to urge appropriators to increase funding on international TB.

When the bill was voted out of committee with a small increase, my staff prepared a floor amendment to provide additional dollars. We looked for Republican cosponsors of the amendment and lined up additional Republicans and Democrats to speak for the amendment. In some instances the chairman was willing to compromise, although appropriators do not like floor amendments because they want to keep the bill roughly the same as it was when it came out of committee. Other times the chairman opposed us. But when he opposed us we beat him on a roll call vote, with almost every Democrat (Ohio's Jim Traficant was the only dissenter one year) and a number of Republicans who had some interest in public health supporting the amendment. The fight continued in the Senate. We were successful there, too, but we always fell far short of what we knew we needed.

As a nation we could do so much. According to economist Jeff Sachs, an annual international commitment of $13 billion for TB, HIV/ AIDS, and malaria—which today kill about six million people a year—could save three million lives a year. Of that amount, if the United States were to put up $4 billion annually, other nations and philanthropists would come up with the rest. But we seem to have other things to do.

We surely had the money. Just in the last year the House of Representatives passed a one-year increase in defense expenditures of $47 billion; that increase alone is greater than the entire defense budget of any other nation in the world. And that does not count spending for war in Iraq. The president signed a farm bill that provided $180 billion over ten years mostly to large corporate farmers. And Congress passed and the president signed a tax cut, most of which goes to the most privileged people in our society, costing $1.1 trillion over the next ten years.

While most Americans think we do much by way of providing humanitarian aid around the world, we rank at the bottom in providing nonmilitary assistance to other nations. In early 2001 the United Nations asked its wealthy members to contribute seven-tenths of 1 percent of their GDP to international aid efforts, primarily health and education programs. Only four countries have reached that goal. The United States allocated about one-tenth of 1 percent of our GDP to international relief efforts. In the end, it is not a question of resources. It is a question of our priorities.

24

War in Iraq

It doesn't matter if war is going well or badly. All that
matters is that a state of war should exist.
> —George Orwell, *1984*

All of us have heard this term "preventive war" since the
earliest days of Hitler. I recall that is about the first time
I heard it. In this day and time . . . I don't believe there is
such a thing; and frankly, I wouldn't even listen to anyone
seriously that came in and talked of such a thing.
> —President Dwight D. Eisenhower, 1953, on being
> presented with plans to wage preventive war to disarm
> Stalin's Soviet Union

The rising tide of the global economy will create many
economic winners, but it will not lift all boats. It will spawn
conflicts at home and abroad, ensuring an even wider gap
between regional winners and losers than exists today.
Globalization's evolution will be rocky, marked by chronic
financial volatility and a widening economic divide.
Regions, countries, and groups feeling left behind will
face deepening economic stagnation, political instability,
and cultural alienation. They will foster political, ethnic,
ideological, and religious extremism, along with the
violence that often accompanies it.
> —*Global Trends 2015* (CIA, 2000)

NEVER HAS A PRESIDENT of the United States changed the subject
more adroitly than in the summer and fall of 2002. All the economic
signs were bad. The stock market was in the tank; the Dow Jones was dropping to a five-year low. President Bush's stratospheric poll numbers were
steadily descending. The corporate abuse scandals were lapping at the feet
of both the president and the vice president. Congress had not passed a

prescription drug benefit, had failed to enact a patient's bill of rights, and
had dropped the ball on retirement security and pension protection. Two
million jobs had been lost since President Bush took office, and economic
growth was lower than at any time in the preceding five decades. Retirement
accounts had shrunk, consumer confidence had eroded, and business investment had declined. Median household income had declined for the first time
in a decade and the poverty rate had risen for the first time in four years.
Another 1.4 million Americans lost their health insurance. Economists and
workers were demanding that Congress increase the minimum wage, which
was lower in real dollars than in 1980, and extend unemployment compensation for hundreds of thousands of laid-off workers whose benefits were
about to expire.

At the same time, executive pay had increased dramatically under both
Clinton and Bush. In 1980 CEOs were paid forty-five times what line workers in their companies were earning. By 2002 that ratio had increased to
almost 500-1. With the scandals at Enron, WorldCom, Adelphia, and Tyco,
Americans were finally beginning to notice.

In June 2002, as the country was still recoiling from the horrors of September 11, a computer disc carrying White House political adviser Karl Rove's
analysis of the 2002 elections was accidentally dropped in the streets of
Washington and picked up by a surprised Democratic Senate staffer. The
memo confirmed much of what the Democrats have long suspected about
an administration that professes to be nonpolitical. A top strategy point
advised Republican candidates to "focus on the war," though the White
House had said the war effort will not be used to win votes. It suggested
that Republicans would gain by keeping the nation's focus on homeland
security and the war on terrorism. "We can also go to the country on this
issue," Rove said, "because they trust the Republican Party to do a better job
of protecting and strengthening America's military might and thereby protecting America." It was becoming increasingly clear that the president's men
had formulated a new direction for our military and a new vision for our foreign policy. In a June commencement speech at West Point, President Bush
hinted at a hegemonic America where he would ensure that our military
power would grow and our military superiority would remain unchallenged.
By the end of the summer the manifestation of that change began to take
shape. The National Security Strategy, a document put out by the president's
National Security Council, stated that other nations "should not use pre-
emption as a pretext for aggression."

The war on terrorism, at least to Republican operatives, had displaced the Cold War and U.S. opposition to communism. From the lowering of the Iron Curtain in the late 1940s until the Berlin Wall fell in 1989, Republicans benefited politically from their vocal and vociferous opposition to communism. It gave Republican presidents and legislators reason and justification to increase defense spending, restrict civil liberties, and squeeze domestic spending. And United States adventurism and unilaterism, especially in Latin America, and all in the name of fighting communism, could be advocated and easily defended.

The war on terrorism, while important and necessary for our country, has begun to serve the same purpose for GOP politicians. In the name of protecting the public, Attorney General John Ashcroft moved aggressively after September 11 to clamp down on civil liberties, something he had wanted to do prior to the terrorism attacks. Huge defense increases were proposed by the White House and their friends in the defense industry, while prodefense members in both parties bid them up. The $47 billion defense increase alone passed by the House was greater than the entire defense budget of any other country in the world; the total amount of United States defense spending is sixty times the combined defense budgets of the "Axis of Evil," the term President Bush used to describe Iran, Iraq, and North Korea.

In September 2002, as storm clouds were gathering over Republican election prospects, President Bush began to warn in the starkest terms of impending danger in Iraq. Every single member of Congress believed Saddam Hussein, Iraq's strongman, to be a tyrant, all of us knew that he had killed hundreds of thousands of his own people, and most of us knew that he had been an ally of the United States during the Reagan-Bush years when we provided his regime with chemical and biological agents to be developed and used against our enemy Iran in the Iran-Iraq war. But many in Congress, and a few in a generally pliant media, were skeptical about the president's timing. The president's chief of staff, Andy Card, was asked about the timing of the Iraq resolution. Why did this issue come before Washington and the country now? Why are we debating it in September? Where were we last year? Where were we last spring? Card answered, "From a marketing point of view, you don't introduce new products in August."

It was clear that President Bush had decided that a unilateral invasion of Iraq was justified. This president, who lost the popular vote, wanted to radically change our decades-old military doctrine from containment, deterrence, collective security, and diplomacy to a policy of preemptive strikes, which National Security Adviser Condoleezza Rice called "anticipatory self-defense." The decades-old military doctrine of containment, deterrence, collective security, and diplomacy had contained and deterred Joseph Stalin and the Soviets, Fidel Castro and his Cuban government, and China and its Communist expansionary tendencies for half of a century. We made no preemptive strike against Cuba. We did not invade the People's Republic of China or the Soviet Union. There had been no mention in Bush's 2000 campaign of this sharp departure from the military strategy that presidents of both parties had followed for more than a century. In its conduct of foreign policy, it had been a "go-it-alone" presidency from the beginning. From its abandonment of the Kyoto Treaty to the un-signing of the International Criminal Court to the withdrawal from the Anti-Ballistic Missile treaty, we as a nation have riled world opinion and isolated ourselves from allies, neutral nations, and much of the world community.

Many of us in Congress asked: What does a unilateral invasion of Iraq tell the world? What does an invasion of a sovereign nation by the United States say to other nations? What does our new military doctrine mean to the rest of the world? Does it embolden Russia to attack the Republic of Georgia in pursuit of Chechen rebels? Does it set an international precedent allowing China to invade Taiwan or to clamp down even harder on Tibet? What would prevent India, a nation with nuclear weapons, from an all-out attack on Kashmir or Pakistan, another nation in the nuclear club, from going into Kashmir from the other direction? And if we invade Iraq unilaterally, will we have the moral standing any longer to step in when a country has, in our minds or in the opinion of the United Nations, invaded another country without provocation? Will we have the moral authority to speak out against an attack by a powerful country against a weaker country? The United Nations' Security Council is charged with preventing UN member states—including veto-wielding permanent members, perhaps *especially* those members—from beginning unilateral, unprovoked wars. A U.S. attack without UN support, many of us believed, would undercut the authority of the UN.

In September three retired four-star generals—John Shalikashvili, Joseph Hoar, and Wesley Clark—testified before the Senate that attacking Iraq without a UN resolution supporting military action could limit aid from allies, "supercharge" recruiting for Al Qaida, and undermine our war on terrorism. Going it alone would not only potentially take valuable resources from the fight against terrorism but would likely break up the coalition that President Bush assembled after the September 11 attacks. And while a UN resolution would isolate Saddam Hussein, going it alone could very well isolate the United States.

The Bush administration asked Congress to scrap the framework that had helped to keep the peace for decades and was promoting a new foreign policy framework that did not have the support of U.S. allies. The departure from the traditional foreign policy of deterrence and containment should require a higher burden of proof for congressional authorization than what the administration had been willing to offer. The administration had yet to provide the proof that moved us beyond the reasonable doubts of liberals and conservatives alike to a consensus that this new approach was what we, as a nation, wished to do in this new era with new threats.

During the International Relations Committee debate on the Iraq resolution, I offered an amendment that would have required that critical questions be answered before Congress authorized war. These questions included a cost estimate for military action *and reconstruction;* an analysis of the impact on the U.S. domestic economy; a comprehensive plan for U.S. financial and political commitment to long-term cultural, economic, and political stabilization in a free Iraq; a statement that details the extent of the international support for military operations in Iraq; and an analysis of the effect on the stability of Iraq, and the region, of any "regime change." It was voted down on a mostly party-line vote, with some pro-war Democrats voting against and a couple of antiwar Republicans voting yes.

The Iraq vote was an opportunity for Congress to reassert its constitutionally mandated authority to declare war, to reaffirm its responsibility to articulate a national security policy in this new era, and to establish a consensus with the American people so that the three key actors—the executive, the Congress, and the American people—are in agreement with the security policy designed to protect them. Bush's policy makes the United States more of a target, more vulnerable to terrorism, and less of a respected leader for the rule of law in the world. George Bush hit a trifecta, and the rest of us were the losers.

Presidents, of course, get their way with Congress when they advocate a march toward war. The House of Representatives gave President Bush the authority that he asked for, 296-133, but with surprisingly greater opposition than the pundits predicted. Actually, those of us who opposed giving the president authority to unilaterally attack Iraq were also surprised by the number of "no" votes. Most interesting was the unanimous opposition from the Democratic members of the Hispanic Caucus and the overwhelming opposition from African American members. In most wars the kids who die are predominantly poor and working class—white, black, and Latino. Equally interesting, those in the Congress and in the Bush administration who were the most vocal advocates for war were mostly those who never served in the armed forces. Vice President Cheney, who never wore a uniform, said that he "had other priorities" during the Vietnam War. So apparently did George W. Bush, who many military people say was AWOL. And Republican Majority Leader Tom DeLay, from Houston, said, according to *Mother Jones* magazine, "When I was that age, the minority kids wanted to get out of the ghetto; they got all the good-paying jobs in the military, and there were none left for us patriots."

After the vote something happened that astounded me. I heard more individual, quiet, sometimes almost whispered comments from constituents—liberals and conservatives, whites and blacks and Latinos, urban and rural, young and old—thanking me "for your courage," "for standing strong," "for your gutsy outspokenness," "for not letting the president push you around on Iraq." I had never before heard that volume of positive response from anything I had done in my twenty-six years of holding public office.

In the end the 133 votes against the resolution, the internal lobbying from a few dissenters like Colin Powell in the Bush administration, and the public opposition to this war forced a reluctant president to pay more attention to the United Nations. A president who initially wanted to unilaterally invade Iraq had shifted his position to supporting a UN resolution calling on thorough, aggressive inspections in Iraq. While the media—owned almost entirely by large conservative corporations—characterized the UN resolution as a win for President Bush, many of us considered it a victory for our country.

As 2002 drew to a close, the public opposition to a preemptive U.S. attack on Iraq seemed to grow exponentially. Religious organizations passed resolutions in opposition to such an attack. The Church of England, for the first time in its history, broke with the government of the United Kingdom on a major policy issue. More than one hundred cities and counties—including Cleveland, Akron, Oberlin, and Lorain County—passed resolutions in opposition. Nelson Mandela and thousands of trade unions spoke out against the war. Grassroots organizations like MothersActingUp.org and MoveOn.org weighed in in a big way. My office drafted the following letter, co-signed by Wisconsin Democrat Ron Kind, who had voted for the October Iraq resolution, urging caution and calling on the president to allow the inspections to continue.

President George W. Bush
The White House
1600 Pennsylvania Ave. NW
Washington D.C. 20500

Dear Mr. President,

On November 8, 2002, the United Nations Security Council unanimously endorsed a resolution designed to force Iraq to give up any weapons of mass destruction. We believe the U.S. should make every attempt to achieve Iraq's disarmament through diplomatic means and with the full support of our allies, in accordance with the process articulated in UN Security Council resolution 1441.

The UN resolution calls for a tough new weapons inspection regime; it requires the government of Iraq to provide inspectors with immediate, unimpeded, unconditional, and unrestricted access, and requires that Iraq permit inspectors to interview officials, scientists, and other individuals as necessary to fulfill the mandate of the resolution. This is an inherently difficult task, requiring patience and perseverance. The report scheduled to be given by Chief UN weapons inspector Dr. Hans Blix and Director General Mohamed ElBaradei on January 27, 2003 will assess whether the United Nations Monitoring, Verification, and Inspection Commission (UNMOVIC) and International Atomic Energy Agency's (IAEA) comprehensive mission is proceeding in the unobstructed and effective manner necessary to realize the aims of UN Security Council resolution 1441. We encourage your Administration to sufficiently weigh future decisions regarding Iraq on the assessment given by UNMOVIC/IAEA, including additional inspection time and resources as appropriate. Your commitment to working through the UN Security Council and your vocal support for resolution 1441 are critical to UNMOVIC/IAEA's eventual success.

In addition, we respectfully urge you to use the opportunity provided in the upcoming State of the Union Address to offer assurances both to the American people and the international community that the United States remains committed to the diplomatic approach and comprehensive inspections process agreed to in UN Security Council resolution 1441.

Thank you for your consideration, and we look forward to your response.

Before sending the letter, Congressman Kind and I sent a "Dear Colleague" letter to other members of Congress, asking them to co-sign our letter. At first the response was positive and heartening; then, at a couple of large demonstrations in Washington and San Francisco in January 2003, the letter became a rallying point for thousands of individuals and hundreds of organizations who were opposed to the war. MoveOn.org and other organizations used the internet to encourage hundreds of thousands of citizens to write, email, fax, and visit members of Congress to sign the Brown-Kind letter. In the space of a couple of weeks in late January and early February, 128 congressmen and congresswomen joined Kind and me in co-signing the letter; twenty-six of them had voted for the resolution and were now asking for the president to slow down in his headlong rush to war.

On Sunday, February 9, the *Morning Journal,* the newspaper in my hometown of Lorain, carried an interview with me at the top of the front page entitled, "The Lonesome Dove: Liberal Rep. Sherrod Brown Explains his Anti-War Stance amid Frantic Hawks." It laid out my opposition to the war and the reasons behind my decision to oppose a preemptive attack against Iraq. I surely did not feel lonesome; in fact, when I had dinner with *Morning Journal* editor John Cole a couple of weeks later, he told me that the response to the article—calls, letters, email—was 75-1 in opposition to the war. Then on February 15, the media, at home and abroad, could no longer ignore the fervor that millions of people felt in opposition to the war. Eight to nine million people marched on six continents. Five million demonstrated in Europe: one million in Madrid and Barcelona; 600,000 in Rome. Millions spoke out in Toronto and Tokyo, in Dhaka and Melbourne, in Tel Aviv and Damascus. At Hyde Park in London, in front of one million Brits at the largest gathering of people in 2,000 years, Mayor Ken Livingstone recalled Mr. Bush's personal history, calling him a draft-dodger, a "stooge for the oil industry," and a stock-market swindler. "And we are asked to send our young women and men to die for this creature? I don't think so."

Great Britain's prime minister, Tony Blair, the only leader of a major power supporting President Bush, was finding that his countrymen were strongly against the war. A European *Time* magazine internet poll asked readers which nation posed the greatest danger to world peace. The response was shocking: out of more than 300,000 answers, 7 percent said North Korea, 8 percent said Iraq, and fully 84 percent said the United States.

At least a million marched and spoke out and rallied and demonstrated in more than 150 cities across the United States—from Billings to Houston, Seattle to St. Petersburg. In New York City hundreds of thousands of people marched against the war. And in Cleveland and Akron more than 2,000 people attended rallies. When I looked out over the crowd at Trinity Episcopal Cathedral in Cleveland, I saw an enthusiasm I had never seen before. And later in the day, from the pulpit of New Covenant Presbyterian Church in west Akron, I saw students and retirees, labor activists and small businesspeople, teachers and nurses and housewives. And even though we knew we had little chance of stopping a president who may have made up his mind about invading Iraq on January 20, 2001, the opposition to this Bush Family War had crystallized. People were paying attention.

POSTSCRIPT

AT ABOUT 8:00 in the evening on January 7, 2003, after I was sworn in for my sixth term in the United States Congress, I walked from my office to the Franklin Delano Roosevelt Memorial. An awesome, inspiring place, a tribute to perhaps our greatest president, this monument is divided by stone and waterfalls into four chambers, each depicting one of Roosevelt's terms. Sitting alone in the cold Washington night, I thought of the responsibilities facing me and my colleagues, the work that Congress would do in the upcoming months, and the proposals that the president had sent us.

I thought about war. I looked at FDR's words engraved on the granite: "I have seen war. I have seen war on land and sea. I have seen blood running from the wounded. . . I have seen the dead in the mud. I have seen cities destroyed. . . I have seen children starving. I have seen the agony of mothers and wives. I hate war."

I thought about social justice. I read what Roosevelt said: "The test of our progress is not whether we add more to the abundance of those who have much; it is whether we provide enough for those who have too little."

And I thought about what I had heard President Bush say about war with Iraq and about tax cuts. George W. Bush has probably never visited the FDR memorial.

I wish he would.

INDEX